THE

INTERNATIONAL

HUMAN

RIGHTS

MOVEMENT

THE

INTERNATIONAL
HUMAN
RIGHTS
MOVEMENT

A History

Aryeh Neier

PRINCETON UNIVERSITY PRESS

Princeton & Oxford

LIBRARY OF CONGRESS CATALOGING-IN-PUBLICATION DATA
Neier, Aryeh, 1937-
The international human rights movement : a history / Aryeh Neier.
p. cm.
Includes bibliographical references and index.
ISBN 9780691135151 (cloth)—ISBN 0691135150 (cloth)
1. Human rights. 2. Human rights—History. 3. Human rights
advocacy—History. I. Title.
JC571.N377 2012
323—dc23   2011043994

British Library Cataloging-in-Publication Data is available

This book has been composed in Garamond Premier Pro

Printed on acid-free paper.

Printed in the United States of America

1 3 5 7 9 10 8 6 4 2

Contents

Acknowledgments   vii

1   The Movement   1

2   Putting Natural Law Principles into Practice   26

3   What Are Rights?   57

4   International Human Rights Law   93

5   International Humanitarian Law   117

6   Defying Communism   138

7   Rights on the Other Side of the Cold War Divide   161

8   Amnesty International   186

9   Human Rights Watch   204

10   The Worldwide Movement   233

11   Accountability   258

12   Rights after 9/11   285

13   Going Forward   318

Notes   335

Index   359

Acknowledgments

Many colleagues in the three organizations with which I have been professionally associated for nearly half a century—the American Civil Liberties Union, Human Rights Watch, and the Open Society Foundations—shaped my thinking and contributed to my knowledge of the human rights movement. They are too numerous to name here, but I express my gratitude to them for what they taught me and for taking part with me in many struggles for human rights. Also, I offer my thanks to the many brave men and women whose efforts to promote human rights took place in far more difficult and dangerous circumstances than those in which I did my work and whose experiences are described in this book.

I express particular gratitude to Leonard Benardo and James Goldston, my colleagues at the Open Society Foundations, and to Professors Andrew Nathan and Eric Weitz, for reading the manuscript and for making critical comments. It is, I think, a much better book because of the changes that I made as a result of their comments. Perhaps it would have been better still, with fewer errors, if I had made more. I also benefited greatly from the editorial pen of Eva Jaunzems, and I thank her, Brigitta van Rheinberg, and their colleagues at Princeton University Press for the conscientious professionalism and generous spirit in which they dealt with the book and with me.

I have been fortunate to have a superb staff in my office at the Open Society Foundations, a staff made up of Claudia Hernandez, Virginia Brannigan, Barbara Meeks, and George Hsieh. Virginia Brannigan did the lion's share of the work on the manuscript, but the others all pitched in from time to time. I am deeply grateful to them.

Finally, I am grateful to Yvette, my life partner, for her indulgence in allowing me to organize our lives over an extended period to make it possible for me to work on this book. This book is dedicated to Yvette.

Aryeh Neier

1

The Movement

AS OF SEPTEMBER 29, 2011

ON THE MORNING OF JULY 15, 2009, NATALYA ESTEMIROVA, A 50-year-old researcher for the Russian human rights organization Memorial and former history teacher who had systematically reported on torture, disappearances, and murders in her native Chechnya for nearly two decades, was abducted as she left her home in Grozny and forced into a car. Her bullet-riddled body was found later by the side of a road. She had become a victim of just the kind of crime that she had so often documented.

For a brief period, the murder of Estemirova was an important news item worldwide. Few outside Russia had even known her name, but a great many now recognized that her death would have serious consequences. Chechnya has a well-earned reputation as a very dangerous place. An unusually large number of journalists, humanitarian workers, and human rights researchers have lost their lives there in the past two decades. Members of professions used to working in some of the world's most dangerous places have learned to avoid Chechnya. Memorial's researchers, led by Estemirova, were virtually alone by the time of her murder in keeping the world informed about the ongoing violent abuses of human rights in the territory. Would even Memorial be able to sustain that reporting after her death? "A question hangs over her execution, the most recent in a series of killings of those still willing to chronicle Chechnya's horrors," wrote a *New York Times* reporter, who described her as "both a trusted source and friend." Is the accounting of the human toll now over? "Without her, will

Chechnya become, like Uzbekistan and Turkmenistan, a place where no one risks asking hard questions openly?"[1]

Though the murder of Natalya Estemirova soon disappeared from news accounts, overtaken by other outrages, among those who paid particular attention to her death and remembered it were thousands of men and women in all parts of the world who do similar work in their own communities. Though only a relatively small number investigate human rights abuses in places as dangerous as Chechnya, a significant number take the risk that they may suffer some form of reprisal: a threat, harassment by officials, a libel suit, an arrest, an assault, or perhaps an attack on a parent or a child. Murder is unusual—though there are a number of cases every year—because it focuses more attention on those intent on silencing their critics. Yet everyone taking on responsibilities like those of Estemirova is aware that it is a possibility.

The international human right movement is made up of men and women who gather information on rights abuses, lawyers and others who advocate for the protection of rights, medical personnel who specialize in the treatment and care of victims, and the much larger number of persons who support these efforts financially and, often, by such means as circulating human rights information, writing letters, taking part in demonstrations, and forming, joining, and managing rights organizations. They are united by their commitment to promote fundamental human rights for all, everywhere. In the period since the end of World War II those rights have been recognized in such international agreements as the Charter of the United Nations, the Universal Declaration of Human Rights, and in a host of global and regional treaties. There is widespread agreement among those who identify themselves with the international human rights movement that the fundamental rights to which they are committed include a prohibition on the arbitrary or invidious deprivation of life or liberty; a prohibition on state interference with the right of all to express themselves freely and peaceably by speech, publication, assembly, or worship; the right of all to equal treatment and equal opportunity regardless of race, ethnicity, nationality, religion, or gender; and a prohibition on such cruelties as torture.

Though identifying with the international human rights movement, many of its adherents may know little or nothing about those promoting the same cause in distant places or even in parts of the world that are relatively close at hand. Even so, a large number recognize that they are part of a struggle that is underway in many places and draw strength from their awareness that they are participants in a movement that does not have boundaries, that is likely to endure, and that values their contributions.

The foremost means of advancing the cause of the international human rights movement that has emerged in the last few decades is the gathering and dissemination of detailed and reliable information on violations of human rights wherever they may occur, including in such places as Chechnya. Information is the lifeblood of the movement. Without knowing her, others in the human rights movement in places remote from Chechnya counted on Estemirova. In turn, she counted on them. Despite the danger, she did what she did every day out of a sense of responsibility to the victims of the crimes she documented; to others in Chechnya, who were the families, friends, and fellow citizens of the victims; to her colleagues in Memorial, who looked to her for information on one of the most dangerous places in Russia; and to her counterparts in the human rights movement worldwide, whose strength as a movement depends on the courage of those like Natalya Estemirova who risk their lives carrying out their self-imposed duties.

The emergence of the international human rights movement as a force in world affairs starting in the late 1970s is not attributable to a single cause. A confluence of unrelated events in different parts of the world that took on added significance because of the Cold War helped to inspire many people to commit themselves to organized efforts to advance the cause. Among those events were the military coup in Chile on September 11, 1973, led by General Augusto Pinochet, and subsequent international outrage at the cruelties committed by the Chilean armed forces under his leadership and at the role of President Richard Nixon and his secretary of state, Henry Kissinger, in supporting the Pinochet coup; the forced resignation of President Nixon from the most powerful post in the world in August 1974 because of his abuses of the rights of Americans; the adoption of the Helsinki Accords in August 1975—an East-West peace agreement with provisions calling for respect for human rights—and, much more important, the establishment soon thereafter of the Moscow Helsinki Group to monitor its human rights provisions. The formation of this group demonstrated that a spark of commitment to rights was alive at the heart of a totalitarian empire. Soviet authorities, however, responded swiftly by imprisoning most Helsinki Group members. Other events contributing to the advent of the human rights movement were the Soweto riots of 1976 and the murder, not long thereafter, of the young black African leader Steve Biko, which turned the spotlight of international attention on the denial of rights in apartheid

South Africa; the advent of Jimmy Carter as president of the United States in 1977 and his decision in the wake of the ignominious end to the war in Vietnam to make human rights the basis for a new moral component within American foreign policy; the awarding of the Nobel Peace Prize to Amnesty International later in 1977, which gave added prominence to a pioneering human rights organization that had taken great care to be even-handed in denouncing abuses by governments of opposing geopolitical alignments and helped it to attract a global membership that today numbers in the millions; and the emergence of the Democracy Wall movement in China in 1978, evidence that even Chairman Mao's decade-long Cultural Revolution, had not extinguished a concern for human rights in another totalitarian state that had, for an extended period, largely isolated itself from the rest of the world.

Like so much else in the Cold War era, many of the 1970s events that led to the emergence of the contemporary human rights movement attracted attention because of their apparent connection to the Cold War struggle. In addition, that context seemed to create links between these events that might otherwise have escaped notice. Resistance to communist and anticommunist tyrannies—sometimes simultaneously and sometimes not—became a defining characteristic of the movement in the years during which it rose to prominence.

The historian Samuel Moyn argues that the failure of the ideologies that lay behind those tyrannies is itself a reason for the emergence of the movement. "The ideological ascendancy of human rights in living memory came out of a combination of separate histories that interacted in an unforeseeable explosion," he has written. "Accident played a role as it does in all human events, but what mattered most of all was the collapse of prior universalistic schemes, and the construction of human rights as a persuasive alternative to them."[2] This view seems mistaken in likening the human rights cause itself to a universalistic scheme, implying that it includes a vision for the organization of society. It does not. On the other hand, Moyn is correct in suggesting that the emergence of the movement was aided by widespread disillusionment with other universalistic schemes. It did not provide an alternative to them, but it did highlight their shortcomings. And in so doing it contributed to their demise.

The emergence of the human rights movement in the 1970s, particularly in the United States, is also due in part to changes in the role of the press that began a decade or so earlier. Up until the Vietnam War, journalists had generally covered armed conflicts as partisans for their own side. During

World War II, for example, British and American correspondents who reported on the Allied forces wore military uniforms.[3] In Vietnam, however, many Western journalists—clad as civilians— questioned the conduct of military operations and, in the United States and elsewhere, helped to create public doubts about the war. Some of the American press skepticism about their own government reflected the experience of a number of journalists in Vietnam who had previously reported on the civil rights movement of the late 1950s and the early 1960s in the South. They had witnessed and reported critically on the performance of state and local law enforcement agencies and the Federal Bureau of Investigation, and they were not ready now to accept on faith what they were told by military commanders in Vietnam. Their approach to their craft was also manifest in the way that the press at home covered the Johnson and Nixon administrations. It reached its apogee with the publication of the "Pentagon Papers" by the *New York Times* and the *Washington Post* and the reporting on Watergate by the *Post* that played a critical role in the forced resignation of Nixon as president in 1974. A new branch of the profession, "investigative journalism," was born. Its targets soon included American participation in the coup in Chile and American involvement in human rights abuses in Latin America and in other parts of the world, such as the role of major corporations in South Africa. One of the early manifestations of the emergence of an American human rights movement was the divestment campaign on college campuses. It led to debates in many institutions across the country about whether their portfolios should include the stocks of companies that did business in the apartheid state and reflected the growing view that Americans shared in responsibility for human rights abuses in other countries.

Interaction between the press and the nongovernmental human rights movement has been an important element in the rise of the movement in many countries. Activists have promoted their cause by seeking media attention for rights abuses, and media exposure of violations and of those responsible for their commission has played an essential role in ending abuse. Simultaneously, in an era in which journalists see themselves in an investigative role, they themselves have taken part in the discovery of abuses and in the identification of those responsible. Often, they look to human rights activists as good sources for information in pursuing their own investigations. The *New York Times* reporter who wrote about the murder of Natalya Estemirova and described her as "both a trusted source and a friend" is typical of many journalists working in territories where it is difficult or dangerous to gather information. He established contact with someone on the scene who was ferreting out just the sort of data that he needed for his reporting, and no doubt she gladly collaborated with him because it was her best means to shine a spotlight on abuses that she had no other means to curb. In many places journalists and human rights activists have formed such symbiotic relationships. A shared sense that they could themselves become the targets of abuse has fostered their alliance. The consequent sharp increase in public awareness of human rights plays a leading role in the story of the rise of the contemporary movement and its influence.

Yet another factor contributing to the emergence of the movement has been the information revolution. As the most important present-day means of protecting human rights is the investigation of abuses, the efficient and rapid dissemination of reports on those abuses is essential. The rise of today's movement took place during a period in which there was also rapid improvement in the ability to transmit information speedily and across borders. This has given the rights movement the ability to become aware of abuses as they take place and to respond instantly.

Today, organized efforts to promote human rights have taken root in most countries of the world. The principal exceptions are a relatively small number of the most repressive countries on earth, including North Korea, Burma, Saudi Arabia, and Turkmenistan, where the authorities will not tolerate the emergence of such organizations. These are also places where it is not possible to engage in investigative journalism. However, in many cities and provincial towns in countries as diverse as Brazil, Russia, India, and Nigeria, local human rights organizations have formed to tackle such issues as police violence, the abuse of persons in detention, and denials of the freedom of expression, as well as other manifestations of official lawlessness. Despite harassment and repression, human rights organizations were active in all those Arab countries that saw political upheavals in 2011 and played an important role in articulating the grievances that led to demands for changes. The movement in such countries often lacks cohesion and a national structure, but it is not short of energy and, over time, it has grown in the sophistication of its methods and in its effectiveness. The extent to which the movement has matured in these regions, and the degree to which it is focused on matters that are universally recognized as core human rights concerns seem to refute the argument that human rights is a Western construct of limited application in other parts of the world. If all restraints on activities to promote human rights were suddenly eliminated in China, there is little doubt that an extensive human rights movement reaching into nearly every corner of that vast country would materialize almost overnight. In fact, wherever abuses are prevalent and mobilization is at least tolerated by the state, the chances are that the human rights movement has established itself.

It is the thesis of this book that the driving force behind the protection of human rights worldwide, today and for roughly the past thirty-five years, has been the nongovernmental human rights movement. Of course, the development of international law and the establishment of international institutions to protect rights is an essential part of the history, and this will be discussed as well. But the emphasis here is on another part of the story, one that has received much less attention elsewhere. Intermittently during the last two-and-a-half centuries, citizens' movements did play important roles in efforts to promote human rights, as during the development of the antislavery movement in England in the eighteenth century and the rise of the feminist movement in the United States in the nineteenth century. The movement that has emerged since the mid-1970s, however, differs from its precursors in that it is global both in its constituency and in its concerns. It has enlisted far larger numbers of adherents than previously, and their efforts involve literally thousands of organizations that though diverse politically, structurally, and stylistically, and operating separately from one another, nevertheless share a sense of being part of one movement. There is little or no prospect that this movement will fade away or decline significantly when it achieves a particular goal, as happened, for example, to the feminist movement for nearly half a century after it won women's suffrage. The contemporary human rights movement responds to victories and defeats by shifting focus from time to time, but it shows signs that it will remain an enduring force in world affairs.

Some accounts of the development of international norms and mechanisms for the protection of human rights suggest that this was a natural development growing out of certain religious and philosophical traditions, or that it was a consequence of historical developments that led states to agree on measures that restrain their authority. What is often m-issing from the analysis is the part played by those outside of government who cared deeply about particular violations of rights and, by making common cause with like-minded others, effectively required governments and intergovernmental bodies to protect rights. Efforts by those outside governments have been particularly important in extending the protection of rights beyond national boundaries, and it is in the present era that they have been most significant. While governments themselves played the leading role in the adoption of previous treaties to protect rights, it is widely recognized that such recent international agreements as the 1997 Treaty to Ban Landmines and the 1998 Rome Treaty that established the International Criminal Court were direct consequences of campaigns by nongovernmental organizations. Governments had to agree to these treaties, but the impetus for them came from citizens' movements. The role of the nongovernmental movement is even more important in exposing abuses of rights and in mobilizing efforts to secure remedies and redress.

Most of the principal U.S.–based organizations concerned with human rights internationally—Helsinki Watch (which became Human Rights Watch), the Lawyers Committee for International Human Rights (which became Human Rights First), the Committee to Protect Journalists, the International Human Rights Law Group (which became Global Rights), Physicians for Human Rights—were formed in the late 1970s or at the beginning of the 1980s. At about the same time human rights associations organized on a national basis were established from El Salvador to Algeria to South Africa to Poland to the Philippines, and in many other countries in between.

There were much older bodies, of course. By far the most important was Amnesty International, established in 1961, whose selection for the Peace Prize by the Nobel Committee in 1977 was a landmark in the recognition of today's international human rights movement. Going back even further, a small U.S.–based group, the International League for Human Rights, was formed during World War II at about the time that a commitment to promote human rights was being developed for incorporation in the United Nations Charter. The roots of the International League go back to an organization to promote rights established in France in the aftermath of the Dreyfus case of the 1890s and an international federation to protect rights, also based in France, that was launched in the early 1920s. Though subsequently eclipsed by other groups, the early participants in those organizations played an important role for a time as voices for human rights at the United Nations and had an impact both on the norms that were established in a number of agreements on rights adopted by the world body and on the development of its machinery for addressing rights issues. Yet the adherents of such early groups—and of an even earlier organization, the London-based Anti-Slavery Society (still in operation as Anti-Slavery International), which goes back to the 1820s—probably did not see themselves as part of a global movement. Rather, they were a small specialized lobby concerned with such matters as, in the case of Amnesty, freeing an individual who had been unjustly imprisoned for reasons of conscience or stopping a particular prisoner from being tortured. Such efforts remain an essential component of the mission of today's movement, in which Amnesty—with scores of national sections and close to three million dues-paying members—plays an important part. But campaigns to protect individual victims of abuse do not constitute the sum and substance of the present-day human rights movement. Today's movement regularly addresses broad issues of public policy that affect the rights of large sectors of the population.

A characteristic that distinguishes the movement that began to take shape in the late 1970s from what went before is that it has enlisted individuals such as Natalya Estemirova in places far from the headquarters of the United Nations and far from Western capitals such as London or Paris; and that those active in it have a strong sense of belonging to a global movement. An essential part of the work of contemporary human rights organizations operating at both the local and national levels is making their concerns and their findings about particular abuses of rights known to those active in international rights efforts. Similarly, organizations operating internationally seek relations with local human rights activists in the countries on which their work focuses. Though they may have little in common linguistically, culturally, or politically, a great many of the millions of persons worldwide who consider themselves human rights activists feel a kinship and seek ties to others within the movement. This helps them to overcome the often well-founded fear of many activists in repressive countries that they themselves may suffer reprisals at the hands of abusive officials.

Prior to the 1970s, the role of the United States in the development of the international human rights movement was not substantial. Both France and England played far more significant roles internationally. As mentioned, the organized movement got underway in France in the 1890s as an outgrowth of the Dreyfus case. It gained momentum following World War I with the establishment of the Fédération International des Droits de l'Homme in 1922 and again with that organization's rebirth after it had been wiped out during World War II. From the start, the outlook of the French-based movement was international, seemingly taking it as a given that the protection of rights is linked to developments that cross national boundaries.

The English rights movement, which began much earlier with the campaign against slavery in the latter part of the eighteenth century, was by its nature international, because the slave trade was international. Rights causes that aroused the British during the nineteenth century, such as various campaigns that focused on cruelties attributed to the Ottoman Turks, were also international. When Amnesty International was established in England, it was intended from the start that it would operate globally.

In contrast, the United States was a latecomer to the cause of international human rights. The nineteenth-century American abolitionist movement and the women's equality movement both focused almost entirely on developments within the United States. Similarly, when major rights organizations such as the National Association for the Advancement of Colored People and the American Civil Liberties Union were established in the early years of the twentieth century, their exclusive concern was the rights of Americans. A few of their leaders, most notably the ACLU's Roger Baldwin, sought to stimulate the development of rights organizations elsewhere, but those activities were kept separate from the work of the organization that Baldwin founded and directed for its first three decades.

When Americans finally became significantly involved in the promotion of rights internationally in the 1970s, however, they quickly became leaders in the field. The decisive factor was their country's leadership in the Cold War struggle. On the one hand, they were in the forefront of denunciations of human rights abuses by America's Cold War antagonist, the Soviet Union, and its client states. On the other hand, many Americans who committed themselves to the international human rights cause also did battle with their own government over its support for anticommunist regimes in various parts of the world that themselves engaged in severe abuses of rights. These struggles propelled them into the forefront of the worldwide human rights movement that was just then emerging and becoming a global force because of its connection to the Cold War. For reasons of language and their differing legal traditions and legal culture, little contact was established between the American-led movement that emerged in the 1970s and the older French-centered movement. Contacts between the British-led movement and the new recruits to the international human rights cause in the United States were, however, quickly and smoothly established. Amnesty International, for example, which had mainly taken hold in Europe up to that point, attracted large numbers of American members, and became a force in the United States. Thus, the "Anglo-Saxons" became the leaders of the worldwide human rights movement, at least until about the beginning of the twenty-first century when the movement became so global in character that it is no longer possible to ascribe leadership to any particular segment.

A factor that contributed to the emergence of United States-based organizations as leaders in the international movement during the last quarter of the twentieth century was the fact that they were better financed than most of their counterparts elsewhere. Amnesty International, which obtained its financial support almost entirely from relatively small contributions from its large membership—concentrated in Western Europe and, subsequent to its receipt of the Nobel Peace Prize in 1977, also in the United States—long dwarfed all other organizations in the field in the size of its budget. Even today, it raises and spends annually a great deal more than the next largest organization, Human Rights Watch. Yet because private philanthropy is far greater in the United States than anywhere else, when in the 1970s Americans finally committed themselves to the promotion of international human rights, a plethora of U.S.-based organizations were able to secure significant financial support. Indeed, American donors quickly became a main source of funding not only for U.S.-based organizations but also for nationally based bodies worldwide.

Much of the organized effort to promote human rights internationally is conducted by organizations focused on ending abuses in their own countries. Yet such bodies are usually well aware that they urgently need support from human rights organizations operating globally, many of which are based in the United States, such as Human Rights Watch, or the United Kingdom, such as Amnesty International. There are three principal reasons for this. First, associations campaigning for an end to human rights abuses in repressive countries may embarrass their governments by calling attention to abuses and, therefore, are themselves particularly susceptible to reprisals. When human rights monitors in one part of the world are under attack, it is essential that organizations operating globally from relatively safe places set up an outcry on their behalf. In this manner, the global organizations provide a measure of protection for national and local groups. Second, many repressive governments can readily ignore complaints from domestic rights monitors. There may be no free press in the country to report their complaints, or the main media in the country—being aligned with the government or controlled by it—may pay little heed to their reports of abuses. Also, it is often difficult for the international press to assess the reliability of complaints issuing from local organizations that are regularly dismissed by their governments as politically biased efforts by opposition groups masquerading under a human rights banner in order to discredit the government with false or misleading information. For such reasons, local or national bodies may get scant attention. The leading global organizations, on the other hand, have reputations that they have established through their work in many countries. A claim that Human Rights Watch is biased against Syria or that Amnesty International is engaged in a conspiracy against the government of Uzbekistan is unlikely to deter the press from reporting their findings. Third, organizations operating globally have ready access to a variety of international fora and established contacts in the international media. It is therefore far more difficult for a government to ignore a global human rights body based far away than a national organization in its own country.

Yet, just as national and local bodies need global organizations for their protection and to give resonance internationally to their complaints, the reverse is also true. The leading global human rights organizations rely on their own investigations of abuses because this is essential in establishing and maintaining their credibility, but they need to be pointed in the right direction, and it is generally national and local human rights bodies that are best able to do this. They tend to establish connections with the victims of abuses and their families, they are familiar with the circumstances and understand the context in which abuses take place, and they often are able to identify those responsible. Without trustworthy and knowledgeable local contacts, a global organization might be able to accomplish little. Often, in fact, the main role of a global body is to validate the findings of national or local human rights organizations. Research in a country lacking a domestic human rights movement is far more difficult for global organizations. This is a reason for the paucity of reports on the abuses committed by such governments as Saudi Arabia and North Korea. Unfortunately, it is the most repressive governments that regularly insulate themselves against human rights pressure by making it exceedingly difficult for bodies operating outside their borders to gather reliable information on their abuses. At times, the neighbors of a repressive regime collaborate in restricting the flow of information. In the case of North Korea, for example, a main source of information is testimony obtained from refugees crossing the border into northeastern China. The Chinese authorities, however, make it very hard to gather the information that these refugees might provide. Without being able to consult domestic human rights monitors in dangerous places, there is little information that international organizations can gather. The interdependence of domestic and global efforts to promote human rights in places where it is possible for local monitors to function has forged strong links between the various components of the movement worldwide and a powerful sense of identification with that movement.

As we have seen, the contemporary human rights movement emerged as a force in international public affairs during a period of intense Cold War competition between East and West, and it made its mark in significant part by exploiting that rivalry. In an earlier era, that competition was sometimes characterized by partisans on both sides in economic terms: in the 1950s and 1960s, for example, it was commonplace to describe the struggle between East and West as communism versus capitalism or, as many Westerners preferred to say, communism versus free enterprise. When those in the West spoke of the virtues of their system, they tended to conjure up images of middle-class suburban houses with cars in every driveway. In contrast, those claiming the superiority of the communist system portrayed happy workers in well-organized factories or riding tractors through endless fields of grain, while their images of the West focused on urban slum housing. By the mid-1970s, when the human rights movement was taking shape, those images were changing. Increasingly, the disparity between the two sides was portrayed in the West in political terms: as repression, or totalitarianism, versus liberty, or human rights. The human rights movement did not bring about that shift in focus. Rather, it developed over time as a result of such political events as Moscow's violent suppression of the Hungarian Revolution in 1956, the construction of the Berlin Wall in 1961, the entry of Soviet tanks into Prague in 1968, and the suppression of Solidarity in Poland in 1981. Influential, too, were writers and thinkers such as George Orwell, Karl Popper, Isaiah Berlin, Czeslaw Milosz, Alexander Solzhenitsyn, Raymond Aron, Leszek Kolakowski, and Hannah Arendt. But the efforts of human rights activists did contribute to the widespread acceptance of the new paradigm. Andrei Sakharov and the Helsinki monitors in the Soviet Union, their counterparts in other East bloc countries— Vaclav Havel and the other signatories of Charter 77 in Czechoslovakia; in Poland, Adam Michnik and his fellow intellectuals in KOR, who made possible the emergence of Solidarity—as well as those in the West who rallied to their support, awakened global consciousness to the repressive character of the states that found it necessary to send such persons to their prisons. Simultaneously, Western human rights activists of the 1970s and the 1980s embarrassed their own governments by pointing out that their claim to represent the forces of freedom was contradicted by their support for military dictatorships in Latin America and Asia, the apartheid regime in South Africa, and many other repressive governments. The American government's involvement in events in Chile in 1973 had a particularly galvanizing effect. Coming at a time when the United States was finally extricating itself from the war in Vietnam, the U.S. role in the Pinochet coup suggested to many Americans and other Westerners that there were no limits on their governments' willingness to assist in the commission of cruelties in the name of the Cold War struggle.

It is possible to point to a number of factors that contributed to the fall of the Berlin Wall in 1989, the collapse of the Soviet empire, and the end to the Cold War. How large a part was played by the human rights movement, East or West, is open to debate. Beyond doubt, however, it was one of the causes, if not the most important cause, of that epic series of events. A former director of the Central Intelligence Agency, Robert Gates, who subsequently served as President George W. Bush's secretary of defense, and was reappointed to that post by President Barack Obama, wrote in his memoir of his service at the CIA: "The Soviets desperately wanted the CSCE [the Conference on Security and Cooperation in Europe, the official name of the 1975 meeting that produced the Helsinki Accords], they got it and it laid the foundations for the end of their empire. We resisted it for years, went grudgingly, [President Gerald] Ford paid a terrible price for going——perhaps reelection itself —only to discover years later that CSCE had yielded benefits beyond our wildest imagination. Go figure."[4] Those benefits derived from the incorporation in the Helsinki Accords of a number of provisions calling for respect of human rights, including the right of an individual "to know and act on his rights." What neither President Ford nor Chairman Brezhnev had imagined when they met in Helsinki in 1975 was that a handful of men and women in Moscow—at the outset, the Moscow Helsinki Group had only eleven members—would seize on the human rights provisions of the Helsinki Accords and take them as a charter to monitor the conduct of their own government; that they would inspire others in the Soviet bloc countries to do similar things; and that a number of Westerners would rally to their defense when they were persecuted for their efforts and insist that freeing the imprisoned Helsinki monitors should become a goal of the foreign policies of their own governments. Robert Gates acknowledged, with some evident chagrin, that the Helsinki human rights monitors did far more to undermine the Soviet system than was ever done by the agency he led, the CIA.

In the late 1970s, when the Helsinki monitors in the Soviet bloc countries were being sent to prison, most countries in Latin America were governed by military dictatorships. Over the next decade and a half, elected governments replaced almost all those regimes. By the 1990s, Cuba remained the Western hemisphere's only out-and-out dictatorship. Some of the other governments in the region, such as those in Guatemala, Colombia, Peru during the years it was ruled by President Alberto Fujimori, Venezuela under Hugo Chavez, and Haiti continued to manifest significant human rights shortcomings, but they should not be compared with the brutal regimes that slaughtered tens of thousands and, in the case of successive military regimes in Guatemala, hundreds of thousands. Here again it is possible to debate how large a part was played by the human rights movement, but it seems incontrovertible that the movement was one of the significant factors in the rapid transformation that took place in that region, beginning with the establishment of a democratic government in Argentina in December 1983, and culminating in the removal of General Augusto Pinochet from his post as dictator of Chile in March 1990.

When the administration of President Ronald Reagan took office in 1981, it was initially determined to abandon the human rights policy associated with Reagan's predecessor, Jimmy Carter. Among other things, officials of the new administration, such as Reagan's ambassador to the United Nations, Jeane Kirkpatrick, blamed the Carter human rights policy for the fall of the Somoza dynasty in Nicaragua and the rise to power of the Sandinistas; and for the fall of the regime of the Shah in Iran and its replacement by Khomeini's Islamic republic.[5] Nothing like that would take place under the new watch, Reagan's secretary of state Alexander Haig, and Ambassador Kirkpatrick made clear. They sought to provide military and financial support to such regimes as the military dictatorships in Argentina and Chile. To no avail. They were stymied by the nascent American human rights movement and its allies in Congress and the press. Eventually, even the Reagan administration shifted ground. In Reagan's second term, he sent an ambassador to Chile, Harry Barnes, who quickly came into conflict with Pinochet over human rights. In Reagan's final year in office, 1988, Pinochet had scheduled a plebiscite to confirm his rule for an additional eight years. At the last moment, realizing he would lose, he tried to cancel his own plebiscite. The Reagan administration, which by then had embraced the rhetoric of human rights and, a few years earlier, in a June 1982 address to the British parliament by the American president, had proclaimed a "crusade" to promote democracy worldwide, forced Pinochet to go forward. He lost the plebiscite he had counted on to ratify his hold on power, setting in motion the democratic transition that culminated in his removal from office a year-and-a-half later. Earlier in Reagan's second term, his administration had reluctantly abandoned two other right-wing dictators it had previously supported: President Ferdinand Marcos of the Philippines and President-for-Life Jean Claude ("Baby Doc") Duvalier of Haiti. Each was forced to flee the country in which he had previously been all-powerful.

Another notable example of the way in which the efforts of the human rights movement contributed to a transition from repression comes from South Africa. Within that country, a rights movement made up of both black and white South Africans played a crucial role. The movement's efforts were aided, as is widely recognized, by the international sanctions imposed by many countries but resisted by two key leaders of the 1980s: Prime Minister Margaret Thatcher in Britain and President Ronald Reagan in the United States. Reagan came, however, under intense public and congressional pressure on the issue and, in 1985, in the face of proposed legislation that would have been adopted over his veto, he signed an executive order that called for "active constructive engagement." That was not good enough. Pressed by the human rights movement, Congress adopted much tougher sanctions in October 1986 and overrode Reagan's veto.

Another factor in the transformation in South Africa is related to events in the Soviet bloc. Despite economic and diplomatic sanctions, and despite an international sports boycott that caused much grief in a sports-mad country, many white South Africans believed that their government was too important an outpost in the East-West struggle to be abandoned by the West. That perception could not survive the collapse of communism, the fall of the Berlin Wall in November 1989, and the end of the Cold War. Yet, retaining their sense that they were a part of the West despite their geographical isolation at the southern tip of Africa, was crucial to many white South Africans. Maintaining that status seems to have mattered even more to some than preserving apartheid. It is probably no coincidence that the announcement by President F.W. de Klerk that Nelson Mandela would be released from prison and that the African National Congress would be legalized took place in February 1990, just three months after the fall of the Berlin Wall. The human rights effort that contributed to the fall of communism and the end of the Cold War seems also to have had an indirect impact on the process of change in South Africa.

For two decades subsequent to the end of the Cold War, it was not possible for the human rights movement to have so dramatic an impact. Yet it continued to play a major role in international affairs in the 1990s and in the first decade of the next century as a consequence, in part, of the stance it had adopted during the 1980s on two related issues: compliance with the laws of armed conflict and the holding accountable of officials responsible for crimes against humanity. To a lesser extent, it also maintained its significance by leading resistance to excesses by governments in combating terrorism. Its attention to armed conflict has meant that many wars, such as NATO's intervention in Kosovo in 1999, Israel's war against Hezbollah in 2006, and Georgia's war in 2008 against Russia were assessed, as they took place, substantially on the basis of the toll they took in civilian casualties. This focus has significantly reduced the numbers killed in some conflicts, as the combatants must modify their conduct in order to gain support in the arena of international public opinion. Those achievements should not be overstated, however, for there are instances where combatants deliberately flout public opinion. This was manifest in Iraq when insurgent forces in the wake of the 2003 U.S. invasion seem deliberately to have killed as many civilians as possible in order to destabilize the country and turn the U.S. victory over Saddam Hussein's forces to ashes. To an extent, this has also been the strategy of the Taliban in Afghanistan, where many in the country blame NATO forces both for their own killings of civilians and for failing to prevent the much larger number of civilian casualties attributable to insurgent forces. Both the Tamil Tigers and the Sri Lankan armed forces demonstrated a readiness to sacrifice large numbers of civilians in the last days of the struggle that in 2009 effectively ended the nation's twenty-six-year-old civil war. Other conflicts in which especially large numbers of noncombatants were killed during the first decade of the twenty-first century include those in Sudan (Darfur) and the Democratic Republic of the Congo. Yet even the magnitude of civilian casualties in these wars in our time is dwarfed by the vast number killed in the years after World War II, before there was an international human rights movement that took up a focus on armed conflict. They include the many millions who died in such conflicts as the partition of India and Pakistan, the military takeover in Indonesia, the Biafran war, the war for the independence of Bangladesh, the Vietnam war, the Cambodian holocaust, Indonesia's annexation of East Timor, the Iran-Iraq war, wars in the African states of Ethiopia, Mozambique, Angola, and Sudan, the counterinsurgency in Guatemala, and the Soviet Union's war in Afghanistan.

The campaign by the human rights movement to bring to justice officials responsible for gross human rights abuses has resulted in criminal proceedings against, among others, the former president of Yugoslavia, Slobodan

Milosevic, who died in prison before his trial was completed; former Prime Minister Jean Kambanda of Rwanda, who is serving a life sentence in prison at this writing; former President Jorge Videla of Argentina who was tried, convicted, imprisoned, amnestied, and then imprisoned again; former President Augusto Pinochet of Chile, who was arrested in London and escaped long-term imprisonment in his own country due only to age, infirmity and, eventually, death; former President Saddam Hussein of Iraq, who was executed by hanging; former President Charles Taylor of Liberia, who is on trial at this writing; Khieu Samphan, the head of state in Cambodia when it was ruled by the Khmer Rouge, who is also on trial for crimes committed more than three decades ago; Omar Hassan al Bashir, President of Sudan, who has been indicted by the prosecutor for the International Criminal Court for war crimes, crimes against humanity, and genocide in Darfur; Alberto Fujimori of Peru, the democratically elected former president, who was convicted by a court in his own country and sentenced to a long prison term for establishing a death squad that committed at least two massacres. The list is growing and now includes as well hundreds of high-ranking political and military officials prosecuted and punished for war crimes, crimes against humanity, and genocide by international tribunals, such as those established to deal with ex-Yugoslavia and Rwanda; by national courts in such countries as Argentina, Peru, and Chile; and by courts in Bosnia, Croatia, and Serbia that have cooperated with the International Criminal Tribunal for the former Yugoslavia. Over time, the impact could be—if it is not already—that officials will consider, before they take actions against noncombatants, whether their decisions might lead to their prosecution and punishment. Recent advances in limiting impunity for such officials were an outgrowth of international revulsion over the great crimes committed in the post–Cold War period in such countries as Bosnia and Rwanda. The human rights movement proved incapable of mitigating those horrors as they took place, but it has translated the revulsion against them into international judicial mechanisms, including a permanent International Criminal Court, that are intended to hold accountable those most responsible. Over time, this should help to deter others from committing comparable crimes. Indeed, it may already be having that effect.

Frequently, the human rights movement's focus on armed conflicts and its effort to promote accountability go hand in hand. Darfur is an example. Organizations such as Human Rights Watch played a leading role in putting the killings, rapes, and mass forced displacement in Darfur on the international agenda. In addition, they successfully campaigned to get the case referred to the International Criminal Court (ICC) in 2005 for the prosecution of those Sudanese officials who could be identified as principally culpable. The efforts of the human rights movement helped to prevent the United States from vetoing a resolution in the U.N. Security Council referring Darfur to the criminal tribunal in The Hague. Although the United States had condemned the crimes committed in Darfur as "genocide," Washington had been expected to block ICC consideration of the case because of the Bush administration's strenuous opposition to the court. A Security Council referral was required because Sudan had not signed and ratified the treaty creating the ICC and, therefore, would not otherwise have come under the jurisdiction of that court. That the United States abstained on the referral rather than vetoing it indicated that even an administration whose relations with parts of the human rights movement were as poor as the Bush administration's could be swayed by the movement's efforts.[6]

It is also important not to overstate the achievements of the international human rights movement in securing accountability. The tribunals it helped to establish have often seemed painfully slow in their proceedings and are expensive to operate. Also, they have so far only demonstrated the capacity to prosecute and punish a relatively small number of the officials who perpetrated the crimes that they investigated, and there seems little prospect that they will be able to cope with a substantially larger number of cases. Perhaps most important, at this writing all those officials who have been called to account have been either leaders or functionaries in states of no more than secondary significance, or leaders of guerrilla groups engaged in combat with such states. There is no realistic prospect that officials of governments as powerful as those of Russia, China, or the United States will become defendants before human rights tribunals in the foreseeable future. Nor does it seem likely that tribunals such as the International Criminal Court will in the near future sit in judgment of officials of regional powers such as Pakistan, Iran, or Venezuela. The human rights movement has far to go in trying to establish a system of international justice that has the authority and prestige to secure universal compliance with its orders and its judgments. Despite these significant shortcomings, however, what has been achieved in the field of international justice in a relatively brief period—less than two decades since the establishment of the Yugoslav tribunal in 1993— seems remarkable.

In 2011, more than two decades after the revolutions in Eastern Europe that brought the Cold War to an end, the world order has again been altered by a set of revolutions, this time in the Arab states of North Africa and the Middle East. As was the case in the former Soviet bloc, the human rights movement played an important but unquantifiable role. Human rights organizations in such countries as Egypt, Tunisia, Bahrain, Syria, Yemen, and Libya, were severely constrained in their ability to operate by the regimes that governed in the region, with some being required to conduct operations outside their own countries. Nonetheless, they had played an important role since the 1970s in documenting abuses and giving voice to those protesting repression. Many of the leaders of these organizations had themselves suffered abuses such as imprisonment or exile. Yet, their role in articulating grievances played an important part in the protests that took place in 2011 in those countries and in the changes that took place. In addition, these same organizations gathered information on abuses committed while the protests were underway, and it is expected that they will have a significant role in promoting accountability for those abuses as well as for the abuses committed over long periods by the governments that were overthrown.

As is apparent, the contemporary international human rights movement faces a host of challenges. It has been in the forefront of efforts in many countries to stop violations of civil liberties committed in the name of the so-called "war on terror" and to prevent what were, in many cases, hasty responses to a perceived emergency from turning into new norms for investigating and regulating the day-to-day activities of citizens. The fact that such measures have been adopted by governments generally respectful of civil liberties, such as the United States and the United Kingdom, has made the challenge especially serious. And the impact is not limited to those countries. Governments in other parts of the world inevitably justify their own practices that violate civil liberties by citing the example of the countries long identified as leading Western proponents of rights. Moreover, the role played by the United States since the Carter presidency in bringing pressure on other governments to respect rights could not be sustained in an era when the U.S. itself practiced and justified long-term detention without charges or trial, denial of habeas corpus, and torture. U.S.–based human rights groups operating globally had in the past tried to leverage the power, purse, and influence of the United States to promote civil liberties in other countries. In the period after September 11, 2001 and the American response, the usefulness of such efforts was drastically reduced. Currently, the U.S.–based human rights movement must rely much more on its own capacity to embarrass governments that abuse human rights. During the years of George W. Bush's presidency, it largely abandoned its previous efforts to use the government of the United States as its surrogate in dealing with other governments. Whether the United States will reclaim the moral high ground in the post-Bush years remains an open question at this writing. The Obama administration has enhanced the international prestige of the United States by its strong stand against torture, but in a number of other respects it has not broken sharply with the human rights practices of the Bush administration. Efforts by Western human rights organizations to enlist the European Union in efforts to promote human rights internationally have not provided an effective substitute for the role previously played by the U.S. The European Union has had a very positive influence on human rights practices in those countries—Croatia, Serbia, and Turkey, for example—that aspire to membership, but it has not been able to exercise significant influence at a global level. In part, this reflects the European Union's unwillingness to appoint leaders who might compete with or overshadow national officials in political influence. In addition, it manifests the difficulty of getting twenty-seven countries to speak with one voice on rights issues. Also, of course, the economic difficulties of some of its member states in recent years have made the E.U. more inward-looking than might otherwise be the case.

The human rights movement, having become capable of exercising significant influence over public policy during the last ten or twelve years of the Cold War, confronted its most significant challenge after the terrorist attacks on New York and Washington, DC, on September 11, 2001. During the Cold War years, the movement essentially prevailed in its argument that the opposing sides were not justified in violating rights—that is, those fundamental rights recognized in the Universal Declaration of Human Rights and in subsequent treaties—by the exigencies of their conflict. It has seemed more difficult, however, to support that argument in the current climate. Because there was always a possibility that the Cold War could have metastasized into global armed conflict between nuclear powers, one could argue that the 1970s and 1980s were actually a much more dangerous period than the first decade of the twenty-first century. While terrorist attacks in various parts of the world have caused carnage, suffering, and havoc, they do not seem to pose an existential threat comparable to what could have happened during the Cold War. Yet, it is not possible to say that the human rights movement is winning its argument with those who would constrain rights so as to increase their advantages in combating terrorists. Debates have not yet been resolved over such issues as extended administrative detention without charges or trials before bodies not providing the safeguards customarily given to criminal defendants. The use of coercive measures up to and including torture against those suspected of involvement in terrorism, though discredited to a greater degree than other abuses, still has significant political support in the United States. Certainly, the international human rights movement has made headway in these areas, but the arguments continue. And with each new terrorist outrage—each attack whether failed or successful, whether in New York, Bali, London, Jakarta, Madrid, or Mumbai—the human rights cause suffers a setback.

The difficulty the movement has had in recent years in securing acceptance of its argument that rights should not be set aside when dealing with terrorism has not, however, seemed to impede its growth. The movement today is made up of a larger number of organizations with more supporters, more resources, operating in more places, and dealing with a wider range of issues than ever before. Globally, only the international environmental movement, which also acquired the characteristics of an enduring worldwide citizens' movement in the 1970s capable of shaping public policy on a range of issues in many parts of the world, is comparably well developed and influential. The two movements exemplify a sea change that has taken place in the making of public policy in recent decades. Previously, when nongovernmental organizations attempted to influence public policy, it was often to advance their own interests, or the interests of their constituents. Not so in the case of the environmental and human rights movements. For the most part, they intervene in public policy matters for altruistic reasons, to improve the lot of others. (The contemporary women's movement became a global force at about the same time, but it failed to develop a comparably influential institutional structure and has played a more limited role in international public policy. On the other hand, it has been very influential in changing personal behavior in many places, both by women and men, and also in securing many adjustments in institutional behavior.) The fact that the human rights and environmental movements have developed so substantially and have come to play such a significant role is a phenomenon that seems worthy of description and analysis.

It is important to note that it does not seem possible to write a history of either the international human rights movement or of the principal events and ideas that shaped it in a linear or chronological manner. This is because several different strands in the fabric of the movement originated at different times and places and were only woven together in the contemporary era. To take one example, considerable effort is today devoted to promoting compliance with the laws of war, the field known as "international humanitarian law." This focus arises from the contemporary recognition that armed conflict is often accompanied by severe abuses and that a principal method of the human right movement, documenting those abuses and measuring them against the norms of international humanitarian law, may be an effective means to mitigate them. Moreover, unlike in earlier times, because of its substantial institutional development and the credibility it has achieved, the contemporary international human rights movement has acquired the capacity to monitor many of the practices of the opposing sides in armed conflicts. It seems appropriate to consider the history of international humanitarian law in a separate chapter because much of its development took place in the period from the 1850s through the 1970s. Mitigating the consequences of armed conflict was beyond the scope of those active in efforts to promote human rights during that era. It was only after the 1970s that the human rights movement identified itself with international humanitarian law and began to promote compliance.

Because the international human rights cause has only acquired the characteristics of a sustained global movement in recent times and continues to develop in ways that are not wholly predictable, it may look quite different in a few years. Three examples. Though it has been impossible up to now for a broad-gauged human rights organization to emerge in China, increasing numbers of Chinese lawyers and others are devoting themselves to efforts to promote human rights. The authorities periodically crack down by imprisoning one or another human rights activist and, in the case of the lawyers, also by disbarring them. But in recent years China has not tried to snuff out the movement entirely. It is impossible to know how things will develop. There could be far harsher and more systematic repression or, consistent with the government's professed desire to extend the rule of law, it might tolerate greater latitude for those attempting to promote rights. It is also possible, of course, that the Chinese authorities will maintain their present somewhat ambivalent and ambiguous policy. Given China's importance both in terms of what happens within the country and its influence globally, the choices made by the country's ruling communist party, and the responses it will elicit from China's emerging civil society, will have enormous impact.

The part that will be played by human rights organizations in the Middle East in the period ahead is also difficult to predict. Though not in the forefront of those organizing the Arab revolutions of 2011, both domestic and international human rights organizations nevertheless played a crucial role by providing the world's press with reliable reports on such incidents as attacks by security forces on unarmed demonstrators. Also, the abuses documented by human rights organizations—such as arbitrary detention, torture, and the prolonged use of emergency laws—figured significantly in demands for change. Governments in the region had in the past generally tolerated the emergence of human rights organizations, harassing them with some regularity, but otherwise paying them little heed. Their complaints were largely ignored both domestically and internationally. As they had little chance to obtain traction in the courts of their own countries, and as the region does not have supranational legal institutions akin to those that exist in Europe, Latin America, and to a lesser extent in Africa, they could not use litigation to protect rights. Before the revolutions of 2011, domestic human rights organizations in most countries of the Middle East were not a significant force. It is impossible to tell whether they will maintain or increase the heightened importance they achieved during the Arab revolutions.

The third example centers on the questions of whether a current trend by governments to try to cut off foreign funding for nongovernmental organizations will be sustained and what will be its impact. At this writing, among the governments that have recently enacted or that are actively considering new restrictions on foreign funding are Russia, India, Israel, and Ethiopia. It is plain that human rights organizations are the main target as they are the NGOs most apt to annoy such governments and also because funding from European and American donors is more available to them than to other organizations (in Israel, members of the Knesset have been explicit in seeking to cut off funds to Israeli human rights organizations, complaining that they are engaged in "lawfare" against the state). Such funding restrictions are also significant because governmental opposition discourages local donors. In Russia, a foundation established by the industrial tycoon Mikhail Khodorkovsky, the Open Russia Foundation, briefly became a major funder of nongovernmental organizations, including human rights groups. That came to an end when the Russian government imprisoned Khodorkovsky and seized his assets.

Despite many such uncertainties, it seems very likely that the international human rights movement will continue to play an important role in public policy for the foreseeable future. The chapters that follow will attempt to provide an account of the history of the movement, describing its philosophic roots, connecting it to the development of international law and international institutions, and exploring the strategies by which it has acquired and exercised political influence. The book will assess as well what the movement has accomplished up to now, what issues are at present its foremost concerns, and the challenges it faces in the years ahead. It is written from the standpoint of one whose career and thoughts were shaped by the international human rights movement and who, in turn, had an opportunity to contribute to its development.

2

Putting Natural Law Principles into Practice

AS OF SEPTEMBER 29, 2011

IT IS POSSIBLE TO CITE ANCIENT ROOTS FOR THE PRINCIPLES OF human rights. Hammurabi's Code, the Bible, Plato, and Aristotle must be considered among the sources for our concept of justice. Roman thinkers such as Cicero and Seneca helped to develop our commitment to freedom of expression. The roots of thinking about rights can also be traced to non-Western sources, such as Mencius and Asoka. In the Christian era, Augustine, Boethius, and Aquinas are among those whose writings about justice were influential and, by the thirteenth century, we may add to this list the English barons at Runnymede who forced King John to accept the Magna Carta limiting the power of kings to infringe on rights. In the late medieval period (early fifteenth century), Christine de Pisan, who wrote about the law of chivalry and the customary laws of war, also called attention to the rights of women.

Yet as the historian Lynn Hunt has argued, "Human rights only become meaningful when they gain political content." Hunt contends that this did not take place until a much more recent period because, as she points out, "They are not the rights of humans in a state of nature; they are the rights of humans in society. They are not just human rights as opposed to divine rights, or human rights as opposed to animal rights; they are the rights of humans vis-à-vis each other. They are therefore rights guaranteed in the secular political world (even if they are called "sacred"), and they are rights that require active participation from those who hold them."[1] To this, it could be added that they are not only the rights of the active participants. They are also the rights of others, which we deem worth defending even though we may not know the beneficiaries. In Hunt's view, this concept of human rights requires a commitment to three principles: that rights are natural and, therefore, inherent in all human beings and not only in those who derive them from their relationship to a particular entity or political regime; that all are equal in their entitlement to rights; and that rights are universal and, therefore, applicable everywhere. There is, of course, considerable overlap between these principles. Belief in any one of them also implies a commitment to the other two. Their interdependence is made manifest in the opening sentences of the American Declaration of Independence of 1776 which asserts the right of the people "to assume . . . the separate and equal station to which the Laws of Nature and of Nature's God entitle them"; "that all men are created equal"; "that they are endowed by their Creator with certain unalienable Rights"; and that rights are not derived from association with a particular government because "whenever any form of Government becomes destructive of these ends, it is the Right of the People to alter or to abolish it . . . ." Paul Gordon Lauren points out that, "It also was a call to revolution . . . not only in the New World, but in the Old as well; for as Jefferson would go on to write: 'a bill of rights is what the people are entitled to against every government on earth'"[2]

Though Hunt considers that it was only in the latter part of the eighteenth century that human rights acquired political content, it seems possible to go back about a century and a half earlier to the struggles of dissenting movements in England in the middle decades of the seventeenth century to find men actively engaged in efforts to uphold rights in which they believed. It was an era of religious strife and parliamentary assertiveness that saw the overthrow of a monarchy and civil war. Christopher Hill, a leading historian of that era, has written:

> For a short time, ordinary people were freer from the authority of church and social superiors than they had ever been before, or were for a long time to be again. . . . They speculated about the end of the world and the coming of the millennium; about the justice of God condemning the mass of mankind to eternal torment for a sin which (if anyone) Adam committed; some of them became skeptical of the existence of hell. They contemplated the possibility that God might intend to save everybody, that something of God might be within each of us. They founded new sects to express these new ideas. Some

considered the possibility that there might be no Creator God, only nature. They attacked the monopolization of knowledge within the privileged professions, divinity, law, medicine. They criticized educational structure, especially the universities, and proposed a vast expansion of education opportunity. They discussed the relation of the sexes, and questioned parts of the protestant ethic.[3]

The religious and political sects of that turbulent period in England—they included the Levellers, the Diggers, the Ranters, the Quakers, the Muggletonians, and many others—were preoccupied not only by their distinctive beliefs but also with the importance that they attached to their right to hold and express those beliefs and by their right to be treated fairly and humanely when the state sought to suppress their beliefs. The Levellers, in particular, insisted upon their "native rights" and "resolved to maintain them with our utmost possibilities." Many rights advocates in our time would find much in common with the views expressed in the 1640s by John Lilburne ("Freedom John"), the best known of the Levellers, whose own commitment to rights encompassed a belief that they were natural, that all were equal, and that rights are universal. Freedom of speech and the press were central to their concept of rights. Levellers demanded of Parliament that the government must "hear all voices and judgments, which they can never do but by giving freedom to the press."[4] Advocates of free speech in the twenty-first century still cite John Milton's great essay of the 1640s, the *Areopagitica*, when they denounce censorship. Anyone reading that essay today readily recognizes that Milton was not merely issuing a pronouncement in abstract philosophical terms. Rather he wrote in the heat of political battle. The pamphleteering that had begun in the previous century on religious and political issues, made possible by the widespread availability of the printing press, had inspired the adoption of legal measures to curb the dissemination of dissent, and Milton wrote to oppose one such measure, a bill in Parliament that would require the licensing of books and pamphlets.[5]

In the more than three centuries that followed the struggle for rights in England by John Milton, the Levellers, and other dissenters, there were episodic attempts to secure rights relevant to such grave issues as slavery, religious persecution, the subordination of women, forced labor, racial segregation, and the suppression of dissent. Citizen movements sprang up from time to time to address these issues and, in some cases, had a major impact. But these movements could not sustain themselves.[6] It is possible that many of their adherents did not have a commitment to the core idea of rights. More likely, however, rights movements could not be sustained because the participants lacked the organizational means to maintain their identification with a citizen movement once a given battle was over. A few such movements attracted significant numbers of followers but, after achieving a victory, such as emancipation of the slaves in the United States or women's suffrage, largely disappeared. In the early part of the twentieth century, a small number of enduring organizations founded to protect rights were established, but they operated only on a national basis, particularly in the United States. A citizens' movement to promote rights across borders on an ongoing basis did not emerge until the post–World War II era.

Not all the great abuses of rights of the previous two or three centuries inspired the emergence of even temporary citizen movements. There was no organized response, for example, to such great historical crimes as the slaughter of much of the indigenous population of the Western hemisphere;[7] to nineteenth- and early twentieth-century genocide in parts of Africa; or to subsequent twentieth-century horrors that included the Soviet gulag, the unprecedented crimes of the Nazis, or the persecution in post–World War II China that caused the deaths of many millions and continued until the death of Mao in 1976.

To some extent, it is possible to attribute the failure of rights movements to arise in response to some of these tragedies to a lack of information. Even events as recent as the famine in China in 1958 to 1961 caused by Mao's "Great Leap Forward" policies that killed perhaps thirty million persons, and the decade long Cultural Revolution that Mao launched a few years later, were not known or barely known in the rest of the world as they were taking place. But not every great abuse of rights was hidden. It is only during our time that a sustained organized movement has developed committed to the idea that severe abuses of rights everywhere should be exposed and denounced, and that, to the extent feasible, measures should be adopted to stop them or to mitigate their horrors. In addition, our time uniquely has produced a plethora of nongovernmental organizations established for those purposes. The possibility that great abuses of rights can be kept out of public view has been greatly reduced not only by the advance and proliferation of communications technology, but also by the emergence of a movement committed to uncovering hidden violations of rights in all parts of the world.

The concept of natural law, which provided the main philosophical basis for the rights movements that did emerge, may be traced back to the

Stoic philosophers in Greece and was also discussed by Aristotle. In Roman times, Cicero was its leading exponent. As the basis for a commitment to the promotion of human rights, it received its greatest philosophic support in the seventeenth century from the works of John Locke. Born in 1632, Locke entered Oxford twenty years later, at a time when the university was immersed in debates between the various religious and political factions of the era. The principles of natural law, which were extensively discussed in the seventeenth century by the Dutch scholar of jurisprudence, Hugo Grotius, who called it "a dictate of right reason," were seen by the philosopher Thomas Hobbes as a context in which all were at war with one another. Hobbes considered that "rights" were not meaningful, because they had to be yielded in the interests of the creation of an orderly state. The contrasting idea of natural law as a guarantor of rights was particularly developed in Locke's *Second Treatise on Civil Government*, published in 1690. Locke diverged from Hobbes in discerning a far more benign aspect of natural law. Describing the "state of nature," he wrote:

> To understand political power aright, and derive it from its original, we must consider, what state all men are naturally in, and that is, a state of perfect freedom to order their actions, and dispose of their possessions and persons, as they think fit, within the bounds of the law of nature, without asking leave, or depending upon the will of any other man. A state also of equality, wherein all the power and jurisdiction is reciprocal, no one having more than another. . . . But though this be a state of liberty, yet it is not a state of license. The state of nature has a law of nature to govern it, which obliges every one, and reason, which is that law, teaches all mankind, who will but consult it, that being all equal and independent, no one ought to harm another in his life, health, liberty or possessions. . . . And that all men may be restrained from invading others rights, and from doing hurt to one another, and the law of nature be observed, which willeth the peace and preservation of all mankind, the execution of the law of nature is, in that state, put into every one's hands, whereby every one has a right to punish the transgressors of that law to such a degree, as may hinder its violation."[8]

Locke's description embodies the essential elements of human rights: namely, that rights have their foundation in natural law and, therefore, are not dependent on particular circumstances that prevail at particular times and places; that all are equal in their entitlement to enjoy and exercise rights; and that they are universal in their application to all human beings and not only to those who are nationals or citizens of a particular political regime. In addition, Locke foreshadows the accountability concerns of our time providing that a limit on rights is needed to protect the rights of others. Moreover, his definition of rights encompasses the right and—as Locke makes clear in his essay—the *duty* to punish those who infringe on the rights of others. Locke also was the precursor of Jefferson in arguing that the people retain the ultimate right to overthrow a government that is destructive of liberty. The concluding paragraph of his *Second Treatise on Civil Government* asserts that "when, by the miscarriage of those in authority [legislative power] is forfeited . . . it reverts to the society, and the people have a right to act as supreme, and continue the legislative in themselves or place it in a new form, or new hands, as they think good."[9] The principles that Locke derives from natural law are the principles on which human rights proponents in our time base their commitment to civil and political rights. (The same cannot be said for economic and social rights, or so-called third-generation rights, which derive from nineteenth-century thinking and lack a foundation in seventeenth-century thought about natural law [see chapter 3].) Natural law has had other great exponents, such as Montesquieu who argued that it precedes the formation of society and is superior to the laws of the state or of religion. It has also garnered strenuous critics, such as the utilitarian philosopher Jeremy Bentham who famously described natural rights as "nonsense upon stilts."[10]

Locke's *Second Treatise on Civil Government* was published at a tumultuous moment in English history. King James II, a Catholic who had attempted to maintain a large standing army contrary to the wishes of Parliament, and who was accused of persecuting religious dissenters and giving preferences to Catholics, was overthrown in 1688. By invitation, William of Orange of the Netherlands (who was of English royal lineage as his mother was Mary Stuart, daughter of Charles I of England) and his wife Mary (the Protestant daughter of James II and William's cousin) assumed the throne jointly in 1689. As part of these events, which came to be called the English Revolution, Parliament adopted a Declaration of Right that in significant respects contributed to the American Bill of Rights and the French *Déclaration des droits de l'homme et du citoyen* (Declaration of the rights of man and of the citizen), which were adopted a century later. It repudiates the ability of the king to exercise certain powers by regal authority, and it asserts that the king may not raise or maintain a standing army in times of peace except with the consent of Parliament. The English Declaration of Right goes on to protect freedom of speech; prohibit excessive bail and excessive fines; prohibit cruel and unusual punishment; set forth the right to trial by jury; prohibit fines and forfeitures before conviction; and provide that "for the redress of all grievances, and for the amending, strengthening and preserving of the laws, parliament ought to be held frequently."

What is lacking in the English Declaration of Right is the principle of universality. Its preamble makes clear that it is based on a series of complaints against King James II, who "did endeavor to subvert and extirpate the protestant religion, and the laws and liberties of the kingdom," and that the rights set forth in the declaration represent a contract with James's successors, King William and Queen Mary. The thinking of the era that is reflected in Locke's notions of a social contract, also set forth in his *Second Treatise on Civil Government*, had plainly influenced Parliament. Yet Parliament was apparently not ready to ground the Declaration of Right in the concept of natural law espoused by Locke.

The 1789 French *Déclaration des droits de l'homme et du citoyen* refers to natural rights and embraces universality in its assertion that "men are born and remain free and equal in rights." At the same time, however, it is rooted in the positive law tradition of continental Europe in asserting that limits on certain liberties, including freedom of expression and freedom from arbitrary arrest, "can only be determined by law." This contrasts with the American Bill of Rights of 1791, which is more sweeping, asserting that "Congress shall make no law" abridging freedom of speech. Natural law principles could be far more readily reconciled with the common law tradition of England that was inherited by the United States than with the civil law legal tradition of a country such as France.

In the seventeenth century, invoking principles of natural law, Englishmen such as John Lilburne defended their own rights. In the next century, other Englishmen, invoking the same principles, went a significant step further: they began to defend the rights of others. And in so doing they gave their movement an altruistic character that foreshadowed the emergence of a global movement. Their concept of altruism resembled that championed in the writing of Immanuel Kant during the same period: that is, it required a concern for the rights of others as a matter of duty and was based on a recognition that freedom matters not as a means to an end but because each human being is an end in herself. She is entitled to respect for her rights. The contemporary human rights movement's concerns with human dignity and autonomy are, thus, direct legacies of the thinking embedded in Kant's philosophy.

The first manifestation of the international movement was the English antislavery crusade of the second half of the eighteenth century. It was grounded in principles of natural law and, in the same era as Kant, though probably not directly influenced by his writing, extended the same concern with respect for all human life to those who had been enslaved. It is, therefore, the parent of all subsequent efforts to defend rights altruistically, putting into practice a philosophy based on respect for individual human dignity and autonomy. The story of its beginnings is well known.

Starting in the 1760s, a handful of antislavery activists led by a musician named Granville Sharp, followed some years later by a Quaker activist, Thomas Clarkson, and a young member of Parliament, William Wilberforce, a convert to evangelical Christianity, began speaking out about slavery, focusing at the outset on the situation of slaves in England. Often those slaves had worked for English masters in the sugar plantations in the West Indian colonies and had accompanied their masters on trips back to the home country. In England some escaped and tried to live free but were hunted down by their masters and returned to bondage. Many struggles over whether those masters could repossess their former slaves ended up in the British courts, which had come under the influence of the most significant work on the common law, Blackstone's *Commentaries*. Published in the 1760s, the *Commentaries* embraced the concept of natural law and held that natural law forbade slavery. The most prominent court case involved a slave from Virginia, James Somerset, who was brought to England by his owner, Charles Stewart. Somerset escaped but was captured in 1772 and put on a ship to Jamaica. With the help of Granville Sharp, the matter was brought to court where it came before England's most prominent judge, Lord Chief Justice William Mansfield. The case dragged on for several months while Mansfield attempted to get the parties to agree to an out-of-court settlement. Eventually, however, Mansfield recognized that a settlement was not possible and that he would have to hand down a decision that would affect an estimated 15,000 slaves then in England, representing a substantial financial investment by their owners. "But if the parties will have it decided, we must give our opinion," Mansfield warned. "[I]f the parties will have judgment, *'fiat justitia, ruat caelum'* [let justice be done though the heavens may fall]."[11] There is disagreement about what Mansfield actually said when he decided the Somerset case on June 22, 1772, but by popular opinion at least he is reputed to have asserted that slavery could not be sustained once a slave had had the opportunity to "breathe the free air of England." As William Cowper wrote in his 1785 poem, *The Task*:

> Slaves cannot breathe in England; if their lungs
> Receive our air, that moment they are free;
> They touch our country, and their shackles fall.[12]

In the eighteenth century, it was widely accepted that *Somerset* had been decided by Lord Mansfield under principles of natural law. Some versions of what Mansfield is supposed to have said when deciding the case make this explicit but, as it is not possible to say which version of his remarks is accurate, or indeed whether any of them is a faithful rendition, this cannot be asserted with confidence.

Having prevailed in the battle to end slavery in England, Thomas Clarkson took up the effort o abolish the slave trade as well. Beginning in 1789, William Wilberforce introduced measures in the House of Commons to secure this goal. Together they succeeded in abolishing the slave trade to the British colonies by 1807. This did not, however, alter the status of those enslaved before it was enacted. The United States abolished the slave trade in the same year (also, of course, not freeing those already enslaved), but the prohibition was violated frequently. In practice, the slave trade to the United States did not end completely until the Emancipation Proclamation more than a half-century later. Before that, slavery had been abolished by every country in Europe and in most other countries of the Western hemisphere. In Britain, where Wilberforce was a founder of the Anti-Slavery Society (in 1823)—which exists to this day as Anti-Slavery International, making it the world's oldest and longest lasting human rights organization—the Slavery Abolition Act that he had long fought for was adopted by Parliament a month after he died in 1833.

In France, the activities of Clarkson and Wilberforce helped to inspire the formation of a group called Amis des Noirs, which persuaded some leaders of the French Revolution to take up the antislavery cause. The impact was most dramatic in Haiti, which had become by the 1780s one of the richest colonies on earth, with an economy that was largely dependent on slave labor. As the historian David Brion Davis has written: "Then the French Revolution ignited a massive insurrection and civil war, which from 1791 to 1804 destroyed this highly exploitative 'pearl of the Antilles.' The slaves and free descendants of slaves defeated not only their masters but the most formidable armies of Spain, Britain and France."[13] In the colonies that France retained in the West Indies, slavery was not abolished until 1848.

The main efforts to abolish slavery in the United States during the later years of the eighteenth century and the early part of the nineteenth were led by Quakers. Though they attracted relatively few others to the abolitionist cause, their efforts did succeed in securing a legal end to slavery in every state north of Maryland between 1777 and 1804. "The contradiction between creed and practice had made some Americans uncomfortable enough in the Revolutionary decades to abolish slavery by statute or judicial interpretation in the Northern states, which accounted for only six percent of the enslaved population," according to a biographer of the antislavery crusader, William Lloyd Garrison. "Massachusetts had immediately swept it away under its state constitution in the 1780s, two decades before Garrison's birth, while New York's gradual abolition law, not passed until 1799, only freed slaves born after the act's passage at age twenty-five for females and twenty-eight for males."[14]

The British not only led the way in abolishing the slave trade in their own colonies. They also attempted to secure an international agreement to end it. The issue was pressed by Lord Castlereagh, the country's foreign secretary, at the Congress of Vienna. "On February 8, 1815, just days before his departure [when the Duke of Wellington arrived to replace him as the British representative at the Congress], Castlereagh could finally point to some success. France, Portugal, Spain, and others had come on board, and the Great Powers issued a joint declaration condemning the practice as 'repugnant to the principles of humanity and universal morality.' [F]or the first time, [human rights] had been made a subject of a peace conference."[15]

Garrison became the foremost white advocate of the abolition of slavery in the United States—the other leading abolitionist was the former slave Frederick Douglass—from the 1830s through Lincoln's Emancipation Proclamation of January 1, 1863 and thereafter. He first acquired his knowledge of the cause by making the acquaintance of a fellow practitioner of the printing trade, Benjamin Lundy. A Quaker, Lundy wrote antislavery articles for a newspaper published by a friend and then learned to become a printer so he could publish his own newspaper. Garrison, who also used his own printing press to publish his newspaper, *The Liberator*, was eager to champion a moral cause and, after his encounter with Lundy, quickly dedicated himself to the immediate abolition of slavery and, in 1833, the year that slavery was abolished in the British colonies, founded the American Anti-Slavery Society.[16]

Ending slavery in the United States, as everyone knows, proved far more difficult than elsewhere. In the north, where the practice did not have a significant economic impact, slavery's incompatibility with widely accepted principles of natural law had made abolition relatively easy. In the South, on the other hand, eleven states had developed a highly successful plantation economy that produced cotton for the textile mills that pioneered the industrialization of the United States and England. This economy depended on slavery. As William Lloyd Garrison rallied support for the abolitionist cause in the northern states by appealing to moral outrage against the enslavement of fellow human beings, many southerners sought to justify their "peculiar institution" not only on the basis of its economic significance to them but also on the claim that it had its own moral virtues. Moreover, they attacked the abolitionists for challenging the provisions of the United States Constitution, which had made slavery a question for determination by the individual states. This marks the origin of what has been known ever since as the "states rights" movement in the United States.

David Brion Davis has pointed out that "with the debatable exception of France, Brazil was the only non-English speaking country in which abolitionism developed as a mass movement. That said, the movement differed markedly from those in Britain and the United States."[17] It consisted mainly of a movement by the slaves themselves who took the initiative in the 1880s and fled the coffee farms, often taking shelter with sympathizers. Brazil finally emancipated its slaves in 1888, one of the last Western countries to do so. The practice of slavery persisted in parts of Africa and the Middle East.

The abolitionist movement in the United States, like that in England which preceded it, was the first substantial effort by groups of citizens to join together to try to protect the rights of others. Many prominent persons, including the poets James Russell Lowell and John Greenleaf Whittier, scions of aristocratic families such as Edmund Quincy and Wendell Phillips, and outspoken former slaves such as Sojourner Truth and Frederick Douglass, were among the thousands who took up the cause. A convention of the American Anti-Slavery Society in New York in 1840, at which there was a split over the role of women in the movement, was attended by more than a thousand delegates.

The right of women to take part as equals in the abolitionist movement, which had been opposed by some of those in the movement as contrary to

God's law, became one of the factors that inspired a number of women who opposed slavery to organize the first women's rights convention in Seneca Falls, New York in July 1848. Led by Lucretia Mott and Elizabeth Cady Stanton—both of whom had been barred from taking part in the World Anti-Slavery Convention in London in 1840—the women who gathered in Seneca Falls called for equal rights in voting, the ownership of property, employment, and family relations. Paraphrasing the Declaration of Independence, they published a "Declaration of Sentiments" that was rooted firmly in the natural law tradition.[18] This convention marked the start of the women's rights movement, both in the United States and internationally, and the movement's agenda has ever since included its themes. The women's movement was thus a direct offshoot of the abolitionist movement and, simultaneously, a rebellion against that movement's discrimination against women. (It may be worth noting that history seems to have repeated itself. More than a century later, in the 1960s, women who participated in the civil rights initiatives of that era sometimes encountered discrimination within the movement. Notoriously, Stokely Carmichael, a leader of the Student Nonviolent Coordinating Committee, responded to a question about the position of women in the movement by saying it was "prone." Such discrimination was a factor in the rebirth of the women's movement that took place later in the decade.)

At Seneca Falls, the most controversial of the resolutions adopted was the one supporting the right of women to vote. It was the only resolution of the twelve adopted that passed with less than unanimous support, and it might not have succeeded but for the intervention of one of the males in attendance, Frederick Douglass, who supported it strongly. Yet voting was to become the central focus of the women's movement in subsequent years. In another part of the world, a quite different issue became the focus of a women's rights movement in the latter part of the nineteenth century and the early years of the twentieth century. The campaign to end the Chinese practice of footbinding was led by foreign missionaries and by Chinese political reformers. Reportedly, an Anti-Footbinding Society, established in 1897, reached a membership of 300,000.[19]

The abolitionist movement eventually achieved success in the period after the Civil War with the adoption of the Thirteenth, Fourteenth, and Fifteenth Amendments to the United States Constitution. The women's movement—or "suffragist movement" as it became known because of its focus on voting—prevailed seventy-two years after Seneca Falls with the adoption of the Nineteenth Amendment in 1920. The fact that former slaves won the right to vote with the passage of the Fifteenth Amendment intensified the focus of the women's movement on that issue until the achievement of suffrage.

Two years after the Seneca Falls meeting, under the leadership of Lucy Stone—whose marriage contract with Henry Blackwell makes clear that she insisted on adherence to feminist principles in her personal life—a women's convention was held in Worcester, Massachusetts; and two years after that, in 1852, another such meeting was held in Syracuse, New York. A participant in the Syracuse meeting was Susan B. Anthony, who was to lead the suffragist movement in the United States for the next half-century. In 1869, Anthony and Elizabeth Cady Stanton formed the National Women Suffrage Association with the specific goal of securing an amendment to the U.S. Constitution. About the same time, Lucy Stone formed the American Woman Suffrage Association, which sought to achieve its goal by amending state constitutions. Eventually, in 1890, the two groups merged and the resulting National American Woman Suffrage Association became the driving force in the crusade for the right of American women to vote.

Though Mary Wollstonecraft had, as far back as 1792, advocated the right to vote for women in her book *A Vindication of the Rights of Women*, and despite the fact that this goal was espoused by a number of nineteenth-century British reformers including, of course, John Stuart Mill (most notably in *The Subjection of Women*, 1869), a suffragist movement did not take shape in Britain until some years later than in the United States. The first suffragist organization was established in 1865. Whereas the movement to abolish slavery began in Britain and only took root in the United States a good many years later, the women's suffrage movement traveled in the opposite direction. Neither country was the first to grant women the right to vote, however. There were instances in which women were allowed to vote in local elections in the United States, as for example in Wyoming, which provided for women's suffrage in state elections from the time it entered the Union in 1890. So far as national elections are concerned, however, New Zealand led the way in 1893, followed by Australia, Finland, and Norway. Many countries, including Britain, Canada, Germany, and a number of others, the U.S. among them, amended their laws to allow women to vote in the aftermath of World War I. The important role that women played in industrial production during the war years contributed to the developing consensus that they should be able to exercise the basic rights of citizenship. Women acquired the right to vote in Soviet Russia with the Russian Revolution in 1917, but the exercise of that right was no more meaningful for them than it was for Russian men.

The virtually single-minded focus on the vote by the women's movement in the United States (and elsewhere) prior to 1920 had an unanticipated consequence. Once it succeeded, the movement all but collapsed. Having achieved its paramount goal, many women's organizations dissolved; others, such as the League of Women Voters, chose not to focus primarily on questions related to the equality of women but instead became important actors in efforts to promote general civic improvement. Some of the energy of the women's movement was diverted into the temperance movement of the 1920s. That movement did have a women's rights component; the Women's Christian Temperance Union, for example, was a proponent of suffrage because its leaders believed that enhancing the political power of women would help them to protect themselves. In an era in which drunkenness was pervasive, drunkards were infamous as wife-beaters. From the standpoint of organizations such as the WCTU and the Anti-Saloon League, obtaining the right to vote for women enhanced the prospects for achieving Prohibition. In the process, efforts languished to address other aspects of the Seneca Falls agenda, including such crucial issues as property rights, equal employment and educational opportunities for women, and women's status in domestic relations. Before winning the right to vote, the women's movement in the United States and Britain was a significant force, and to the extent that the struggle led by Margaret Sanger to promote the availability of the means of birth control is considered a part of that movement, it continued to have a significant impact.[20] With that important exception, however, for nearly another half century until its rebirth in the late 1960s, the women's movement made little headway.

The abolitionist movement met a similar fate following the abolition of slavery. Though the post–Civil War decades were a period of widespread violence against newly freed blacks in the southern states, as evidenced by the rise of the Ku Klux Klan, frequent lynchings, the systematic deprivation of the right to vote supposedly guaranteed by the Fifteenth Amendment, and the introduction of racial segregation that endured *de jure* into the second half of the twentieth century, the pre–Civil War movement for the rights of blacks died away. No substantial organized efforts to promote racial equality were evident during the crucial years of the 1870s and the 1880s when "Jim Crow" was becoming both law and universal practice in the South. Segregation had not been a feature of slavery in the South— though it was often practiced in the North—because enforced servitude ensured that blacks and whites lived in close proximity to one another. It was introduced as a rigid, legally enforced system only after slavery was abolished.

The most significant challenge to racial segregation in the South in that era was spearheaded by a lawyer from upstate New York, long-since forgotten, named Albion Winegar Tourgée. A carpetbagger during the years after the Civil War, and for a period a judge, Tourgée was also a popular novelist and the author of a weekly newspaper column, "Bystander," that appeared in a Chicago newspaper and was regularly reprinted by many other papers. Adopting an approach that in subsequent years would typify the strategy of U.S. rights movements, Tourgée challenged Jim Crow in the courts and, simultaneously, rallied public opinion against the practice through his newspaper column and through an organization he established, the National Citizens' Rights Association.[21] His crusade warrants attention because it seems to have been the first substantial organized effort to promote racial equality in the period following the disappearance of the abolitionist movement.

Tourgée's outspoken denunciations of segregation prompted a group of eighteen black men in Louisiana, calling themselves the Citizens' Committee, to contact him in 1891 and ask his help in mounting a constitutional challenge to a law adopted the previous year that would require segregation on trains passing through the state. Other southern states adopted similar laws in the same period. Tourgée advised the group to select a person who was nearly white as the subject of a test case designed to highlight the absurdity of racial classifications. In this respect, as in others, Tourgée's approach anticipated a tactic employed by contemporary public interest lawyers who try to ensure that test cases involve helpful fact patterns. The leader of the Citizens' Committee, Louis Martinet, himself a lawyer and also the editor of a New Orleans newspaper for blacks, was discomfited by Tourgée's suggestion, however, because discrimination against very light-complected blacks was relatively mild. Even so, he and the Citizens' Committee went along. On June 7, 1892, Homer Adolph Plessy, who described himself as "seven-eighths Caucasian and one-eighth African," boarded a train in New Orleans and entered a car reserved for whites. He was arrested and charged with violating the segregation law.[22]

The U.S. Supreme Court disposed of the question of Plessy's color by saying simply that such matters were to be determined by the laws of each state.[23] The Court refused to acknowledge that segregation violated the

Fourteenth Amendment's requirement of equal protection under the law, explaining in a passage that has become infamous and that had a devastating impact, that "[if] the enforced segregation of two races stamps the colored race with a badge of inferiority . . . it is not by reason of anything found in the act, but solely because the colored race chooses to put that construction on it. . . . If the two races are to meet upon terms of social equality, it must be the result of natural affinities, a mutual appreciation of each other's merits, as a voluntary consent of individuals. . . . Legislation is powerless to eradicate racial instincts, or to abolish distinctions based upon physical differences."[24] Only Justice John Marshall Harlan dissented, writing that "the judgment this day rendered will, in time, prove to be quite so pernicious as the decision made by this tribunal in the Dred Scott case" (the 1857 decision that overturned an act of Congress limiting slavery and helped propel the country into the Civil War).[25] Many years later, Yale law professor Charles Black commented that in the majority's assertion that segregation only implies inferiority because the colored race puts that construction on it "the curves of stupidity and callousness intersect at their respective maxima."[26]

The National Citizens' Rights Association, formed to challenge racial segregation and the systematic disenfranchisement of black voters then underway in the southern states and promoted by Tourgée through his newspaper columns, claimed a membership of more than a hundred thousand within a year after its foundation. Given what we know about membership recruitment of fledgling twentieth-century groups such as the American Civil Liberties Union (ACLU) and the National Association for the Advancement of Colored People (NAACP), this figure seems improbable. In any event, the organization was short-lived. It disappeared within a few years and left behind no trace of its activities.

The same was true of another organization established in the same era, the Free Speech League. It was the vehicle of a crusading lawyer, Theodore Schroeder, who opposed all forms of censorship. Created by Schroeder in 1902, it enlisted prominent journalists, including Lincoln Steffens, in its efforts. For a brief period, the organization was prominent in opposing efforts to suppress the increasingly frank discussion of sexuality in early twentieth-century publications. The League disappeared about the time the United States entered World War I.[27]

· · ·

In England, where the antislavery movement originated in the latter decades of the eighteenth century and, after an early victory in the home country, turned its attention to slavery in the colonies, other movements concerned with violations of human rights in distant places became important forces a century later. One of these was the campaign mounted by William Gladstone against his arch-rival, Benjamin Disraeli, on account of the latter's failure to express outrage over what were known as "the Bulgarian atrocities."

After suffering a major electoral setback in 1874, Gladstone had largely retired from politics, but he reentered the fray when reports of Ottoman cruelties in putting down a rebellion in the Balkans began to circulate in the British press. Gladstone published a pamphlet on the subject in 1876 entitled, "Bulgarian Horrors and the Question of the East." Hundreds of thousands of copies were sold. His denunciations of Disraeli for his silence on these horrors were so effective that they made it possible for Gladstone to regain his post as prime minister. It is difficult to think of other situations in which a government's policy towards human rights abuses in a far-distant land figured so significantly in the political process. Undoubtedly, one important factor in creating such a powerful popular reaction in this case was that the perpetrators were Muslims (the Ottoman Turks) persecuting Christians (the Bulgarians). On the other hand, it would be unfair to attribute Gladstone's passionate involvement in this cause solely to religious bias. He had manifested his concern for human rights a quarter of a century earlier following a visit to Naples by launching a campaign against the cruelty of Neapolitan prison conditions. In that instance, both the victims and their persecutors were Christians.[28]

Rights issues also gained adherents in continental Europe during this era, though most often through professional and intellectual activities rather than through causes such as those that inspired Gladstone or the American feminists and opponents of racial segregation. A legal scholar, John Fabian Witt, has argued that a factor was the development of internationalism, attributable in part to the adoption of a plethora of international treaties in the century following the end of the Napoleonic wars. According to Witt, "The crowning achievements of the late-nineteenth-century international lawyers were the Hague conferences of 1899 and 1907 [landmarks in the development of international humanitarian law]," which established rules that were cited in the prosecution of the top Nazi war criminals at Nuremberg and still play an important role in the protection of rights during armed conflict. Witt also cites the emergence of a number of associations of lawyers and the appearance of journals concerned with international law in the countries of Western Europe during the last decades of the nineteenth century.[29]

In the last decade of the nineteenth century, some years after Gladstone's campaign to denounce the Bulgarian atrocities and at about the same time as Albion Winegar Tourgée and Louis Martinet were waging their battles against harsh racial policies in the American South, another struggle got underway in England. Its aim was to mitigate the extraordinary cruelty of the rule of King Leopold II of Belgium in the huge swath of Africa then know as the Congo Free State. From 1885, when Leopold acquired control, until 1908, when the Belgian parliament voted to annex the Free State, the Congo was the king's personal fiefdom.

The story is familiar thanks to Adam Hochschild's 1998 book, *King Leopold's Ghost*.[30] Leopold secured vast riches by exploiting the natural resources of the Congo, especially ivory and rubber. An Englishman named Edmund Morel, employed in Antwerp in the 1890s by a Liverpool-based shipping company, noticed that there was something strange about the vast quantities of these goods being delivered to Belgium: hardly anything was being shipped to the Congo in exchange. The only significant shipments to the Congo were weapons that were being sent to various Belgian "trading companies." Morel deduced—correctly—that the mountains of ivory and rubber were being secured for Leopold through forced labor. In fact, the conditions under which these resources were extracted were so cruel that it is estimated that Leopold's wealth was secured at a cost of as many as ten million lives. It is possible that in all of human history only Hitler, Stalin, and Mao have more blood on their hands.

Morel transformed himself into an investigator who published numerous articles about his findings. He founded his own journal, the *West African Mail*, as well as a crusading organization, the Congo Reform Association. Hochschild quotes historian A.J.P. Taylor as writing that, "Morel has never had an equal as organizer and leader of a Dissenting movement. . . . He knew exactly where to look for rich sympathizers; and he took money from them without altering the democratic character of [his movement]. Millionaires and factory workers alike accepted his leadership."[31] Morel enlisted thousands of supporters for his efforts in England and in the United States. One of his American supporters was Mark Twain, who published a pamphlet in 1905, *King Leopold's Soliloquy*, an imaginary monologue by the king.[32] Hochschild describes Morel's campaign, which eventually brought to an end most of Leopold's atrocities, as the first human rights movement of the twentieth century. It is an apt description, but it is important to note that, like other movements in the era, it was not sustained after it had achieved its immediate goal. Though not on the scale of Leopold's crimes in the Congo, there were many other wrongs being committed in Africa in that period by the continent's European colonizers, and these did not give rise to international campaigns.

In 1909, more than a decade after the movement's stunning defeat in *Plessy v. Ferguson* in the U.S. Supreme Court and the disappearance of Albion Winegar Tourgée's National Citizens' Rights Association, a new organization was established to challenge racial segregation in the United States. The incident that inspired men like William English Walling, a white southerner, and W.E.B. DuBois, the leading black public intellectual of the period, to organize the National Association for the Advancement of Colored People was a lynching in Springfield, Illinois, Abraham Lincoln's home town. Walling and DuBois enlisted many prominent white liberals to serve on the association's board: feminist and social worker Jane Addams; philosopher John Dewey; Rabbi Stephen Wise; Oswald Garrison Villard, publisher of the *Nation*; Arthur Spingarn, a well-to-do Jewish businessman; and John Haynes Holmes, a well-known Unitarian Minister in New York. More soundly managed and, therefore, more enduring than the National Citizens' Rights Association—although it, too, has had its ups and downs over the past century—the NAACP established local branches across the United States and enlisted hundreds of thousands of members. Many of its largest and most active branches were in the South, where black clergy and members of their congregations made up a significant part of the membership.

The call to the meeting at which the NAACP was launched made plain the founders' vision that much of the organization's work would take place in the courts. At the same time, they acknowledged the difficulty of the task that lay ahead, given the segregationist views that had prevailed in *Plessy* and in the Supreme Court's decisions in voting rights cases. "The Supreme Court of the United States," the call stated, "supposedly a bulwark of American liberties, had refused every opportunity to pass squarely upon this disenfranchisement of millions. . . . [T]he Supreme Court . . . had laid down the principle that if an individual state chooses, it may make it a crime for white and colored persons to frequent the same market place at the same time, or appear in an assemblage of citizens, convened to consider questions of a public or political nature in which all citizens, without regard to race, are equally interested."

Though progress through litigation would be difficult in light of the make-up of the U.S. Supreme Court, it seemed the only option. Moreover, a large portion of the country's black population lived in the South where, having had the vote taken away from them by a variety of means, they had no ability to influence the representative branches of government. Efforts to challenge racial segregation in the United States Congress were, therefore, similarly doomed to fail. Not only were southern blacks excluded from voting for members of Congress from their states, but members of Congress from the South, who only represented white voters, completely dominated both the U.S. Senate and the House of Representatives. In that era, the South was solidly Democratic and, once elected, members of Congress from the region were reelected over and over again. The congressional seniority system ensured that southern Democrats with secure seats dominated all committees that might deal with questions affecting segregation. But at least in the courts, litigation challenging discrimination would get attention and, over time, might have an impact.

Choosing its cases with care, the NAACP did make progress in the courts. The first case the organization brought before the U.S. Supreme Court was *Buchanan v. Warley*, decided in 1917.[33] It involved a white man's sale of a building lot in Louisville to a black man in violation of a city ordinance that required residential segregation. The case was well chosen because the ordinance could be portrayed as a violation of the property rights of the white man as he was denied the right to dispose of his property as he saw fit. Also, it was difficult for the Court to suggest that, as in *Plessy*, "natural affinities" kept whites and blacks apart because, in this case, the white man who sold the property and the black man who bought it had acted in concert. The Supreme Court decided that Louisville's ordinance violated "the fundamental law enacted in the Fourteenth Amendment of the Constitution preventing state interference with property rights except by due process of law."[34] In basing the holding on the due process clause of the Fourteenth Amendment and not on the equal protection of the laws clause, the Court avoided deciding *Buchanan* in a way that would have overruled its decision twenty-one years earlier in *Plessy*. Even so, the *Buchanan* decision confirmed the wisdom of the founders of the NAACP who believed that, by selecting their cases with great care and by litigating them with skill, they would be able to chip away at *Plessy* and gradually use the courts to undermine segregation.

In 1917, the year that the Supreme Court decided *Buchanan*, the United States entered World War I. An early by-product was a wave of nationalist sentiment and strong popular antagonism against those who dissented from the decision to go to war. Hundreds of state and federal prosecutions were launched against vocal opponents of the war or the draft.[35] Also, conscientious objectors, other than those affiliated with traditional peace churches such as the Quakers or the Mennonites, were given short shrift in the courts and imprisoned. In response, a new organization was established in 1917, the Civil Liberties Bureau (later, the National Civil Liberties Bureau) to defend those persecuted for reasons connected to the war. Its principal organizers were Roger Baldwin—who was himself imprisoned for resisting the draft—and Crystal Eastman, and they were joined by some activists who were also associated with the NAACP, Jane Addams and Rev. John Haynes Holmes among them. This was a period when "Federal legislation effectively criminalized antiwar speech; the Post Office banned antiwar and radical literature from the mails; mobs brutalized and even lynched antiwar speakers; and federal agents and allied vigilantes led lawless raids on labor unions and radical organizations."[36] Intended as a temporary organization to meet the wartime emergency, the National Civil Liberties Bureau merged after the war with another World War I organization, the American Union Against Militarism, to form a permanent body, the American Civil Liberties Union. Established in 1920, the ACLU began by challenging the attack on free speech that persisted after the war ended and was exacerbated by widespread alarm over anarchists, who were responsible for a number of terrorist bombings, and communists sympathetic to the regime recently established in Soviet Russia. The assault on free speech was more intense during this period than at any other time in American history. It produced literally thousands of federal and state prosecutions of dissenters. In 1919, Attorney General A. Mitchell Palmer, whose own home had been destroyed by an anarchist bomb, launched the "Palmer Raids" in which thousands of suspected radicals were rounded up and detained arbitrarily, and hundreds of them were summarily deported to Soviet Russia. A court case, in which a federal judge invited two ACLU lawyers to take part, successfully challenged the constitutionality of the Palmer Raids[37] and required the cancellation of deportation orders for an English couple.

Like the NAACP, the American Civil Liberties Union focused much of its effort on the courts. Between them, the two organizations played a leading role—indeed, *the* leading role—in transforming the role of the courts in the United States so that, for much of the past century, they functioned as the principal institutional protectors of the rights of Americans.

Indirectly, the two organizations also exercised worldwide influence, because litigation in time became an important means of protecting rights in other countries as well. Prior to the twentieth century, there had only been a handful of court cases—most notably, Lord Chief Justice Mansfield's decision in the slavery case in England—that had played a significant part in the protection of rights. Yet as a result of the pioneering work of the NAACP (and, eventually, its offshoot, the NAACP Legal Defense Fund) and the ACLU, the idea that courts should play a leading role in safeguarding and expanding rights came to be accepted in a substantial number of countries. Ultimately, this vision of the role of courts is rooted in the concept of natural law. Judges, whose job it is to discover the applicable law and apply its principles, are the persons best suited to protect rights. Growing international acceptance of this concept has helped to bring about the establishment of such international bodies as the European Court of Human Rights and the Inter-American Court of Human Rights, which provide supranational judicial protection of rights in regions that otherwise maintain civil law legal traditions based on the supremacy of positive law. Constitutional courts that have been established in recent decades in many countries in different parts of the world provide such protections at a national level and bring concepts derived from the common law into a number of civil law systems.

A note of explanation may be in order here. At the turn of the century and in the early years of the new century, courts in countries with a civil law tradition played a markedly different role in rights struggles than British and U.S. courts. In France, partisans of Captain Alfred Dreyfus denounced the proceedings that took place in a military court in 1894, in which the Jewish soldier was convicted of espionage in a climate marked by anti-Semitism and the withholding of evidence from the defendant. The trial resulted in Dreyfus's conviction and sentencing to Devil's Island. The unfairness of the trial was captured in Clemenceau's famous aphorism that "military justice is to justice as military music is to music." After an extensive campaign by those who came to be known as "Dreyfusards,"—they included Émile Zola (who was himself convicted of libel for his famous attack on the military justice system, "J'Accuse," published in Clemenceau's newspaper, *L'Aurore*), Marcel Proust, Anatole France and many other leading artists and intellectuals of the era—a new trial was eventually held in a civilian court. The civilian Cour d'Appel cleared Dreyfus in 1906 and reversed all previous convictions. Controversy ignited by the case played a role in French rights debates over an extended period and contributed to both the ascendancy of a strong anti-clerical movement in France that remains an important force today, and to the implementation in 1905 of measures designed to sharpen the separation between church and state inherited from the period of the French Revolution. Fallout from the case also helped to make the question of anti-Semitism a long-term and intense subject of dispute between French liberals and a segment of French opinion that contributed to the rise of fascism in Europe.

During this same period, a rights struggle in South Africa—where the judicial system reflected the continental civil law system of Europe more than the British common law tradition—was led by a lawyer, who did not, however, focus most of his efforts in the courts. Mohandas Gandhi had gone to South Africa in 1893 to take a job with an Indian law firm in Durban. During a court appearance soon after his arrival, the judge told him to take off his turban. Gandhi refused and walked out of the court. Soon thereafter, he boarded a train to Pretoria but was thrown off for attempting to ride in a first-class carriage for which he had purchased a ticket.[38]

Gandhi's experiences led him to take up the cause of equal rights for Indians in Natal, the province where he lived, which was also home to the largest part of South Africa's Indian population. In 1894 he organized the Natal Indian Congress to try to promote equal rights and in a vain effort to prevent passage of legislation stripping the province's Indian population of the right to vote. He made speeches, drafted petitions, and focused the attention of the press in South Africa, India, and England on the grievances of the Indians. In 1906, in an action that presaged the role he would play when he returned to India, he organized the Indian population of the Transvaal province in a nonviolent campaign of defiance against legislation requiring that all Indians register with the state. The episode resulted in the jailing of hundreds of Indians, and thousands more lost their jobs. Eventually, the government backed down and Gandhi was able to negotiate a compromise.

Gandhi returned to his home country in 1914 and, drawing on his experiences in South Africa, soon began leading rights struggles in India. As he had organized Indians in Transvaal to defy the requirement to register, so he led a campaign in India in which citizens pledged not to obey an anti-sedition law, the Anarchical and Revolutionary Crimes Act (the "Rowlatt Act"). It was in this period that Gandhi introduced *satyagraha*, a pledge to rely on a "truth force" rather than violence. The British colonial forces that ruled India responded violently to Gandhi's nonviolent movement, and

British soldiers killed four hundred Indian civilians who were holding a peaceful demonstration at Amritsar.

In 1920, Gandhi's prominence as a leader who championed nonviolence and his organizing ability propelled him into the leadership of the Indian National Congress, established in the 1880s. From then on, he was simultaneously the leader of a rights struggle in India and the leader of a nationalist movement seeking the country's independence. Rights issues, such as equal treatment for the "untouchables" (or "Dalits"), continued to play an important role in his efforts, but his primary identification in India and worldwide was as the leader of a nonviolent struggle for independence.

■ ■ ■

When in 1915 the Ottoman Turks massacred as many as a million Armenians, the strongest official reaction came from American Ambassador Henry J. Morgenthau, Sr., who remonstrated forcefully with Turkish officials and sent many messages home denouncing the atrocities. Morgenthau also attempted—without success—to save the lives of survivors by arranging for their admission to the United States and by offering personally to raise the money needed to pay for their transportation. The strongest public reaction, however, took place in Britain. In certain respects, British response to the "Armenian horrors" echoed the reaction inspired by Gladstone to the "Bulgarian horrors" a generation earlier. Once again, it was the Ottoman Turks who were the perpetrators and, once again, it was Christians being persecuted by Muslims.

Among those in Britain who led the denunciation of the atrocities were Viscount James Bryce, founder of the Anglo-Armenian Association, and the historian Arnold Toynbee, who was a leader of another group, the British Armenia Committee. After the end of World War I, when the British took the lead in seeking prosecution of Kaiser Wilhelm II and other German officials for war crimes, they also sought prosecution of the "Young Turks"—the Ottoman officials generally considered to be principally responsible for the massacres of the Armenians. A British Foreign Office list of ninety-seven suspected war criminals who warranted prosecution included nine Turkish leaders charged with responsibility for the Armenian massacres.[39] Indeed, a number of arrests and trials for the Armenian massacres did take place in Turkey, including a case in which an official, Kemal Bey, was sentenced to death and hanged. There were also cases in which British authorities arrested Ottoman Turk officials with the intent to bring them to trial before British courts, an early example of an attempt to invoke principles subsequently labeled "universal jurisdiction." The plan for these trials was disrupted by Turkey's descent into civil war in the years following World War I, and a few year later, in 1923, all proposed trials before British courts or an international tribunal were finally scuttled with the adoption of the treaty of Lausanne that brought an end to the conflict between Britain and Turkey. With the failure of international justice, Armenian nationalists pursued efforts to take vengeance individually against Turks associated with the massacres. This led to a number of assassinations. Today, nearly a century after the massacres, they remain a sore spot in international relations, and a dispute as to whether it is appropriate to use the term "genocide" to describe them continues at this writing.

■ ■ ■

Roger Baldwin, the principal founder of the American Civil Liberties Union in 1920, and its executive director for the next thirty years, never confined his concern with rights to the United States. The same year that he launched the ACLU, Baldwin also took part in the establishment of two groups to promote human rights internationally: the International Committee for Political Prisoners and the American League for India's Freedom. The latter group, as its name suggests, was at least as concerned, if not more concerned, with India's independence from England as with rights in India.

The International Committee for Political Prisoners began with a focus on the anarchists and communists deported to Soviet Russia (which became the Soviet Union a few years later)—and, in a smaller number of cases, to other European countries—by the United States in the course of the Palmer Raids.[40] Others associated with the ACLU who joined in establishing the ICCP included Jane Addams, Clarence Darrow, Felix Frankfurter, and Norman Thomas. Baldwin chaired the group. Very soon the organization also began to call attention to the plight of political prisoners in Russia. In large part, this reflected Emma Goldman's influence on Baldwin. Goldman, the best-known anarchist leader of the period, was one of those deported to Russia during the raids. She had been initially enthusiastic about the revolution, but upon her arrival in the new Soviet state quickly became disillusioned by the political repression that she encountered. Making her views clear to Russian leaders, including Lenin, Goldman became liable to arrest and imprisonment in Russia and, therefore, made her escape.[41] Baldwin, who had first met her in 1909 when he was still a social worker in St. Louis, and admired her greatly, was persuaded by Goldman that it was important to call attention to Soviet abuses of rights. Accordingly, in 1925, he wrote the introduction for a book, *Letters from Russian Prisons*, that was edited by Alexander Berkman, like Goldman a well-known anarchist and, for many years, her lover. Though a leftist at the time who had sympathized with the Russian Revolution, Baldwin began his introduction with a scathing observation: "Russia presents the unique spectacle of a revolutionary government based on working-class and peasant power imprisoning and exiling its political opponents in other revolutionary parties."[42] Baldwin did not challenge the legitimacy of Soviet Russia, but his readiness to criticize its treatment of political dissenters was significant in 1925 when many Western liberals were inclined to sympathize with the young Soviet state. Emma Goldman was far more critical of political repression in Russia but, under her influence, Baldwin was willing to go well beyond what was customary in his circle at that time. A decade-and-a-half later, from about the time of the Moscow purge trials of the late 1930s and the 1939 Hitler-Stalin pact, Baldwin became strongly anticommunist.

Roger Baldwin's involvement in organizations promoting India's independence brought him into contact with many of those prominent in that struggle, including Jawaharlal Nehru. This eventually led to the formation of an Indian Civil Liberties Union, with Nehru as its chair. The group was not very significant in India, but it continued in existence until India's independence in 1947, when Nehru became the new state's first prime minister. According to a member of its board, a friend of Nehru named Tarkunde who subsequently became a High Court judge, Nehru then sent a letter to his fellow board members noting that, as he was prime minister, the organization was no longer needed. He suggested that it should dissolve. "And we did," said Tarkunde, who founded another civil liberties group many years later in the mid-1970s when Nehru's daughter, Prime Minister Indira Gandhi, declared a state of emergency and imprisoned thousands of political critics of her government.[43] The group organized by Justice Tarkunde, the People's Union for Civil Liberties, remains active at this writing.

Though rights organizations were established in a number of countries in the period before and after World War II, none of them acquired anything like the significance of the American Civil Liberties Union. They tended to be very much smaller, even relative to the size of the country in which they were formed and, in that era, demonstrated little ability to influence the course of public policy. Paul Gordon Lauren has noted the involvement of prominent intellectuals such as Carl von Ossietzky of Germany (a leading anti-Nazi and later a winner of the Nobel Peace Prize), Miguel de Unamuno of Spain, and Giacomo Matteotti of Italy (subsequently murdered by the fascists) in organizations established in Europe after World War I. In association with Victor Basch of France, they established, in 1922, the Paris-based Fédération Internationale des Droits de l'Homme (FIDH), which was snuffed out when the Nazis occupied Paris during World War II and revived a few years after the war.[44]

Established somewhat later, in 1934, was the National Council for Civil Liberties in England.[45] Initially associated with the Labor Party, it came under the influence of communists in the World War II period and refused to defend civil liberties for fascists and Trotskyists. A particular controversy erupted over the issue of free speech in the case of Sir Oswald Mosley, a former Conservative member of Parliament, who organized the British Union of Fascists in 1932. Mosley, whose wedding to Diana Mitford Adolph Hitler attended, was imprisoned in England in 1940 and not released until 1943. When the war ended in 1945, free speech advocates such as George Orwell and E. M. Forster, who had resigned from the National Council for Civil Liberties over its failure to defend civil liberties for individuals like Mosley, joined with other prominent intellectuals and artists including Augustus John, Herbert Read, and Osbert Sitwell to form a new group, the Freedom Defence Committee.[46] When the NCCL changed its policies and agreed not to place political conditions on its readiness to defend free speech, the Freedom Defence Committee's reason for existence ended, and the organization dissolved. The National Council for Civil Liberties went through a similar struggle in the 1980s when the question was whether it would defend free speech for racists. Again, the issue provoked resignations. At this writing, renamed Liberty, the organization is faring well and its policy is closer to that of the American Civil Liberties Union, which prides itself on its readiness to defend free speech for all. In recent years, Liberty has been the leader of efforts in the United Kingdom to resist restrictions on civil liberties advocated by political figures such as Tony Blair and Gordon Brown in the name of the battle against terrorism. Along with the ACLU, it has taken the lead in organizing a global association of civil liberties groups that encompasses organizations in Canada, Ireland, Argentina, Hungary, and South Africa. The association's groups distinguish themselves from other human rights groups by the broad range of issues with which they are concerned, including the rights of the developmentally disabled, drug addicts, and other such marginalized groups, and also by their readiness to engage in litigation and lobbying as well as in the gathering and disseminating of information in their efforts to protect rights. In practice, however, there is often not a sharp dividing line that separates civil liberties groups from some other human rights organizations.

Though there is little or no value in speculating about how history might have turned out if one or another circumstance had been different, it is perhaps worth pointing out that the non-existence of either a sustained international human rights movement or a broader array of civil liberties groups during the decade that preceded World War II is particularly regrettable. It was a period of especially severe abuses of rights in different parts of the world: Nazi Germany where Jews, leftists, and others were persecuted; Soviet Russia where Stalin's Gulag was taking shape; Spain where German and Italian planes pioneered in the indiscriminate bombardment of a civilian population; Ethiopia where Mussolini's forces used poison gas; and China where Japanese troops committed countless atrocities. The 1930s—Auden's "low dishonest decade"—foreshadowed and helped make possible the unparalleled horrors of World War II. In turn of course, it was World War II that demonstrated the connection between abuses of human rights and war. During the war years, as Paul Gordon Lauren has pointed out, a number of prominent writers and intellectuals drafted or supported proposed declarations of rights. They included the futurist writer H. G. Wells, historian James T. Shotwell, journalist Clarence Streit, and the philosopher Jacques Maritain.[47] It seems possible that their efforts contributed to the decision of the authors of the United Nations Charter to incorporate a commitment to promote human rights among the responsibilities of an institution established to preserve peace. The emergence of the contemporary human rights movement in the postwar decades is in part attributable to a widespread understanding that the failure to unite in denouncing crimes such as those of the 1930s contributed to the calamity that followed.[48]

▪ ▪ ▪

In January 1947, Roger Baldwin received a letter at the American Civil Liberties Union from the U.S. War Department telling him that General Douglas MacArthur wanted him to go to Japan and Korea as a consultant on civil liberties. A legacy of the three months Baldwin spent in Japan was the establishment of a Japanese Civil Liberties Union, a small organization that continues in existence at this writing. The following year, also at the invitation of the War Department, Baldwin and two ACLU Board members, lawyer Arthur Garfield Hays and editor Norman Cousins, went to Germany. Baldwin took advantage of that trip to visit Austria as well. Though no lasting institutions resulted from those visits, his activities in countries under American occupation reflected his interest in promoting rights internationally, not just in the United States. In the postwar period, Baldwin also took on a leadership role in two new organizations, the International League for the Rights of Man (later, the International League for Human Rights, ILHR), which he helped to establish during the war; and the Inter-American Association for Democracy and Freedom (IAADF).

The International League for Human Rights was, in part, an outgrowth of the much older French Fedération des Droits de L'Homme, founded in the early years of the twentieth century as a result of the dispute over the Dreyfus case. Baldwin had established contact with the group on a trip to France in 1927. His association with it was renewed in 1942 when French exiles in New York, including Henri Bonnet, subsequently the French ambassador to the United States, sought to continue its activities despite Nazi occupation of their own country. They invited Baldwin to join them on the Board of Directors of the new group they established. He became chair in 1946, while still serving as executive director of the ACLU.[49]

The ILHR, with Baldwin heading its efforts during his final years at the ACLU in the late 1940s and for many years thereafter until his death at the age of 97 in 1981, played a significant role for a period as a lobby group at the United Nations promoting the adoption of the Universal Declaration of Human Rights and a number of treaties giving legal force to the provisions of the Declaration. Its representatives were frequently the only group prowling the hallways of the U.N., buttonholing delegates on human rights issues. When others took part in such efforts, it was often representatives of organizations established along religious lines. Later on, after Amnesty International was established and became active at the U.N., and still later when many other human rights bodies emerged and rose in significance, the ILHR, which never effectively diversified its activities to deal with changed circumstances, was readily eclipsed. During its first two decades or so, however, and to a much more limited extent thereafter, it helped in establishing the norms of international human rights.

The Inter-American Association for Democracy and Freedom held its first major gathering in Havana, Cuba in 1950. A close colleague of Baldwin's, Frances Grant, his American contemporary who seemed to know the struggling democrats in every Latin American country in an era when military dictatorships were common in the region, led the organization as its secretary general. The IAADF played a role in calling attention to the terrible human rights record of Rafael Trujillo, the dictator of the Dominican Republic. It also helped to establish something of a mutual support network among democratic leaders in the hemisphere, such as Romulo Betancourt of Venezuela, José Figueres of Costa Rica, and Eduardo Frei of Chile, each of whom served for a period as his country's president. Yet the organization was so closely identified with Frances Grant that when she died in the early 1970s, the organization died with her.

· · ·

As this record indicates, over a period of close to two centuries, from the start of the antislavery movement in Britain in the second half of the eighteenth century, a number of efforts were made to promote human rights internationally. Most of them, though not all, got their starts in England or the United States, both countries in which the concept of natural law had taken root to a far greater extent than in the countries of continental Europe. Their common law traditions have a strong intellectual kinship with the concept of natural law. In contrast, the countries of continental Europe, and countries in other parts of the world that derive their legal systems from the Continent belong to the civil law tradition in which positive law is supreme and may not be set aside because of a conflict with principles of natural law or higher law. (As noted above, a shift towards a common law approach has taken place in recent years in different parts of the world with the emergence of supranational courts to enforce international human rights treaties and with the development of national constitutional courts in continental Europe and in some countries of Africa and Asia.) It is important to recognize the valor of the continental European intellectuals who created the organizations that joined to form FIDH in the years after World War I. Many of them paid with their lives for standing up against fascism and Nazism. Yet in the period prior to 1961, when Amnesty International was launched in England (see chapter 8), none of the international rights movements resulted in the creation of a substantial enduring movement or of organizational structures capable of exercising influence on a range of rights issues over the long term. None had the staying power and capacity of such early-twentieth-century national bodies in the United States as the NAACP and the ACLU, nor were domestic rights organizations created in other countries that exercised comparable influence. That is not to depreciate the significant achievements of international campaigns during that period. They played a major role in the abolition of slavery, in curbing the worst cruelties of King Leopold's savage rule of the Congo, in securing for women the right to vote, and in helping to define the norms of human rights. Though some of the international campaigns of the era from the middle of the eighteenth century to the middle of the twentieth century were joined by large numbers of people whose collective efforts contributed to important changes in public policy, those efforts did not result in the formation of a sustained international human rights movement. No doubt, the difficulty of operating internationally in an era prior to the age of air travel and rapid communications was a major factor. The same factors impeded the long-term survival of significant national organizations. Once a particular goal had been achieved, such as the adoption of the Nineteenth Amendment in the United States and its counterparts in other countries giving women the right to vote, the great majority of the many thousands of women and men who had fought for suffrage did not continue to struggle for the rights of women to equal treatment in education, employment, or domestic relations. Nor did they take up other human rights issues. An international human rights movement with staying power had not yet been born.

3

What Are Rights?

AS OF SEPTEMBER 30, 2011

AMONG THOSE ENGAGED IN THE PROMOTION OF HUMAN RIGHTS, there is general agreement that rights are an aspect of humanity. They are not dependent on such characteristics as race, nationality, or gender, nor do they depend on a person's presence within the territory of a particular political entity. Rights, most proponents agree, are ethical norms with a legal content that requires that they should be honored and enforced by public institutions. Some rights, it is generally conceded, may be temporarily abridged by the state because of exigent circumstances; others may never be violated, no matter the context or the purported justification. Disputes over rights generally involve three questions. Which norms warrant universal legal enforcement? What circumstances warrant temporary abridgements of rights? What abridgements are permissible in such circumstances? This chapter addresses the first of those questions. The other two are considered in connection with the discussion of rights after September 11 in chapter 12.

In the eighteenth century, when discussion of "rights" became widespread, the word was used in a number of phrases in English and French, the two languages in which the concept developed. These included "natural rights," the "rights of mankind," the "rights of humanity," the "rights of man" and, infrequently, "human rights." Not exactly interchangeable, these usages had in common that they were all based on the emerging idea of individual autonomy and referred to what today we would call "civil" and "political" rights.

Possibly the most sweeping concept of rights in that era was Jefferson's as expressed in the Declaration of Independence. His idea of "unalienable rights" included not only "Life" and "Liberty," but also the "pursuit of Happiness"—a right that might be considered to fall on the "positive liberty" side of Isaiah Berlin's mid-twentieth-century equation[1]—and, perhaps even more far-reaching, echoing Locke—"The Right of the People to alter or abolish [a form of government that does not serve those ends], and to institute a new Government, laying its foundation on such principles and organizing its powers in such form as to them shall seem more likely to effect their Safety and Happiness." In other words, a government that does not respect rights lacks legitimacy and, therefore, may be overthrown. The other great revolutionary document of the age, the French Declaration of the Rights of Man and of the Citizen of 1789, seemed in its opening sentences to have a comparably wide reach. The "natural and imprescriptible rights of man," it read, were "liberty, property, security and resistance to oppression." The right to resist oppression sounds similar to Locke's view and Jefferson's about the right to alter or abolish a government that does not respect liberty. Yet liberty was defined in a way that Isaiah Berlin could comfortably classify as "negative liberty" because, the French Declaration asserted, it "consists in the ability to do whatever does not harm another; hence the exercise of the natural rights of each man has no other limits than those which assure to other members of society the enjoyment of the same rights. These limits can only be determined by the law." The French Declaration went on to list many of the civil and political rights that would be set forth today in any document focusing on these issues, including the right of all citizens to take part in governmental decisions either in person or through their representatives; the right to count equally; the right not to be arrested except in accordance with law; the right not to be punished as a consequence of laws adopted *ex post facto*; the presumption of innocence (though Americans regard such a presumption as one of their basic rights, it is not articulated in any of the foundational documents of the United States but has been absorbed into our thinking from the French Declaration); freedom of opinion, expression, and religious belief; and the right not to be deprived of property arbitrarily and without compensation. The American Bill of Rights adopted two years later provided a similar set of guarantees of civil and political rights, adding as further provisions: protection against unreasonable searches and seizures, the right not to be forced to incriminate oneself, the right to counsel, and the right not to be subjected to cruel and unusual punishment; but not, however, including Jefferson's assertion of a right to pursue happiness or the right to alter or abolish an abusive government. As seen from the perspective of James Madison and those who contributed to the thinking that went into his writing of the American Bill of Rights, the concept of rights referred exclusively to civil and political rights: that is, rights that limit the power of the state to interfere with certain actions of citizens and that empower citizens to influence the actions of the state.

In our time, it is customary for many—but not all—proponents of rights to define rights more broadly than in the French Declaration or the American Bill of Rights. The Universal Declaration of Rights, adopted by the United Nations in 1948, widely seen as both the source and the lodestar for the contemporary human rights movement, follows the French Declaration of Rights and the American Bill of Rights in its first twenty-one articles, which are devoted to civil and political rights, adding several that were not mentioned in those earlier documents. These include the right to an effective remedy when rights are violated; the right to freedom of movement within a state; the right to live in one's country and to return to it; and the right to seek asylum from persecution. But in Articles 22 through 26, the Declaration made a radical break with its predecessors. The rights set forth in these articles are not civil and political rights but, instead, economic and social rights. They include a right to social security, a right to employment, a right to rest and leisure, and a right to education. Other international agreements on rights adopted in subsequent years added to this list a right to food, a right to health care, and a right to housing.

In the view of many of their proponents, the rights set forth in the Universal Declaration of Rights are "indivisible." By this the authors mean that there is no difference in significance or hierarchy between civil and political rights on the one hand and economic and social rights on the other. Moreover, calling this list of rights indivisible implies that the enjoyment of rights of one sort is dependent on the protection of both sets of rights. They are complementary. Mary Ann Glendon, author of a history of the adoption of the Universal Declaration, calls them a "geodesic dome of interlocking principles."[2] Some advocates of economic and social rights go further. They contend that economic and social rights must have priority because only those who have adequate food, shelter, and health care are in a position to enjoy civil and political rights.

What brought about the shift from the almost exclusive focus on civil and political rights in the eighteenth century to the twentieth century's according of equal or even superior status to economic and social rights, of course, was the rise of socialism and communism in the nineteenth century. As the historian Lynn Hunt has pointed out, "Socialists and Communists wanted to ensure that the lower classes would enjoy social and economic equality and not just equal political rights. Yet even as they drew attention to rights that had been shortchanged by the proponents of the rights of man, Socialist and Communist organizations inevitably downgraded the importance of rights as a goal. Marx's own view was clairvoyant; political emancipation could be achieved through legal equality within bourgeois society and its constitutional protections of private property. Socialists and Communists nonetheless raised two enduring questions about rights; are political rights enough [or as the issue is often posed by advocates of economic and social rights, 'is the right to speak meaningful to a man who does not have enough to eat'], and can the individual's right to the protection of private property co-exist with society's need to foster the well-being of its less fortunate members?"[3]

An 1840 essay by Pierre-Joseph Proudhon, one of the founding fathers of socialist and communist thought, known for his aphorism that "property is theft," explicitly attacked the inclusion of property in the list of natural rights set forth in the French Declaration of the Rights of Man and of the Citizen. He wrote that property "is a right outside of society; for it is clear that if the wealth of each was social wealth, the conditions would be equal for all, and it would be a contradiction to say: *Property is a man's right to dispose at will of social property.* Then if we are associated for the sake of liberty, equality and security, we are not associated for the sake of property; then if property is a *natural* right, this natural right is not social, but *anti-social.*"[4] Proudhon's use of terms such as "*social* wealth" and "*social* property" is reflected in contemporary usage of the phrase "economic and *social* rights" as the preferred label for economic rights.

Though the Marxist thought of the previous century played a crucial role in the incorporation of economic and social rights in the mid-twentieth century Universal Declaration of Human Rights, it did not prevent continued adherence to the eighteenth-century view, expressed in the American Bill of Rights as well as in the French Declaration, that a catalogue of rights should include the protection of private property. Article 17 of the Universal Declaration provides that "(1) Everyone has the right to own property alone as well as in association with others," and "(2) No one shall be arbitrarily deprived of his property."

The United States, represented by Eleanor Roosevelt, whose husband, President Franklin D. Roosevelt, had led the country out of the Great Depression and who had included "freedom from want" in his "Four Freedoms" address of 1941, accepted the incorporation of economic and social rights in the Universal Declaration of Human Rights. Indeed the enumeration of such rights reflected Franklin Roosevelt's thinking. In his 1944 State of the Union address, the President had said: "We have accepted, so to speak, a second bill of rights, under which a new basis for security and prosperity can be established for all—regardless of station, race or creed." He then went on to list its components, citing "a useful and remunerative job"; "the right to earn enough to provide adequate food and clothing and recreation"; "the right of every family to a decent home"; "the right to a good education"; and several more. Roosevelt concluded his list with the assertion: "All these rights spell security. And after this war is won, we must be prepared to move forward, in the implementation of these rights, to new goals of human happiness and well-being."[5] Nor was it Roosevelt alone in the United States who championed economic and social rights. Also in 1944, a committee of the American Law Institute, an influential body made up of judges and legal scholars, published a draft International Bill of Rights. In addition to the civil and political rights set forth in the American Bill of Rights, it incorporated rights to education, work, food, housing, and social security—the last of these including health care—in its compilation.[6]

The influence of Franklin Roosevelt on the Universal Declaration, mediated through the handiwork of Eleanor Roosevelt, is most evident in the Declaration's preamble. The second paragraph states:

> *Whereas* disregard and contempt for human rights have resulted in barbarous acts which have outraged the conscience of mankind, and the advent of a world in which human beings shall enjoy *freedom of speech and belief and freedom from fear and want* has been proclaimed as the highest aspiration of the common people (emphasis added).

It was, of course, Franklin Roosevelt who used those exact words in proclaiming the four freedoms of "freedom of speech and belief and freedom from fear and want."

Though the United States contributed to the inclusion of economic and social rights—freedom from want—in the Universal Declaration, it would not go along with a failure to protect the right to own property. And its espousal of economic and social rights did not persuade the Soviet Union and its satellites to vote in favor of adoption of the Declaration, as Moscow objected to the provisions dealing with freedom of movement, as well as freedom of thought, religion, and expression. The Soviet bloc countries abstained, as did two others: Saudi Arabia on account of the provision on freedom of religion, which includes the right to change one's religion, and because of the guarantee of equal rights for women and men, particularly "as to marriage, during marriage and at its dissolution"; and South Africa because of the provision that all are "equal in dignity and rights" in Article 1, and on account of Article 7, which provides that "All are equal before the law and are entitled without any discrimination to equal protection of the law." No government among the fifty-six states that were then members of the world body voted against adoption of the Universal Declaration of Human Rights.

Since the adoption of the Universal Declaration by the United Nations General Assembly in 1948, there have been many efforts to expand further the scope of rights. Advocates of economic and social rights have succeeded in getting a number of national and international agreements, including the International Covenant on Economic, Social and Cultural Rights, to recognize rights to food, health care, and housing. Because it is apparent that some countries with limited resources would be hard pressed to accord their nationals all the economic rights to which proponents of such rights consider them to be entitled, another economic right has also emerged, though it has not yet been incorporated in any global agreement: the right to development. This carries with it the implication that, as a matter of right, the resources of wealthy countries should be used to raise the standard of living of poor countries so as to enable them to meet the economic and social rights of their populations. An obvious justification for seeking such a transfer is that a significant part of the wealth of the wealthy is derived from their exploitation of the resources of the rest of the world. Hence, calling for a right to development does no more, in the view of some of its proponents, than provide a measure of redress for those who have not shared in those advances or who may have been impoverished in the process.[7]

As economic and social rights are sometimes referred to as "second-generation" rights, the right to development is considered a third-generation right. It is not alone in this category, which is comprised of purported rights that tend to be inherently international in character. That is, it would be difficult or impossible to implement them effectively except on an international scale through bodies that engage in global governance. They include the right to a clean or a healthy environment and the right to peace. (At times, first-generation rights are referred to as blue rights; second-generation rights as red rights; and—as they include the environment—third-generation rights are designated green rights.)

Another characteristic of rights to development, to a healthy environment, and to peace, of course, is that unlike the first-generation rights set forth in the American Bill of Rights, the French Declaration of Rights and the first twenty-one articles of the Universal Declaration of Human Rights, they are collective rather than individual. That is, it is difficult to imagine how an individual, on her own, could enjoy the right to development. It is only possible to imagine that, in common with her fellow citizens of a poor country and of other poor countries, she would benefit from the transfer of knowledge, skills, and resources that would enhance opportunities for the population as a whole to achieve greater economic and social well-being. Moreover, it is difficult to identify a particular individual or a finite group of individuals who could be held accountable in such a way as to secure someone else's development. Enforcement of this right could take place only through the collective action of an entire society, or of many societies acting together under the direction of global authorities to bring about the necessary transfer of resources. The same is true of a healthy environment or of peace. Without some international institution owning the capacity to regulate the practices of the world's governments, these rights could not be secured. Of course, goals such as development, a healthy environment, and peace may be promoted through voluntary agreements among states, such as an international agreement on climate change. It is calling them "rights" that suggests the need for enforceability against recalcitrant states even in the absence of an international agreement.

There is yet another collective right that has been incorporated as the first article in both the International Covenant on Civil and Political Rights and the International Covenant on Economic, Social and Cultural Rights, the two international treaties that were promulgated by the United Nations in 1966 in order to transform the provisions of the Universal Declaration of Human Rights—which is, after all, only a declaration of the U.N. General Assembly—into binding international law enforceable in the states that ratify these treaties or, at the least, providing a basis for assertions that those states have a legal obligation to comply with their provisions. The collective right that precedes all of the others enumerated in these two treaties is the right to self-determination.

The period in which virtually all the colonial nations in Asia, Africa, and the Caribbean were gaining their independence was still in its early stage in 1948 when the Universal Declaration of Human Rights was adopted by the U.N. General Assembly. In contrast, by 1966, when the two covenants were adopted by the United Nations and submitted to member states for ratification, many former colonies had already gained their independence and had become members of the world body. Recognition of a right to self-determination was immensely important to them in the early years of their existence as independent states, and so took precedence over other rights. It is a collective right, of course, because no individual on his or her own can claim this right, and as such it is set forth in the two covenants as a right of "peoples only." It can only be enjoyed by an individual by virtue of his or her affiliation with a "people" that enjoys this right collectively because geography, history, ethnicity, religion, language, culture, or some combination of these factors gives them status as a people and, therefore, a basis for the formation of a state of their own.

Twentieth-century assertions that economic and social rights deserved the same degree of recognition and protection as civil and political rights was in part a reaction to the rise of communism and socialism in the nineteenth century. In like manner, twentieth century endorsement of a right of self-determination derives from the rise of another ideology during the nineteenth century: nationalism. Nineteenth-century nationalist movements included those that led to the unification of states such as Germany and Italy and demands for the break-up of the Ottoman and Austro-Hungarian empires into their ethnic and linguistic components. And, though it came after the end of the nineteenth century at the conclusion of the First World War, the Versailles Peace Treaty's attempt to give every ethnic/linguistic group its own state was in the spirit of the previous century. A direct ancestor of the right to self-determination set forth in the two U.N. covenants of 1966 was President Woodrow Wilson's famous assertion: "Every people has a right to choose the sovereignty under which they shall live." With that statement, Wilson ranks not only as a leading proponent of collective rights, but perhaps also as an avatar of the twentieth-century anti-colonial and separatist movements that led to the proliferation of independent states in today's world.

With the passage of time, a number of the states that were newly independent in 1966 when the two covenants were promulgated, or that were about to achieve their independence, have become strenuous opponents of further efforts to secure independence for groups claiming a right to self-determination. Many secessionist movements have been vigorously opposed by African governments and by the Organization of African Unity and its successor, the African Union, which have adhered to the view that redrawing colonial-era boundaries would have disastrous consequences despite the fact that those boundaries were arbitrary and established in disregard of tribal and linguistic territories. Indeed, African states have been so successful in adhering to this view that, until recently, there was only a single instance in which a new country that previously was part of another African country had gained international recognition; namely Eritrea, which became independent of Ethiopia in 1993. A factor in making that possible was the fact that during most of the colonial era, Eritrea had not been part of Ethiopia. (As this is written, South Sudan has just become an independent state and is gaining international recognition. On the other hand, though Somaliland and Puntland both function autonomously, there is no sign that their separation from the failed state of Somalia will be recognized internationally any time soon. Nor does there seem any likelihood that a long-standing independence movement, the Polisario, will gain recognition in the foreseeable future for the proposed state of Western Sahara in its attempt to break away from Morocco.)

The situation has been somewhat similar in Asia, though of course there is no regional body on the continent that is a counterpart to the African Union. Individual governments have been on their own in resisting separatist tendencies. Pakistan separated from India when the two countries became independent in 1947, but Pakistan fought a war more than two decades later, marked by great cruelties, in an unsuccessful attempt to prevent independence for geographically separate Bangladesh. Two other former colonies, India and Indonesia, have fought protracted wars against secessionist movements, and China, which was only colonized in bits and pieces, has made strenuous opposition to separatist movements in such territories as Tibet, Taiwan, and Xinjiang a centerpiece of its policy.

Many new states have emerged during the past two decades as a result of the fall of communism. The Soviet Union disintegrated in 1991 and became fifteen new states. Some of them, in turn, have had to struggle against independence movements such as the Chechen rebellion in Russia and separatist movements such as those of the Abkhazians and South Ossetians in Georgia and the Transnistrians in Moldova. At this writing, no fewer than seven states have been internationally recognized since the breakup of Yugoslavia began in 1991. The Czech Republic and Slovakia became separate states in 1993.

Can such issues be decided on the basis of rights? Some supporters of independence movements continue to adhere to the view that they can, but the question that necessarily arises is how are those rights to be determined? Is it enough that a majority of the population in a particular territory wishes to be independent? And if so, how are the boundaries of that territory to be determined? What about those within a territory who do not wish to lose their nationality—the Serbs in Bosnia, for example, or the Unionists in Northern Ireland? What if—as has happened in a number of countries—separatist movements arise in resource-rich territories, such as Aceh or Papua in Indonesia, where the wealth derived from the exploitation of those resources becomes a factor? Does that wealth or the taxes on it belong to those in the immediate vicinity or to the entire country?

Some of those who have followed developments in the former Yugoslavia were partisans of independence for Kosovo but expressed little interest in the separatist movement in Montenegro. It was not only that Montenegrins and Serbs seemed almost indistinguishable ethnically, religiously, and linguistically, but also that there was no history of Serb persecution of Montenegrins. Under the circumstances, what was the justification for self-determination and independence? In contrast, particularly in the period subsequent to Slobodan Milosevic's accession to power in the late 1980s, Albanian Kosovars suffered severe persecution. This, far more than their ethnic, linguistic, and religious differences from Serbs, seemed to many the main justification for self-determination. Once a people have achieved their goal of the collective right to an independent state, however, there is no guarantee that individual rights will be protected. Though Albanian Kosovars were persecuted in a united Yugoslavia under Milosevic, this did not prevent some of them from persecuting the Serb and Roma minorities in their territory once they became its masters.

It is evident that a great many factors must be weighed in making decisions about self-determination and independence. Some of those issues were raised by Eleanor Roosevelt at a 1952 meeting of the U.N. Human Rights Commission. Speaking for a country that had suffered its greatest national trauma in the previous century over just this question, she asked: "Does self-determination mean the right of secession? Does self-determination constitute a right of fragmentation or a justification for the fragmentation of nations? Does self-determination mean the right of people to sever association with another power regardless of the economic effect upon both parties, regardless of the effect upon their internal stability and their external security, regardless of the effect upon their neighbors or the international community?"[8] To these, one might add the question, if it is a "people" that is entitled to self-determination, how does one define a people? Which of the various attributes of a people should be considered and which disregarded? Does the concept of a people have room for minorities? For our purposes, the issue is whether these questions can be resolved by decisions on rights?

As one contemplates the vast landscape that is potentially subject to rights, it is inevitable that one must ask not only what are "rights," but also what are the limits on rights? In addition to traditional issues of civil and political freedom, are such major issues as peace, development, the environment, the independence of states, and the allocation of their economic resources to deal with health, education, food, and shelter to be resolved on the basis of rights? Do all of these aspects of humanity require legal enforcement? If so, what happens when upholding one right comes into conflict with honoring another? What scope is there for political choices that are not determined by assertions of rights?

These are, it should be pointed out, largely hypothetical questions. No state or collection of states is organized in a manner that permits issues of significant magnitude outside the field of civil and political rights to be decided on the basis of rights that take precedence over legislative and executive decision-making. Courts may decide questions that have important consequences for the economy or the environment, but—with few exceptions—they do so by interpreting or applying legislation rather than on the basis of rights derived from natural law. Moreover, it is difficult to imagine that any body exercising governmental power, whether organized democratically or in some other way, will be required by its constituents to make major decisions that involve the allocation of the resources of the society on such a basis.

If the idea of rights is meaningful, it is because it is accepted that a right takes precedence over other considerations. In the realm of civil and political rights, this idea is well understood. Even though the vast majority of citizens in a state that respects rights may be offended, scandalized, or hurt by the expression of an idea or a point of view, each person has a right to speak and to say what she will. Though evidence of an individual's criminal guilt may be overwhelming, she still has a right to counsel and the right to a fair trial. Despite the potential advantages to be derived from coercing a suspect to divulge information or to name the names of others who are involved in a conspiracy, torture is prohibited. Rights, as Ronald Dworkin has argued, trump all else.[9] If the entire body politic is on one side and a minority of one is on the other, if it is a question of that individual's rights, he or she should prevail. That is the theory on which the great charters of civil and political rights are based. It is epitomized in the first five words of the American Bill of Rights; "Congress shall make no law . . . ." That is, civil and political rights, such as those set forth in the First Amendment, are not subject to democratic control.

Another necessary feature of rights is that they are not merely aspirational; they should be enforceable. The mechanism that seems best suited for this purpose is the courts. Legislatures are not the ideal institutions to uphold rights because an essential role of their members is to advance the interests of their constituents and to engage in negotiations and compromises with those representing other interests until either a mutually acceptable outcome is reached or one side prevails because it can muster a greater number of votes at a certain moment (and not because it necessarily embodies justice). Nor is the executive situated especially well to serve this purpose, for it is the duty of that branch of government to do its best to advance the welfare of the citizenry as a whole. It asks a great deal, perhaps too much, to require that the executive should have the ultimate responsibility to safeguard the rights of the discordant individual whose actions may seem inimical to the well-being of all others.

The courts, on the other hand, have a responsibility to find the law and then to apply it in the particular case that comes before them. It is not their responsibility to weigh the competing interests that must be considered by a legislative body. Nor are they bound by the practical realities that dominate the thinking of the executive. If the law recognizes a right, it is the duty of judges to uphold that right. On such grounds, the justiciability of questions involving rights and their judicial enforcement seems crucial to making rights a reality. It is hard to imagine how rights could be upheld in practice without a body that is insulated from the regular political process playing a decisive role. Rights are not abstract. They are, if one adopts a social contract approach, part of the relationship between a citizen and a state in which the citizen has ceded certain powers to the state in return for the state's commitment to use those powers for the common good. In the zone known as rights, however, the citizen has expressly reserved to herself the regulation of her own conduct and has limited the state to taking only such action as is required to facilitate the citizen's exercise of those rights and to prevent interference with the rights of others. The same is true if one adopts a universalist approach in which rights are an aspect of one's humanity. Resort to judicial intervention seems the most appropriate means both for enforcing the citizen's contract with the state and for recognizing the fundamental human interest in exercising rights.

Though third-generation rights have been extensively discussed, few attempts have been made to put them into practice. It is true, of course, that there has been a great deal of litigation in the United States, and to a lesser degree in other countries, over environmental issues; and the environmental movement appropriately regards the courts as an important venue for its efforts. By and large, however, such litigation has not involved sweeping claims of environmental rights, and where such claims have been made they have generally not prospered. Rather, the focus of successful environmental litigation has been an effort to compel executive agencies to comply with specific legislative requirements that involve the management of natural resources, that regulate industries, or that concern public or private projects with environmental consequences. Litigation in the environmental field must be sustained by positive law. It is not grounded in principles of natural law.[10]

It is in the realm of second-generation rights, that is, economic and social rights, that most of the debate over the purview of rights has taken place and where the most extensive efforts have been made to seek remedies through the courts, as is the regular practice in the field of civil and political rights. Two countries where especially significant efforts have been made to advance economic and social rights through the courts are India and South Africa.

The Indian Constitution of 1950 has a section, Part III, which deals with "fundamental rights" that are civil and political rights. A separate section, Part IV, deals with "directive principles of state policy" that are a mixture of civil and political rights and economic and social rights. The first of these principles holds that "the citizens, men and women equally, have the right to an adequate means of livelihood." To the extent that the focus is on the equal rights of men and women, this belongs on the civil and political rights side of the spectrum. The same is true of another of the "directive principles," which requires that there be "equal pay for equal work for both men and women." On the other hand, the "right to an adequate means of livelihood" and other passages that deal with such questions as ownership and control of the material resources of the community, operation of the economic system so that it does not lead to concentrations of wealth, opportunities for children to develop in a healthy manner, and the provision, within the state's resources, for the right to work, to education, and to public assistance are assertions of economic and social rights.

When the Indian Constitution was drafted, it was explicitly stated in that document that the directive principles were not justiciable. They were included in the Constitution to provide guidance to the executive and legislative branches of government rather than to constitute judicially enforceable rights. The directive principles were, it was said, "the soul" of the Constitution. Over time, however, as a consequence of decisions by the Supreme Court of India, constitutional amendments, and extensive public debate, the courts have become deeply engaged in efforts to uphold them. In essence, they do so by interpreting broad principles of fundamental rights, such as the right to life, the right to liberty, and the right to equality in light of the directive principles.

Though there have certainly been court cases in India that have significantly improved the economic well-being of some citizens, the ability of the courts to adjudicate questions arising under those provisions of the directive principles that concern economic and social rights cannot be said to have made a substantial difference in the lives of the vast majority of the country's impoverished people. The most comprehensive recent study of litigation on social and economic rights in India finds that "in health and education, the patterns show low impact of courts on policies, the reluctance of judges to penalize government providers as compared to private providers, and the corresponding lack of emphasis by NGOs and others on litigation as a strategy to obtain social goods."[11] No judicial means has been found to make it possible to redistribute the rapidly growing wealth of India in a manner that benefits the poor. On the contrary, as in the other great Asian power that has dazzled the world by the speed of its economic gains, China, the gap between rich and poor has been expanding at a fast pace despite the ostensible commitment of both countries to economic and social rights.

Arthur Chaskalson, the first chief justice of the Constitutional Court established in South Africa after the Apartheid era gave way to a democratic government elected by citizens of all races, has argued that it is particularly appropriate for the constitution of his country to incorporate protections for social and economic rights because of the need to overcome the racial discrimination on which the previous government was based. Unlike India and several other countries where constitutions treat economic and social rights separately, the South African Constitution puts them on the same plane as civil and political rights. Chaskalson has called attention to his differences with the general approach to rights of the legal philosopher, Ronald Dworkin, expressed in such works as *Taking Rights Seriously*.[12] According to Chaskalson:

Dworkin is unlikely to have any quarrel with the achievement of equality as a constitutional value nor with its being very closely linked with the value of human dignity. He may, however, quarrel with other provisions of the [South African] Constitution that impose positive duties on the state to address the legacies of the past, and, he may argue that such rights raise policy considerations closer to the political process than legal principles relevant to the judicial process. Provision is made in the South African Constitution for socioeconomic rights that require the state to take action to achieve the progressive realization of access to housing, health care, food, water, social security and land. . . . Claims for enforcement of these rights represent hard cases. Governments are elected to deal with these issues, and socioeconomic rights are at the border of the separation of powers between the judiciary and the executive.[13]

At the time Chaskalson wrote in 2003, nine years after the establishment of the Constitutional Court, it had considered just three cases involving social and economic rights. In *Soobramoney*,[14] the first of these cases, the court ruled against a man suffering from kidney disease who sought dialysis at state expense. The Court reasoned that if such expenses were extended to all patients suffering from serious life-threatening diseases, the health care budget would have to be dramatically increased or the funds made available for primary care would have to be drastically reduced. Also, it noted that the state had to use its limited resources to provide for housing, food and water, employment and social security, as well as health care, and that "this requires [the state] to adopt a holistic approach to the larger needs of society rather than to focus on the specific needs of particular individuals."[15] Denied the care he needed, Mr. Soobramoney died right after the Constitutional Court ruled against him.

The second social and economic rights case considered by the South African Constitutional Court was *Grootboom*.[16] Mrs. Grootboom had lived in a shantytown settlement near Cape Town that became waterlogged during the winter rains. Along with about a thousand others from the area, many of whom had been on waiting lists for subsidized low-cost housing for several years, she and her children moved to a nearby hillside where there was vacant land. After being forcibly removed from that spot, they relocated in a local sports field and, with the help of a lawyer, wrote to the municipal council asking for assistance in obtaining housing. No assistance was forthcoming, so Mrs. Grootboom sued. Eventually, the Constitutional Court decided that the state's housing program was unreasonable because "it failed to make reasonable provisions within its available resources for people . . . with no access to land, no roof over their heads, and who were living in intolerable conditions or crisis situations."[17] Yet the Court refrained from ordering a specific remedy in Mrs. Grootboom's case. It left it to the state to decide how best to provide a remedy by devising a program that would deal with persons in her situation. The Court did not suggest that a right to housing required any change in the "available resources" that had been allocated by the state to deal with housing.

The third such case decided by the South African Constitutional Court is much the best-known ruling by a court anywhere in the world in a matter involving social and economic rights. It was brought to the Court by the Treatment Action Campaign (TAC), a nongovernmental organization in South Africa that spearheaded a challenge to the bizarre HIV/AIDS policies of President Thabo Mbeki's government. As its name indicates, it sought treatment (with anti-retroviral drugs) for those infected with HIV.

The specific issue in the TAC case[18] was the government's failure to provide Nevirapine in public hospitals to prevent the transmission of HIV from mothers to their newborn children. A single dose of Nevirapine administered at the time of birth can, in a high percentage of cases, prevent the disease from being passed on. Cost was not a factor. The treatment is not expensive and the government had been offered a five-year supply of Nevirapine free of charge. Rather, it seemed, the government did not provide this treatment because the president and his minister of health did not accept that HIV causes AIDS and considered that, despite the overwhelming medical evidence to the contrary, the administration of such drugs could do more harm than good.

In the court case, the South African government argued that the making of health care policy is the responsibility of the executive branch. It is not up to the courts to sit in judgment of its policies and to require that changes be made when judges disagreed with those policies. The Constitutional Court rejected that argument on the basis that the government's policy was not reasonable. Under its terms, the children denied access to Nevirapine were denied the right to enjoy all the rights to which they would be entitled under the South African Bill of Rights. Justice Chaskalson argued, "The difference between *Soobramoney* and *TAC* was that the policy governing the use of dialysis machines was rational. . . . In contrast, in *TAC* the budget was not a material issue—the policy viewed objectively in the light of the evidence, was unreasonable."[19]

It is possible to applaud the outcome in the TAC case and still to be troubled by the distinction drawn between that case and *Soobramoney*. Both cases involved health care. Both involved situations in which the failure to provide the treatment that was sought would result in death. In adopting the view that denying Soobramoney the care he needed was reasonable because of the cost, the Court made the kind of decision that is constantly made by health ministries in all parts of the world. But is it appropriate for a court dealing with a question of rights to base its judgment on utilitarian principles that deny a man life-saving care? What if such principles were applied in a case involving civil and political rights? Could a court rule that torture is unreasonable in most cases but reasonable in some cases where grave crimes are involved? Or could it deny the right to counsel in a complex case because the expense was too great? What about freedom of speech? Should it only be protected when a court finds that the government acted unreasonably in banning the expression of a particular point of view?

Of course, courts make judgments about the reasonableness of the actions of the executive all the time. But, it is not an approach that results in the robust protection of rights. Reasonableness should not be the issue in political rights cases. Rather, the question is whether the government has ventured into territory where it is forbidden to go by such actions as torturing a defendant in a criminal case, withholding counsel from her, or denying her the right to speak. On the other hand, in cases involving economic and social rights, it seems almost inevitable that courts will engage in a cost-benefit analysis. The outcome is likely to be judicially determined social policy rather than some equivalent of a decision on a civil and political rights question. Moreover, there is the question raised by the South African government in the *TAC* case: Is a court the appropriate body to make decisions about health policy? Suppose, for example, that a novel form of treatment were proposed for patients suffering from cancer. Having heard about this treatment, some patients—desperate for any care that might save their lives—want it provided at state expense. If the state does not provide it, should a court overrule the decision of the physicians who rejected the treatment as unreasonable? What gives judges a basis for making such decisions? Shouldn't they be made by executive branch officials acting pursuant to policies made by the legislature? If judges have a role, should it be limited to instances where the executive branch of government disregards legislative policy? Or to cases in which there is evidence of invidious discrimination—as on grounds of race or gender—in the manner in which policies are carried out? The latter, of course, implicates civil and political rights.

It should be noted that the South African Constitutional Court acted in a very restrained way in those first three cases involving economic and social rights. Apparently, the Court was intent on not usurping the authority of the other branches of government to allocate the economic resources of the state. In *Soobramoney*, it rejected a claim for sophisticated health care because of the high cost. In *Grootboom*, it ruled for the plaintiff but left it to the state to determine how to deal with those lacking habitable homes without requiring the state to come up with extra resources to address the issue. In *TAC*, it ordered access to a life-saving benefit in circumstances in which the costs to the state would be negligible. It appears that the South African Constitutional Court was intent on neither trying to determine the tax burden that should be borne by the country's citizens nor on determining how large a share of the state's budget should be allocated to particular social services. It limited itself to ruling on what it considered to be just and reasonable ways to make those services available to those with great needs. On the other hand, in two of those three cases, it did overrule the decisions of the elected branches of government on how to spend the funds allocated for particular services. As the beneficiaries of the Court's decisions had not been denied those services for invidious reasons, it still may be asked what gives a court a legitimate basis for overruling the judgments of the branches of the government that are accountable to the electorate? It is, of course, true that in the *TAC* case the president and his minister of health held bizarre views on HIV/AIDS and that great numbers of South Africans suffered severely as a consequence. Though the scope provided by the South African Constitution for judicial involvement in public policy raises questions, giving the courts such authority worked out very well in this case.

In *Courting Social Justice: Judicial Enforcement of Social and Economic Rights in the Developing World*, a book published in 2008, several legal scholars provide detailed examinations of litigation to enforce social and economic rights in major countries that have specific constitutional provisions dealing with such rights.[20] The book focuses on South Africa, Brazil, India, Nigeria, and Indonesia. Writing about South Africa, Jonathan Berger, one of the contributors, argues that the *TAC* case—as well as other litigation in the lower courts involving arbitrary denial of treatment for those infected by HIV— has saved "hundreds of thousands of lives." At the same time, he acknowledges that *Grootboom* was "a failure" and that "the existence of a right to education—arguably a stronger right [than the right to health care] in as much as the constitution does not expressly refer to its progressive realization—appears to have done little. Although the state apportions the largest portion of its social spending to education, it has yet to be compelled to prioritize its resources in a manner that fundamentally addresses the country's key educational challenges." Berger attributes the inconsistent results to the high level of social mobilization by South African civil society around the right to health care for those who were deprived of treatment for HIV/AIDS by the policies of President Mbeki. No comparable mobilization has taken place on other social and economic issues. He argues that while "litigation remains an indispensable tool, without which the inertia of a flawed political process may never be broken, it becomes most effective when its use is limited and targeted. Simply put, broad social change will not be won in the courts alone."[21]

It is, of course, also possible to imagine a circumstance in which the elected branches of government act in enlightened ways and in which unelected judges thwart them by imposing their own social and economic policies. That happened in the United States following Franklin D. Roosevelt's election as President of the United States during the Great Depression. Roosevelt's famous "court-packing" plan was a response to decisions by the U.S. Supreme Court, grounded in the economic theories favored by the judges rather than by the Constitution, that jeopardized "New Deal" legislation designed to promote both economic recovery and a more just distribution of economic benefits. If the Supreme Court had not shifted ground—the famous "switch in time that saved nine"—under a combination of presidential pressure and the fortuitous fact that Roosevelt had to make new appointments, most of the economic reforms of the New Deal would have been struck down. Empowering judges to decide important public policy questions involving economic issues that go beyond its primary function of interpreting legislation is a two-edged sword. There can be no guarantee that it will always promote the cause of distributive justice. At times, as in the cases that thwarted Roosevelt's reforms, the consequences of judicial decision-making may be just the opposite.

In a recent work, *The Idea of Justice*, the philosopher and Nobel Prize winning economist Amartya Sen endorses the concept of economic and social rights.[22] A section of Sen's book entitled, "The Plausibility of Economic and Social Rights," focuses on two of the criticisms of the concept:

what Sen calls "the institutionalization critique," by which he means the criticism that it is not always possible to correlate claims for such rights with the obligations of institutions to honor those rights; and "the feasibility critique," by which he means the inability of governments in most of the world to provide the resources to fulfill those rights. He responds to the first of these by arguing that, "Even the classical 'first-generation' rights, like freedom from assault," may not correspond perfectly with the obligations on others. Sen adds: ". . . the ethical significance of [social and economic] rights provides good grounds for seeking realization . . . through agitation for new legislation, or through helping to generate greater awareness of the seriousness of the problem." Missing from this response to the "institutionalization critique" is any suggestion that it might be appropriate to address questions on economic and social issues, such as distributive justice, in the manner that civil and political rights are regularly addressed: namely, through judicial process. This may reflect Sen's awareness that the judiciary is not well equipped to deal with such matters. As to the "feasibility critique," Sen argues that "not just social and economic rights, but all rights—even the right to liberty—would be nonsensical, given the infeasibility of ensuring the life and liberty of all against transgression. . . . We cannot prevent the occurrence of murder somewhere or other every day. Nor, with the best of efforts, can we stop all mass killings, like those in Rwanda in 1994, or in New York on 11 September 2001. . . . The confusion in dismissing claims to human rights on grounds of incomplete feasibility is that a not fully realized right is still a right, calling for remedial action. Non-realization does not, in itself, make a claimed right a non-right."[23]

There are a number of flaws in Sen's argument. One mistake is that he draws an analogy between social and economic rights and first-generation rights by labeling "freedom from assault" or "prevent[ion] of the occurrence of murder" as first-generation rights. They are not. The fact that it is crucially important to protect people against assault and murder does not make these into first-generation rights. We attempt to prevent assault and murder by devising public policies to serve those ends. Those policies include teaching that assault and murder are wrong; establishing a police force to protect us and to investigate cases in which assault and murder nevertheless take place; and by creating a system of justice that will punish those who engage in such transgressions. In ordinary circumstances, those who commit assault and murder are private persons. We do not attempt to defend ourselves against their crimes by asserting our rights. Rather, we endow the state with certain powers to protect us against those crimes.

There may also be circumstances, as in Rwanda in 1994, in which the state itself is culpable for assault and murder. The use of state power for such purposes does involve a gross violation of rights. In these circumstances we may devise mechanisms, such as the International Criminal Tribunal for Rwanda, to punish state officials responsible for abuses.

Classical first-generation rights, however, are in alignment with the obligations of states and, although violations may occur with varying degrees of frequency, it is entirely feasible to realize these rights. They may be divided into five broad categories: (1) freedom of inquiry and expression, meaning that the state may not obstruct an individual's right to gather information and ideas nor prevent their expression through speech, publication, peaceable assembly, or worship; (2) due process of law, meaning that the state may not deprive an individual of life or liberty or otherwise impose a severe punishment without according that person fair procedures for determining whether such punishment is warranted; (3) the right to equal treatment, meaning that a person's race, religion, nationality, gender, sexual preference, or disability should not be a basis for denying a person the same opportunities and benefits as others; (4) the right not to be treated cruelly, meaning that punishments may not involve such practices as torture or otherwise be cruel, inhuman, or degrading; and (5) the right to privacy, meaning that the state is limited in its power to intrude on a person's body, home, communications, or personal relationships.

Sen, ordinarily among the most astute thinkers on the public policy questions of our age, fails to recognize the essential differences between civil and political rights and economic and social rights. Civil and political rights are limitations on the power of the state. In contrast, the realization of economic and social rights, like the prevention of assault and murder to which Sen draws analogies, require the state to exercise certain powers. In some circumstances, of course, it is highly desirable for the state to exercise power. Prevention of assault and murder are very good examples. Similarly, it is highly desirable for the state to exercise power to address such critical issues as education, health care, housing, and the availability of food. Not calling these "rights" does not diminish their significance. Differentiating them from civil and political rights does, however, help to clarify what means are appropriate to bring about desired results. Matters of social and economic concern, unlike first-generation rights, must be addressed through the bodies of government that have the power of the purse and the power of the sword: that is, the legislative and executive branches. They cannot, and should not, be vindicated through judicial process, as is most often the case where civil and political rights are concerned. Because state power is required to address economic and social issues, Isaiah Berlin referred to the realization of what are called social and economic rights as "positive liberty." Because restraints on state power are needed to protect civil and political rights, Berlin referred to these as "negative liberty."

Underlying Amartya Sen's approach to social and economic rights is his understanding of the very concept of rights. He argues: "The assertion of the importance of a 'right' must not be confused with the interpretation that Ronald Dworkin chooses, and Thomas Scanlon supports, that a right must, by definition, 'trump' every contrary argument based on 'what would be good to happen.' . . . I would argue that taking rights seriously requires us to recognize that it would be bad—sometimes terrible—if they were violated. This does not imply that the recognition of a claim as a right requires us to assume that it must always overwhelm every other argument in the opposite direction (based, for example, on well-being, or a freedom not included in that right)."[24]

Sen's position might be termed a "soft" approach to the idea of rights. It is one in which rights may be trumped by a concern for "well-being." If that soft approach prevailed, the right to speak could be trumped, for example, by the need to prevent dangerous ideas; the right not to be deprived of liberty without due process of law by the need to ensure that a fair trial does not exonerate someone thought to be guilty; and the right not to be punished cruelly by the need to use torture to extract information deemed crucial; and so on. Economic and social rights are about well-being, and it makes sense that these should be trumped from time to time by conflicting concerns that are also about well-being. But for those like Dworkin and Scanlon who take what may be called a "hard" approach to rights, Sen's position underscores their reasons for not equating civil and political rights with economic and social rights.

Though the legal scholar Cass R. Sunstein is a proponent of economic and social rights and has published a book celebrating Franklin D. Roosevelt's espousal of such rights,[25] he has acknowledged that courts are not suited to their enforcement. According to Sunstein, the reason that such rights are not given constitutional status in the United States "begins with the fact that the American Constitution is enforced by courts." He continues:

Some nations regard constitutions as a place for setting out general goals and aspirations—symbols not meant for real world implementation. But in America, rights are not aspirations. Citizens are entitled to expect independent judges will ensure that the government respects those rights in practice. If we emphasize this point, we might conclude that the American Constitution does not recognize social and economic rights for one simple (as well as good) reason: Judges cannot enforce those rights. Inevitably the second bill would become a set of goals rather than rights. When other nations place all or part of the second bill in their constitutions, it is because they believe that their founding document need not be limited to provisions with real meaning in the world.[26]

A point that Sunstein does not address is whether incorporating rights that are only aspirational in a constitution or in an international agreement on rights, and that lack what he refers to as "real meaning in the world," undermines the significance of guarantees of civil and political rights in those documents. Does it convey the view that such rights, too, are merely generally desirable goals rather than legally enforceable contracts between the citizen and the state?

Kenneth Roth, the Executive Director of Human Rights Watch since 1993, has proposed that human rights organizations such as the one he directs, should focus on economic and social rights in circumstances that resemble those that prevail when there are abuses of civil and political rights.[27] He bases this proposal on the notion that it would be best to concentrate on implementable goals, arguing, for example, that simply deploring the fact that some people go hungry or lack shelter has little effect. What makes efforts to promote civil and political rights meaningful is that they identify the violation of rights, the violator, and the remedy. Where the violation is torture, the violator might be identified as a secret police agency, and the remedy sought would then be prosecution and punishment of the torturers and of those who exercise authority over the torturers. Accordingly, Roth has argued, in the economic and social rights field as well, "we should look for situations in which there is relative clarity about violations, violators, and remedies."[28]

Roth then goes on to contend that the "nature of the violation, violator, and remedy is clearest when it is possible to identify arbitrary or discriminatory governmental conduct that causes or substantially contributes to an ESC [economic, social and cultural] rights violation. These three dimensions are less clear when the ESC shortcoming is largely a problem of distributive justice. If all an international human rights organization can do is argue that more money be spent to uphold an ESC right—that a fixed economic pie be divided differently—our voice is relatively weak. . . . On the other hand, [if] the government . . . is contributing to the ESC shortfall through arbitrary or discriminatory conduct, we are in a relatively powerful position to shame the institutions or the officials who are to blame."[29]

The *TAC* case in South Africa presents an example of the kind of arbitrary conduct by the government that Roth had in mind. When it comes to matters involving discriminatory conduct by a government, it is important to note that these may also be seen as violations of civil and political rights. For example, if a portion of a municipality in the United States in which blacks reside, or an area in an Eastern European town inhabited by Roma, or a part of an Israeli city populated by Israeli Palestinians, lacks such services as paved roads and sewage and trash removal that are available to the other parts of the community, the remedy that is required may be economic as it requires providing the missing services to those suffering the deprivation, but the discriminatory basis for shortchanging the disfavored racial group makes such matters, first and foremost, violations of civil and political rights. Having embraced the principle of economic and social rights under Roth's leadership, Human Rights Watch has in practice, for the most part, addressed economic issues in circumstances where they are closely linked to civil and political rights.

Roth's argument did not address the legitimacy of a judicial role in enforcing social and economic rights. With rare exceptions, Human Rights Watch does not engage in litigation. Its principal means of promoting rights is by documenting abuses, calling attention to the discrepancies between the practices of a government and its commitments and obligations under international law; and publicizing its findings widely in order to embarrass the authorities responsible for the abuses and, thereby, to persuade them to change their ways. It is important that those pursuing this approach accept the main tenets of international law on human rights as they have been adopted, because they provide the standards against which to measure a government's performance and the grounds for accusing a government of not living up to its responsibilities. Accordingly, the fact that there is positive law concerning economic and social rights—that is, international treaties have been adopted, signed, and ratified in which governments undertake to comply with rights to food, housing, education, and health care—is central in Roth's argument that Human Rights Watch should be concerned with these issues, though only in circumstances where violations, violators, and remedies can be clearly identified.

Although Roth's focus is not on litigation, the elements that he identifies as essential from the standpoint of an organization engaged in "naming and shaming" are also critical for those going to court to try to enforce economic and social rights. A clear violation of an existing obligation must be identified; the individuals or institutions named as defendants in a lawsuit must have apparent responsibility as the violators; and, in seeking a ruling from a judge, it is necessary to point out what remedy is appropriate. Without these ingredients, litigation is fruitless. Though Roth's approach does not completely assuage the concerns of those with philosophical objections to the concept of economic and social rights, it inspires less apprehension that efforts in this area will undermine efforts to secure strong protection for civil and political rights.

To set forth the arguments against efforts to address economic and social issues in a rights context is not to dispute that a fairer distribution of economic resources, whether at a national or an international level, is a laudable cause in itself. The issue is not the goal; it is, rather, the means for pursuing the goal. The main criticism of the concept of economic and social rights comes from those who believe that efforts to redress gross economic inequities or economic suffering should focus on the political process; and that addressing these issues from a rights perspective while bypassing democratic decision-making is both futile and inappropriate. Of course, there are many countries where it is not possible to rely on democratic decision-making to deal with inequities in the allocation of resources, because they are subject to authoritarian rule. An example is China where the gap between those benefiting from the country's economic progress and those left behind has been growing significantly. Yet in such circumstances, it is impossible to imagine that the country's rulers would allow a court to revise its economic policies on the basis of assertions of economic rights. The leaders of states that are not democracies do not give courts the power to make major revisions of their policies. It is in states where democratic decision-making customarily takes place that it is possible even to imagine that rights claims that contradict state policies might obtain serious consideration in the courts and be put into practice if judges upheld them.

The enforcement of certain civil and political rights itself may have economic consequences. In practice, the state cannot limit itself entirely to negative enforcement. If law enforcement officials obtain evidence showing that an individual has committed a serious crime, they will not leave that person at liberty. Rather, they will probably try to imprison her. To do so, however, they are required to accord her due process of law, and that entails expense. It can be costly to provide defendants with fair trials in which they are properly represented by counsel and to ensure that those sent to prison are housed in decent circumstances that do not violate the prohibition on cruel and unusual punishment. Yet the economic ramifications of efforts to enforce civil and political rights in these circumstances do not require a broad redistribution of a society's resources or of its economic burdens. In contrast, if one goes beyond the cautious and restrained jurisprudence of the South African Constitutional Court in trying to provide remedies for shortages of housing and health care, a substantial measure of economic redistribution is required.

Attempts to address invidious discrimination may have even more substantial economic consequences than is involved in fashioning remedies for other violations of civil and political rights. For example, if members of a racial minority have systematically been victimized by inferior public education, the costs of a remedy that not only equalizes education opportunities prospectively but also attempts to compensate past victims could be considerable. Yet even in such circumstances, the economic burdens imposed on those required to pay taxes to cover the costs are unlikely to be so great as to entail substantial economic redistribution. Moreover, while providing expensive remedies to minorities who have suffered discrimination may arouse resentment by some of those required to bear the costs, it also seems possible to make a strong moral argument to them that the compensation is justified by past abuse and, thereby to secure a measure of public acceptance for such actions even when they are mandated by the decisions of unelected judges. Inevitably, of course, some will resent sharing the burden of such costs when they do not see themselves as individually responsible for the discrimination. On such grounds, judicial decisions may inspire widespread objections. Yet the likelihood is that there would be far greater resentment against the courts if they attempted to impose a general redistribution of wealth merely on the basis of economic rights.

Where redistribution is sought on the basis of rights to health care and housing or some other form of economic benefit, those promoting such "rights" effectively contend that the benefits must be provided outside the political process. This is so because, if an economic benefit is a right, it must be honored whether or not it commands political support; it should not be subject to the negotiations and compromises that inevitably take place in the political process. Courts are appropriate bodies to enforce rights precisely because they are not, or should not be, accountable politically. Moreover, they are not well suited to engage in negotiations and compromises.

Opponents of efforts to promote distributive justice through assertions of rights argue that the central purposes of the political process are to deal with two questions: public safety and the allocation of resources. Alexander Hamilton, writing in the *Federalist Papers*, famously called the judiciary "the least dangerous" branch of government because it has "neither the power of the purse nor the power of the sword."[30] Economic and security matters ought to be, and are, constant questions of public debate. Frequently, as in the United States in the elections of 2010 that shifted political power in Congress and in many state governments, elections turn on these issues. Citizens hold their representatives accountable for the stands that they have taken and the votes that they have cast. Some who question the concept of economic rights believe that to withdraw such questions from politics, and to attempt to settle them on the basis of rights in circumstances in which there has been no invidious discrimination against a disfavored minority, is to carve the heart out of the democratic process. These are not matters that should be settled by a judge claiming superior wisdom and exercising the powers of a Platonic guardian. Working within the democratic process, advocates for a more equitable distribution of economic resources ought to put forward vigorous arguments and build coalitions to help them prevail. But neither proponents nor opponents of distributive justice should be able to circumvent that process on the basis of assertions of rights. Nor is it likely that they could succeed in securing substantial economic redistribution solely by the invocation of rights. If judges attempt to resolve such questions without demonstrating that their decisions are firmly grounded in efforts to remedy severe deprivations of civil and political rights, such as clear-cut racial discrimination, their decisions are not likely to be respected by the other branches of government. And the judiciary would be hard pressed to implement decisions on economic matters if they were ignored by the executive and legislative branches. Most likely, the only practical effect of such judicial decision-making—unless implementation of the ruling were cost-free, as in the decision of the South African Constitutional Court in *TAC*—would be to weaken the courts as instruments for the protection of civil and political rights.

Compliance with judicial decision-making, in all societies, is largely dependent on the prestige of the courts. If that prestige is sacrificed by intruding too deeply into areas where legislative decision-making is more appropriate, it probably cannot be reclaimed on a case-by-case basis when important questions of civil and political rights come before judges. A recognition that more assertive enforcement of the South African Constitution's provisions on economic and social rights could undermine its authority in other areas may have contributed to the restrained manner in which that country's Constitutional Court has acted up to this writing.

Moreover, where economic and social issues are concerned, choices must be made that seem to lie beyond the competence of courts. Consider the question of health care. One person, such as Mr. Soobramoney, requires kidney dialysis. Another needs a heart by-pass operation. Still another needs life-long anti-retroviral therapy. And a cancer patient may require bone-marrow replacement surgery. All of these, and many more, are life-saving measures, but they can draw on scarce resources—such as organs for transplant—and they are expensive in varying degrees. Hospitals have committees of physicians and ethicists who consider factors of cost effectiveness and the prospects for recovery when a patient seeks expensive or exotic forms of treatment. Should a judge substitute her judgment for those of such a committee because a patient has a right to health care? The answer is yes if the denial of care reflects some improper discrimination. But if the denial is based on a judgment that other health needs must take precedence, the intervention of a court becomes more questionable. And if a court decides that the right to health care requires that all patients must receive whatever treatment they require to sustain life, no matter the cost, the implication is that resources must be withdrawn from other components of the state budget or that taxpayers must increase their contributions to the state. What gives a court grounds for saying that increases to the health care budget must take precedence over other state responsibilities such as national defense, police protection, firefighting, transportation, sanitation, economic development, education, or other social services? Also, what is it about courts, or about statements of rights, that makes judicial judgments on such questions worthy of implementation by the other branches of government?

Such questions are not limited to the field of health care. They arise in other areas of economic and social rights, such as education. No great difficulty arises if a constitution states that every child has a right to a primary school education or a secondary school education. The legislative specificity of such a rule makes it readily enforceable by a court. More difficulty emerges, however, if an international treaty or a national constitution invokes a more general "right to education." Elected officials may decide that a state requires some persons with a secondary school education who will work in manufacturing and service industries, while others need the kind of elite education that produces engineers, scientists, diplomats, and surgeons. Does the right to education entitle everyone to obtain the highest level of education provided by the state? Can one deal with such questions on the basis of rights? Or, consider the question of employment. Does the right to a job mean that everyone is entitled to obtain at least menial work, or can an individual who has such a right insist on more satisfactory or more remunerative employment?

Some critics of the concept of economic and social rights base their skepticism or outright opposition on the apprehension that, if too many matters are treated as rights, the effect will be to weaken civil and political rights. There are at least two ways in which this could take place. If economic rights are weighed in the balance against other state economic interests, as seems inevitable and as is reflected in the jurisprudence of the South African Constitutional Court, similar balancing might take place where civil and political rights are concerned. The right not to be tortured will be weighed against the state's need for information. The right to free speech will be weighed against the state's interest in preventing social unrest. And so forth.

The other danger is that states may claim that their shortcomings in protecting civil and political rights should be balanced against the progress they have made in fulfilling economic and social rights. Such claims were regularly made by communist states in the era prior to the collapse of the Soviet Union, and they have been made since by some Asian states. In practice, the governments making such claims typically have less than stellar records on economic issues, but it is often difficult to document their shortcomings because of their denial of civil and political rights. For decades China made such arguments on the international stage, but we now know that as many as thirty million Chinese starved to death during the years of Mao's "Great Leap Forward" in the late 1950s and early 1960s, because the lack of civil and political rights made it impossible for Chinese to criticize the regime's disastrous agricultural policies. Thereafter, the absence of free speech and freedom of the press delayed Beijing's knowledge and recognition of the scale of the problem it had created. It also prevented international disaster relief, because the rest of the world was never informed of the suffering in rural China. Even in contemporary times, when China enjoys greater civil freedom and much more affluence, the fact that a right to education is set forth in the Chinese Constitution has not prevented the exclusion from the public schools of many millions of children of migrant workers. In some cities, they are not considered eligible to attend public schools because their families are not recognized as legal residents. Freedom to discuss the circumstances of these children without restraint might do more to get them into the schools than the constitutional declaration of a right to education. At the least, the situation of these Chinese children suggests that, in practice, when claims are made that denials of civil and political rights are offset by economic and social rights, it may be that neither kind of right is respected.

Civil and political rights mean the same thing everywhere. Freedom of speech, freedom of assembly, freedom of religion, the right to be treated equally and fairly, and the right not to be tortured do not depend upon economic contexts. On the other hand, it is inevitable that social and economic rights have to be applied differently in different circumstances. Resource allocation has to play a role in determining the benefits to be provided. It is appropriate that countries should deal with such matters in different ways depending on their resources. This is explicitly recognized in various international agreements on economic and social rights, which state that those rights should be realized progressively. It will be difficult to prevent that idea from carrying over to the field of civil and political rights if economic and social rights are put on the same plane.

. . .

When Jefferson wrote of "unalienable" rights and the French Declaration of the Rights of Man and of the Citizen discussed "imprescriptible" rights, the implication was, as noted, that these rights are human attributes that endure for all time and are universal in their application. The evolution of the term "human rights" has carried with it that idea, and it was made explicit in the name given to the Universal Declaration of Human Rights.

Yet the idea of universality has been challenged. The fact that the concept has its origins in the work of Western thinkers is itself a factor in some efforts to reject it. One such challenge took place in the 1990s when officials of several Asian states—notably Singapore, Malaysia, Indonesia, and China—began discussing so-called "Asian values" and proclaimed, to use the title of an article on the subject by a Singaporean diplomat, Bilahari Kausikan, "Asia's Different Standard."[31]

According to Kausikan, "the hard core of rights that are truly universal is smaller than many in the West are wont to pretend. . . . It is not only pretentious but wrong to insist that everything has been settled once and forever.

The Universal Declaration is not a tablet Moses brought down from the mountain. It was drafted by mortals. All international norms must evolve through continuing debate among different points of view if consensus is to be maintained. Most East and Southeast Asian governments are uneasy with the propensity of many Americans and some European human rights activists to place more emphasis on civil and political rights than on economic and social rights."[32] Going on to dispute the idea expressed in a report by Human Rights Watch that political and civil rights that promote democratic accountability are not mere luxuries to be enjoyed after a certain level of economic development is achieved, Kausikan argued that the East Asian and Southeast Asian experience "sees order and stability as preconditions for economic growth, and growth as the necessary foundation of any political order that claims to advance human dignity."[33]

Kausikan added that, "The Asian record of economic success is a powerful claim that cannot be easily dismissed. Both the West and Asia can agree that values and institutions are important determinants of development. But what institutions and which values? The individualistic ethos of the West or the communitarian traditions of Asia? The consensus-seeking approach of East and Southeast Asia or the adversarial institutions of the West? . . . [M]any East and Southeast Asians tend to look askance at the starkly individualistic ethos of the West in which authority tends to be seen as oppressive and rights are an individual's 'trump' over the state."[34]

Kausikan accepted that it is legitimate to consider the prohibition of genocide, murder, torture, and slavery as universal. Accordingly, he made clear that he does not object when Western governments or nongovernmental organizations campaign on these issues. Indeed, he says, "The West has a legitimate right and moral duty to promote those core human rights . . . ."[35] On the other hand, when it comes to such issues as detention without trial or freedom of the press, he contended that Westerners should "accept that no universal consensus may be possible and that states can legitimately agree to disagree."[36]

Kausikan painted with too broad a brush when he characterized the West as individualistic and adversarial and the East as communitarian and consensus seeking. In fact, both parts of the world draw on both traditions. For a time, the communist system in China suppressed individual entrepreneurship, but today, nearly two decades after Kausikan's essay was published, much of that giant country's rapid economic development reflects traits Kausikan attributed to the West. Similar individualistic approaches to the creation of wealth were evident even earlier in Hong Kong and

Taiwan and among overseas Chinese in several Southeast Asian countries. That suggests that if communitarianism is characteristic of China, it is so at least in part because it was enforced by a regime that subsequently relaxed its controls. Likewise, it might be more appropriate to speak of consensus-imposing authoritarian regimes than of a consensus-seeking people. When Kausikan published his essay, the oppressive Suharto regime was still in power in Indonesia and it dealt with criticism by suppressing media, as for example when the media reported on the vast wealth acquired by the first family. In Singapore and Malaysia, governments have sometimes suppressed critical media directly; at other times, officials such as the long-time prime minster of Singapore, Lee Kuan Yew, filed libel suits against critics in which the Singaporean judiciary could be counted on always to uphold his claims. It would seem inaccurate to describe such methods of silencing critics as "consensus-seeking."

As Kausikan contended, Asia's record of economic success cannot be easily dismissed. At the same time, however, it is far from clear that the authoritarian character of a number of states in the region was an indispensable factor in making that success possible. Politically oppressive Singapore has flourished economically, but so has Hong Kong where civil liberties have been respected. Among larger states of the region, by far the most economically successful from the standpoint of the standard of living of its citizens is Japan, which is democratic and, while inhospitable to ethnic minorities and foreigners, is largely respectful of individual rights. South Korea was rigidly authoritarian until the latter part of the 1980s, but has subsequently developed as an open society and has continued to succeed economically. Taiwan has followed a somewhat similar path. Democratic India is doing far better than the neighboring states of Pakistan and Bangladesh where individual rights enjoy less protection. The greatest economic growth in the region is now taking place in China, but that growth did not begin until the death of Mao and the end of the extreme suppression of rights that characterized his rule. Because China was held back for so long, it will be many years before the standard of living of its citizens catches up to that of Japan, South Korea, or Taiwan, where rights are respected even if present-day economic growth rates are maintained.

Is there a connection between development and rights? Yes, certainly, if one considers as Amartya Sen does, that freedom is a constitutive part of development.[37] From Sen's standpoint, the well-being that is the aim of development will be achieved to the extent that human capabilities are given the freedom and means to develop. The concept of capability implies not only that the resources are available to permit people to fulfill their ambitions and desires, but also that they have the opportunity to put those resources to effective use. The right of women to take part as equals in the political process, in domestic relationships, and in the professions is as essential as education, health care, and shelter if they are to secure the benefits of development. So too is a woman or a man's ability to speak freely without fear of persecution by the state.

On the other hand, if one assesses only the direct economic consequences of the protection of rights, it is more difficult to make a case. During the Cold War era, and for a number of years thereafter, it was fashionable in the West to argue that the protection of rights simultaneously fostered economic development. It is, however, increasingly difficult to maintain that argument in the face of China's spectacular economic progress over the past two decades.

Nor are China and Singapore the only examples of repressive states that are doing well economically. Vietnam is another Asian state that is now making economic progress despite a regime that shows little or no respect for rights. In contemporary Africa, such states as Sudan, Rwanda, Uganda, and Ethiopia are repressive in varying degrees, but they are among the African countries where in recent years economic gains have been significant. There are, of course, contrary examples in Africa and elsewhere. Botswana, democratically governed, possessed of substantial mineral resources, and, unlike most African states, respectful of rights, is a model of successful development. Ghana seems to be headed in a similar direction. The same is true of a Latin American state, Costa Rica, that is almost entirely lacking in marketable resources. Observers of these states tend to link their economic success in such matters as health care, education, and income distribution to their well-established democratic political culture and their scrupulous respect for civil and political rights.

In our time, however, the evidence seems neither to favor those who claim that respect for rights fosters economic development nor those who argue that an authoritarian model provides a quicker or surer path towards that goal. Rather, it appears that many factors play a part in development and that states with contrasting records on democratic processes and civil and political rights may achieve economic success.

What Asia's economic success, and the economic success of certain Asian states, does suggest is that the contrary claim—that is, that only democratic states that also respect rights thrive—cannot be sustained. Rights are not principally instrumental means to achieve other ends, though at certain times and places they play that role. It is their intrinsic significance that makes most of us prize our rights. We want to think our own thoughts, speak our own minds, publish our views, not suffer arbitrary punishment or cruel treatment, count equally regardless of our race, our ethnicity, our religion, or our gender, and we want to reserve a certain amount of space for private behavior where the state may not intrude. Those rights are fundamental and universal because they define us as autonomous human beings. By and large, people everywhere will not consent to give them up except in the face of superior force.

The four Asian governments that led the challenge to the universality of rights in the 1990s were not then democracies. (One of them, Indonesia, has subsequently undergone substantial democratic development. Another, Malaysia, has also made some headway in a democratic direction.) Their rejection of such rights as freedom of speech and the prohibition on arbitrary detention also raises the question of whether it is only under a democratic government that these rights can be protected.

The contemporary record does indeed suggest that democratic government is almost always a necessary but not sufficient condition for respect for rights. Examples of non-democratic governments that honor rights tend to involve special circumstances. Civil liberties are, for example, zealously protected by the citizens of Hong Kong, though Hong Kong is not a democracy. The elected members of its legislature sit alongside appointed members; the chief executive is appointed by the Chinese authorities; and ultimate power rests with the government of China. Yet the people have maintained and even strengthened the civil liberties they enjoyed before control of the territory was transferred from Britain to China in 1997, because the Chinese authorities are honoring the commitments they made at that time. The authorities have the power to withdraw the rights that prevail in the territory, but they could only do so through a violent crackdown that would exceed many times over what happened at Tiananmen Square in 1989 in damaging the country's international reputation.

While democracy is almost always needed if rights are to be protected, and participation in self-government is itself an aspect of human rights, the record also shows that many democracies violate rights. One has only to think of the history of the United States. It was founded as a democracy while slavery was widely practiced. That cruel violation of rights was legally enforced for the first third of American history. After the slaves were freed, many legal measures were adopted, and, until half a century ago, implemented to require racial segregation. Also, large parts of the indigenous population of the United States were driven from their lands and some were exterminated during an extended period following the establishment of American democracy. Other democracies have also mistreated and continue to mistreat racial minorities. Indeed, it is sometimes the case that minorities that receive a measure of protection during periods of authoritarian rule suffer greater mistreatment following the advent of democracy. This has been the experience of the large Roma minority in the countries of Central Europe. It reflects the fact that popular prejudice may have greater political force in a democratic state than in a dictatorship. Abuses against racial minorities are not the only significant violations of rights that take place in democracies, but they seem the least amenable to correction through the democratic process.

■ ■ ■

The 1990s Asian challenge to the universality of rights was the most substantial and sustained effort in that direction of recent times. Yet it faded with the advent of democracy in Indonesia, the relaxation of the authoritarian character of Malaysia's government, and the evolution of a different approach in China. Over time, there have been slow but perceptible improvements in the willingness of the Chinese authorities to permit a larger scope for free expression, though with many reversals along the way. Today, Chinese journalists explore issues that were previously off limits, and they may do so in depth.[38] Some Chinese lawyers provide criminal defendants with a more vigorous defense than had been customary and, from time to time, they prevail in court or embarrass the regime in ways that require it to circumscribe repression. Along the way, some of the lawyers have themselves suffered prosecutions, detentions, and disbarments, but the legal profession as a whole continues to manifest more independence than in the past. The torture of detainees seems to take place less frequently. Minorities that were persecuted, such as gays and people living with HIV/AIDS, now organize and speak out. Harassment continues intermittently, but there has been a gradual acknowledgment that minorities have rights. The Chinese government occasionally acknowledges shortcomings with respect to the protection of rights while pointing out that critics, such as the government of the United States, also commit abuses. It has become standard practice for the Chinese government to publish a report on rights abuses committed by the United States about the time that the State Department releases its annual report on human rights abuses in other countries worldwide. In doing so, Beijing expresses backhanded support for the concept of rights and for the principles of civil and political rights that are the main focus of both the State Department's report and, to a lesser extent, of China's counter-report.

■ ■ ■

As noted, the majority of contemporary rights advocates accept the view that the concept of rights should extend to economic and social rights, though probably not to such controversies as self-determination or third-generation rights. Even so, by far the largest part of the work done by the international human rights movement focuses on civil and political rights. To the extent that there has been a shift in focus in recent years in the actual work of nongovernmental human rights groups operating at the local, national, or international level, it has been primarily in their increased attention to international humanitarian law; that is, to the application of the principles of civil and political rights in the context of armed conflict and military occupation (see chapter 5). The rights movement's commitment to economic and social rights, though widespread, is to a large extent rhetorical. It is possible that proponents of such rights will in time discover new means to enforce them and that jurisprudence will evolve more effective ways to promote such rights through litigation. A dwindling minority of rights proponents are skeptical that this is possible; and an even smaller number—which includes the present author—doubt that it is desirable. For the time being, those within rights movements who contend that the concept of rights should be circumscribed and limited to civil and political rights, are on the losing side of the argument.

4

International Human Rights Law

AS OF OCTOBER 3, 2011

THERE ARE TWO SOURCES OF INTERNATIONAL LAW: CUSTOM AND
treaties. Customary international law is the term used to describe rules that
are so widely accepted and so deeply held that they help to define what it
means to belong to a civilized society. The question of whether customary international law is binding on the United States came before the U.S.
Supreme Court as long ago as 1900 in a case called *Paquete Habana*.[1] It
involved two fishing boats flying the Spanish flag that were seized by armed
vessels of the United States during the Spanish-American war as they were
fishing along the coast of Cuba. Their American captor sold the two boats
at auction. The capture was unlawful under the customs of war, the Supreme Court held, and the proceeds from the sale of the boats, together
with damages and costs, should be paid to the Spanish owner of the two
boats.

Treaty law—or conventional law, as it is sometimes called, because the
treaties that are the source of such law are multilateral conventions (at
times, also referred to as covenants)—often covers the same ground as customary international law. Torture is forbidden by customary international
law, for example, and prohibitions against torture are also set forth in several multilateral treaties. The effect is to reinforce recognition that a particular norm set forth in a treaty has the status of customary law. On the other
hand, not every provision contained in a treaty has the status of customary
law. In order for it to attain that status there has to be additional evidence

of its wide acceptance as a norm and of the depth of commitment to that norm. Customary international law, which evolves over time, is binding everywhere; treaty law is binding on the parties to the treaty.

Some treaties create institutions, and those institutions contribute to the further development of international law by adopting rules that are within their mandate. Accordingly, bodies such as the United Nations, the World Trade Organization and the International Criminal Court, each created by a multilateral treaty, are themselves sources of international law. In the case of the United Nations, it is the Security Council, as the world body's most important entity, that has the principal role in the making of international law.

In the mid-1970s, when the United States started making commitments in domestic law to promote human rights internationally, it did so by recognizing that international law protects human rights. An example is Section 502B of the Foreign Assistance Act, adopted by Congress in 1975. It is the most important of the U.S. laws on human rights as it denies security assistance to governments that grossly abuse human rights, establishes the post of Assistant Secretary of State for Human Rights, and requires the preparation of country reports on the human rights practices of other governments. The law states: "The President is directed to formulate and conduct international security assistance programs of the United States in a manner which will promote and advance human rights and avoid identification of the United States through such programs, with governments *which deny to their people internationally recognized human rights and fundamental freedoms, in violation of international law* or in contravention of the policy of the United States" (emphasis added).

Although American law explicitly recognizes international law as the source of human rights protection, it was the practice of the George W. Bush administration to avoid references to international law when it denounced human rights abuses by other governments. The Bush administration did not explicitly repudiate international law; but by avoiding citations to international law, it made plain its lack of enthusiasm for any suggestion that it promoted compliance with international rules that would be binding on the United States as they are binding on others. In this, the Bush administration reflected a strain in American thought, often referred to as "American exceptionalism," that is hostile to the very concept of international law. On the other hand, the predecessor Clinton administration and the successor Obama administration have tended to base their denunciations of abuses of human rights on international law, often citing specific provisions that have been violated. Elsewhere in the world, it is generally accepted that international law is the source of legitimacy for efforts to deal with abuses of human rights committed beyond the borders of one's own country. The United States may be the only country in which, though many of its citizens acknowledge that human rights abuses abroad are an appropriate area of concern for its government, there is also a sharp division over the grounds that make such concerns legitimate. Some American advocates of rights hold the view that was reflected in the policies of the Bush administration. It was often an outspoken proponent of international human rights on the basis that it was legitimate and appropriate for it to call on other governments to uphold the same values as the United States. This is contrary to the approach preferred by the mainstream of the American-based nongovernmental human rights movement, but it has often been convenient for that movement to make common cause with other Americans who do not share the worldwide movement's commitment to international law.

Though there were precursors, for all intents and purposes the recognition of human rights as a central component of international law began with the adoption of the United Nations Charter in 1945. The main forerunners included prohibitions on slavery and the slave trade; limits on the conduct of armed conflicts that form a separate branch of law; namely, international humanitarian law (discussed in chapter 5), which protects the rights of combatants and noncombatants; and the minority treaties promulgated following World War I, which required new states created through the peace negotiations at Versailles, as well as states that acquired new boundaries during those negotiations, and that were principally organized along ethnic/linguistic lines, to accord certain rights to minorities as a condition of admission to the League of Nations.

The United Nations Charter went far beyond what existed previously both in the breadth of the principles incorporated in it and in the universal acceptance of those principles manifested in the ratification of the Charter by all countries seeking to become members of the world body. The preamble to the Charter states: "We the people of the United Nations . . . reaffirm faith in fundamental human rights, in the dignity and worth of the human person, in the equal rights of men and women . . . ." Article 1 goes on to state that one of the purposes of the United Nations consists in "promoting and encouraging respect for human rights and for fundamental freedoms for all without distinction as to race, sex, language or religion." Article 55 provides that "the United Nations shall promote . . .

universal respect for, and observance of, human rights and fundamental freedoms for all without distinction as to race, sex, language or religion." And, Article 56 states: "All members pledge themselves to take joint and separate action in cooperation with the Organization for the achievement of the purposes set forth in Article 55." This last provision was an especially important departure from what had previously been the generally accepted norms of international relations, as it legitimized worldwide efforts to promote rights within the borders of any sovereign state.

The language of the Charter does not reflect any particular theory of rights. Unlike Thomas Jefferson's Declaration of Independence of 1776 or the French Declaration of Rights of 1789, there is no reference to "unalienable" or "imprescriptible" rights, such as would indicate a grounding in the concept of natural rights. Rather, as the words of the preamble indicate, rights are seen as a means to recognize the worth and dignity of each person. To the extent that the words of the Charter define rights, it is by a focus on the right of all to be treated equally. As the United Nations was intended mainly to be an institution that would further the cause of peace, a commitment to the promotion and observance of human rights was perceived by the authors of the Charter as a means to that end. The human rights provisions were incorporated in the text of the Charter in June 1945, just a few weeks following the first publication in May 1945 of photographs of the Nazi concentration camps and death camps. The crimes that were recorded in those photos demonstrated the connection between gross abuses of human rights and a cataclysmic international conflict. Stopping such abuses, and emphasizing individual dignity and the right to be treated equally, seemed to be a way to promote peace. Accordingly, it was important not only to recognize that all have rights not to be subjected to such abuses, but also that all the members of the United Nations have a responsibility to try to prevent or stop abuses of rights.

Although the inclusion of a number of provisions with respect to human rights in the United Nations Charter has had revolutionary significance, it is doubtful that most of those involved in the process grasped its importance at that time. A number of nongovernmental groups were present in San Francisco, where deliberations about the Charter took place, and some of them supported incorporation of references to human rights. Yet such groups, which were principally organized along religious lines, did not constitute a human rights movement. There was no such movement at the time, and there was no experience to draw upon to indicate how crucial the existence of such a movement would become in the crusade for the recognition of rights in international law. Diplomatic support for the rights provisions of the Charter came mainly from some of the smaller states represented at San Francisco, such as the Philippines, Lebanon, and Australia, whose representatives were personally concerned with the issue. The United States was a supporter of the inclusion of the rights provisions, but it might have had more difficulty if the language of Article 1 and Article 55 had simply declared that rights should be respected for all regardless of race. At the time, racial segregation was required by law not only in the southern states, but was also practiced by the federal government in such institutions as the armed forces. But as the Charter only required the United Nations to "promote and encourage" respect and observance of equal rights for all, the State Department considered that it could support inclusion of these provisions.

The other country that emerged from World War II as a great power, the Soviet Union, apparently did not feel threatened by references to "fundamental human rights" because of the provision in Article 2 stating: "Nothing contained in the present Charter shall authorize the United Nations to intervene in matters which are essentially within the domestic jurisdiction of any state . . . ." Ever since, states criticized by the United Nations as a body or by others outside its borders, whether governmental or nongovernmental, have invoked that provision of the Charter to denounce such criticism as illegitimate intervention. The tension between the passages in the Charter requiring the promotion of human rights and joint and separate action by members to that end, and the provision for nonintervention, continues up to the present day.

Another provision of the United Nations Charter, Article 68, provided that one of the institution's standing bodies, the Economic and Social Council, set up a number of commissions to carry out its responsibilities, including a commission for the promotion of human rights. The Commission on Human Rights was established in 1946 and the U.S. delegation to the U.N. designated one of its members, Eleanor Roosevelt, to serve as its representative on the Commission. She was elected as its first chair. One of its initial responsibilities was to draft an international bill of rights. On December 10, 1948, its proposal was adopted by the General Assembly of the United Nations as the Universal Declaration of Human Rights. In addition to Mrs. Roosevelt, key figures in the adoption of the Declaration included John Humphrey, a Canadian professor of law from McGill University in Montreal, who was appointed the first director of the U.N. Human Rights Division and who prepared an early draft; René Cassin, the French delegate to the commission, also a law professor, an important figure in the Resistance during World War II and, many years later, a recipient of the Nobel Peace Prize, and also the author of a draft; Charles Malik, the Lebanese delegate, a former professor of philosophy, his country's ambassador to the United States as well as chair of the Economic and Social Council at the U.N. and a powerful intellectual proponent of individual rights; Pengchun Chang, the Chinese delegate, who had studied philosophy with John Dewey at Columbia University and had been a teacher and a playwright in China before joining his country's diplomatic service, and was sometimes allied with Malik and sometimes differed with him in the framing of the Declaration; Carlos Romulo, the Philippine ambassador to the U.N., who had been a prominent journalist in the United States and then a member of the Philippine government in exile at the time of the Japanese conquest and a combatant against the Japanese, and a leading proponent of decolonization; and Hernán Santa Cruz of Chile, a champion of leftist causes in Latin America who was a strong advocate of the inclusion of economic and social rights in the Declaration. As this array indicates, the Declaration was far from being exclusively an expression of Western views. There were no Africans among those who shaped it, because as decolonization had not yet begun in sub-Saharan Africa, there were hardly any African members of the United Nations. But Asia, the Middle East, Europe, South America, and North America were all represented among those who took the lead in determining the contents of the Declaration.[2]

The Universal Declaration of Human Rights was adopted by the General Assembly of the United Nations without dissent but, as discussed in chapter 3, with eight abstentions. In itself, it did not constitute binding international law. Resolutions of the General Assembly lack that status. On the other hand, it was significant for international law in two respects. First, the commitment to promote fundamental human rights in the United Nations Charter *is* binding international law as a treaty signed and ratified by the member states. By adopting the Universal Declaration without dissent, the General Assembly provided an authoritative interpretation of what it is that is meant by fundamental human rights. Second, as in a number of instances when the General Assembly took a stand by adopting a declaratory resolution, the Declaration was followed by the drafting of a treaty—in fact in this case, two treaties were drafted—for submission to the member states for signature and ratification. The ratification of the treaty would transform the contents of the resolution into binding international law.

A third factor should also be weighed in considering the significance of the Declaration, and that is its symbolic importance. It was the first time in history that a comprehensive charter of rights was adopted by a globally representative body. Among the individuals who were most deeply involved in the process were persons, such as Eleanor Roosevelt and René Cassin, who enjoyed international recognition and stature. The absence of dissents—despite the abstentions—suggested worldwide acceptance and approval. These combined to provide the Declaration with great prestige. As a consequence, the anniversary of the adoption of the Declaration is celebrated in much of the world as International Human Rights Day. It has become customary for nongovernmental human rights organizations in many countries to hold commemorative events on December 10 each year and for many government officials to issue statements on that day expressing their commitment to the cause of human rights. In some places, more elaborate arrangements are made. In Tuscany, for example, twelve or thirteen thousand secondary school students study human rights during the fall semester each year, and then on the anniversary of the Universal Declaration, the majority go to an indoor stadium in Florence to attend and take part in an event that is part spectacle and part tutelary built around some aspect of the Declaration.

Of course, as noted in the discussion of natural law in chapter 2, the most important contribution of the Universal Declaration was its assertion that rights are universal. They are not attributes of nationality or citizenship. Rather, they are an intrinsic part of what it is to be human.

The day before adopting the Universal Declaration of Human Rights, the General Assembly put in place another of the principal building blocks of international human rights law: it adopted unanimously, without debate, the Convention on the Prevention and Punishment of the Crime of Genocide. The Genocide Convention is, of course, even more inextricably connected with World War II and the Holocaust than any other component of international human rights law. Indeed, the word "genocide"— and the very understanding that there is a need for a word to designate attempts to exterminate a people for reasons of race, ethnicity, religion, or nationality—did not exist prior to the war. The word was coined by an American legal scholar of Polish Jewish provenance, Raphael Lemkin, during the war. Lemkin was the originator of the proposal for the Genocide Convention and a tireless advocate for it both prior to its adoption by the General Assembly and thereafter, when it was submitted to the member states for ratification. His efforts paid off as the Convention was ratified by enough states that it went into effect by 1951, an impressively swift process by the standards of most human rights treaty negotiations. The speed is especially noteworthy because the Convention embodied an important innovation in international law.

In 1945, when the World War II allies that had fought against Nazi Germany met in London to draw up the charter for the prosecutions at Nuremberg, they provided for the prosecution of "crimes against humanity." Yet the Nuremberg Charter specified that only crimes committed in connection with the war met that definition. Nazi crimes prior to the war did not fall under the jurisdiction of the Nuremberg Tribunal. This was consistent with international humanitarian law in effect up to that point, which did not cover crimes that a government might commit against its own nationals during times of peace. Having observed the conduct of Nazi Germany, especially during a period when he served as a member of the staff of the prosecution at Nuremberg, Lemkin wanted to go further. Accordingly, the Genocide Convention makes no distinction based on whether the crimes are committed during a war and thus crosses the boundary between international humanitarian law and international human rights law. This has made the Genocide Convention a much more significant instrument than would otherwise be the case, because some genocides in the period subsequent to World War II have been attempts by a government or an armed force to exterminate a segment of its *own* population during an internal armed conflict, as happened in Guatemala in the early 1980s; or an attempt to carry out such an extermination during what was essentially peacetime, as in Rwanda in 1994.[3]

The application of the Genocide Convention in times of peace was one of the factors that prevented ratification of the Convention by the United States until 1988, forty years after its adoption by the United Nations General Assembly. It aroused fears in some southern senators that the Convention would be invoked against racial segregation. Another factor that long prevented ratification was the antagonism by some in the United States toward international law, or indeed anything that seemed a step in the direction of "world government." The Convention was finally ratified when President Ronald Reagan found it politically convenient in the wake of criticism of a visit he paid to a cemetery in Germany where S.S. officers were buried. Even then, it was only possible to secure ratification with two reservations, one declaration, and five understandings that substantially diminish the significance of the action by the United States. Of these, by far the most important is a reservation effectively nullifying application to the

United States of Article IX of the Convention, which permits a state party to the Convention to go to the International Court of Justice—popularly known as the World Court—to resolve disputes related to the Convention, including findings of responsibility for the commission of genocide. According to the reservation, "the specific consent of the United States is required in each case" where the United States might be brought before the Court to adjudicate a matter arising under the Convention.

While the Genocide Convention speedily became international law, the effort to transform the provisions of the Universal Declaration of Human Rights into a legally binding agreement (or two agreements) proceeded at a snail's pace. The most important reason was the hardening of lines in the Cold War that was still in its earliest stages when the Declaration was adopted by the United Nations in December of 1948.

Another factor slowing the process was a shift in the American position. Eleanor Roosevelt was a crucial advocate for the support that the U.S. initially gave for inclusion of economic and social rights in the Declaration. That support did not last. Defining such issues in terms of "rights" was alien to the American tradition. The U.S. stand contributed to a decision by the U.N. Commission on Human Rights in 1952, the last year of the Truman administration, to divide the provisions of the Universal Declaration into two treaties. One eventually became the International Covenant on Civil and Political Rights, and the other became the International Covenant on Economic, Social and Cultural Rights.

Truman was succeeded by Eisenhower as president of the United States, and Eisenhower appointed as his secretary of state John Foster Dulles, one of the foremost opponents of the entire effort to establish rights internationally. This appointment ensured that, even though the Declaration had been divided in two, in part out of deference to the United States, Washington would not support either proposed treaty. Lacking strong proponents, and beset by Cold War difficulties, the process of drafting the two treaties slowed almost to a halt. It was not until 1966 that the two Covenants were finally approved by the General Assembly and submitted to member states for ratification. It would take another ten years before they were ratified by enough states to go into effect.

One reason for the extremely slow progress is that there was as yet no substantial nongovernmental human rights movement. Hence, there was no body to exert significant pressure for swift action. The International League for Human Rights was present in the corridors of the U.N., and it helped to enlist a few other groups that would weigh in from time to time, principally religious groups or groups organized along religious lines, such as the World Council of Churches and the World Jewish Congress. Other nongovernmental organizations that were active during that era and influenced the world body on human rights matters included the Paris-based Fédération Internationale des Droits de l'Homme, which got a fresh start after World War II; and the Geneva-based International Commission of Jurists, launched in 1955. With the establishment of Amnesty International in the 1960s, however, a public constituency for international human rights began to make its presence felt. Through the mid-1970s the main role of such groups in shaping international law was to provide helpful advice on legal issues to a few sympathetic government officials. Over time, Amnesty began to attract more public attention to the cause by publicizing the cases of individual victims of human rights abuse in different parts of the world and by identifying governments responsible for extensive abuses. This gave impetus to efforts to codify human rights in international law, particularly in Western Europe where Amnesty's membership and influence grew most rapidly.

The International Covenant on Civil and Political Rights (ICCPR) differs in several significant respects from the provisions of the Universal Declaration of Human Rights dealing with civil and political rights. The differences include:

- An assertion of the right of self-determination that is contained in Article 1 of the ICCPR. It also appears as Article I of the International Covenant on Economic, Social and Cultural Rights (ICESCR). (See chapter 3 for a discussion of this "right".)
- A provision, contained in Article 4 of the ICCPR that permits a state to suspend certain rights "in time of public emergency which threatens the life of the nation and the existence of which is officially proclaimed ... to the extent strictly required by the exigencies of the situation ..."

Under the Covenant, rights that may never be suspended are: the right to life; the prohibition against torture or cruel, inhuman, or degrading treatment; the ban on slavery or enforced servitude; the prohibition on imprisonment for inability to fulfill a contractual obligation; the prohibition on *ex post facto* punishment; and the right of all persons to legal recognition. Moreover, where rights may be restricted—as in the case of free expression or the prohibition on arbitrary arrest or detention—no discrimination may take place on grounds of race, color, sex, language, or social origin. Accordingly, if the Covenant had been in effect during World War II, for example, and the United States were a party to it, and a public emergency had been declared after Pearl Harbor, detention of those thought to pose a threat to the life of the country would have been permissible, but not on the basis that they were Japanese-Americans. Or, to bring the issue closer to the present day, if the United States had declared a public emergency after 9/11, the first question would be whether the life of the country was threatened. Assuming the answer was yes—not necessarily a valid assumption—detentions without charges or trial would have been permissible if it were shown that they were strictly required by the emergency, but only if no racial or religious discrimination determined the choice of detainees. The detention of Muslims because they were Muslims would have been forbidden. Torture or cruel, inhuman, or degrading treatment would be prohibited.

In practice, Article 4 of the ICCPR has been much abused. Many countries have declared emergencies and kept them in place for extended periods when there is no threat to the life of the country. For example, a state of emergency was kept in place almost continuously during the more than three decades that the dictator General Alfredo Stroessner ruled Paraguay and for nearly as long in Egypt under President Hosni Mubarak. (One of the principal demands of the vast numbers who demonstrated in Tahrir Square in Cairo starting on January 25, 2011 and who forced Mubarak to resign eighteen days later was an end to the state of emergency.) Detentions and other restrictions of rights during such "emergencies" often bear little or no relationship to the ostensible cause for declaring the emergency.

- Article 19 of the Universal Declaration and Article 19 of the ICCPR both protect freedom of opinion and expression, and Article 20 of the Declaration protects freedom of assembly. Yet Article 19 of the ICCPR explicitly allows restrictions that are not mentioned in the Declaration. It states: "The exercise of [freedom of expression] carries with it special duties and responsibilities," and restrictions "should only be such as are provided by law and are necessary: (a) For respect of the rights or reputations of others; (b) For the protection of national security or of public order (*ordre public*), public health or morals." Articles 20 and 21 of the ICCPR add to the restrictions on free expression provided in Article 19 of the Covenant. Article 20 states: "(1) Any propaganda for war shall be prohibited by law. (2) Any advocacy of national, racial or religious hatred that constitutes incitement to discrimination, hostility or violence shall be prohibited by law." Article 21 recognizes the right of peaceful assembly, but allows exceptions "in the interest of national security or public safety, public order (*ordre public*), or the protection of public health or morals or the protection of the rights and freedom of others."

As is apparent, the exceptions to freedom of expression and assembly in the ICCPR are so broad that they substantially nullify the rights supposedly protected. One consequence has been that, for an extended period, organizations concerned with rights in the United States paid very little attention to the field of international human rights. The organization that long epitomized disdain for international human rights as embodied in international law was the American Civil Liberties Union. By far the largest and best-organized defender of rights in the United States, the ACLU is dedicated above all to the defense of First Amendment rights. Ever since its establishment in 1920, it has vigorously resisted efforts to create exactly those exceptions to the protections provided by the First Amendment that are allowed by Articles 19, 20, and 21 of the ICCPR. Accordingly, the ACLU never played a significant role in efforts within the United States to ratify the ICCPR and barely took note when it was ratified in 1992. Among the many reservations required by the U.S. Senate prior to ratification were those involving the provisions of the ICCPR that conflict with the First Amendment. By 1992, the ACLU stand on First Amendment issues was too widely accepted in American law to permit endorsement of the restraints on free expression that are set forth in the ICCPR and accepted in most other countries in the world.

Except in matters related to free expression, disregard for the domestic application of international human rights law has abated significantly in the United States since about the late 1990s, including in the ACLU, in part because the United States Supreme Court has become less protective of rights under the U.S. Constitution; in part because European institutions such as the European Court of Human Rights and the European Court of Justice have gained recognition as leaders in the protection of rights; and in part because discrete bodies of international law, such as the Geneva Conventions, have been invoked successfully in American courts to protect rights. Yet if it were not for the U.S. reservations with respect to Articles 19, 20, and 21 of the ICCPR in ratifying the treaty, it is possible that international law would still be considered by domestic rights advocates as more of a burden than a protection of rights.

- Article 17 of the Universal Declaration protects the right to own property and prohibits arbitrary deprivation of property. There is no mention of such a right in either the ICCPR or the ICESCR.

  The classic charters of rights—that is, the American Bill of Rights and the French Declaration of Rights—protect the right to property. Though the Soviet Union and its client states objected to the inclusion of this right in the Universal Declaration of Human Rights, American influence over the drafting of the Declaration ensured that it would be included. The fact that it was not included in either of the Covenants reflects, at least in part, the decline in the influence of the United States in the drafting of those later documents and the rise in influence of former colonies in Africa and Asia that aligned themselves on such questions with the Marxist principles of the Soviet bloc states.

- Article 27 of the ICCPR sets forth a right that is not mentioned in the Declaration. It states: "In those States in which ethnic, religious or linguistic minorities exist, persons belonging to such minorities shall not be denied the right, in community with the other members of their group, to enjoy their own culture, to profess and practice their own religion, or to use their own language."

  This is a valuable addition to the rights protected by the Declaration. Most significant is the wording artfully addressing rights that must be exercised collectively—that is, "in community with other members of their group"—that at the same time protects them within the framework of individual rights by asserting that "persons belonging to such minorities shall not be denied the right . . . ." If it is respected, this right is especially important because almost no country is homogeneous. A handful of countries—such as Switzerland, which has four official languages (French, German, Italian and Romansch); Finland, which has elaborate protections for the linguistic and cultural rights of its Swedish-speaking minority; and Italy, which, after long conflict, protects the rights of the German speakers in the

Tyrol—have addressed the problem of linguistic and cultural minorities satisfactorily, but most have not. As disputes over language and related cultural questions have often led to severe and long-lasting internal armed conflicts, as in Sri Lanka (in the case of the Tamil minority) and Turkey (in the case of the Kurds), this remains an area where the ICCPR has the potential, as yet largely unfulfilled, to have great positive impact.

The International Covenant on Civil and Political Rights includes a number of other provisions that add to the rights set forth in the Universal Declaration of Human Rights. These include: a requirement that accused persons should be separated from convicts in detention and that juvenile offenders should be segregated from adults (Article 10); more detailed protections for criminal defendants, such as adequate time and facilities for the preparation of a defense, the right to be tried without undue delay, the right to examine witnesses against one and to present witnesses on one's own behalf, the right not to be compelled to testify against oneself, the right to an interpreter and a prohibition against double jeopardy (Article 14); and the right to recognition as a person before the law (Article 16).

The provisions of the International Covenant on Economic, Social and Cultural Rights also diverge substantially from the economic and social rights provisions of the Universal Declaration of Human Rights. The economic rights set forth in the Declaration are social security (Article 22); work and protection against unemployment (Article 23); rest and leisure, including limits on working hours and holidays with pay (Article 24); an adequate standard of living that makes it possible for a family to obtain food, clothing, housing and social services, and security in the case of restrictions on an individual's ability to earn a livelihood beyond that person's control (Article 25); and education, including free elementary education (Article 26).

The ICESCR introduced the idea that economic rights should be available "to the maximum of [a state's] available resources, with a view to achieving progressively the full realization of the rights recognized in the present Covenant . . ." (Article 2). On the one hand this reflects a realistic recognition that poor states would find it difficult or impossible to comply with all the standards that are identified as economic rights in the Covenant and simultaneously to address such other interests as water, utilities, roads, transportation, sanitation, police and fire protection, the administration of justice, and national security. On the other hand, it raises a question as to the meaning of rights, as it is not suggested in the Article that they must take precedence over the other economic concerns that a state should address (see chapter 3). Also, it raises the question of how one determines when a state has reached the maximum of its available resources. What criteria could be used in deciding at what point its spending on roads, bridges, sanitation, or national defense should be capped to make more funds available to deal with those matters identified as economic rights? The concept of progressive realization, moreover, implies that all states will have increasing economic resources over time, which will allow them to come closer to fulfilling economic rights. But what if states decline economically, as has happened in a number of cases? What if there is a worldwide recession or depression in which the great majority of states decline? What if a pandemic produces both economic decline and, simultaneously, a greatly heightened need for expensive health care? What is the significance of a progressive realization of economic rights in such circumstances?

The assumption that economic circumstances will consistently improve is an essential characteristic of the Covenant. Article 11, which guarantees "the right of everyone to an adequate standard of living for himself and his family" goes on to assert a right "to the continuous improvement of living conditions." Article 12, which recognizes "the right of everyone to the enjoyment of the highest available standard of physical and mental health" requires that states shall provide: "for the reduction of the stillbirth-rate and of infant mortality"; "the improvement of all aspects of environmental and industrial hygiene"; "the prevention, treatment and control of epidemic, endemic, occupational and other diseases"; and "the creation of conditions which would assure to all medical service and medical attention in the event of sickness."

A difficulty not addressed in the Covenant is what happens when measures taken to fulfill some of the rights it guarantees have side effects that produce violations of other rights. China is an obvious example. Its spectacular rate of economic growth in the last decade of the twentieth century and the first decade of the twenty-first century has greatly increased the capacity of the country to provide its citizens with certain improvements in living conditions, including food, clothing, housing, and education. On the other hand, there has been a heavy cost in the form of a severe deterioration in environmental hygiene. Air quality and water quality have declined drastically as a consequence of the immense industrial effort that is responsible for the improvement of other aspects of China's standard of living. What is there about the identification of all of these issues as rights that provides guidance to Chinese authorities in determining which should take precedence, or what balance to strike?

Despite their shortcomings, most states have ratified both Covenants. At this writing the ICCPR has been ratified by 167 countries and the ICESCR has been ratified by 160 countries. In combination with the Universal Declaration of Human Rights, they are sometimes referred to as the "international bill of rights." Worldwide, these agreements are generally regarded as foundational for the legitimacy of the international human rights movement. Attempting to hold governments responsible for compliance with the provisions of the Covenants and the Declaration are central to the activity of the global movement.

Over time, a host of additional treaties have been adopted at both a global and a regional level that, in combination with the Covenants, make up the main body of international human rights law. At the global level, these include the Convention on the Elimination of All Forms of Racial Discrimination (CERD), the Convention on the Elimination of All Forms of Discrimination Against Women (CEDAW), the Convention Against Torture and Other Cruel, Inhuman or Degrading Treatment or Punishment (CAT) and the Convention on the Rights of the Child (CRC). At the regional level, they include the European Convention for the Protection of Human Rights and Fundamental Freedoms, a treaty signed and ratified by governments seeking to join the Council of Europe; the Lisbon Treaty establishing a Charter on Fundamental Rights for the member states of the European Union; the American Convention on Human Rights, a treaty that binds the members of the Organization of American States; and the African Charter on Human and Peoples' Rights, an agreement originally promulgated by the Organization of African Unity that is now linked to the OAU's successor, the African Union. In 2009, an agreement was reached by the Association of Southeast Asian Nations (ASEAN) establishing an ASEAN Intergovernmental Commission on Human Rights with limited and poorly defined powers to address rights issues in its ten member states. There are no regional rights agreements in other parts of Asia or in the Middle East.

There are a number of differences among these agreements. Among the most important are provisions in the American Convention for a right to reply and the right to asylum. In addition, the influence of the Catholic Church in Latin America is reflected in a provision that the right to life "shall be protected by law and, in general, from the moment of conception." The African Charter not only recognizes the right to self-determination but goes further to assert: "Colonized or oppressed peoples shall have the right to free themselves from the bonds of domination by resorting to any means recognized by the international community." It also provides so-called third-generation rights: "the right to development"; "the right to national and international peace and security"; and "the right to a generally satisfactory environment favorable to their development" (see chapter 3).

Enforcement of the rights set forth in international law may take place in two ways. The first, and much the most important means of enforcement, takes place within states that comply with international agreements that are binding on them because they have signed and ratified them. In addition, certain norms set forth in international agreements on human rights—such as the prohibition on torture—have, as noted, achieved the status of customary international law and are universally binding regardless of whether a particular state has ratified the International Covenant on Civil or Political Rights, or one of the regional human rights treaties, or the Convention Against Torture and Other Cruel, Inhuman or Degrading Treatment or Punishment, all of which forbid torture. In addition to prohibiting torture, it is generally accepted that customary international law forbids genocide, crimes against humanity, a policy or practice of murder or disappearances, systematic racial discrimination, and a policy or the practice of prolonged arbitrary detention.[4]

In some countries, it is accepted that participants in domestic court cases may directly invoke international protections for human rights and may expect that national courts will apply these protections just as they apply relevant portions of domestic law. Elsewhere, however, courts do not generally take into account international protections of rights when reaching judgments or do not accept them as binding. Even so, state officials are supposed to adhere to guarantees of rights that are applicable to them as a consequence of either conventional or customary international law. Failure to do so is a basis for denunciation of their shortcomings. Such denunciations often enjoy enhanced legitimacy when they are able to include a reference to a state's failure to comply with the commitments it made when becoming a party to an international human rights treaty. (It was this legitimacy that the Bush administration renounced by its unwillingness to cite international law. In the view of some of its critics, this greatly reduced its effectiveness as a proponent of human rights despite its readiness to be outspoken on the subject.)

The other means of enforcement is by appeal to an international body that has jurisdiction over an aspect of international human rights law, either because it was given such authority in the charter of the agency, such as the United Nations, that established it; or because it was formed under the terms of a particular treaty and entrusted with the responsibility to enforce the terms of that treaty.

Though the United Nations Human Rights Council—which succeeded the U.N. Commission on Human Rights in 2006—is the world body's principal institutional mechanism for human rights protection, in practice most of its activities have little impact. The Council lacks authority to enforce its decisions. To the extent that the Commission and its successor, the Council, have been effective in the protection of rights, it is primarily through criticism of the general practices of particular governments. Even in that role, the Commission and Council have a poor record, infrequently adopting resolutions that are critical of powerful states or of states that are protected by powerful blocs of governments such as the African bloc, the Latin American bloc, or the Islamic bloc. The bright spot in the performance of the Commission and, more recently, the Council, is their designation of Special Rapporteurs to look into the human rights practices of particular countries or to look into particular categories of human rights violations such as torture or violations of the rights of human rights defenders. Many of the Special Rapporteurs have performed their responsibilities with distinction, issuing well-documented, carefully considered, and hard-hitting reports on the practices of abusive regimes or on the kinds of abuses that fall within their mandates. One example of many that might be cited is the work of the former Polish Prime Minister, Tadeusz Mazowiecki, who served as Special Rapporteur on Bosnia during most of the period of conflict in that country in the early 1990s. His reporting, which began before the International Criminal Tribunal for the Former Yugoslavia was functioning effectively, became a leading source of information for the world community on the terrible crimes that were being committed.

There have been exceptions, of course. In the early 1980s, the Reagan administration used its influence at the United Nations to secure the appointment of a few Special Rapporteurs who could be counted upon to serve its interests. One of those was Lord Colville, a close associate of British Prime Minister Margaret Thatcher. He served as Special Rapporteur for Guatemala during the period when the country's military forces were engaged in a genocidal counterinsurgency campaign. Reagan himself had characterized allegations of gross human rights abuses against the country's president, General Efrain Rios Montt, as "a bum rap" when he met with Rios Montt in Honduras in December 1982. Colville's reporting, in a period when hardly any foreign journalists were based in Guatemala, helped to cover up the slaughter that was taking place in the sections of the country's highlands populated by most of its Mayan Indians.

In recent years, no U.N. Special Rapporteur has performed as badly as Colville. On the contrary, the great majority of those focusing on particular countries, and those dealing with thematic issues such as torture, extrajudicial killings, internally displaced persons, freedom of religion, and attacks on human rights defenders have done outstanding work in gathering information, making representations to governments, and issuing timely and well-documented reports. This has made them a valuable part of the international system for the promotion of human rights. The same is true of some of the bodies at the United Nations created through the adoption of particular treaties, such as the Committee Against Torture established through the Convention Against Torture and Other Cruel, Inhuman or Degrading Treatment. The treaty bodies, generally made up of experts in the fields in which they operate, have been less deferential to powerful states and to states that are members of powerful blocs than the Commission and the Council. They lack enforcement powers, but their investigations, their hearings, and their reports have often been helpful in dealing with particular cases of human rights abuse. Yet another United Nations body, the office of the U.N. High Commissioner for Human Rights, established in the early 1990s, did not play a significant role in its first decade or so, and it badly bungled its management of the World Conference Against Racism in Durban, South Africa in 2001, allowing that event to be dominated by denunciations of Israel, some of which had an anti-Semitic character. The office began to be a more effective body a little later in the first decade of the new millennium with the appointment of a Canadian judge, Louise Arbour, as High Commissioner. Arbour, who had previously served as chief prosecutor for the International Criminal Tribunal for the former Yugoslavia, upgraded the professionalism of her office's operations. After serving a five-year term, she was succeeded in 2008 by a South African, Navanethem Pillay, who had served as chief judge of the International Criminal Tribunal for Rwanda and then as a judge on the International Criminal Court. Based on her performance up to this writing, it appears that Judge Pillay is building on the achievements of Judge Arbour and that their efforts over the past several years are making the office of the High Commissioner a factor in the protection of human rights. Another fairly new U.N. office that is also making a valuable contribution is the post of Special Advisor on the Prevention of Genocide. As Secretary General of the world body, Kofi Annan chose a prominent human rights advocate of Argentine origin, Juan Mendez, as the first Special Advisor. (In 2010, he was appointed U.N. Special Rapporteur on Torture.) As Mendez's successor as Special Advisor, Secretary General Ban Ki Moon appointed Francis Deng, a highly regarded Sudanese. (He had previously served as the Special Rapporteur on Internally Displaced Persons.) The role of Mendez and Deng in dealing with ethnic conflicts that could escalate into more serious violence has proven significant. Unfortunately, the fact that the U.N. Council on Human Rights—much the most visible of the rights instruments of the world body—has not performed well tends to undermine the efforts of other U.N. bodies that do valuable work on their own and that, unlike the Council, are not politicized.

In practice, regional human rights bodies have in general been more effective than those that are global in scope. Perhaps the most effective body anywhere in the world for international rights enforcement is the European Court of Human Rights, which is associated with the Council of Europe that enforces the European Convention on Human Rights. To become a member of the Council of Europe, states must sign and ratify the Convention. The European Court of Human Rights has decided a host of cases involving abuses by a government, including Turkey's mistreatment of its Kurdish minority and violations by Russia of the rights of Chechens. In 2010, Russia accepted a number of procedural reforms affecting the Court that it had previously blocked. Those reforms had been accepted by all other states subject to the Court's jurisdiction, but unanimity was required before they could go into effect. The consequence will be to enhance the Court's efficacy, including its effectiveness in deciding cases against Russia. Another country where the protection of rights has been greatly advanced by the European Court is Ukraine. At an earlier stage in its history, the Court decided a landmark case involving abuses by British forces against detainees in Northern Ireland. More recently, it has issued a number of important decisions that protect the rights of the Roma minority in the countries of Central Europe. The Court has the status to secure compliance with many but not all of its decisions and, in some countries that are parties to the European Convention, its decisions are considered to have binding authority as precedents in domestic jurisprudence. At this writing, the Council of Europe is pursuing efforts to enhance the authority of the European Court of Human Rights to secure compliance with its decisions.

Another body, the European Court of Justice, has jurisdiction in cases involving the member states of the European Union. As the twenty-seven member states of the EU have now adopted a Charter on Fundamental Rights, the European Court of Justice is likely to play an increasingly important role in the future. In the past its jurisdiction was limited to certain areas of rights that were part of the law of the EU. One of these is gender discrimination, and the Court's jurisprudence on that subject is widely considered to be among the most progressive anywhere.

The Inter-American Court of Human Rights and the Inter-American Commission of Human Rights, which refers cases to the Court and itself publishes reports on the basis of its hearings and investigations, are also very important instruments for the enforcement of rights. At this writing, an African Court of Human Rights has only recently been established. Those promoting the African Court look to it to follow in the path of the European Court and the Inter-American Court. The African Commission on Human Rights has approximately the same powers as the Inter-American Commission, but has not been comparably effective. There are also subregional courts in Africa that may play an increasingly valuable role over time in rights protection. One of these is the ECOWAS Court, a body connected to the Economic Community of West African States. One of its important decisions, rendered in 2008, was to order the payment of compensation to a woman who had been held in slavery in Niger. There are no regional treaties or agreements on rights in the other parts of the world except the 2009 ASEAN decision that established the ASEAN Intergovernmental Commission on Human Rights. It is not yet known how that body will use its relatively vague mandate. There are no provisions for a court to enforce the ASEAN agreement, and there is little prospect for the establishment soon of other regional judicial bodies to enforce rights.

Up to now, the most significant practical contribution of international human rights law has not been the actual enforcement of its statutes through the actions of domestic or international bodies such as commissions or courts. Rather it has been its role in providing a basis for citizens' groups to monitor the practices of states, to document abuses, and to call attention to the discrepancies between those practices and the standards prescribed by international law. Such monitoring is most effective when a state has itself accepted those standards by ratifying an international agreement; or in cases where the standard is so universally accepted as to reach the status of customary international law. Such monitoring may be effective even when it would be futile to try to seek enforcement of rights through domestic litigation and in circumstances where no regional judicial body exists through which the enforcement of international law may be sought. Indeed, as many of the most severe violations of rights are perpetrated in just such circumstances, monitoring and denouncing abuses is essentially the only means to protect the victims. While United Nations bodies have lacked the capacity to enforce rights, they have played a part in the monitoring process through the efforts of the Special Rapporteurs, of the High Commissioner and the treaty bodies, and because some nongovernmental groups publish their findings in the form of reports to those bodies. It is in their role as recipients of such reports that components of the U.N. human rights system sometimes aid the cause. The fact that monitoring has proven so effective has contributed significantly to the emergence and development of the contemporary international human rights movement and is the principal factor that has made it an international force. In essence, therefore, it has been the role of international human rights law in making possible the mobilization of global public opinion that is its main contribution.

The organization that pioneered in demonstrating the significance of monitoring was Amnesty International. As will be discussed in chapter 8, at the outset, in the 1960s, its efforts focused on individual victims of human rights abuse. Over time, it went further and began issuing reports documenting the practices of governments that regularly committed abuses. Subsequently, literally thousands of other organizations established on a local, national, regional, or global basis, also engaged in monitoring, with Amnesty International and a younger organization, Human Rights Watch (discussed in chapter 9), leading the way. Today, government officials all over the world have come to recognize that citizens' groups are paying attention to their practices with respect to human rights and that the abuses, the victims, and the identities of the perpetrators may be identified in a human rights report. No other aspect of law, domestic or international, has previously been enforced primarily in such a fashion. The international human rights system is unique in depending for compliance with its requirements above all on monitoring by a citizens' movement. Monitoring is effective because most governments worldwide have come to realize that it is important that they at least pretend to abide by the provisions of international law with respect to human rights. Gathering data about abuses demonstrates that these pretenses are often not warranted and thereby embarrasses the governments whose violations are revealed. In popular parlance, this is referred to as "naming and shaming." Often, it results in a hostile relationship between the governments that are the targets of monitoring and the groups that document and denounce abuses. Although governments often engage in strident exchanges with human rights monitoring groups, at some point they may decide instead to make changes in their practices so as to shore up their side of the debate or to relieve themselves of embarrassment. It is in this manner that abuses are often curbed and progress on human rights takes place. Were it not for international law setting standards against which the conduct of governments can be measured, monitoring would not be so effective.

In the years ahead, it is likely that human rights litigation in international courts will grow in significance relative to monitoring. Indeed, in countries subject to the jurisdiction of the European Court of Human Rights or the Inter-American Court of Human Rights, it is already difficult to say which of the two is more important. And in practice of course they play a complementary role. Yet as there is no forum—certainly no effective forum for international human rights litigation—in most other parts of the world, monitoring is likely to remain of primary importance for the foreseeable future.

Though earlier efforts to develop international human rights law were mainly driven by governments and government officials, with nongovernmental organizations playing a supporting role, by the 1990s the main impetus for further development of the field came from the international citizens' movement. By then, of course, the movement had attracted large numbers of supporters worldwide and had become a political force. It was a period when substantial headway was possible because of the end of the Cold War, and the nongovernmental human rights movement seized the opportunity to take on the issues at the top of its agenda.

In an earlier era, the study of international human rights law had a somewhat exotic aspect. It could seem that there was little connection between the law on paper and real world events. No longer. Today, it is widely recognized that this body of law is an integral part of the system of governance worldwide. International human rights law has come a long way since the brief references to it that found their way into the Charter of the United Nations in 1945.

5

International Humanitarian Law

AS OF OCTOBER 3, 2011

SINCE ANCIENT TIMES, SOME WHO TAKE PART IN ARMED COMBAT have recognized that placing certain limits on the way in which they conduct hostilities can be advantageous. It can be a sign of civilized behavior, enhancing their own prestige; it may be a way to encourage their opponents to behave in a similar manner; and it may contribute to the reestablishment of peaceful relations in which the rule of law prevails. Whether or not these limits confer advantages, they do most often have the effect of asserting a commitment to humane principles.

A story Herodotus tells indicates that the value of such limits was recognized by the Persian king Xerxes. In violation of the customs of war, Sparta (known also as Lacedaemon) had murdered heralds sent by Xerxes to conduct negotiations. Subsequently, Sparta sent envoys to the Persians, who were supposed to pay for those crimes with their own lives. When they arrived, however, Xerxes refused to kill them. He said he "would not be like the Lacedaemonians, for they have broken what is customary usage among all mankind by killing the heralds; but I will not myself do what I rebuke them for, nor by counterkilling will I release the Lacedaemonians' guilt."

The notion that truly "civilized" peoples should set boundaries even in war was not confined to those who founded Western civilization. The Chinese military strategist Sun Tzu, whose writings about the relationship between warfare and politics anticipated much contemporary thought on such matters, also discussed the subject in the period not long after Herodotus. He advised armies to "treat captives well, and care for them."

In the West, some of the leading figures in the Christian Church also called for restraint in combat. Saint Augustine, in the fourth century, wrote that war might be justified in certain circumstances, but that it becomes criminal if it is conducted "with a malicious intent to destroy, a desire to dominate, with fierce hatred and furious vengeance." To Augustine, the goal of war was not more war but peace. Accordingly, conducting hostilities in a manner that contributes to the restoration of peace is essential.

Prior to the last century-and-a-half, the most significant development of codes imposing restraints on the conduct of hostilities took place during what is sometimes called "the age of chivalry": that is, the late medieval period, lasting from about the twelfth to the fifteenth century. The period of chivalric rules—which applied to those who held honored posts as knights, or "chevaliers"—may have begun even earlier, as it is reported that in 1066 "William the Conqueror expelled from his militia a knight who struck at the dead Harold's body on the battlefield with his sword."[1] During the age of chivalry, special courts—The Court of Chivalry in England and the Parlement of Paris in France, among others—tried cases involving violations of chivalric rules. For the most part, the rules of chivalry protected those with the rank of knighthood from being treated cruelly or dishonorably by others holding like rank. They did little to safeguard common soldiers or noncombatants from the ravages of war. Even so, the rules of chivalry are generally regarded as the antecedents of the laws of war of our era. Other precursors include efforts at codification in the seventeenth and eighteenth centuries, most notably by the Dutch scholar Hugo Grotius in 1625.[2] The essence of what became (much later) humanitarian law was captured by Jean Jacques Rousseau in *The Social Contract*, published in 1762. According to Rousseau:

> . . . war is something that occurs not between man and man, but between States. The individuals who become involved in it are enemies only by accident. They fight not as men or even as citizens, but as soldiers: not as members of this or that national group, but as its defenders. A State can have as its enemies only other States, not men at all . . . . Even when war has been declared, the just Prince, though he may seize all public property in enemy territory, yet respects the property and possessions of individuals, and, in so doing, shows his concern for those rights on which his own laws are based. The object of war being the destruction of the enemy State, a commander has a perfect right to kill its defenders so long as their arms are in their hands: but

once they have laid them down and have submitted, they cease to be enemies, or instruments employed by an enemy, and revert to the condition of men, pure and simple, over whose lives no one can any longer exercise a rightful claim.[3]

It is customary to begin accounts of the development of contemporary international humanitarian law—the laws of war (*ius in bello*, as opposed to *ius ad bellum*, which refers to the law dealing with the resort to armed conflict)—with the battle of Solferino in 1859. A young businessman from Geneva, Switzerland, Henri Dunant, was traveling in Italy and came upon a battlefield in northern Italy, near the village of Soliferno, where the French and Italians were fighting the Austrians. Dunant was horrified at the carnage. He was less concerned with those who had been killed than with the many thousands who had been wounded and were, for the most part, lying where they fell. Many were dying of thirst or because nothing was being done to staunch their bleeding. Together with a few local women, a doctor or two, and some tourists, Dunant ministered to as many of the wounded as possible. Subsequently, he wrote a book about the incident, *A Memory of Solferino*. It led directly to Dunant's role in the establishment of the International Committee of the Red Cross in 1863 and the adoption of the First Geneva Convention in 1864, which focused on the protection and care of the sick and the wounded in war. The signatories were Switzerland, Belgium, Denmark, France, Italy, the Netherlands, Portugal, Spain, and four of the states that joined together several years later to form Germany: Baden, Hesse, Prussia, and Wurtemberg. In 1882, the United States acceded to this treaty.[4]

Without detracting from Dunant's achievement, it is worth noting that public concern with the suffering caused by war entered a new phase during the 1850s and the 1860s because of a technological innovation of the era: the invention of the telegraph. This permitted another innovation, the advent of the war correspondent. Previously, news of battles traveled slowly and much of what the public eventually heard were self-serving accounts by military commanders touting their glorious deeds. Now, with the telegraph, journalists were able to accompany armies and send back timely reports that went into graphic details not previously disclosed in accounts of military campaigns.

The first conflict that was reported by correspondents using the new technology was the Crimean War of 1854–56. The most famous of the journalists who covered that war was William Howard Russell of the *Times* of London. One of his dispatches, published on October 9, 1854—five years before the battle of Solferino—sounded much like the subsequent writing of Henri Dunant. Russell wrote:

> It is with feelings of surprise and anger that the public will learn that no sufficient preparations have been made for the care of the wounded. Not only are there not sufficient surgeons . . . not only are there no dressers and nurses . . . there is not even linen to make bandages. . . . Can it be said that the battle of the Alma has been an event to take the world by surprise? Yet . . . there is no preparation for the commonest surgical operations! Not only are the men left, in some cases for a week, without the hand of a medical man coming near their wounds, not only are they left to expire in agony, unheard and shaken off, though catching desperately at the surgeon as he makes his rounds through the fetid ship, but now . . . it is found that the commonest appliances of a workhouse sick ward are wanting, and that the men must die through the medical staff of the British Army having forgotten that old rags are necessary for the dressing of wounds.[5]

Russell's dispatches inspired Florence Nightingale to set sail for the Crimea to care for the sick and wounded, taking with her a large party of nurses and helping to revolutionize the nursing profession. Soon thereafter, telegraphed dispatches from the front line by correspondents covering the Civil War in the United States elicited a similar response from Clara Barton. Some two decades later, Barton established the American National Red Cross and played a leading role in getting the United States to sign the first Geneva Convention.

Reporting on the Civil War in the United States was a crucial factor in producing a far more comprehensive compendium of restrictions on the conduct of armed conflict than that contained in the first Geneva Convention. Francis Lieber, a German-born professor of law at Columbia University in New York who had highly placed contacts in the administration of President Abraham Lincoln, suggested the preparation of a code of conduct for Union forces. He was appointed a member of a committee to prepare such a code.

In April 1863, the secretary of war promulgated Lieber's code as General Orders No. 100, entitled "Instructions for the Government of Armies of the United States in the Field." Its 157 articles embodied principles that remain central to the contemporary laws of armed conflict. One of these is that it is permissible for armed forces to engage in conduct that is militarily necessary in order to prevail. It states: "Military necessity admits of all destruction of life or limb of *armed* enemies, and of other persons whose destruction is incidentally *unavoidable* in the armed contests of the war . . . ." (emphasis in the original; Article XV). Yet it also provided that "Military necessity does not admit of cruelty—that is the infliction of suffering for the sake of suffering or for revenge, nor of maiming or wounding except in fight, nor of torture to extort confessions . . . . ." (Article XVI). It provided that, in circumstances in which Union soldiers occupy enemy territory, "All wanton violence committed against persons in the invaded country, all destruction of property not commanded by the authorized officer, all robbery, all pillage or sacking, even after taking a place by main force, all rape, wounding, maiming, or killing of such inhabitants, are prohibited under the penalty of death, or such other severe punishment as may seem adequate for the gravity of the offense . . . ." (Article XLIV). And it commanded that "A prisoner of war is subject to no punishment for being a public enemy, nor is any revenge wreaked upon him by the intentional infliction of any suffering, or disgrace, by cruel imprisonment, want of food, by mutilation, death, or any other barbarity" (Article LVI).

Not all of the provisions of the Lieber Code would stand up today, given the evolution of the laws of war. To cite one example, Article XVIII states: "When a commander of a besieged place expels the noncombatants, in order to lessen the number of those who consume his stock of provisions, it is lawful, though an extreme measure, to drive them back, so as to hasten on the surrender." Yet on the whole, the Lieber Code was a great advance in establishing that principles of humanity should prevail even in the context of warfare and in specifying what conduct comports with those principles. It is ironic, therefore, that in our time, proponents of measures by the Bush administration that departed from those principles in the wake of the terrorist attacks of September 11, 2001 should cite the actions of President Lincoln during the Civil War as a precedent. Though Lincoln did suspend habeas corpus in Maryland in April 1861 in connection with his effort to prevent that state from joining the insurrection—an act that he justified on grounds that the Constitution provides that the writ may be suspended in case of rebellion or invasion if the public safety requires it[6]—taken as a whole, his administration was greatly concerned to uphold the rule of law during a devastating war that posed a serious threat to the continued existence of the Union. One of its finest contributions was its adoption of the Lieber Code, which became the basis for successive field manuals of the U.S. Army up to the present day, and also for codes adopted by the armed forces of other countries. The latter include the Prussian army code of 1870, which helped to place limits on what was permissible combat behavior during the Franco-Prussian War. Other governments that used it as a model for their own manuals included the Netherlands (1871), France (1877), Serbia (1879), Spain (1882), Portugal (1890), and Italy (1896).[7]

The Lieber Code was one of the factors that led to an effort at the end of the nineteenth century to adopt an international agreement codifying the laws of war. Czar Nicholas II of Russia issued a call for a peace conference in August 1898, motivated primarily by his concern that European countries were building up the size of their armed forces and that advances in technology would make armed conflict more devastating than ever before. The Czar's initiative resulted in the Hague Convention that took place from May to July 1899. Russia's proposed agenda included limits on the expansion of armed forces, a freeze on military budgets, and controls on the development of new weapons. Though the conference was a failure in that it did not achieve these purposes, it was more successful in addressing the Russian government's subsidiary concern with adopting rules for the conduct of hostilities. It was the first international treaty that placed significant limits on the conduct of land warfare. It also produced a Convention on warfare at sea and declarations on what those assembling at The Hague considered to be inappropriate means of warfare: namely, the use of balloons to discharge explosives (this was just before the invention of the airplane); the use of projectiles to spread asphyxiating gases; and the employment of expanding dumdum bullets.

Among the important achievements of the Convention were a requirement that prisoners of war must be humanely treated, and rules on the manner of their treatment; a provision asserting that "the right of belligerents to adopt means of injuring the enemy is not unlimited" and prohibiting such practices as killing or wounding an enemy who has laid down arms, or destroying or seizing the property of an enemy unless destruction or seizure is "imperatively demanded by the necessities of war"; an attempt to protect noncombatants by prohibiting attacks on "towns, villages, habitations or buildings which are not defended"; an agreement to protect "edifices devoted to religion, art, science, and charity, hospitals, and places where the sick and wounded are collected"; and a prohibition of pillage.

Perhaps more important even than any of these specific rules was a sentence known as the "Martens clause" that was incorporated into the preamble of the Convention. It is named for the Russian diplomat and legal scholar, Fyodor Fyodorovich Martens, who proposed it. The clause states:

> Until a more complete code of the laws of war is issued, the high contracting Parties think it right to declare that in cases not included in the Regulations adopted by them, populations and belligerents remain under the protection and empire of the principles of international laws, as they result from the usage established between civilized nations, from the laws of humanity, and the requirements of the public conscience.

Theodor Meron, a leading scholar of the laws of war and a judge at the International Criminal Tribunal for the Former Yugoslavia has pointed out that the Martens Clause is deeply rooted in concepts of natural law and customary law and in historical affirmations of their importance even when details are not spelled out. Meron cites as a precedent the concluding provision of the Articles and Ordinances of War adopted in 1643 by the Kingdom of Scotland, which states:

> Matters, that are clear by the light and law of nature are presupposed; things unnecessary are passed over in silence; and other things may be judged by the common customs and constitutions of war; or may upon new emergents, be expressed afterward.[8]

Echoes of the Martens clause are present in the statute adopted by the Allied powers after World War II specifying that the Nazi leaders arraigned at Nuremberg would be tried for the commission of "crimes against humanity." It was cited by the prosecutors and the judges at Nuremberg and has been restated or paraphrased in many international agreements of the twentieth century. It is also referred to in the military manuals of a number of countries, including the United States and the United Kingdom. The treaty establishing the International Criminal Court adopted at Rome in 1998 contains what has become the most authoritative definition of crimes against humanity, spelling out the elements of this crime.

A second Hague Convention in 1907 also failed to agree on limits on the size of armed forces or on the production of weapons. It expanded the rules applicable to naval warfare and largely repeated the rules for land warfare adopted eight years earlier, including the Martens clause (with a

couple of minor changes of wording: "inhabitants" instead of "populations," for example). Forty-four governments took part in the adoption of
the second Hague Convention, including the leading countries of Europe
and Latin America, the United States, Japan, the Ottoman Empire, and
Persia. A planned third Convention never took place because of the outbreak of the First World War.

One of the important aspects of the way that the Martens clause has
figured historically is that its significance is accepted by countries with civil
law systems, such as those of continental Europe, as well as by those with
common law traditions such as the United Kingdom, many of its former
colonies, and the United States. In general, civil law systems are based exclusively on the law as written and enacted by legislation or decree—that
is, "positive law"—while common law systems rely also on precedent and
usage over time. Although Martens himself came from a civil law background, the Martens clause reflects a common law approach, in which
unwritten customs that are widely accepted acquire as much force as positive law. As the pace at which warfare has evolved has greatly exceeded the
frequency at which international conventions take place and the speed at
which they agree on rules and go through the cumbersome process of ratification, a common law approach has been essential in ensuring that the
law reflects evolving humanitarian standards. In addition, of course, as not
everything may be thought of in advance by the authors of international
agreements, it is helpful to have an approach that permits the application
of general principles to unanticipated circumstances. Customary international law, reflecting deeply held and widely accepted norms, and considered universally binding, plays an important role in the laws of armed
conflict. The Nuremberg Tribunal ruled in the *Krupp* case that the Martens
clause "is much more than a pious declaration. It is a general clause, making the usage established among civilized nations, the laws of humanity,
and the dictates of public conscience into a legal yardstick to be applied
if and when the specific provisions of the Convention [that is, the Hague
Convention] and the Regulations annexed to it do not cover specific cases
occurring in warfare or concomitant to warfare." The phrase "usage established among civilized nations" is, in effect, an assertion in the Martens
clause that customary international law relating to the conduct of war is
binding in matters not specifically addressed in the Hague Conventions.

Unhappily, the Hague Conventions did not prevent German use of poison gas during World War I. Gas was used to great effect on the western
front starting in April 1915 and, soon thereafter, also on the eastern front.

In retaliation, the British used poison gas against German troops later in the same year. There were many other deviations by both sides from the agreements reached at The Hague. In addition, the conduct of the war demonstrated that there were numerous gaps in the protections that had been agreed upon in those Conventions. After the war, Germany was required by the Treaty of Versailles to surrender some members of its armed forces for trial on charges that they had violated the laws of war but, thereafter, arrangements were made for them to be tried by a German court. Only a handful were convicted and punished.

Perhaps because the Hague Conventions were not regarded as having significantly limited the barbarity of World War I, there was no great impetus in subsequent years to adopt additional international agreements limiting the conduct of hostilities. A new treaty on gas warfare was agreed upon at Geneva in 1925, but many of the states ratifying it adopted reservations asserting that it would cease to be binding on them if an enemy used gas against them. Also, Conventions were adopted at Geneva in 1929 at which the rules on the treatment of the sick and wounded were updated and a new agreement was reached on prisoners of war. The latter was a significant advance, but two of the major powers that became leading combatants in the Second World War a decade or so later—the Soviet Union and Japan—did not become parties to this treaty. Both countries subsequently became notorious for their gross mistreatment of prisoners of war who should have enjoyed the protections for captured combatants that had been growing in acceptance internationally and that were respected to an extent by German forces when dealing with the prisoners of war they captured on the western front. On the other hand, on the pretext that the Soviet Union's failure to join the Geneva Convention on prisoners of war excused its own mistreatment of captured Soviet troops, the Germans murdered literally millions of them during the war. The Oxford scholar of the laws of war, Adam Roberts, has pointed out that a contributing factor was the attitude of the Soviet Union itself, which "never completely abandoned its view that soldiers who fell into enemy hands were traitors who deserved no protection from their government, and it refused to cooperate with the International Red Cross about prisoners."[9]

The laws of war, which only apply during periods of armed conflict or military occupation, did not govern Germany's treatment of the Jews within its borders prior to the start of the war. Also, as understood at that time, they did not apply to the Jews of Germany itself once the war had started, because that was an issue involving the relations between a government and its own nationals. It was to address such gaps in international law that the Charter of the United Nations, adopted at the end of the war, committed the governments of the world to respect human rights; and that such postwar agreements as the Genocide Convention were made applicable to governments whether or not grave crimes against human rights were committed during wartime and whether or not they were committed against a government's own nationals (see chapter 4).

On the other hand, a vast number of atrocious crimes were committed during World War II to which the laws of war as then recognized were applicable. By far the greatest number were committed by Germany and Japan. The victorious allies convened tribunals at Nuremberg and at Tokyo at which some of those with major responsibility for these crimes were tried. While crimes by the Allies were overshadowed by those of Germany and Japan, they were far from trivial and accounted for the deaths of hundreds of thousands of civilians in such aerial attacks as the firebombings of Hamburg, Berlin, Dresden, and Tokyo, and the atomic bombs dropped on Hiroshima and Nagasaki. In addition, many thousands of rapes were committed by Russian troops in Eastern Europe and in Germany; and by Moroccan troops under French command in Italy. Russian forces murdered thousands of Polish officers at Katyn and, at Nuremberg, falsely attributed those killings to the Nazis. The crimes of the victors were not prosecuted.

Before the outbreak of World War II, during the Spanish Civil War, in response to the bombing of Barcelona in 1938 by the forces of Generalissimo Francisco Franco in which more than a thousand residents were killed, Britain's Prime Minister Neville Chamberlain—no great antagonist of Franco—had told Parliament that, "The one definite rule of international law . . . is that the direct and deliberate bombing of noncombatants is in all circumstances illegal."[10] Expanding on this a few weeks later in another address to the House of Commons, Chamberlain said:

> In the first place, it is against international law to bomb civilians as such and to make deliberate attacks upon civilian populations. That is undoubtedly a violation of international law. In the second place, targets which are aimed at from the air must be legitimate military objectives and must be capable of identification. In the third place, reasonable care must be taken in attacking those military objectives so that by carelessness a civilian population in the neighborhood is not bombed.[11]

A very good statement of the terms of today's international humanitarian law as applied to aerial bombardments, Chamberlain's remarks were repeated in substance in statements by other Allied leaders, including President Franklin D. Roosevelt, during the early days of World War II when such attacks were carried out in Europe exclusively by German planes and, in Asia, by Japanese forces. Later in the war, however, when British and American proponents of aerial bombardments, such as General Arthur "Bomber" Harris and General Curtis LeMay, carried out attacks that killed scores of thousands of civilians in the cities of the Axis powers, Allied leaders fell silent on such practices. At Nuremberg, Field Marshall Hermann Goering, the chief among the twenty-two top Nazi defendants in the first trial—who escaped execution by hanging after his conviction by taking poison in his cell—was prosecuted for the bombings that destroyed Warsaw, Rotterdam, and Coventry, but was not convicted on those charges. If he had been convicted for such indiscriminate attacks against civilians, it could have been awkward to explain why Allied leaders responsible for similar bombardments were not prosecuted.[12]

Though the proceedings that took place at Nuremberg and at Tokyo were criticized at the time and ever since as "victors' justice," and though they were flawed in many respects, they represented a great advance in the rule of law internationally. Many of the individuals who were principally responsible for the ghastliest crimes ever known were tried in dignified proceedings in which they were provided ample opportunity to defend themselves as best they could with the assistance of counsel of their choice and then, in full public view, duly convicted and punished. In the process, a vast amount of evidence was put on the public record and, because the defendants and their attorneys had every opportunity to challenge its accuracy and its relevance, the trials established clearly the nature, extent, and culpability for the crimes that were committed. Thereby, the trials played an important part in undercutting efforts to rewrite history and, at least in Germany, contributed over time to a widespread and deep sense of general responsibility for those crimes. The Tokyo tribunal was far less successful in promoting public acceptance of responsibility, and this for a number of reasons: the decision by General Douglas MacArthur not to prosecute Emperor Hirohito who, more than anyone else, symbolized the Japanese nation and probably bore ultimate responsibility for the crimes ordered by his military commanders; a strong Japanese view that the firebombing of Tokyo and the use of the atomic bomb at Hiroshima and Nagasaki made them the victims; and the failure of the American military authorities, who wanted Japan as a bulwark against the advance of communism in Asia following the triumph of Mao Zedong in China in 1949, to press the Japanese to hold war crimes trials in their own courts. Whereas German courts convicted thousands of Germans for Nazi war crimes, not a single such prosecution ever took place in a Japanese court, even though Japanese forces had slaughtered as many as ten million civilians in such countries as China, the Philippines, and Korea during the war. Because it is widely recognized that many Germans accepted full responsibility for the crimes committed by the Nazis during World War II—a process that began at Nuremberg, but did not end there—there is no significant enduring antagonism today against Germany by those in such countries as Israel, Poland, and Russia whose kin were among the victims. In contrast, hostility against Japan is a continuing factor in several countries of Asia.

Four years after the end of World War II, the governments of the world met again at Geneva and adopted four Conventions that were then signed and ratified by virtually every country in the world. The 1949 Conventions made several important advances. Among them were the identification of certain violations of the Conventions as "grave breaches" (war crimes that warrant prosecution and punishment); a requirement that all parties to the Conventions are "under the obligation to search for persons alleged to have committed, or to have ordered to be committed, such grave breaches" and to bring such persons to trial before its own courts or before the courts of another country that is ready to put them on trial; and a provision applying the fundamental rules embodied in the Geneva Conventions to armed conflicts that are "not of an international character." As by far the majority of war victims since World War II have suffered harm either in internal conflicts or in conflicts in which one of the parties was not an internationally recognized state, the last of these rules—known as Common Article 3 because the same language appears in Article 3 of each of the four Conventions—is especially important. The language of Common Article 3 makes clear that its provisions for the circumspect treatment to be accorded to prisoners of war apply not only to those who would qualify in the context of international armed conflicts, but also to all caught up in armed conflict. Much of the effort of the international human rights movement in the past three decades to limit the abuses that are committed in armed conflicts has focused on wars covered by Common Article 3.

Further advances took place in 1977 with the adoption of two Additional Protocols to the Geneva Conventions. In combination, the four

Geneva Conventions of 1949 and the two Additional Protocols of 1977 are now considered the fundamental laws that govern the conduct of all wars, international or internal. The First Additional Protocol adds to the rules that apply to international armed conflicts; the Second Additional Protocol supplements Common Article 3 and applies to non-international armed conflicts. Each of the Additional Protocols includes detailed rules that attempt to enlarge the protection that is provided to civilian noncombatants in situations of armed conflict. For example, Protocol I prohibits indiscriminate attacks and provides that, among others, the following types of attacks are to be considered as indiscriminate:

(a) an attack by bombardment by any methods or means which treats as a single military objective a number of clearly separated and distinct military objectives located in a city, town, village or other area containing a similar concentration of civilians or civilian objects; and

(b) an attack which may be expected to cause incidental loss of civilian life; injury to civilians, damage to civilian objects, or a combination thereof, which would be excessive in relation to the concrete and direct military advantage anticipated (quotations from Article 51, Section 5).

Protocol I also lists a series of protections for those held by a party to a conflict who may not be entitled to the privileges of prisoners of war. In addition to prohibiting such practices as torture, outrages upon personal dignity and degrading treatment, Article 75 requires that no punishment may be imposed on such a person without a series of protections for due process of law, including conviction "by an impartial and regularly constituted court respecting the generally recognized principles of regular judicial procedure." This has been one of the provisions of the Geneva Conventions cited by critics of the procedures ordered by President George W. Bush and partially retained by the Obama administration that were used against those labeled by the Bush administration as "unlawful combatants" and detained at places such as Guantanamo in Cuba. Even if those captured in Afghanistan are not entitled to prisoner of war status, as the Bush administration insisted, they are entitled to the protections provided by Article 75, which supplements the provisions of Common Article 3.

Though vast numbers of violations of the laws of war took place in the many internal armed conflicts of the decades following World War II, and in such international wars as those in Korea and Vietnam, as well as in the Iraq-Iran War of the 1980s, these were rarely criticized publicly on grounds that governments had failed to adhere to their obligations under the Geneva Conventions. Awareness of the rules imposed by those agreements was largely confined to some in the armed forces who underwent instruction in international humanitarian law, and to the personnel of the International Committee of the Red Cross. The ICRC regularly interceded with military commanders to try to persuade them to respect the laws of war, but it did so quietly and confidentially rather than through public denunciations. The Geneva-based body's practice of not speaking out publicly on abuses, or of doing so only in extremely rare circumstances, is based on its conviction that it is most effective in mitigating abuses of international humanitarian law when it is able to obtain access to places that are off limits to all others, such as those where security prisoners are detained. In addition, the organization prizes its ability to speak directly to military commanders. If it were to engage in public denunciations, the ICRC would lose its access and, with it, the ability to provide protection and services to victims of abuse whom no other institution is able to reach.

At times, the ICRC's refusal to engage in public denunciations has aroused great controversy. The most extreme instance was the decision of the organization's leaders during World War II not to denounce publicly the Nazi extermination of the Jews of Europe at a time when ICRC personnel had gathered extensive information on what was taking place but the general public internationally was not aware of the systematic genocide that was underway. The ICRC's public silence became an issue many years after the end of World War II, during a period when scholars and others were debating what was known about the Holocaust as it took place: Who knew about it, when did they know it, and what did they do (or not do) to alert others?[13] Another occasion when the ICRC's approach was questioned was in the late 1960s during the Biafran war in Nigeria. Some young French doctors who served as ICRC volunteers broke away at the time to form a new organization—Médecins Sans Frontières (Doctors without Borders)—which would provide humanitarian assistance *and* speak out on abuses.[14] On the whole, however, despite these debates, the ICRC's distinctive role has been widely accepted both by those providing humanitarian assistance and also by those engaged in denunciations of human rights abuses, and the organization is greatly admired for the bravery of its representatives, and for their skill, professionalism, and effectiveness in mitigating the barbarities of armed conflict. Speaking out is essential, many of the ICRC's admirers would agree. But in contemporary circumstances—unlike the situation in World War II, when there was no international human rights movement with the capacity to gather information on atrocities—it is accepted that this should be done by others, while the ICRC sticks to the distinctive role that only it can play. Of course if the ICRC were today confronted with a situation similar to what it encountered during World War II, it would have a stronger case for maintaining confidentiality than at a time when there was no international human rights movement to raise an alarm about mass atrocities. Its silence in that era, when it had information that no one else was making publicly available, is a cloud that continues to hang over the history of an organization with an otherwise splendid record.

Starting in the 1980s, some in the international human rights movement began monitoring armed conflicts in accordance with the standards of international humanitarian law. Human Rights Watch led the way (see chapter 9) and, over time, others followed. Today, gathering and disseminating information on violations of the laws of war and on efforts to curb such abuses is a significant part of the work of human rights organizations in any country where there is an armed conflict, and of most of the human rights groups that operate globally. As a consequence, awareness of the Geneva Conventions and of other aspects of international humanitarian law is far greater than ever previously. In some cases, this has had an impact on the practices of armed forces. An example is NATO's entry into the war in Kosovo in 1999, when significant efforts were made to limit the number of civilian casualties. Human Rights Watch criticized NATO for not taking greater care to ensure that noncombatants were not victimized. Yet by the standards of most earlier wars to which comparisons would be warranted, the number of civilian casualties that resulted from NATO's bombardments was relatively small. (It would have been even smaller if NATO had not required that all bombings should take place from an altitude of 15,000 feet or higher. That requirement was intended to ensure that NATO planes would not be shot down. It was successful, as not a single NATO combatant was killed during the war in Kosovo.)

In the 1990s, international humanitarian law greatly increased in effectiveness due to the emergence of a system of international criminal justice to adjudicate and punish those responsible for war crimes, crimes against humanity, and genocide. The new era began in 1993 with the decision of the United Nations Security Council to create the International Criminal Tribunal for the Former Yugoslavia; the world body's subsequent decisions to create additional ad hoc tribunals to deal with atrocities in other parts of the world; and the creation within just a few years of a permanent International Criminal Court (see chapter 11). The statutes governing these tribunals all followed closely the provisions of international humanitarian law as codified in the Geneva Conventions and Protocols. And, the extensive jurisprudence of these tribunals has provided authoritative interpretations of the various provisions of those statutes and, therefore, also of the international treaties and of the customary law that make up international humanitarian law. As a result, the application of these requirements to particular circumstances is now more precisely defined than ever previously. And of course the fact that international humanitarian law has now been enforced through criminal sanctions that the various tribunals have imposed on hundreds of high-ranking military officials, guerrilla leaders, civilian officials, and heads of governments has contributed immensely to awareness of the rules for the conduct of warfare and for the seriousness with which they must be regarded.

Yet in the first decade of the twenty-first century, the United States launched two wars in which the question of the proper application of international humanitarian law, and of whether American practices complied with the requirements of the Geneva Conventions aroused unprecedented controversy. In October 2001, the United States invaded Afghanistan in reprisal for the terrorist attacks a few weeks earlier on New York and Washington, DC, which were directed from that country, and because the Taliban regime that ruled Afghanistan refused to turn over to the United States the al-Qaeda leaders responsible for the attacks. Having never recognized the Taliban as the legitimate government of Afghanistan, the administration of President George W. Bush declared that the Geneva Conventions did not apply to the conflict. In addition, the administration argued that the Geneva Conventions were not applicable to its conflict with al-Qaeda either, and that, consequently, neither captured al-Qaeda members nor members of the Taliban were eligible for prisoner of war status under the Geneva Conventions. The fact that they did not wear uniforms was a prominent factor among those cited by the Bush administration to support its contention that Taliban fighters did not warrant treatment as lawful combatants.[15]

The administration's arguments were widely criticized. Particularly harsh comments at an early stage of the war focused on a memorandum by Alberto Gonzales—then counsel to the president and, subsequently, his appointee to serve as attorney general of the United States—labeling certain provisions of the Geneva Conventions "quaint." In subsequent years, far more information emerged demonstrating that many officials of the Bush administration, led by Vice President Dick Cheney, espoused the abuse of detainees (by means of "enhanced interrogation" in the language often used by advocates of such practices) to elicit information that could be used for such purposes as proving a link between al-Qaeda and Saddam Hussein's regime in Iraq. Critics pointed to disparagement of the Geneva Conventions as conducive to an atmosphere in which the torture of detainees was condoned.

In 2003, the United States invaded Iraq in order to remove the government of Saddam Hussein. This time, however, the Bush Administration acknowledged the applicability of the Geneva Conventions on the basis that Saddam's regime was internationally recognized. In addition, as members of Saddam's armed forces wore uniforms, it did not argue that they were exempt from the consideration due prisoners of war. Nevertheless, significant violations of the Geneva Conventions took place after American forces and their allies defeated Saddam's regular forces and an insurgency was begun by Iraqis seeking to end the occupation of their country. A scandal erupted in April 2004 when photos surfaced showing Iraqi detainees at Abu Ghraib Prison being sexually humiliated and tortured by their American prison guards. The guards' actions elicited worldwide condemnation, with many critics linking these abuses to the Bush administration's earlier disparagement of the Geneva Conventions. Abu Ghraib, along with Guantanamo, became a global symbol of American disregard for international humanitarian law.

In the wake of Afghanistan and Iraq, an important question about the application of international humanitarian law remains. Does it apply to the so-called "war on terror"? Are those alleged to be members of al-Qaeda entitled to any of the protections of the Geneva Conventions? Even if it is acknowledged that captured Taliban fighters are entitled to the minimum due process protections of Common Article 3 and Article 75 of the First Additional Protocol, if not the protections afforded to prisoners of war, what about al-Qaeda members apprehended in Afghanistan or elsewhere in the world?

Many commentators have criticized the term "the war on terror." It suggests, they have noted, a war against a state of mind that has neither a beginning nor an end. As one scholar of international humanitarian law put it: "Wars against proper nouns . . . have anyway advantages over those against common nouns (e.g., crime, poverty, terrorism), since proper nouns can surrender and promise not to do it again."[16] (See chapter 12 for discussion of another aspect of the label "war on terror" and its adoption by the Bush administration.)

Whether or not the metaphor of "war" is used to describe the struggle against terrorists, it is clear that not all measures adopted by governments in that struggle are subject to international humanitarian law. Some terrorist acts—however terrorism is defined—take place outside the context of armed conflict. In such circumstances, acts of terrorism are crimes covered by domestic criminal law and, in certain cases, also by international criminal law. Limits on the conduct of governments in situations not arising in connection with armed conflict derive from relevant domestic laws and international human rights law. International humanitarian law only comes in to play when incidents of violence reach the level of armed conflict or take place as part of an armed conflict. In the latter circumstances, however, labeling them as "terrorism" does not exclude them from the realm of international humanitarian law.

The attempt to blow up the World Trade Center in New York in 1993 is an example of a terrorist act that was not covered by international humanitarian law. Though several people were killed, a great many were injured, and there was much damage to property, the episode did not take place in the context of an armed conflict, and, in and of itself, did not rise to the level of an armed conflict. Moreover, no armed conflict was set off by the crime, and the group that planned and carried out the attack does not appear to have been organized to such an extent that it could be held accountable under international humanitarian law. Those responsible for the attack were properly prosecuted, convicted, and punished under the laws of the United States while enjoying the same protections provided by those laws to all other criminal defendants. As they were afforded those protections, there was no reason to invoke international human rights law in their behalf.

The attacks on the World Trade Center and the Pentagon on September 11, 2001 are a more complicated case. There too, there was no on-going armed conflict. On the other hand, the scale of the killing and destruction of property was so great that it rose to the level of armed conflict. Moreover, the attack was organized by a group, al-Qaeda, which had training camps and a substantial organization; and it had the backing of the Taliban, which controlled most of the territory of a state, Afghanistan. Also, of course, the United States responded to the attacks as an act of war and undertook to destroy al-Qaeda, to remove the Taliban from power, and to occupy Afghanistan. Once that response was effected, international humanitarian law clearly applied. Its application did not prohibit the United States from doing what was militarily necessary to subdue al-Qaeda and their backers, the Taliban. But, at the very least, the actions of the United States should have been constrained by the rules governing a non-international armed conflict set forth in Common Article 3. Those rules include prohibitions on torture and the cruel treatment of detainees; "outrages upon personal dignity, in particular, humiliating and degrading treatment"; and "the passing of sentences and the carrying out of executions without previous judgment pronounced by a regularly constituted court affording all the judicial guarantees which are recognized as indispensable by civilized people." Respecting such principles of humanity as the foundational principles of international humanitarian law provide, would not stand in the way of the military measures necessary to defeat those who had made war on the United States.

The treatment of alleged al-Qaeda and Taliban combatants violated these principles of humanity. Abuses include the use of waterboarding and "wall slamming" to elicit information from detainees and the establishment of military commissions to try them and pass sentences on them without such "judicial guarantees . . . recognized as indispensable by civilized peoples" as the right to assistance by counsel of their choice, the right to know the evidence against them and to cross-examine witnesses against them, the right to present evidence and witnesses of their choice, the right to an impartial judge, the right to be tried in a regularly constituted court, and the right to appeal to a regularly constituted appellate court.

In the early period following the terror attacks of 2001, some in the international human rights movement who had been in the forefront of the effort to monitor compliance with international humanitarian law and to secure compliance with its provisions feared that the Bush administration would succeed in its argument that such agreements as the Geneva Conventions and Protocols were outdated and no longer relevant to the kind of warfare required in a war on terror. For the time being, however, it appears that those efforts did not succeed. Questions about how detainees should be treated are still being debated at this writing in the U.S. courts and in the Congress. The Obama administration has not joined in the criticism of the relevance and importance of the Geneva Conventions. Indeed, it has proclaimed its adherence to them, but it has nonetheless not abandoned the practice of long-term detention without trial that was a hallmark of the Bush administration's war on terror policies. Also, apparently bowing to political pressure, it has indicated that it too will rely on military commissions—with expanded due process protections—to try some of the Guantanamo detainees, while others will be tried in regular federal courts, raising the question as to why different detainees are obtaining different measures of justice. At this writing, hardly any trials have taken place, and it is far from certain how matters will develop.

Several high-level Bush administration appointees have had their careers damaged by their participation in efforts to circumvent the requirements of the Geneva Conventions. They include a number of those whom President Bush attempted to appoint to serve as members of federal appellate courts, such as Stephen Haynes, former General Counsel of the Department of Defense, who were denied confirmation by the Senate. (One of the authors of memos justifying torture, Jay Bybee, was confirmed for appointment to the Ninth Circuit Court of Appeals before his role in advising the CIA that it could engage in torture was made public.) Another Bush appointee, Michael Mukasey, who was not himself involved in any of the efforts to evade or disparage the Geneva Conventions, came close to being rejected by the Senate for appointment to the office of attorney general for failing to take a clear stand on whether the waterboarding of detainees accused of involvement in the 9/11 attacks constituted torture in violation of American commitments under domestic and international law. Mukasey seemed to want to avoid clarity on the issue because he feared that if he acknowledged that waterboarding is torture, his testimony would be used in civil suits against CIA officials involved in such conduct. On the other hand, had he insisted that such treatment of detainees is permissible, he would most likely have been denied confirmation. President Barack Obama's choice to serve as attorney general, Eric Holder, stated emphatically that waterboarding is torture in response to the first question he got at his Senate confirmation hearing. Yet Holder subsequently made clear that he was not in favor of prosecuting those who had engaged in or authorized such practices if they had relied on legal advice, however mistaken, that such practices are permissible.[17]

Unquestionably, difficult issues will continue to arise about the application of international humanitarian law to the asymmetric conflicts of our time that are not confined in the time or space in which they take place. Some have suggested that it may be appropriate to supplement international humanitarian law as we know it today to ensure that previously unanticipated developments and circumstances are covered. Yet it appears that international humanitarian law, as it has evolved over the past century-and-a-half, is sufficiently comprehensive so as not to leave major gaps in its application. Also, it appears that those who wished to disregard it—symbolized by Alberto Gonzales, whose footnote in history may rest on his description of the Geneva Conventions as "quaint"—failed. If anything, the requirements of international humanitarian law are more widely known than ever before, and the belief that they should be respected in practice enjoys enhanced public support.

Though international humanitarian law and international human rights law developed independently, in our time they have converged and are now deeply interwoven. Theodor Meron has written: "Human rights enrich humanitarian law, just as humanitarian law enriches human rights. The recognition of customary norms rooted in international human rights instruments affects, through application by analogy, the interpretation and eventually the status, of the parallel norms in instruments of international humanitarian law. The influence of processes followed in the human rights field on the development of customary law by humanitarian law tribunals is well known . . . . The fact that the law of war and human rights law have different historical and doctrinal roots has not prevented the principle of humanity becoming the common denominator of both systems."[18]

6

Defying Communism

AS OF OCTOBER 3, 2011

THE RISE OF THE INTERNATIONAL HUMAN RIGHTS MOVEMENT AS A significant force in world affairs cannot be separated from the Cold War context in which it took place. The Cold War magnified the importance of citizen efforts to promote rights and, though many of those involved in the movement during the Cold War era took significant risks and suffered severe consequences, it was the the circumstances of the East-West conflict that attracted many of them to the cause in the first place. Rights activists on both sides of the Iron Curtain became aware that calling attention to abuses of rights by their own governments carried extra weight in an era when a global competition was underway for hearts and minds. Embarrassing their governments sometimes put them in extra danger, but, because reprisals against them created further embarrassment, sometimes provided a measure of protection as well.

The leading nongovernmental human rights organizations operating globally, Amnesty International and Human Rights Watch, were born at different stages of the Cold War era and the *modus operandi* of each in turn, at least during their early years, was shaped by the Cold War (see chapters 8 and 9). Their efforts, as well as the efforts of indigenous human rights activists both in the Soviet bloc countries and in countries aligned with the United States were not only influenced by the Cold War context; in addition they had an impact on the way the Cold War played out and eventually ended. This chapter discusses the emergence of the human rights movement in the communist countries, and the following (chapter 7) discusses its development on the other side of the Cold War divide.

In the autumn of 1965, the citizens of Moscow discovered that two prominent writers, Andrei Sinyavsky and Yuli Daniel, had been arrested. Sinyavsky was a literary critic known for his articles in the journal *Novy Mir*. Daniel was a translator. According to the authorities, Sinyavsky was Abram Tertz and Daniel was Nikolay Arzhak, writers whose works were published abroad under those pseudonyms. They were arrested not long after a coup that ousted Nikita Khrushchev as the Soviet leader. As Khrushchev was noted for his speech to a Communist Party Congress nearly a decade earlier disclosing crimes of the Stalin era, the arrest of Sinyavsky and Daniel seemed ominous. It appeared to be part of an effort to reassert hard-line Communist Party control, and also an attack on *Novy Mir* and its well-known editor, Alexander Tvardovsky. Under Tvardovsky's direction, *Novy Mir* had led the way in opening up the Soviet Union's cultural life in the period after Stalin's death in 1953, through measures that included the publication of Alexander Solzhenitsyn's powerful short novel, *One Day in the Life of Ivan Denisovich*.

Many Russians first learned about the arrest of Sinyavsky and Daniel from Western radio broadcasts to the Soviet Union. The broadcasts helped to stimulate what was probably the first human rights demonstration since the advent of the Soviet regime nearly a half century earlier. It took place on December 5, 1965, in Moscow's Pushkin Square. The date was apparently selected because December 5 was Constitution Day in the Soviet Union, and leaflets were circulated expressing concern that Sinyavsky and Daniel would be tried in secret in violation of their constitutional right to a public trial. The location, of course, was chosen because the square is named for its monument to one of Russia's most revered literary figures. It is not clear how many persons gathered to take part in the demonstration. Ludmilla Alexeyeva, in her 80s at this writing, the doyenne of Russian human rights activists and the leading historian of dissent in the Soviet Union, has pointed out that Vladimir Bukovsky, a well-known critic of Soviet psychiatric repression, "estimates that about two hundred people gathered at the appointed time, but I was there and it seemed to be a much smaller number of demonstrators. However, KGB agents in plainclothes and volunteer militia had been sent, so it was difficult to tell who was who .... Twenty people were pushed into automobiles and detained. They were easy to spot because of the flashbulbs [the demonstration took place at

6:00 in the evening when it would have been dark on December 5 in Moscow] of Western correspondents who had heard of the affair and who came to see the unusual event in the Soviet capital. Fortunately, the detainees, most of them students, were released after a few hours. Together with others who had been noticed on the square that night, about forty in all, they were expelled from their institutes."[1]

The demonstration over the arrests of Sinyavsky and Daniel in 1965 was the beginning of the emergence of a human rights movement in the Soviet bloc countries. It was not, however, the beginning of dissent. National groups that had suffered persecution, such as the Crimean Tatars, had previously organized to express their grievances. Writers such as Solzhenitsyn had published accounts of persecution in the Soviet Union and others, such as Boris Pasternak and Joseph Brodsky, had published abroad. And, of course, there had been uprisings years earlier against Soviet oppression in East Germany, Poland and, most notably, in Hungary in 1956. Yet the December 1965 demonstration was distinctive in being a peaceful gathering focused on a constitutional right, the right to a public trial. It inspired others in Moscow to engage in systematic efforts to document abuses of human rights and to disseminate that information internationally.

Another characteristic of the demonstration in Pushkin Square is that it looked similar to demonstrations that were taking place at that time in Western countries, particularly in the United States. The early 1960s was a time that saw great numbers of peaceful street demonstrations taking place in the United States against racial segregation. By the middle of the decade, as many or more demonstrations were taking place against American involvement in the war in Vietnam and against military conscription for the war. It served Soviet purposes to publish news reports on those U.S. demonstrations and on anti-war protests in Europe as well. But it must have come as something of a shock to the authorities in Moscow when a hundred or two hundred of their citizens employed the same means of public protest over a question of rights within the Soviet Union.

The demonstration in Pushkin Square apparently achieved its purpose. International news reporting on the demonstration called attention to the question of whether the trial of Sinyavsky and Daniel would be public, and that may have played a part in the decision that it should be open. It was covered extensively in the Western media and, thanks to Western radio broadcasts, Soviet citizens also heard about the proceedings. Daniel got a five-year prison sentence and Sinyavsky was sentenced to seven years.

Many writers and other intellectuals circulated letters protesting the sentences and some of these were collected and published in *samizdat* editions [that is, underground editions that were not officially sanctioned]. These contributed to the emergence of a human rights movement. An important figure in the birth of that movement was Yuli Daniel's wife, Larissa Bogoraz. She became one of its leaders and, later on, in the late 1970s and the early 1980s, when many other human rights activists were in prison or in exile, Bogoraz played a leading role in circulating internationally carefully documented information on Soviet abuses of human rights. The accuracy and detail that characterized her reports—which were verified years later after the Soviet system opened—suggests that many persons must have collaborated in the collection of this information and that the Soviet dissenters were intent on getting it right and not publishing information that could be discredited.

The first human rights organization known to have formed in the Soviet Union was the Initiative Group for the Defense of Human Rights, established in 1969. One of its founders was a 39-year-old biologist, Sergei Kovalev, who seemed to be embarked on a promising scientific career. Kovalev had previously made clear that he was prepared to challenge Soviet orthodoxy by criticizing the theories of T. D. Lysenko, Stalin's favorite biologist, who had achieved a cult-like status in Russian scientific circles. Many of the others who took part in early human rights efforts in the Soviet Union were also mathematicians and scientists—including Alexander Esenin-Volpin, a mathematician who was the principal organizer of the Pushkin Square demonstration for Sinyavsky and Daniel; Pavel Litvinov, a physicist whose grandfather had been foreign minister of the Soviet Union and who was noted for demonstrating in Moscow's Red Square in 1968 against the use of Soviet troops to crush Czechoslovakia's "Prague Spring"; Valery Chalidze, a physicist who was stripped of his passport and his Soviet citizenship on a visit to the United States in 1972 and, thereby, forcibly exiled; Tatyana Velikanova, a mathematician; and Yury Orlov, a physicist who became the founding chair of the Moscow Helsinki Group, established in 1976. The most prominent Soviet dissident scientist was, however, Andrei Sakharov, renowned as the "father" of the Soviet hydrogen bomb, who joined with Chalidze and another physicist to form the Moscow Human Rights Committee in 1970. Sakharov and Kovalev became close friends and collaborators, as became evident to Western human rights activists many years later when Sakharov was freed by Mikhail Gorbachev from internal exile and allowed to travel to the United States. Sakharov insisted that Kovalev, still haggard after a long prison sentence followed by a period of internal exile, should accompany him. When those meeting with Sakharov, including the present author, started asking questions, Sakharov regularly said that, before he responded, he would like to hear the views of Sergei Adamovich. Though Kovalev was the younger of the two, the great physicist gave the impression that he considered the biologist his mentor, at least in the human rights field.

The leading role of mathematicians and scientists in the human rights movement in the Soviet Union is probably attributable to at least two factors. Especially in the period following World War II and the dramatic end to the war in Japan brought about by the nuclear attacks on Hiroshima and Nagasaki, it was evident to Soviet authorities that the country's military might would be crucially dependent on scientific advances. It was in their interest, therefore, to permit scientists a somewhat greater degree of contact with the outside world than was enjoyed by others. Another factor was that scientists enjoyed great prestige, none more than Andrei Sakharov. This provided them with a little more latitude than others to speak their minds. Of course, the fact that so distinguished a scientist as Sakharov embraced the human rights cause must itself have inspired other scientists.

Although Kovalev was a scientist, within the nascent human rights movement he was known as a "legalist." That is, he was intent on avoiding association with those within the Soviet Union or in exile groups who proclaimed that they sought to overthrow the Soviet system. His focus was close attention to rights abuses that violated Soviet law. It is possible, of course, that the Soviet system might not have been able to survive if it had adhered to its own laws. Those who got to know Kovalev did not think, however, that his legalist emphasis was merely a more sophisticated attempt to undermine the regime than overt calls for an overthrow. Rather, he impressed both colleagues in the Soviet Union and observers in the West as a man of principle whose public utterances were synonymous with his deepest beliefs. Other scientists, including Tatyana Velikanova who became his co-editor at *The Chronicle of Current Events*, a human rights bulletin that began publishing in *samizdat* in the late 1960s, and Valery Chalidze, were also legalists. Perhaps this reflected the concern of scientists and mathematicians for accuracy, detail, and evidence. But whatever the explanation, their approach became the main current of the Soviet human rights movement.

In December 1974, Kovalev was arrested and, a year later, he was put on trial in Vilnius, Lithuania, on charges of anti-Soviet agitation and propaganda. As foreign journalists could not travel to Vilnius, they were restricted in their ability to cover the trial. Even so, the case was publicized internationally, particularly through the efforts of Andrei Sakharov. The winner of the 1975 Nobel Peace Prize for his efforts to place controls on the nuclear weapons that his own scientific work had helped to develop, Sakharov did not go to Oslo to receive the award. Instead, he stood outside the courthouse in Vilnius—he was not allowed inside—to call attention to his friend's trial. Sakharov's wife, Elena Bonner, travelled to Oslo to receive the prize in his place and to read his speech in which he talked about the trial of Kovalev. Sakharov's efforts did not prevent the court in Vilnius from sentencing Kovalev to seven years in prison to be followed by three years of internal exile, a sentence that the biologist served in its entirety.

A few months prior to Kovalev's trial, in August of 1975, heads of the governments of thirty-five countries of Europe and North America gathered in Helsinki, Finland for a conference to adopt a formal peace agreement recognizing the end of World War II thirty years earlier and, of great importance to the Soviet Union, also recognizing the national boundaries resulting from the war. To some in the West, participation in the conference by U.S. President Gerald Ford was a betrayal. He was accused of attaching greater importance to the policy of détente promoted by his secretary of state, Henry Kissinger, than to freeing the "captive nations," such as Estonia, Latvia and Lithuania, that had been incorporated into the Soviet Union during World War II after enjoying two decades of independence following the First World War. Though it was barely noticed at the time, a few State Department officials, collaborating with a small number of their counterparts in the foreign ministries of some Western European governments, took advantage of the eagerness of the Brezhnev regime in the Soviet Union to adopt an agreement perceived as favoring the Soviet bloc, to incorporate provisions in the Helsinki Accords requiring respect for international human rights. The Soviet Union and the governments it controlled in Eastern Europe had abstained in 1948 when the United Nations General Assembly adopted the Universal Declaration of Human Rights, and they had not signed and ratified the International Covenant on Civil and Political Rights, but now those charters of freedom were incorporated, by reference, into the Helsinki Accords. The Accords also state that citizens of the thirty-five signatory countries enjoy the right "to know and act" on their rights. Brezhnev and his colleagues in the Soviet leadership probably did not imagine that the human rights provisions of the Helsinki Accords, hardly noted at the time, would come to be recognized as by far the most important feature of the Accords, and they certainly could not have foreseen that they would play a leading role in the downfall of communism and the Soviet system.

The Accords were not a treaty, and thus did not have the binding legal status of an agreement subject to a formal ratification process. President Gerald Ford recognized that congressional opposition to the policy of détente with the Soviet Union pursued by Kissinger would have made it highly unlikely that two thirds of the U.S. Senate would vote to ratify a treaty. Hence, it was preferable from Ford's standpoint to scale down the legal significance of what was done at Helsinki rather than face the humiliation of a rejection by the Senate. It soon became evident, however, that the Accords adopted at Helsinki were nevertheless very important. In the Soviet Union, a contributing factor was the manner in which the Brezhnev regime celebrated their adoption. A front-page photograph in *Pravda* showed the Communist Party leader signing the Accords in Helsinki, and the newspaper printed the entire text. That was how the small group of human rights stalwarts in Moscow, who were at that moment preoccupied with such disturbing developments as the arrest of Sergei Kovalev the previous December and his forthcoming trial in Vilnius, learned about the human rights provisions. Except for the Soviet Union's ratification of the United Nations Charter, which referred to human rights in a general way, it was the first time their government had committed itself to respect internationally recognized human rights. Eleven of those human rights stalwarts—among them the historian Ludmilla Alexeyeva, Elena Bonner (Sakharov's wife), Pyotr Grigorenko (a former general who had championed the cause of the Crimean Tatars and, as a result, had spent five years as a psychiatric prisoner in a mental hospital), Anatoly Marchenko (who had protested against the Soviet crackdown on the Prague Spring and who eventually died in prison while serving a fifteen-year sentence for dissent[2]), and Anatoly Schcharansky (a leader of the Jewish "refuseniks" who sought to emigrate to Israel and eventually became a cabinet minister in Israel[3] after a long prison sentence in the Soviet Union)—formed the Moscow Helsinki Group. They chose the physicist Yury Orlov as their chairman.

Ludmilla Alexeyeva has written that:

> Yuri Orlov saw an opportunity to use the Final Act [as the Helsinki Accords were widely known][4] . . . to spur the West on to a mediating role. The Final Act pointed out to the signatory countries the legitimacy of mediatory functions in the area of human rights by declar-

ing them to be an indissoluble part of the major goal of the Helsinki Accords: the preservation of peace. In this light the question of the degree of freedom given to citizens and the freedom of information available under different governments ceased to be a simple matter of internal affairs and became a general concern.[5]

In keeping with this view that the Helsinki Accords recognized and legitimized the internationalization of concern for human rights in the signatory states, the Moscow Helsinki Group issued a call for citizens in other countries to form similar groups. The response from other parts of the Soviet Union was rapid and there were soon Helsinki groups operating in Ukraine, Lithuania, Georgia, and Armenia. Not all these groups exactly resembled the Moscow Group, however. Some of those who became their leaders were not legalists like Kovalev. Though they were concerned with human rights issues such as freedom of expression and the right to a public trial, they also had another cause: national liberation. From the standpoint of the Soviet authorities, this of course made them even more dangerous than the Muscovites who had launched this movement, and their treatment was correspondingly harsh.

Intellectuals in other Soviet bloc countries also responded to the call from Moscow. In September 1976 in Warsaw, the historian Adam Michnik and the political activist and theorist Jacek Kuron were among the founders of KOR, the Polish initials for the Workers Defense Committee, a group formed to defend the rights of industrial workers who were then subject to severe reprisals for protesting the economic policies of Communist Party leader Edward Gierek.

The decision of the Polish intellectuals to identify themselves with the cause of industrial workers was crucial because, even under communism, the country was sharply divided by class. In Poland, unlike in other countries in the region, class distinctions were still so significant under communism that it was customary for children born to parents who came from the "intelligentsia"—that is, civil servants and others whose work involved the use of their minds, as distinct from agricultural and industrial workers, who relied primarily on their hands—to have this noted on their birth certificates. By bridging the gap between industrial workers and intellectuals, and thereby earning the trust of the workers, the founders of KOR paved the way for the emergence of Solidarity four years later.[6] In that era, intellectuals such as Michnik, Kuron, Bronislaw Geremek (a medieval historian who became foreign minister of Poland in the period following the fall of communism) and Tadeusz Mazowiecki (a lawyer who became Poland's first prime minister after the fall of communism)—became close allies of Lech Walesa, an electrician in the shipyards of Gdansk who emerged as the leader of Polish industrial workers, then the leader of Solidarity and, eventually, president of post-communist Poland.

At about the same moment that KOR was being created in Poland, Czech intellectuals were circulating a statement that many of them signed and that was published in January 1977. It became known as Charter 77.

Originally signed by 242 persons[7], Charter 77 over the next decade garnered more than a thousand additional signatures, representing a large part of the country's intellectual elite. The three men who took the lead in drafting the Charter, enlisted others to sign it, and then became its first three spokespersons, were Jiri Hajek, Jan Patocka, and Vaclav Havel. Hajek was an historian, a former Communist Party member, and a diplomat who had served as ambassador to Great Britain, ambassador to the United Nations, and foreign minister until September 1968, when he was forced by the Soviet authorities to resign from that post after they sent troops and tanks into Prague to suppress Czech liberalization. Hajek remained a Marxist after signing the Charter and after serving as a spokesperson for the signatories during the first two years after its publication.

Jan Patocka was widely regarded as Czechoslovakia's most important philosopher. Though well known internationally, his teaching career in Czechoslovakia was blocked by the Nazis when they took over in 1939, and then again by the Communists after they took power in 1948. He died in March 1977 of a cerebral hemorrhage, two months after the publication of Charter 77 and three days after the police subjected him to an eleven-hour interrogation.

Vaclav Havel was, of course, Czechoslovakia's best-known playwright—a practitioner in the movement known as "theater of the absurd"—and he became the country's first president after the "Velvet Revolution" of 1989 brought about the downfall of communism. He spent much of the period between the publication of Charter 77 and the time that he became president, some thirteen years later, in prison.

The text of the Charter begins with a statement noting that the International Covenants on Civil and Political Rights and on Economic, Social and Cultural Rights had been incorporated into Czech law in October 1976 after the Czech government confirmed its adherence to these agreements at Helsinki in 1975. It then goes on to describe the way that the rights set forth in the covenants were being violated in practice, stating:

"The right to freedom of expression, for example, guaranteed by article 19 of the first-mentioned covenant, is in our case purely illusory. Tens of thousands of our citizens are prevented from working in their own fields for the sole reason that they hold views differing from official ones . . . ." As in the Soviet Union and elsewhere in the Soviet bloc, in Czechoslovakia, too, the Helsinki Accords and their affirmation of international human rights agreements provided legitimacy for the establishment of a human rights movement.

Charter 77 was both a manifesto and an organization. In its latter role, it tried to avoid dependence on a few leaders by always selecting three spokespersons and changing those designated to speak for it every year or so. One of those chosen was, like Jiri Hajek, always a former member of the Communist Party. Often, like Hajek, these were men and women who continued to count themselves as Marxists. In this manner, Charter 77, like the legalists in the Soviet Union, signaled that its concern was human rights and that it was not trying to overthrow the communist system.

Of course, there were some in the regime, as there were many Chartists, who recognized that if human rights such as the freedom to speak and to publish were protected, it would be difficult or impossible to maintain communist rule. Yet by eschewing association with regime change, and by ensuring that those who spoke for Charter 77 included self-proclaimed Marxists who had been Communist Party members, they made it more difficult for the regime to characterize them as subversives. Thereby, they also allied themselves firmly with those espousing human rights internationally and contributed to the emergence of a worldwide human rights movement.[8]

The emergence of the movement in the Soviet bloc countries in the 1960s and 1970s astonished many in the West by its audacity in confronting the all-powerful communist authorities and by the readiness of many of those active in it to endure hardships: ouster from their jobs, exclusion of their children from universities, the break-up of their families through internal exile or expulsion from the country, and, in a large number of cases, long years of imprisonment at hard labor. Even more amazing, however, was the appearance of the Democracy Wall movement in China in 1978.

At the time, there was little contact between China and the West or, for that matter, between China and Soviet bloc countries. The split between China and the Soviet Union in the late 1950s—which coincided with Mao's Great Leap Forward and the resulting three years of mass starvation—had left China almost completely isolated from the rest of the world. From 1966 to 1976, China suffered through the Cultural Revolution, a period of turmoil and upheaval in which millions of urban residents were sent to the countryside to "learn from the workers and peasants" by doing farm labor; schools across the country were shut down; and gangs of Red Guards roamed the country destroying significant parts of China's cultural heritage and persecuting those deemed to have a bourgeois family background or thought not to be enthusiastic devotees of Mao. Though China's isolation had been interrupted while the Cultural Revolution was underway by the diplomatic initiative of President Richard Nixon's national security advisor, Henry Kissinger, and by Nixon's own visit to China, this was not accompanied by any opening within China.

Changes began in 1976 with the death of Premier Zhou Enlai that January. Many Chinese, and many in other parts of the world as well, were under the impression that the urbane Zhou was more liberal than Mao and had done his best to soften the impact of the Cultural Revolution. Though there is some evidence for this—for example the role he played in preserving a Lamaist temple in Beijing that probably would have been destroyed had it not been for his intervention—it is also clear that Zhou was himself capable of ruthless conduct and that any thought that he might harbor liberal tendencies was a fantasy. Even so, vast numbers of Chinese flooded Tiananmen Square in Beijing on April 5, 1976 (grave-sweeping day in China, when the recently deceased are honored) in a demonstration to mourn the death of Zhou and, thereby, to signify their opposition to the terrible crimes of the decade-long Cultural Revolution.

One of those who took part in what became known as the April 5th Incident was a young electrician at the Beijing zoo, Wei Jingsheng. Wei had been a Red Guard during the early years of the Cultural Revolution and had subsequently joined the army. Like many others in China, he got a close-up look at the suffering caused by the Cultural Revolution. The death of Mao in September 1976 and the arrests soon thereafter of Mao's widow Jiang Qing, as well as other hard-line supporters of the Cultural Revolution in what was known as the "Gang of Four," spurred Wei and others to express their own political convictions. In 1978, some of them began posting their views at a spot in Beijing that quickly became known as the "Democracy Wall." The most important essay posted was one entitled "The Fifth Modernization," written by the young electrician at the zoo. Wei's essay, put up on December 5, 1978, referred to the "Four Modernizations" that were being promoted by China's new post-Mao leader, Deng Xiaoping. In his essay, Wei argued that the modernizations proposed by Deng of agriculture, industry, science and technology, and defense, would not transform China unless they were accompanied by a fifth: democracy. Wei wrote: "Our history books tell us that the people are the masters and creators of everything, but in reality they are more like faithful servants standing at attention and waiting to be 'led' by leaders who swell like yeasted bread dough."[9]

Soon after posting his "Fifth Modernization" essay, Wei and a few others founded a periodical called *Exploration*, which became a forum for the publication of reports on human rights abuses. Wei himself wrote an article for *Exploration* about Qincheng, a prison that was used at the time, and subsequently following the demonstrations at Tiananmen Square in 1989, to confine high-ranking political prisoners.

Exploration did not survive for long. Though Deng Xiaoping had turned China away from the extreme policies of the Cultural Revolution, and though he visited the United States about the time *Exploration* began publishing and was hailed by the Carter administration for his reforms, he quickly ordered a crackdown on the Democracy Wall movement and its offspring, including the small journals in which Wei and others were speaking out in a manner unknown in China since the Communist takeover three decades earlier. Wei was arrested on March 29, 1979 and, later that year, on October 16, 1979, was put on trial. It was one of scores of trials of Democracy Wall activists that took place at about that time but, unlike most of the others, Wei's ordeal was publicized by the Chinese authorities. Apparently, the intent was to use the trial to frighten others. Wei appeared in court in a prison uniform with his head shaven, as if he had already been found guilty. His alleged crime was divulging military secrets, a charge based on a conversation he had had with a journalist from Reuters in which he discussed widely known information about China's war at that time with Vietnam. Writing about that trial, the political and cultural essayist Ian Buruma has pointed out that:

> One of the most indelible images of human dignity is that of Wei Jingsheng reading his defense statement. . . . The photograph is simple with no great dramatic action. Wei stands in the foreground, looking young and thin, fragile almost, in his shabby convict's clothes, one buttonless sleeve hanging loosely around a slender wrist. His shaven convict's head and calm, studious expression make him resemble an earnest monk. Behind him is a blur of faces. . . . Wei's speech was every bit as devastating as his Democracy Wall manifestos. He made

a simple, beautifully argued case for the right to criticize. The logic was so impeccable that it embarrassed the judges, who shuffled their papers, cursed the defendant's impertinence, and called for an early lunch. One of the things Wei said was: "The Constitution grants citizens the right to criticize their leaders, because these leaders are human beings and not gods. It is only through the people's criticism and supervision that those leaders will make fewer mistakes, and only in this way that the people will avoid the misfortune of having their lords and masters ride roughshod over them. Then, and only then, will the people be able to breathe freely."[10]

Wei was sentenced to fifteen years in prison, a long enough period to deter others from engaging in dissent. One of those who protested the sentence was Andrei Sakharov, who would soon thereafter be sent into internal exile in the Soviet Union for criticizing his own government's invasion of Afghanistan later in 1979.

International press reports in the late 1970s about individuals such as Sergei Kovalev, Andrei Sakharov, Adam Michnik, Vaclav Havel, and Wei Jingsheng speaking out in communist countries and enduring harsh reprisals, was one of the main factors galvanizing the emergence of an international human rights movement in that period. With the world sharply divided between East and West, and the communist world split between the half ruled by Moscow and the half in which Beijing was supreme, those making great sacrifices to proclaim their commitment to rights in Moscow, Warsaw, Prague, and Beijing symbolized the universality of the cause. This was also the period in which those identifying themselves with the nascent human rights movement in Western countries were rallying to the defense of those persecuted by Pinochet in Chile, by the military junta that had seized power in Argentina in 1976 and perfected the crime of "disappearances," and also of course by the apartheid state in South Africa that murdered Steve Biko. Simultaneously defending the victims of communist repression was essential to the new movement, for it made clear that their purpose was not to support those for whom they had ideological sympathy, but rather to defend rights for all. Some, of course, only championed victims of repression by right-wing regimes; others focused exclusively on communist tyranny. But the mainstream of the international movement that developed in the late 1970s identified itself with victims of rights abuses irrespective of the ideological character or the geopolitical alignment of the governments responsible for violations.

Two countries at the periphery of the communist world that became important objects of concern to the emerging international human rights movement were Cambodia and Cuba. Cambodia loomed large because it was the site of the greatest mass killing of the 1970s anywhere in the world. The slaughter by the Khmer Rouge from 1975 to 1979 had ideological links to Mao's Cultural Revolution but was carried to an even greater extreme. It caused the deaths of about a million-and-a-half persons, about twenty percent of the population. The carnage was eventually ended when Cambodia was occupied by the forces of its communist neighbor, Vietnam. Though the regime installed by the Vietnamese stopped most of the killing, it did not provide space for the exercise of rights.

Many leftists in the West hailed Vietnam's victory in Cambodia because of the ouster from power of the Khmer Rouge. Some Western rightists held their noses and supported the claim by Democratic Kampuchea (the Khmer Rouge, who remained active as a guerrilla force controlling parts of the country) that it should hold on to Cambodia's seat at the United Nations rather than allow it to be occupied by the regime installed by Vietnam, against which the United States had recently fought, and lost, a long war. Vietnam's own violations of rights in the aftermath of the war included the confinement of tens of thousands in reeducation camps and the persecution that led thousands more to risk their lives seeking refuge as "boat people." The repressive character of the victor in the Southeast Asian struggle was stressed by those leading the campaign to deny Cambodia's seat at the U.N. to the government installed by Hanoi. Steering a course that required it to oppose strenuously any effort to confer legitimacy on Democratic Kampuchea, while simultaneously denouncing vigorously Vietnam's abuses of human rights, was one of the early tests for the international human rights movement. The struggle over Cambodia separated the movement from many on both the Right and the Left who used the language of rights to espouse their opposing stands.[11]

Cuba was significant as an outpost of communism on the American doorstep. So far as its violent abuses of rights are concerned, by far the largest number took place during the first several years after Fidel Castro took power on New Year's Day, 1959. Just how extensive those abuses were is difficult to assess. At the time, there was no rights movement either domestically or internationally attempting to compile detailed information on such matters. It was a period when many Cubans resisted Fidel Castro's imposition of a communist system, some of them emulating Castro by going to the mountains and waging guerrilla warfare to challenge the new revolutionary regime. The best researched and most authoritative history of the period expresses considerable uncertainty about how many Cubans were incarcerated or killed:

> Numbers of prisoners killed or imprisoned under the Revolution are impossible to estimate fairly: Castro himself admitted to the existence of 20,000 political prisoners in 1965 [it is important to interject here that the term "political prisoners"—*presos politicos*—in Latin American usage refers to all those imprisoned for political opposition to a government, whether violent or non-violent]; a pessimist might well suspect the figure to be closer to the 40,000 named by the exiles, if those in forced labor or "rehabilitation" camps are included. The total number of executions by the Revolution probably reached 2,000 by early 1961, perhaps 5,000 by 1970. But who can be certain of figures in this realm? Further, accounts by ex-prisoners of appalling conditions during interrogation or in Cuban political prisons in La Cabaña, the Principe or (until 1965) the Isle of Pines are too numerous to be discounted. It is true that most accounts of inhumanity date back to 1960–61, when invasion was daily expected, but no good regime should be capable, even under any provocation, of such malign behavior to its opponents.[12]

By the late 1970s, the Cuban regime was more secure and both the total number of prisoners and the number held for violent and nonviolent opposition to it had declined substantially. Executions were relatively infrequent, and most of those who could accurately be termed political prisoners were those still incarcerated for offenses committed in the early days of the revolution. As the maximum sentence in Cuba for those not executed is imprisonment for thirty years, and the most defiant prisoners, known as *plantados*, served every day of their sentences, several scores of them remained in prison until the 1990s. But the number of new political prisoners during the 1970s and thereafter was relatively small, reflecting the regime's consolidation of control as well as the emigration of many dissenters. Also, most physical abuses were discontinued. The most severe abuse found by a few foreign human rights monitors who gained access to the Cuban prisons in the late 1980s, aside from the imprisonment of several scores of peaceful dissenters, was the use of tiny, dark punishment cells with concrete bunks, usually for periods of about three weeks at a time, to confine a small number of rebellious inmates.[13]

Many on the Left in Western countries were reluctant to criticize the Cuban government on human rights grounds, because they saw the country as the victim of long-standing efforts by the United States to do it harm. Also, the physical abuses taking place in the late 1970s and early 1980s, when the human rights movement began to become a factor in international affairs, seemed minor in comparison to those that were pervasive in the anticommunist military regimes that ruled most Latin American countries in that era. Yet another factor was the tendency of the Right—as exemplified by leading spokespersons of the Reagan administration in the 1980s—to misstate the abuses by Cuba. They talked of numbers of political prisoners, as if there had been no changes since the 1960s, and of alleged tortures of the sort commonly used by Latin America's right-wing military regimes. In fact, the situation was more analogous to that in the Soviet Union under Brezhnev. There was pervasive political surveillance by the Committees for the Defense of the Revolution, no right to dissent, and a judiciary that was completely subservient to the Communist Party, and long prison sentences were given to those who nevertheless continued to denounce the regime. But there was little use of physical abuse other than the abuse that is more or less inherent in a system that relies on imprisonment to deal with dissent. As with complaints leveled against the regime installed by Vietnam in Cambodia, criticizing the Castro regime for its actual abuses of rights required the international human rights movement to steer a course that did not satisfy either the Right or the Left.

It is, of course, difficult to say how large a part the human rights movement played in the momentous events of 1989, when communist regimes in Central and Eastern Europe collapsed, the Berlin Wall was breached and then torn down, and the Cold War came to an end. Certainly, it was one of the important factors that helped to bring about those changes. Another, of course, was a desire by the inhabitants of the communist states to acquire the material goods that seemed so plentiful in the West. Also, to some degree, rights and prosperity were linked in the minds of many in the Soviet bloc states, because the West had succeeded in conveying the belief that freedom is an indispensable ingredient of economic success.

For a brief period, it appeared to many around the world that 1989 would also transform China. One of the small developments that quickly led to the enormous demonstrations in Tiananmen Square in Beijing and in other cities across China that spring was an effort by a few intellectuals to secure the release of Wei Jingsheng on the tenth anniversary of his imprisonment. The effort began with an essay published by Ren Wanding, a human rights activist who had also been imprisoned in 1979 at about the same time as Wei, but who had been released several years earlier. The matter was taken up by the prominent astrophysicist, Fang Lizhi, who was being hailed by some as "China's Sakharov." Fang pressed the case for Wei's release in an open letter to Deng Xiaoping. Next, the poet Bei Dao enlisted thirty-two other intellectuals to join him in sending an appeal on behalf of Wei to the National People's Congress and the Central Committee. Their letter said that the release of Wei "would create a positive atmosphere advantageous to reform as well as being consistent with today's steadily growing trend across the world of respect for human rights."

Fang Lizhi's open letter and Bei Dao's petition were sufficiently unusual in China that Wei Jingsheng's case was placed on the agenda of the meeting of the Politburo that took place on April 8, 1989. During the meeting, a former premier of China, Hu Yaobang—who had been stripped of all political power but still attended Politburo meetings—collapsed and had to be taken to a hospital. Hu, regarded by many Chinese as a reformer because he had strongly opposed corruption and, though less strongly, espoused political reforms, was a sick man who had suffered a heart attack the previous year and was just recovering from the flu when he attended the Politburo meeting. He died in the hospital after a few days. It was news of Hu's death that inspired large numbers of students and others to go to Tiananmen Square, just as crowds had flocked to the square to mark Zhou Enlai's death in 1976. The fact that Hu's collapse was widely believed to have been linked to the Politburo discussion of Wei Jingsheng's case connected the demonstrations in Tiananmen Square to demands for human rights.[14]

Those demands did not succeed. On the night of June 3–4, 1989, following a declaration of martial law, the Chinese armed forces occupied the square, driving out the students and others who had been demonstrating there since April. Along the way through Beijing to the square, the Chinese military encountered opposition from neighborhood residents and others. In some cases, barriers were erected to impede their route. The tanks that led the military deployment readily brushed these aside. In the process, a few hundred persons were killed.[15] In the following weeks, the Chinese authorities seized many hundreds more for their part in the demonstrations of that spring and imprisoned them for long periods. A number of workers were executed for their part in the protests, and the small human rights movement in China, which had gradually rebuilt itself after the crackdown on the Democracy Wall activists in 1979, was again snuffed out.

After 1989, it did not seem possible to rebuild a human rights movement in China that could accurately describe itself as such. The emergence of a movement with the characteristics of human rights movements in other countries would have been a direct challenge to the Chinese authorities. Instead a different kind of movement has emerged in China, one in which Chinese lawyers are playing a prominent role. They established organizations to advance the legal rights of vulnerable sectors of the population, such as migrants, the children of migrants, women, gays, those infected by HIV/AIDS, and the disabled. In addition, individual lawyers and law firms became known for taking on human rights cases, representing, for example, journalists and bloggers prosecuted for various offenses—often, on charges of disclosing state secrets or for publishing information that embarrassed the authorities—or those arrested for their participation in labor protests or protests over such issues as corruption, pollution, or land seizures. For the most part, those defending rights in this manner have tried to avoid confrontations with the government. The same is true of journalists publishing information about rights. In the 1990s, and in the first decade of the twenty-first century, many Chinese devoted themselves assiduously to efforts to expand freedom. In the process, they made slow but steady progress, though with many reversals along the way, in expanding the permissible scope of public discourse in China and in bringing China a little closer to the rule of law. Many important issues still cannot be discussed in the media or in public assemblies in China at this writing, and the arbitrary exercise of state power remains commonplace. The eleven-year prison term imposed on literary critic Liu Xiaobo on Christmas Day 2009, for his role in drafting and circulating Charter 08—modeled on Charter 77 in Czechoslovakia three decades earlier—was particularly disheartening to many of those in China and abroad who were eager to see advances in rights. On the other hand, Chinese proponents of rights were greatly encouraged by the awarding of the 2010 Nobel Peace Prize to Liu, because it helped ensure that the rest of the world would pay heightened attention to the human rights struggle in China. Much as it might like to thumb its nose at world opinion, the Chinese government would have to make some accommodations.

Many Chinese, and many outsiders who observe developments in China, would agree that the cumulative consequences of efforts by lawyers, journalists, and some others to expand rights in China, even without directly challenging the government in the manner of Liu Xiaobo and his fellow signatories of Charter 08, has had a significant impact. Few issues, if any, are off limits today in communications that do not involve public dissemination, including in such settings as university classrooms. The main goal of the Chinese government in restricting the circulation of information seems to be to stop local protests from spreading. This is reflected in vigilant policing of the Internet. Those posting information on protests on their websites report that it is wiped out almost instantaneously. Estimates—that cannot be confirmed—of the number of those employed as "Internet police" range in the tens of thousands. Dissent in China today is possible; the organization of dissenters is not. The long prison sentence imposed on Liu Xiaobo was intended not so much to punish him for the views expressed in the document as for enlisting others to join with him in signing Charter 08 and thereby turning it into an organized body of dissent.

In the former communist countries of Europe on the other hand, the situation after 1989 has been altogether different. Strong human rights movements have come of age in many countries. Helsinki committees initially formed before the fall of the Berlin Wall now play a prominent part in such countries as Russia, Poland, Hungary, Romania, the Czech Republic, and Bulgaria. There are also in these countries many new groups, established after 1989 to address such issues as pervasive discrimination against the Roma minority and the rights of women, gays, the mentally disabled, drug users, and others disadvantaged in various ways. Indeed the rights movements in the former communist countries of Europe tend to be better organized and more highly developed than those in most West European countries.

Not surprisingly, the legalists continued to speak out for human rights after regime change took place. The activities of Sergei Kovalev in post–Soviet Russia exemplify a commitment to the defense of rights that does not regard the political character of the regime responsible for violations. In the last years of the Soviet Union, Kovalev had joined the historian Arseny Roginsky as a founder of Memorial, a group originally focused on documenting and preserving the record of Stalin-era persecution that had evolved into a leading human rights organization in post–Soviet Russia. When Boris Yeltsin became president of Russia following the collapse of the Soviet Union in 1991, he appointed Kovalev—who had been elected in 1990 as a member of the Russian Federation's Congress of People's Deputies, the Duma—chairman of the Presidential Human Rights Commission. In that capacity, Kovalev spoke out strongly to oppose Yeltsin's decision to go to war in Chechnya and, when it became apparent that Russian forces would bomb Grozny (which was controlled by Chechen rebels), Kovalev moved into the city to call attention to the attacks on its civilian inhabitants and, by sharing their dangers, to rally public opinion against the bombardment. Kovalev led efforts to document and denounce abuses committed during the two wars in Chechnya and played a major role in promoting international condemnation of those abuses.

In a letter to Yeltsin that he published in *Izvestia*, Kovalev wrote:

> In this conflict we have seen in full measure contempt for the law, flouting of the Constitution, demoralization and disintegration of the army, outrageous incompetence on the part of the security services, inept careerism on the part of the chiefs of the power ministries, and awkward and cynical ties orchestrated by the first persons of the state. . . . Perhaps you believe that you are building a Great Russia for the good of its citizens. Not at all! Your current policies will only rapidly resurrect a state predisposed to illegality and the abuse of rights.[16]

When Vladimir Putin succeeded Yeltsin as President of Russia, Kovalev became an outspoken critic of his authoritarian rule and of violations of human rights committed by the Russian government. Putin's rise, and the glorification of the Russian state that his rule epitomized, was a bitter draught for Kovalev, a lifelong champion of human rights, to swallow. It meant, as he wrote:

> . . . the defeat of all those who naively supposed that the cold war confrontation between 1946 and 1991 was not a geopolitical competition between two superpowers but a historical struggle for freedom, human rights and democracy. "You wanted freedom? You thought that human rights were a universal concept equally applicable in any corner of the globe? Just look what has become of Russia after communism! They chose Putin themselves"—So antiliberals of both the left and right will say. And what can those of us who have not lost faith in the constructive power of democracy answer?[17]

It seems likely that only the international stature that Kovalev had earned through his role as a Soviet-era dissenter—and perhaps also his age (he turned 80 in 2010, and the Russian authorities probably calculated that they would not have to put up with him indefinitely)—spared Kovalev from reprisals by the Putin regime. Reprisals would have dramatized internationally the similarities between Soviet repression and repression in the post–Soviet Putin era.[18]

A factor in the development of strong rights movements in the former communist countries of Europe is the availability of international legal remedies for rights violations. As the governments of these countries belong to the Council of Europe, they are required to ratify the European Convention of Human Rights and to submit to the jurisdiction of the European Court of Human Rights, which enforces the Convention.[19] Before 1989, litigation had mainly been a means to enforce rights in countries with a common law tradition—the United Kingdom, the United States, and India, and also South Africa where the legal system rests on both common law and civil law traditions. In the last two decades, however, litigation is becoming an increasingly important means of protecting rights in civil law countries as well, particularly in the former communist countries of Europe. The combination of a rights movement made up in part of Helsinki committees that were launched before the fall of the Berlin Wall, the establishment of constitutional courts in many countries, and the possibility of recourse to the European Court of Human Rights, has helped make this possible. Though lawyers were not prominent in rights movements in Eastern Europe during the communist era—except in Poland, where a part of the legal profession was not state controlled—they have come to the fore in the last two decades because of the availability of international legal remedies for rights abuses. Bulgarian lawyers especially have been in the forefront of international human rights litigation, but Russian lawyers and Ukrainian lawyers have also played a significant role in cases brought before the European Court of Human Rights.

Another factor has been the availability of financial support for the human rights movement in former communist countries from Western donors. This support has come from governmental donors such as USAID and from the aid agencies of the Scandinavian countries; from intergovernmental bodies, such as the European Union; and from a few private foundations in Europe and the United States (including the foundation directed by the present author, which has been the source of the largest amount of assistance). Some human rights groups in the former communist countries are better funded than their counterparts in some Western countries, because international donors believe that the latter should be supported by domestic contributors. In practice, however, such support has not been easy to obtain.

Some former communist countries remain too repressive at this writing for human rights organizations to operate there, except on a largely clandestine basis. These include Turkmenistan and Uzbekistan in Central Asia, as well as Cuba (which maintains its communist system), Laos, and Vietnam. North Korea, of course, remains a hard-line communist state. Not only is it inconceivable that a human rights organization might operate there; control is so tight that it is virtually impossible for external groups to collect information on conditions within the country, except by interviewing the small number of refugees who manage to cross the border into China. (Even that is difficult as the Chinese authorities are hostile to human rights monitors.) While human rights groups continue to operate throughout Russia, Moscow has armed itself with legal measures that could be invoked at any time to curtail their operation; and Russian human rights monitors are already subject to violent assaults such as those that have also victimized many journalists whose reporting embarrasses or irritates the Kremlin. At this writing, the human rights movement in Russia is alive and reasonably well, but nevertheless in serious peril. Rights defenders have been assassinated, as have journalists and others whose work involves rights. The impunity with which such killings have taken place suggests the vulnerability of the human rights movement. Having gotten its start in the communist world in Moscow in the 1960s, it would be ironic, and tragic, if it were to be snuffed out in its birthplace nearly a half century later, in the post-communist era. As there are also a few positive signs in Russia, such as increased acceptance of the jurisprudence of the European Court of Human Rights, that outcome is unlikely. Russia will probably remain a battleground for the human rights movement—as it has been since the 1960s.

China will, of course, also continue to be a battleground. The rights struggle there has a number of components. It includes demonstrations for autonomy or independence by minorities in Tibet and Xinjiang that sometimes turn violent; protests by peasants and workers across China against abuses of authority by local officials often suspected of corruption; attempts by journalists, lawyers, and other members of the intelligentsia to expand the boundaries of public discourse; and, apparently most threatening to the regime, an effort to launch a general human rights movement such as that attempted by Wei Jingsheng in the late 1970s and by Liu Xiaobo thirty years later. All of these represent significant challenges to the Chinese central authorities, who seem eager, on the one hand, to show that they are moving in the direction of a state that abides by the rule of law; but, on the other, manifest fear that tolerance of dissent could lead to a loss of control that might produce an upheaval. China is a powerful state that has been extraordinarily successful economically, but it exhibits a lack of self-confidence when it confronts rights issues. Its responses to attempts to expand rights do not seem to reflect a clear strategy. Almost certainly, demands for rights will become more widespread and more intense, and, in the years ahead, it seems safe to say that China—like Russia—will be at the center of the worldwide struggle for rights. The movement that began in those countries during the Cold War era when communist regimes had a firm hold on power still has a long way to go to secure the rights for which it has fought for the past half century.

7

Rights on the Other Side of the Cold War Divide

AS OF OCTOBER 5, 2011

MANY AMERICANS TOOK PART IN STRUGGLES FOR RIGHTS DURING the period from the mid-1950s to the mid-1970s. In the last half of the 1950s, and the first half of the 1960s, efforts to promote racial equality in the South took center stage, starting with the Montgomery bus boycott of 1955, which came at a time when southern cities and states were resisting compliance with the U.S. Supreme Court's 1954 decision in *Brown v. Board of Education*. During those same years, there were also battles on college campuses and elsewhere over restrictions on speech and association left over from the early 1950s, when Senator Joseph McCarthy was riding high. By the mid-1960s, the issues that galvanized rights advocates in the United States were protests over the war in Vietnam and the closely connected issue of the rights of opponents of the draft. In the early 1970s, President Richard Nixon's violations of civil liberties had the unanticipated effect of mobilizing additional support for the rights cause, which contributed to his own forced resignation from office.

Though it was a fertile period for those promoting rights within the United States, few Americans were concerned in those years with efforts to secure rights in other parts of the world. The emergence of a rights movement in the Soviet Union in the 1960s was little noted, and relatively few in the U.S. joined Amnesty International, which developed far more rapidly in Europe. Americans concerned about rights in that era could be mobilized to deal with American violations of rights, but not with rights abuses by other governments. The fact that the governments of the world had joined together in committing themselves to protect rights by adopting the United Nations Charter, the Genocide Convention, the Universal Declaration of Human Rights, and the 1949 Geneva Conventions, and in establishing mechanisms at the United Nations to look into violations of rights, barely registered on the consciousness of even those most preoccupied with struggles over rights in the United States. Internationalism, and with it the commitment to protect rights through international law, which had been represented by Eleanor Roosevelt, was not sustained. Inattention to such matters by those deeply engaged in domestic rights struggles was, in a way, a counterpart to the disdain for international law frequently expressed by partisans of American exceptionalism. When Americans began at last to react to rights abuses in other countries, it was because some had become aware that their government bore a large share of responsibility for certain abuses committed by foreign governments.

The events that particularly focused American attention on U.S. involvement in rights violations in other countries took place in Chile a year or so before Richard Nixon was forced to resign. September 11 became an inauspicious date in that country long before airplanes hijacked by al-Qaeda terrorists crashed into the World Trade Center in New York and the Pentagon in Virginia. On that date in 1973, General Augusto Pinochet gave the order for two Hawker Hunter fighter jets to attack the presidential palace in Santiago, setting the building on fire. Soldiers under Pinochet's orders stormed the palace as it was burning and discovered the body of the leftist President, Salvador Allende, his head destroyed by bullets from an automatic rifle. Whether Allende died at his own hand using a weapon that had been a gift from Fidel Castro, or whether he was killed resisting the attack, remains in dispute.

A roundup of Allende's civilian supporters followed Pinochet's coup. Many were tortured to death; others were killed by firing squads. About two thousand persons in the custody of the armed forces died. Additional thousands were imprisoned. Many—perhaps the majority—also endured torture. If an event in any part of the world can be said to have transformed the human rights cause into an international movement, it was the military coup in Chile and the cruelty that accompanied it.

Two factors played crucial roles in making the events in Chile so significant. One was the response in Chile by the Catholic Archdiocese of Santiago under the leadership of Cardinal Raúl Henriquez Silva in defending human rights. The other was the worldwide reaction which, like the American reaction, focused on the role that the U.S. played in the coup through the actions of President Richard Nixon and Secretary of State Henry Kissinger, who used the Central Intelligence Agency to carry out their decision to topple Allende's government. Kissinger is famously reputed to have said, "I don't see why we need to stand idly by and watch a country go communist due to the irresponsibility of its own people."[1] The American part in the coup had particular significance at that moment, when millions of Americans, and millions in other countries as well, were taking part in protests against U.S. conduct in the war in Vietnam. What they found out about the Nixon Administration's role in Chile seemed to many to justify their antagonism toward American foreign policy.

Whether the role of the United States was limited to a campaign to destabilize the government of Allende by causing economic upheavals and fomenting strikes, or whether it extended to direct support, to plotting the details of the coup with Pinochet and his military brethren, was long unclear. More recently, however, thanks to the declassification of large quantities of U.S. government documents, it has become evident that the Central Intelligence Agency was deeply implicated in the actual planning of the coup.[2] There was never a secret about the eagerness of the Nixon administration to prevent a leftist government with close ties to Fidel Castro's regime in Cuba from succeeding in Chile. The fact that Allende had been duly elected and governed democratically did not mitigate the hostility of the American president and his secretary of state.

In Chile, Cardinal Henriquez Silva established two organizations, the National Committee to Aid Refugees and the Committee of Cooperation for Peace, to provide legal assistance to those persecuted by the military regime established under the leadership of General Pinochet. Protestant and Jewish leaders in Chile cooperated with the Catholic Archdiocese in the formation of these groups. The Committee to Aid Refugees assisted the many leftists from other countries in Latin America and elsewhere who had flocked to Chile during Allende's tenure as president. Some of them were among those rounded up, tortured, and murdered in the immediate aftermath of the coup. (One of the executed was an American, Charles Horman, whose story eventually became the subject of the 1982 Hollywood film, "Missing," directed by Costa Gavras.) The Committee of Cooperation for Peace attempted to provide legal protection to Chileans facing ill treatment. The Committee enlisted about fifty lawyers in its work and, in two years, provided representation in more than seven thousand cases, filing some 2,342 habeas corpus petitions.[3] The lawyers who brought these cases did not enjoy immunity from reprisal; among those targeted were two who subsequently acquired international recognition: José Zalaquett and Hernán Montealegre. Both were seized and forcibly exiled. Following his expulsion, Montealegre became the first director of the Inter-American Institute for Human Rights in Costa Rica, an organization that has played a key role for more than three decades in training Latin American human rights leaders. He was imprisoned and tortured before being sent out of the country. Zalaquett was spared torture. In exile, his intellectual abilities and his charisma made him a central figure in the formation of the international human rights movement. He served for a period as chair of the International Executive Committee of Amnesty International (see chapter 8). Another well-known lawyer who was forced into exile several years later was Jaime Castillo, a former minister of justice in the Christian Democratic government that preceded Allende. He was physically seized by Chilean secret police operatives and dumped across the Argentine border. At the time, Castillo was chairman of another nongovernmental organization that played a leading role in opposing Pinochet's abuses, the Chilean Commission on Human Rights.[4]

Internationally, events in Chile provoked strong reactions in many countries. In addition to the evident involvement of the United States, other factors that combined to elicit a much greater response than was customary for a Latin American military coup were the fact that it was a democratic government that was overthrown; the mass detentions that accompanied the coup, including thousands who were held at a soccer stadium; the summary executions of large numbers; the inclusion of nationals of other countries among the victims; and reports of the widespread use of torture by Pinochet's forces. The Nixon administration's support for Pinochet's regime after it took power contributed to the anti-American character of the international response.

Reaction in the United States included condemnation of both the new regime in Chile and of the actions of the Nixon administration by members of Congress. Democrats in the House of Representatives, led by Donald Fraser of Minnesota and including Tom Harkin, Michael Harrington, George Miller, and Toby Moffett, and in the Senate, led by Edward Kennedy of Massachusetts, James Abourezk, and George McGovern, denounced the coup, its accompanying cruelties, and the involvement of the United States. At the time there was no human rights movement focused on international affairs in the United States and there were no laws linking the conduct of American foreign policy to human rights conditions abroad. Yet on October 2, 1973, three weeks after the coup, Senator Kennedy proposed a sense of Congress resolution calling on the president to "deny economic or military assistance other than humanitarian aid, until he finds that the Government of Chile is protecting the human rights of all individuals, Chilean and foreign."[5]

Kennedy's resolution inaugurated politically significant and effective U.S. congressional involvement in the protection of human rights internationally.[6] It was also a period of rising concern in Congress over Soviet abuses of rights. The issues that played the leading role in generating this concern were not those that were the focus of Sergei Kovalev and Andrei Sakharov's efforts. Rather, members of Congress were particularly concerned with the treatment of the so-called refuseniks, Soviet Jews who were refused the right to leave the U.S.S.R. and sometimes punished for trying to emigrate to Israel. A *de facto* alliance was formed. As a consequence, between 1973 and 1976, Congress adopted major legislation that places human rights conditions on the conduct of American foreign policy, most of which remains in effect at this writing. Because supporters of these laws included both those intent on condemning Pinochet's abuses and those condemning the abuses of the Soviet Union, they were adopted with sufficient support to enable Congress to override vetoes of some of the legislation by President Gerald Ford. Ford, who came into office in August 1974 following the forced resignation of Richard Nixon over the Watergate scandal, had retained Henry Kissinger as his secretary of state. Kissinger did not believe that the human rights practices of other governments should be a factor in American foreign policy and he most probably interpreted the actions of Congress in adopting laws on human rights as a repudiation of his policies in Chile—as indeed was intended by at least some of their sponsors.

The most important of the laws adopted during this period was Section 502B of the Foreign Assistance Act. As discussed in chapter 4, it bars the United States from providing security assistance "to any country the government of which engages in a consistent pattern of gross violations of internationally recognized human rights." Such gross violations, the law said, include "torture or cruel, inhuman, or degrading treatment or punishment, prolonged detention without charges and trial, causing the disappearance of persons by the abduction and clandestine detention of those persons, and other flagrant denial of the right to life, liberty or the security of the person." Security assistance includes military assistance, military training, and sales of military, police, or intelligence equipment. The law also required the secretary of state to publish annually a report on the human rights practices of countries worldwide, inaugurating a practice that has continued ever since. Aside from providing some of the most detailed information that is available on many countries, the compilation of these reports has made it necessary for every U.S. embassy in the world to develop the capacity to monitor closely the human rights practices in the country where it is based. Accordingly, the post of "human rights officer" has become a feature of all American embassies and has made them important venues for human rights protection, irrespective of the policies of the administration holding office in Washington.

Another of the laws adopted during this period was an amendment to the Trade Act that is popularly known as "Jackson-Vanik" for its sponsors, Senator Henry Jackson of Washington and Representative Charles Vanik of Ohio. In the absence of a presidential waiver, it denies most favored nation trading status to any government with a non-market economy that denies its citizens the right to emigrate. This was a law specifically intended to help Soviet Jews. Its adoption reflected the consensus shared in that period by members of Congress of different ideological persuasions who came together in support of international human rights. A decade and a half later, after the killings in Tiananmen Square, Jackson-Vanik became an important factor in America's relations with China as well. The date when China's presidential waiver was due each year happened to be June 3, the anniversary of those killings, which took place during the night of June 3–4. The right to emigrate was never an issue so far as China was concerned; Deng Xiaoping is reported to have asked an American visitor, "How many do you want? A hundred million? Two hundred million? Three hundred million?" Even so, human rights activists rallied for a few years around a campaign to deny annual renewal of most favored nation status for China on the anniversary of the events in Tiananmen Square. As trade was the main factor in American relations with China, Jackson-Vanik was the only provision in U.S. human rights law that could have a significant impact. Disputes over most favored nation status persisted until 1994 when President Clinton announced that he was severing the link between trade relations with China and human rights. Thereafter, American trade with China grew so rapidly that no further effort to condition such commerce on human rights had any prospect of being considered seriously. (At this writing, Jackson-Vanik remains part of U.S. law and, though it has no practical effect, it is considered by some to be an obstacle in the way of good relations between the United States and Russia. That is because its main use had been to block trade with the former Soviet Union.)

The emergence of an international human rights movement in the United States and elsewhere in the years subsequent to the adoption of laws in the mid-1970s placing human rights conditions on the conduct of American foreign policy was greatly influenced by those laws. It is, therefore, appropriate to consider members of Congress such as Donald Fraser, Tom Harkin, and, above all, Edward Kennedy, as among those who helped to give birth to that movement, or at least to the branch of it that developed in the United States. As they were primarily reacting to the events in Chile, Pinochet's coup and the reaction to it by Cardinal Raúl Henriquez Silva also should be recognized for the crucial role they played. The Cardinal continued to play a leading role as he transformed the ad hoc Committee of Cooperation for Peace into an important arm of the Church known as the Vicaría de la Solidaridad and gave it quarters in the main building of the Archdiocese in Santiago. That meant that to attack the "Vicaría"—as it came to be widely known, not only in Chile but also internationally—Pinochet's forces would have to raid the Church itself in one of Latin America's most Catholic countries. Cardinal Henriquez Silva had been inspired by another churchman, Cardinal Paulo Evaristo Arns in San Paulo, who had spoken out against military abuses in Brazil. In turn, Cardinal Henriquez Silva's example, along with that of Cardinal Arns, helped to inspire Catholic Church leaders in a number of other countries, such as El Salvador, Guatemala, Peru, the Philippines, South Korea, East Timor, and Zimbabwe, who also put the Church in the forefront of human rights protection in their countries. On the other hand, in neighboring Argentina, where a military coup took place in 1976, the Church hierarchy collaborated with the armed forces that committed massive human rights abuses.[7] In communist Cuba, too, the Catholic Church hierarchy has until recently kept silent about abuses of human rights.[8] It seems that policies on such matters are not set in Rome but are largely determined at the archdiocesan level. It was Cardinal Henriquez Silva's personal actions under the influence of one of his colleagues in the Latin American Church, and their influence on other Latin American Church leaders and on Church leaders in some other parts of the world, that made their role so significant in the development of the international human rights movement.

. . .

As invoking international law is not taken seriously by many in the United States, and indeed arouses outright antagonism in partisans of American exceptionalism, it would have been difficult for a human rights movement to gain traction in this country if that were the movement's only means of influencing American foreign policy. Those who led the formation of the human rights organizations that were established in the United States in the late 1970s and early 1980s did not suffer that handicap. They could cite American laws recently enacted under the leadership of Senator Kennedy and company. Those laws gave enhanced domestic status to international law, because they referred to "internationally recognized rights" and specified that these included such matters as prohibitions on torture and disappearances. Through the legislation of the mid 1970s, international law became part of American law, not only because certain provisions of international law are binding on the United States, but also because American domestic law on the promotion of human rights in relations with other governments explicitly accepted international law; and because it made such American practices as military assistance and sales of security equipment to foreign governments directly dependent on the government's adherence to international law. The infant human rights movement in the United States achieved legitimacy here not only by monitoring the human rights practices of other governments in accordance with international agreements but, to a much greater extent, also by monitoring compliance by the United States with its own laws placing human rights conditions on the conduct of American foreign policy.

The adoption of Section 502B of the Foreign Assistance Act in 1975 required the administration of President Gerald Ford, under the direction of Secretary of State Henry Kissinger, to compile the first volume of the *Country Reports* that have been published annually ever since on human rights practices worldwide. The work covered developments during 1976, the last year in office for Ford and Kissinger, but it was not ready for publication until early in 1977. As Jimmy Carter took office on January 20 of that year, it was his administration that actually published the first volume of *Country Reports* and became associated with their issuance.

1976, the year that Carter campaigned to become president and won election, was also a year of heightened international attention to South Africa. Much of that attention focused on an upheaval in the giant township of Soweto, near Johannesburg, under the influence of the Black Consciousness movement led by a charismatic young black leader, Steve Biko. Large-scale protest in Soweto began in June that year when the Department of Bantu Education—as it was known because all black South Africans had been deprived of their nationality and were designated by the apartheid government as nationals of Bantustans in isolated parts of the country that most of them had never even visited—required that instruction would take place in Afrikaans as well as English. Riots took place in Soweto on an almost daily basis and spread to other parts of the country. The South African security forces struggled to suppress the protests. The following year an incident took place that added to interest in developments in South Africa worldwide, including in the United States. The police murdered Steve Biko. As in the case of the Nixon administration's role in Pinochet's coup in Chile, it was the American connection to events in South Africa that made the practices of the apartheid state an issue for Americans. That connection was the high level of investment in South Africa by American businesses, and it led to a disinvestment campaign in churches and on college campuses, and to opportunities to publicize the campaign at the annual meetings of stockholders of many corporations. It was another case in which the cause of human rights internationally became a domestic issue in the United States.

· · ·

As originally adopted, the provision of Section 502B requiring the State Department to compile and publish country reports on human rights practices applied only to countries that were recipients of United States military or economic assistance. The rationale of the proponents of the law was that Congress should be informed about the human rights situation in any country before determining whether to provide it with such assistance. In the Cold War circumstances of the period, this meant that only governments that were aligned with the United States were the subjects of such reports; almost all communist countries were excluded as they did not receive U.S. military or economic assistance. Later, 502B was amended so as to apply universally, as Congress recognized that it was a mistake to exempt communist countries from such scrutiny of their human rights records.

The first set of *Country Reports* was a relatively slender volume of mostly superficial information, some of it not completely reliable. Yet, as it focused on countries aligned with the United States and was published by the Carter administration, it helped to convey the impression that Carter was particularly concerned about abuses by right-wing governments. Loud protests against the *Country Reports* by some of those governments reinforced that impression.

To oversee the compilation of the *Country Reports*, and because the legislation adopted during the Ford era required the establishment of the post, the Carter administration created the office of assistant secretary of state for human rights. There had never been such a post previously. The first appointee, chosen by Carter, was a political ally of the president, Patricia Derian of Mississippi. Derian had no background in international affairs. She had been a housewife in Jackson, married to a surgeon on the faculty of the University of Mississippi, who had led an effort to keep the city's schools open when local officials closed them to avoid court-ordered desegregation. Derian's involvement in that struggle led her to regional prominence in the civil rights cause. She became a national board member of the American Civil Liberties Union and president of an organization known as the Southern Regional Council, which played a leading role in the registration of black voters in the South in the 1960s and the early 1970s. In addition, she became a Democratic National Committee Woman when an integrated slate successfully challenged the credentials of the all-white Mississippi delegation at a national Democratic political convention. It was in her role as a member of the Democratic National Committee that she became a friend and an ally of her fellow white southern liberal, Jimmy Carter, when he ran for President in 1976. Carter's choice of Derian apparently reflected his view that her leadership in the civil rights struggle in the United States qualified her to serve as the country's first assistant secretary of state for human rights.

The establishment of this post was not popular with many of the career professionals in the State Department. American foreign policy, most of them believed, should reflect the country's security interests and its economic interests. They did not like being told by the Congress that promoting human rights should also be a foreign policy goal, especially in circumstances when it seemed to come into conflict with long-established interests that they were attempting to advance in such areas as security and trade. The fact that the person charged with fostering human rights had never been professionally concerned with the other goals of American foreign policy and lacked any background in international affairs exacerbated the resentment that some felt over the new post.

Despite the hostility that Derian encountered in some quarters of the State Department, and from American embassies in some of the countries to which her efforts were devoted, she set about her mission with determination and with a measure of bureaucratic dexterity that many professionals in the Department might not have expected from a Mississippi housewife (before raising a family, Derian had been a nurse). Career Foreign Service officers who thought they could easily thwart the efforts of a foreign policy neophyte found their work cut out for them.[9] At the outset of her State Department career, Derian focused particularly on Argentina. A military coup had taken place there in March 1976, and when Derian began work in the Carter administration in early 1977, political imprisonment without charges and trial, torture, and disappearances—the crime for which the Argentine military became particularly known—were epidemic. More than a few Argentine survivors of that era believe that Derian saved their lives or the lives of family members. When the military dictatorship ended in December 1983 and a civilian, Raúl Alfonsín, was elected president, the Reagan administration—which took office in January 1981—sent Vice President George H. W. Bush to Buenos Aires as its official representative at the inaugural ceremony. As the present author, who also attended that event, was able to observe, Bush's visit was accepted in a perfunctory manner. Derian, who was again a private citizen after the end of the Carter administration, was greeted with enthusiasm. The new civilian government of Argentina celebrated her arrival as that of a great friend.

The Carter administration's criticism on human rights grounds of the military dictatorship in Argentina, and of other right-wing dictatorships in the hemisphere—those of Generals Romeo Lucas García in Guatemala, Augusto Pinochet in Chile, and Anastasio Somoza in Nicaragua—became the object of attack by many prominent in the foreign-policy establishment of the successor Reagan administration. No one articulated the views of the Reaganites more effectively or more memorably than Jeane Kirkpatrick, a political scientist chosen by Reagan to serve as his administration's ambassador to the United Nations. Indeed, it appears that the main factor that convinced Reagan to appoint Kirkpatrick to that post was that he had read an essay she published in the neoconservative monthly *Commentary*, in which she attacked the Carter administration, claiming that its human rights policy had precipitated the overthrow of Somoza in Nicaragua and of the Shah in Iran. She described their governments as "friendly autocratic" regimes and said they had been replaced by far worse, the Sandinistas in Nicaragua and Khomeini in Iran. Kirkpatrick claimed that the Carter administration failed to distinguish between autocratic societies with the potential to evolve into more democratic systems, and totalitarian regimes that are incapable of ever becoming more democratic. In Kirkpatrick's view, Somoza and the Shah were friendly autocrats who deserved support by the United States. In contrast, the Sandinistas and the Khomeini regime were in the totalitarian camp.[10]

In line with this thinking, the Reaganites defended the human rights performance of regimes that they considered to be aligned to the United States, including the military governments in El Salvador and Guatemala, which were engaged in struggles with left-wing insurgents; the kleptocratic dictatorship of "President-for-Life" Jean Claude "Baby Doc" Duvalier in Haiti; Asian military governments, such as those of presidents Marcos in the Philippines, Chun in South Korea, and Suharto in Indonesia; the military regime in Turkey; the apartheid government in South Africa; others elsewhere in Africa, such as those of presidents Moi in Kenya, Mobutu in Zaire, and Doe in Liberia; as well as South American military regimes in Argentina, Chile, Brazil, and Uruguay. After failing to secure U.S. Senate confirmation of its original nominee for the post of assistant secretary of state for human rights (see chapter 9), the Reagan administration installed a young neoconservative lawyer, Elliott Abrams, in the post. Abrams made it plain that alignment with the United States in the Cold War struggle with the Soviet Union was a positive factor influencing his bureau's assessment of the human rights records of other governments. Under his leadership, the annual *Country Reports on Human Rights Practices*, which by this time covered all countries and not only those that were the recipients of U.S. military and economic assistance, were skewed so that they assessed the practices of left-wing governments far more harshly than those that portrayed themselves as anticommunist allies of the United States. Nongovernmental human rights organizations in the United States, such as Human Rights Watch and the Lawyers Committee for Human Rights (later known as Human Rights First) published critiques of the *Country Reports* each year, pointing out that the sections dealing with right-wing regimes often left out important information on abuses or presented the information in such a way as to make the State Department an apologist for abuses. Leaders of those groups, and of organizations like Amnesty USA and the Washington Office on Latin America, established a contentious relationship with the Bureau of Human Rights at the State Department that contrasted sharply with their friendly relations with the Bureau during the Carter administration.

The Reagan administration's vigorous championship on human rights grounds of many governments aligned with the United States, in which there were in fact severe abuses of human rights, contributed inadvertently to the emergence of a strong human rights movement in the United States that denounced administration policies. What Reagan, Kirkpatrick, Abrams, and other members of the administration had failed to grasp is that by becoming apologists for rights abuses in countries allied with the United States, they contributed to the view by many Americans that those were *American* abuses of rights. This helped to mobilize efforts against their policies by rights proponents who had not previously paid much heed to international affairs. Their new focus helped to transform the international human rights cause into a domestic issue. Indirectly, this also contributed to the development of national rights groups in many of the countries that were the subjects of dispute. Factors that played a role in this development included international public attention to the findings of human rights organizations in the United States and in countries over which disputes took place when they contradicted the State Department; and financial support for those organizations from donors in the United States and Europe intent on countering the policies of the Reagan administration.

An example was El Salvador. The war there in the 1980s between the Salvadoran armed forces and left-wing guerrillas operating under the banner of a group known as the FMLN was characterized by many thousands of killings by death squads aligned with and controlled by the military and often made up of members of the armed forces; and also by massacres of peasants in villages where the Salvadoran military believed that the guerrillas had supporters. One such massacre in December 1981 involved a number of hamlets in the vicinity of a village called El Mozote and left more than a thousand dead, most of them young children. It was the largest number killed in any such episode in the Western hemisphere since World War II. As the massacre was committed by a U.S.–trained battalion of the Salvadoran military, and as officials of the Reagan administration testified before Congress in February 1982 denying that the massacre had taken place, El Mozote became a particular focus of controversy between the human rights movement and the administration. (Some years later, long after the end of the Reagan administration, the dispute over whether in fact there had been a massacre was definitively resolved by the forensic exhumation of the bodies of a large number of the victims. They included many skeletons of infants who had been killed violently.[11])

In El Salvador, up to 1982, the Catholic Archdiocese had supported a human rights organization known as Socorro Juridico. Its leaders had been close to Archbishop Oscar Arnulfo Romero, who established the organization, and who was himself murdered by a death squad in March 1980 as he was saying Mass. Subsequently, Socorro Juridico came under fire from the Reagan administration, ostensibly on the grounds that it was biased against the Salvadoran armed forces because it only reported on their abuses and not also on those of the guerrillas. In fact, this was standard in the human rights field at that time, as nongovernmental organizations worldwide, including Amnesty International, limited themselves to reporting on violations of international human rights law, which only applied to governments. The first shift in practice in the field did not take place until 1982 when Americas Watch, one of the components of the future Human Rights Watch, began monitoring armed conflicts in accordance with international humanitarian law, which also applies to groups engaged in combat with government forces (see chapter 5).

The conflict with the Reagan administration led Archbishop Rivera y Damas, successor of the murdered Archbishop Romero, to disaffiliate Socorro Juridico in early 1982 and to create a new Church human rights office with enhanced status and resources. Called Tutela Legal, it was housed in the headquarters of the archdiocese, like the Vicaría in Chile. Tutela Legal did monitor both sides of the conflict in El Salvador and, because it quickly established a reputation for reliable reporting, the human rights cause in the war-torn country achieved heightened prominence. It was one of many instances in which the Reagan administration's assaults on elements of the human rights movement backfired and contributed unintentionally to the strengthening of the movement.

Seeing that its conflict with the infant human rights movement over El Salvador was going poorly, the Reagan administration attempted to shift the focus. In June 1982, the president made a speech to the British parliament in which he launched what he called a "crusade for democracy."[12] Reagan equated advances in the direction of electoral democracy with human rights, and he argued that El Salvador was doing better on human rights than nearby Nicaragua, because the Sandinistas, who had toppled Anastasio Somoza's dictatorship in 1979, had declared that they would not hold elections until 1985. In contrast, although a fairly high intensity war was underway in El Salvador, with many thousands of Salvadorans being killed in the fighting and even larger numbers being murdered in death squad killings or as the victims of "disappearances," the country had recently conducted an election. The election had, however, scant effect on the exercise of political power in El Salvador, as civilian officials wielded little influence over the armed forces. Even so, the election did serve the public relations purposes of the Reagan administration, because it produced television footage of long lines of Salvadorans waiting patiently in the hot sun for their turn to cast their vote. It was powerful visual evidence that El Salvador was a democracy.

It is unclear to what degree Reagan's call for a crusade for democracy was intended at the time as a tactical maneuver in the struggle for public opinion over the American role in the wars in Central America and to what degree it was, from the outset, a considered and deliberate innovation in American foreign policy. Whatever the initial inspiration for the speech, the way forward that it enunciated has had a profound impact. In the three decades that have elapsed since that speech, every American administration has committed itself in significant measure to the promotion of democracy on the international stage. Also, though the extent to which different administrations have equated the promotion of democracy with the promotion of human rights has varied to some degree, in general the two are not distinguished by those who have spoken for the U.S. government in the period since Reagan's address at Westminster.

From the standpoint of many in the human rights movement, however, equation of the promotion of democracy with the promotion of human rights is troubling. Almost all human rights advocates would agree that the right to take part in self-government through the electoral process is itself a fundamental right and, therefore, a key component of human rights. Human rights advocates would readily agree as well that such essential aspects of democracy as the freedom to communicate by speech, press, or assembly are also central aspects of human rights. Disagreement begins with the claim made by the Reaganites and their successors in Washington that governments based on electoral democracy may be counted on to protect human rights. In reality, the human rights movement has often been at odds with democratically elected governments over such issues as minority rights, the abuse of detainees, and restrictions on the liberties of their critics. Some of those equating the promotion of democracy with the effort to secure human rights have argued that the deficiencies of a democracy are self-correcting, whereas the shortcomings of other forms of government are less susceptible to change. Whether or not this is the case, it has been the experience of the international human rights movement that many significant abuses are committed by governments that are democratic. In contemporary times, Colombia, Peru, Russia, Israel, and Sri Lanka could be cited as examples of countries in which the popular will, periodically expressed at the polls, has produced governments that have engaged in significant human rights abuses over a sustained period of time. India is the world's largest democracy, but it has committed substantial abuses in conflict areas such as Kashmir, and violations of rights against impoverished detainees in the criminal justice process are endemic. In some countries of Central and Eastern Europe, the advent of democracy after the fall of communism was accompanied by the rise of populist movements that have fostered discrimination against national minorities and against the Roma population of the region. In countries in other parts of the world, including Zimbabwe, Venezuela, and Iran, leaders such as Mugabe, Chavez and Ahmadinejad have come to power by democratic elections and subsequently perpetuated their rule by undemocratic means that include severe violations of rights. Documenting and denouncing such abuses internationally remains an important part of the effort to curb their violations. The self-correcting characteristics of democracy cannot be counted on to secure that result. Moreover, even if democracies may eventually change their ways, their abuses cause much suffering before reforms take place.

Whatever the motivations of the Reagan administration in launching its crusade for democracy, the policy shift that this represented had a significant impact. It produced the establishment through legislation by Congress of such bodies as the National Endowment for Democracy (NED), which provides funds openly to organizations in other countries that it considers to be promoting democracy and human rights. Earlier, since the beginning of the Cold War, the United States had often covertly financed groups in other countries that were perceived to be anticommunist in their outlook. The primary mechanism for such funding was the Central Intelligence Agency, using a wide range of intermediaries, but exposés in the 1970s of those CIA activities disrupted the flow of funds. In part, NED financing was a way of doing openly what had previously been done covertly, though it also included support for rights efforts that probably would not have qualified for the kind of aid that had been given previously by the CIA. In addition, through the legislation creating the NED, the United States also established such bodies as the National Democratic Institute, the International Republican Institute, and the International Foundation for Electoral Systems, all government-funded. These have played a significant role in efforts to promote electoral democracy worldwide during the past three decades.

The Reagan administration's announced commitment to promoting democracy also had an important impact on its own policies towards some countries where struggles were underway to replace dictatorships with elected democratic governments. The impact was most profound during

Reagan's second term as President, which began in 1985. Governments that had previously enjoyed unwavering support from the Reagan administration but came under pressure from the United States to democratize during the second term included those in Haiti, the Philippines, and Chile.

In Haiti, a new law was promulgated in 1985 requiring all political parties to support the hereditary dictatorship of President Jean Claude Duvalier. In July, a referendum was conducted and, according to the Haitian government, about 90 percent of the country's eligible voters took part and no fewer than 99.8 percent of them endorsed perpetuation of Duvalier's "Presidency for Life" and his right to designate his successor. Even so, Reagan's secretary of state, George Shultz, reported to Congress in October that, "the Government of Haiti is making progress toward implementing political reforms which are essential to the development of democracy in Haiti, including the establishment of political parties, free elections, and freedom of the press."[13] Preposterous statements of this sort were typical of those made by the Reagan administration about many dictatorships that were politically aligned with the United States and, as a result, elicited relatively few raised eyebrows.

Then there was a change. Shortly after Shultz issued this statement, which was part of a report to Congress required to continue U.S. military and economic aid to Haiti, demonstrations against the Duvalier regime broke out. One of them in a provincial town, Gonaive, was put down when the army fired on a peaceful gathering, killing three schoolchildren and critically injuring a fourth. With the Haitian citizenry up in arms over this episode, which it had learned about through a broadcast on a Catholic Church radio station, the State Department let it be known in December that it might not be able to continue to certify that the conditions for U.S. aid were being met in Haiti. In January 1986, the Department took the next step and declared that it would no longer certify. Withdrawal of U.S. support led to an intensification of the protests and, on February 7, 1986— not long after Duvalier declared memorably that his rule of the country was "as strong as a monkey's tail"—the "President for Life" fled Haiti.[14] Subsequent to his departure, Haiti has been intermittently democratic, but has fared badly. By far the most impoverished country in the Western hemisphere, it has secured little support from the United States. The main focus of U.S. policy since the end of the Cold War, when its geopolitical alignment no longer mattered, has been to limit undocumented Haitian migration to the United States and, secondarily, to limit Haiti's use as a way station for drug trafficking. When a devastating earthquake struck in early 2010, the United States led the way in providing international assistance, but the Haitian government was so weak and ineffectual that it had great difficulty using the aid to good advantage.

In the case of the Philippines, American policy up to 1985 had been shaped by the concern of successive administrations not to jeopardize U.S. relations with a country that was the site of major Air Force and Navy bases. While Jimmy Carter was president, Patricia Derian had struggled to limit U.S. support because of systematic human rights abuses. In this case, however, she was thwarted by State Department officials, led by Richard Holbrooke, then the assistant secretary of state for East Asia, who focused on security interests. Those interests contributed to the muted reaction of the Reagan administration in 1983 when opposition political leader Benigno Aquino, the father of the country's current president, was assassinated at the airport on his return to the country from exile.

Following the Aquino assassination, the human rights situation in the country continued to deteriorate and, in 1985, the Reagan administration—which had up to then been a firm supporter of the corrupt and dictatorial Filipino president, Ferdinand Marcos—began to speak out critically. That November, Reagan sent Senator Paul Laxalt of Nevada to Manila to deliver a letter to Marcos about the deteriorating situation. In an effort to shore up his own power, Marcos set a presidential election for February 1986, a year-and-a-half ahead of schedule.

The Reagan administration's increasing commitment to electoral democracy was demonstrated in the president's request that Senator Richard Lugar of Indiana head a delegation to observe the election. It was marked by massive fraud and extensive violence as Marcos pretended that he had prevailed. Reagan's own lack of enthusiasm for a process that would result in the ouster of Marcos was indicated in his public assertion that there had been fraud on both sides. That had the effect of prolonging Marcos's hold on his post, but it produced denunciations from human rights organizations, members of Congress, and from the press in the United States. The outcry forced the Reagan administration, after a great deal of bloodshed in the Philippines, to tell Marcos that it was time to go. He was given refuge in Hawaii (Duvalier went to France). In the aftermath of Marcos, the Reagan administration was supportive of the administration of President Corazon Aquino, widow of the assassinated Benigno Aquino, who defeated Marcos in the February 1986 election in which he had tried to claim victory.

In Chile, the constitution that had been promulgated by a decree of President Augusto Pinochet provided that his role would be extended for eight years at a time on the basis of a national plebiscite. There would be no opposition candidate, only a "yes" or "no" vote. Pinochet conducted such a plebiscite in 1980 and, as his critics had no opportunity to express their views through the media, to hold rallies, or otherwise to reach voters, had no difficulty in prevailing. Another plebiscite was scheduled for 1988, Reagan's last year in office.

In keeping with its commitment to promote democracy, forcefully set out in the speech at Westminster in 1982 and then evolving further during the latter part of Reagan's tenure, the administration made statements calling on the Chilean government to allow opponents of Pinochet an opportunity to reach voters through the media. Eventually, Pinochet agreed to allow those favoring a "no" vote in the plebiscite five minutes on national television every day during the period leading up to the election. In addition, opponents of Pinochet, though still restricted in many ways, were given far greater latitude to campaign than eight years earlier. The National Endowment for Democracy contributed a million dollars to nongovernmental groups in Chile for voter education.

The plebiscite was set for October 5, 1988. As the date approached, Pinochet became aware that he was likely to lose. At the last moment, he prepared a coup that involved cancellation of the plebiscite. The U.S. Ambassador to Chile, Harry Barnes, who took up his duties in Santiago in 1985 at the start of Reagan's second term, learned what was planned and alerted Washington. Since his arrival, Barnes had made clear his own espousal of the restoration of democracy in Chile and had established close ties to Chilean human rights organizations, a stance in sharp contrast to the performance of the Reagan administration during the President's first term. Backing up Barnes, Deputy Secretary of State John Whitehead summoned the Chilean ambassador in Washington to his office and insisted that the plebiscite should go forward. In addition, the State Department contacted Pinochet's fellow military commanders in Chile to deliver the same message. The plebiscite was held as scheduled and Pinochet was defeated 55 percent to 45 percent, paving the way for the restoration of democratic government. Today, Chile is widely regarded as the most successful democracy in Latin America.

Pinochet's defeat in the October 1988 plebiscite, followed by the successful conduct of contested elections in Chile in March 1990 that were won by the opposition to Pinochet, may be considered the culmination of a remarkable series of transitions in Latin America and East Asia in the 1980s, in which one right-wing military dictatorship after another gave way to democratic governments that were significantly more respectful of human rights. In Latin America, dramatic improvements in human rights took place in Argentina, Brazil, Uruguay, and Honduras, as well as Chile. In Guatemala, where human rights abuses had reached genocidal proportions in the early 1980s under the military rule of Generals Romeo Lucas García (1978–82) and Efrain Rios Montt (1982–83) and then had abated somewhat under the next military dictator, General Oscar Mejía Victores (1983–86), civilian democratic rule began in January 1986 with the election of President Vinicio Cerezo the previous December. By most standards, Guatemala under Cerezo's democratic government and that of his elected successors continued to be a dangerous place from a human rights standpoint, but the violence was not comparable to what it had been under the various military dictatorships. A shift towards democracy took place in Peru as well, but it did not lead to any measure of improvement in the human rights situation. On the contrary, the advent of democracy was marked by the beginning of armed struggle against a messianic Maoist guerrilla movement, Sendero Luminoso (Shining Path), with a concomitant substantial increase in human rights abuses by both sides in the conflict. The presidency of Alberto Fujimori (1990–2000) was particularly marked by violations, many of them quite serious. Early in the 1990s, armed conflicts in El Salvador and Nicaragua came to an end, and substantial reductions in human rights abuses took place in these two war-ravaged Central American countries.

In East Asia, a few right-wing military dictatorships were supplanted by democratic governments during this same period. Following the fall of Ferdinand Marcos's dictatorship in the Philippines in 1986, President Chun Doo Hwan, the military leader of South Korea, was forced to resign in 1987. Chun's fall may be attributed, at least in part, to the Olympic games that were scheduled to take place in Seoul a year later. Playing host to the Olympics was the cause of great pride to many Koreans, who saw the games as an opportunity to show the world their country's achievements. Though overshadowed in world recognition by its neighbors, China and Japan, Korea had made immense headway economically since its devastation and impoverishment less than four decades earlier during the Korean War. By the late 1980s, Seoul was a shining contemporary city, and most South Koreans were relatively well off. In 1987 a giant electronic billboard was erected in the center of Seoul that counted off the number of days remaining until the Olympics.

The one cloud on the horizon was the country's reputation for human rights abuses. Posters appeared in various parts of the world with the tag line: Torture is Not an Olympic Sport. There had been boycotts of the Olympics in Moscow in 1980 (over the Soviet Union's invasion of Afghanistan) and in Los Angeles in 1984 (in retaliation for the American boycott of the Moscow Olympics), and there seemed a distinct possibility of a boycott of the 1988 Seoul Olympics over human rights abuses. University students in Seoul who opposed the Chun dictatorship took advantage of the situation to hold demonstrations against the regime.

On previous occasions when students demonstrated, the dictatorship in South Korea had cracked down violently. The most notorious episode took place in the southwestern city of Kwangju in 1980, where as many as two thousand students and other demonstrators were massacred by the police in putting down a demonstration. Clearly the Chun government could not react in the same manner in 1987. The world's eyes were on South Korea because of the forthcoming Olympics, and a violent crackdown would have greatly increased the likelihood of a boycott. The demonstrations got larger and larger, but Chun's forces could only respond with plastic shields and with teargas (one student was killed when a teargas canister hit him in the head, the only known death during these demonstrations). Increasingly, non-students joined the demonstrations, with the numbers reaching as many as a quarter of a million persons at their peak. Caught between the need not to take any action that would endanger the Olympics so ardently desired by most Koreans and the inability to control the demonstrations, President Chun was forced to resign. He did so in a speech apologizing to the nation for human rights abuses and corruption, and then committed himself to a monastery. His resignation inaugurated a shift to democratic government and produced a dramatic improvement in the human rights situation.

In Taiwan, political reform took place in a far less dramatic and confrontational manner. In July 1987, the same month that Chun resigned in South Korea, President Chiang Ching-Kuo lifted martial law, which had been imposed thirty-eight years earlier by his father, General Chiang Kai-shek. The decree was replaced by a National Security Law that contained explicit guarantees of individual rights. At the time, President Chiang was seventy-seven years old and in ill health. Though there had been protests in Taiwan, his actions were not forced upon him. Rather, they seemed a prudent response to the improvement of relations between China and Taiwan's protector, the United States; and to the emergence of a domestic political opposition movement intent on pursuing a peaceful democratic transition. Shifts towards democracy and increased respect for human rights in other countries of the region probably influenced events in Taiwan.

In certain respects, the moves away from right-wing military dictatorships and systematic abuses of human rights in Latin America and East Asia during the 1980s were as remarkable as the collapse of the communist regimes of Eastern and Central Europe at the end of the decade. Though the kinds of abuses that were characteristic of the right-wing dictatorships and those committed by the communist governments differed greatly, the changes were of comparable significance in producing human rights improvement. Of course, the changes in the communist countries also produced an end to the Cold War. By ending the military standoff between East and West, while at the same time reducing the involvement of the two sides in proxy shooting wars in Africa, Asia, and Latin America, those changes had greater geopolitical significance. Yet the momentous events symbolized by the fall of the Berlin Wall should not obscure the historic importance of events in other parts of the world in roughly the same period.

As indicated previously, the dramatic shifts away from right-wing military dictatorships that took place in Latin America and East Asia in the 1980s were related to the shifts away from communist dictatorships in Central and Eastern Europe in the same era. Because the struggle of the West against communism since about the mid-1970s had focused increasingly on denunciations of human rights abuses by governments linked to Moscow, violations of rights by their own geopolitical allies became more and more embarrassing to Western states. This was particularly true in the case of the United States. Washington spearheaded criticism of Soviet-backed governments for systematic violations of rights, especially during the presidency of Ronald Reagan (1981–89). As made manifest by the actions of his administration during his second term, Reagan's commitment to promote democracy also led Washington to withdraw support from dictatorial regimes it had previously backed. If the Carter administration's policies were responsible for contributing to the collapse of authoritarian dictatorships friendly to the United States, as had been alleged in 1979 by Jeane Kirkpatrick, the policies of the president who appointed Kirkpatrick on the basis of her criticism of Carter ultimately had similar consequences, and in a larger number of countries. Carter was often an eager proponent of human rights. Reagan was, at most, a reluctant convert to the cause, at least so far as abuses by right-wing governments were concerned. In practice, however, their successive presidencies may be regarded as a period in which the promotion of human rights became an institutionalized component of American foreign policy. The American-based international human rights movement, which first became a factor in the making of foreign policy during the Carter years, had a leading role in requiring the Reagan administration to abandon the policies with which it came into office in 1981 and instead help to perpetuate efforts to foster human rights during its later years.

Developments in the early 1990s, after the end of Reagan's presidency, continued along the same path in at least two countries in different parts of the world, El Salvador and South Africa. Throughout the 1980s, because of the great number of death-squad killings that took place in El Salvador, and also because of a number of large-scale military massacres of peasants thought to be sympathetic to the Marxist guerrillas battling the military regime, the small Central American country was a leading international symbol of right-wing human rights abuses. A particularly horrifying crime took place in the country's capital, San Salvador, on November 16, 1989. Soldiers raided the campus of the country's Jesuit university, the University of Central America, focusing on the residence of the clerics who headed the university's faculty. Six Jesuit priests, their housekeeper, and the housekeeper's daughter were executed by the soldiers. On previous occasions when comparably outrageous crimes had been committed in El Salvador, U.S. government officials had either denied that they took place at all or had attempted to explain them away. At first, it seemed that this situation would be treated in the same way. The U.S. ambassador to El Salvador, William Walker, speculated publicly that the killings were the work of the guerrillas, the FMLN. He suggested that they committed the murders in order that they be blamed on the armed forces, thereby discrediting them. The assistant secretary of state for inter-American affairs, Bernard Aronson, said that they were the work of the "violent right."[15] Aronson's statement, like that of Ambassador Walker, was apparently intended to exculpate the armed forces.

This time, however, the United States had to retreat quickly from this position. The killings took place just a week after the fall of the Berlin Wall, and even members of the U.S. Congress who had been strong supporters of the Salvadoran military out of Cold War considerations no longer considered it crucial to serve as apologists for such crimes. By January 1990, both the administration of President George H. W. Bush and the Salvadoran government had conceded that the armed forces carried out the murders.

The episode figured significantly in signals that the Bush administration sent to the Salvadoran military that U.S. support was coming to an end. Those signals made the military more amenable to a negotiated settlement of the war than it had been previously. As it happened, geopolitical developments had a similar effect on the Salvadoran guerrillas. The end of the Cold War made communist governments less eager to provide support for such insurgencies. Also, aid to the Salvadoran guerrillas from the Soviet Union and Cuba had flowed through the Sandinista regime in nearby Nicaragua. That government's loss of power in an election in February 1990, and changes in the Soviet Union, meant that aid to the guerrillas was no longer available from those sources. With both sides in the conflict losing their principal funding, serious negotiations got underway and, by 1992, the war ended and the vast number of human rights abuses associated with the conflict declined dramatically.

In South Africa, the apartheid regime had long considered itself an outpost of the West of such importance in the Cold War struggle that it could rely on continued backing by the West. Indeed, on such grounds, both President Ronald Reagan in the United States and Prime Minister Margaret Thatcher in the United Kingdom had resisted the imposition of sanctions on South Africa. In the United States, however, in 1986, Congress imposed tough economic sanctions against South Africa in an act adopted over Reagan's veto.[16] When the Cold War ended in 1989, it was a signal to the South African government that it could no longer count on Western support. In February 1990, just three months after the fall of the Berlin Wall, President F. W. de Klerk, who had been elected the previous September, announced that Nelson Mandela would be released from prison (where he had been held for more than twenty-seven years) along with hundreds of other opponents of apartheid; that the African National Congress and other previously prohibited organizations would be legalized; and that he was ready for negotiations to adopt a new national constitution that would provide equal rights to all, regardless of race. The process by which South Africa would be transformed by the election in which Mandela became President in 1994 was underway.

Looking back on those years, it now seems that the period of the 1980s and the very beginning of the 1990s, when dictatorships right and left collapsed, was a golden age in the history of human rights. A handful of those active in that era consciously struggled to take advantage of the geopolitical forces unleashed by the rising importance of human rights in the East-West struggle. In all likelihood, however, many of those active in the rights struggle were largely oblivious to the ways in which their own efforts both shaped and were shaped by those larger-scale forces. The impact of their efforts was not, however, diminished by their failure to appreciate its significance in reordering global political alignments.

8

Amnesty International

AS OF OCTOBER 3, 2011

AMNESTY INTERNATIONAL, THE BEST KNOWN AND BY FAR THE largest human rights organization in the world—in membership, in global income, and in the number of its national sections—was established in London in 1961. Its creation was a major milestone in the emergence of an enduring human rights movement. From the start it was intended to be a global organization. That is, those who would participate in its efforts would come from all over the world, and those on whose behalf it campaigned would be persons everywhere who suffered abuses of human rights.

Amnesty was established at a time when Cold War tensions were at a high point. The previous October, Soviet leader Nikita Khrushchev at a meeting of the United Nations General Assembly had interrupted British prime minister Harold Macmillan by pounding his fists on the table, jumping to his feet, and shouting, "You sent your planes over our territory, you are guilty of aggression." At a subsequent session of the General Assembly, when the delegate from the Philippines said something the Soviet leader did not like, he took off his shoe, waved it at the delegate, and banged it on the table. In the United States, John F. Kennedy was sworn in as president in January 1961. A few days later, in his State of the Union address, Kennedy warned, "We must never be lulled into believing that either power [the Soviet Union or China, which were undergoing estrangement from each other at that moment] has yielded its ambition for world domination . . . ." Two days after that, the United States test-fired the Minuteman Intercontinental Ballistic Missile, which it would soon aim at the Soviet Union. Almost inevitably, the Cold War context played a crucial role in shaping a new institution that had the intention to operate worldwide and that wished to address the abuses of rights committed by those on all sides of the global struggle.

Amnesty's principal founder was Peter Benenson, a lawyer and a convert to Catholicism from a wealthy family of Russian Jews who had immigrated to England. Benenson attended Eton and Oxford and, for at least a decade and a half prior to taking the lead in the formation of Amnesty, was active in efforts to promote civil liberties. An admirer of the American Civil Liberties Union, he avoided involvement in its British counterpart, the National Council for Civil Liberties, because, in the 1950s, it was partially controlled by communists and communist sympathizers. Instead, in 1956, the year that saw the Hungarian Revolution and other challenges to Soviet subjugation of Eastern Europe, Benenson launched a group, Justice, which became the British affiliate of the International Commission of Jurists. The ICJ is a Geneva based organization established after World War II that was reliably anticommunist. For a time, in its early years, it was covertly supported by the Central Intelligence Agency.

An article Benenson said he read in a London newspaper about two students in Portugal imprisoned for toasting freedom in a Lisbon bar reportedly inspired him to publish his own article on "The Forgotten Prisoners" in another British paper, the *Observer*. At the time, the paper's editor was David Astor, a strong supporter of efforts to promote human rights who made a practice of giving prominence to articles on the subject. Astor placed Peter Benenson's article on the front page of the *Observer Weekend Review*. It was illustrated by photos of six well-known political prisoners, three held by communist dictatorships and three imprisoned by right-wing anticommunist regimes. A sidebar stated:

> On both sides of the Iron Curtain, thousands of men and women are being held in gaol without trial because their political or religious views differ from those of their Governments. Peter Benenson, a London lawyer, conceived the idea of a world campaign, APPEAL FOR AMNESTY, 1961, to urge Governments to release these people or at least give them a fair trial. The campaign opens today, and *The Observer* is glad to offer it a platform.[1]

Benenson's article described the purposes of the Appeal for Amnesty and the method it would use. Its aims were to work impartially to release those imprisoned for their views; to secure fair trials for them; to expand the right to asylum and assist political refugees in obtaining jobs; and to secure international legal protections for freedom of opinion.

Newspapers in a number of countries—among them *Le Monde*, the *Journal de Genève*, *Die Welt*, and the *New York Herald Tribune*—reprinted Benenson's article from the *Observer*, and other media reported on it. This helped to ensure that the response was international. Some of the respondents volunteered to work for the Appeal for Amnesty and others sent financial contributions. The effort was off to a flying start.

One early respondent was Sean MacBride, who four decades earlier had been a well-known fighter for Irish independence during the war for liberation from England. Subsequently, MacBride became a leading Irish political figure, a foreign minister of Ireland and, in 1974, the recipient of the Nobel Peace Prize for his efforts on behalf of human rights. MacBride also served for a period as the secretary general of the International Commission of Jurists. MacBride's mother, the Irish actress and revolutionary heroine Maud Gonne (Yeats wrote his first play, *Cathleen ni Houlihan*, for her), had herself been a campaigner against political imprisonment in her time; and his father was executed by the British in 1916 for his role in the Irish liberation struggle. Sean MacBride became the chair of Amnesty's board and one of those who helped to make it an influential organization. Another early recruit who played a leading role in the organization was the noted British civil liberties lawyer, Louis Blom-Cooper. Still going strong at this writing half a century later, Blom-Cooper was at the time the author of a regular column on legal issues in the *Observer*. Many prominent artists also responded to the Appeal for Amnesty, including the violinist Yehudi Menuhin, the sculptor Henry Moore, and the actress Julie Christie.

Amnesty International's strategy was to establish a research office in London to identify and gather information on individual "prisoners of conscience." Amnesty would then distribute information worldwide about them and the abuses they suffered. Those advocating or condoning violence, or engaged in efforts to overthrow their governments, would not be included. On this basis, Nelson Mandela, who had been designated by Amnesty as a prisoner of conscience in 1962, when he faced charges for leading a labor strike, was not considered eligible for that status subsequently as he had justified violence in the struggle against apartheid during his speech to the court in 1964, following his conviction on a charge of sabotage. It was for this crime that he spent twenty-seven years in prison.[2] The organization would publicize information about prisoners of conscience, taking care to choose those on whom it would focus from different parts of the world. The implication was that this would ensure a measure of balance, so that those on whose behalf it campaigned would be victims of abuse by both communist and anticommunist regimes, as well as by governments not aligned with the principal Cold War antagonists. Amnesty International accordingly adopted a "statute" providing that it would "at all times maintain an overall balance between its activities in relationship to countries adhering to the different world political ideologies and groups."[3]

Peter Benenson's insistence that the organization he founded should clearly articulate its intention to campaign against political imprisonment without regard to the geopolitical alignment of the governments that it confronted was soon translated into the organization's *modus operandi*. The local campaign groups that took up the cause of those identified as prisoners of conscience by Amnesty's researchers at its headquarters in London would each work on three cases: one each of prisoners held by communist, anticommunist, and nonaligned countries. They would write letters to officials of those governments, publicize the cases as best they could in their own communities, organize assistance for the families, assist released prisoners in securing asylum, and raise funds for Amnesty's research operations in London. Enlisting volunteers in such efforts proved an excellent means of recruiting members to Amnesty. Only a minority of the members took part in such volunteer activities, but a significant number did contribute time and energy as well as membership dues, and those who only supported the organization financially and by swelling the ranks of its membership apparently derived satisfaction from the knowledge that they were helping to underwrite such an extensive volunteer effort.

Many of the beneficiaries of those volunteer efforts subsequently informed Amnesty of the organization's impact on their treatment, and Amnesty used these testimonials in its promotional literature, attracting additional volunteers. Probably the statement from a former prisoner of conscience that was reproduced most widely was that of Julio de Pena Valdez, a trade union leader imprisoned by the authorities in the Dominican Republic in 1975 and reportedly held naked in an underground cell. Following his release, he wrote to Amnesty International:

> When the first two hundred letters came the guards gave me back my clothes. Then the next two hundred letters came and the prison

director came to see me. When the next pile of letters arrived, the director got in touch with his superior. The letters kept coming and coming: three thousand of them. The President was informed. The letters still kept arriving and the President called the prison and told them to let me go.

After I was released the President called me to his office for a man to man talk. He said: How is it that a trade union leader like you has so many friends all over the world? He showed me an enormous box full of letters he had received and when we parted, he gave them to me. I still have them.[4]

Even today, a half century after its founding, Amnesty relies heavily on volunteers. Some have contributed volunteer services to the organization for decades.

Amnesty grew rapidly. A year after Peter Benenson published his appeal in the *Observer*, the organization reported that it had groups working or in formation in some twenty-five countries in all parts of the world except in the Soviet bloc countries. (Later on, national sections of Amnesty were also established in some of those countries, including in the Soviet Union itself.) The organization's rapid development as an international movement reflected Benenson's eagerness to operate globally. He was especially intent on establishing operations in the Francophone countries of Europe, so that Amnesty would not be seen as an Anglo-Saxon effort. The 1962 meeting at which the decision was made to establish Amnesty International as a permanent organization was held in Luxembourg.

Though Peter Benenson led the establishment of Amnesty in 1961 and originated many of the ways of conducting its affairs that shaped the organization, he stepped aside a few years later. It is unclear to what degree his departure from its leadership was due to health reasons or to disaffection with some of the others who played prominent roles in its direction. Probably both were factors. The disaffection—in the 1980s he reconciled with the organization he had founded—apparently stemmed from concern that one of the other leaders of the organization had ties to the British government that allowed it to exercise influence. According to one history of the organization, "there was an internal fight over a damning Amnesty International report on British use of torture in Aden (now Yemen), which had been a British colony. Benenson, at this time, had handed over the day-to-day operations of Amnesty. Under his handpicked successor, Robert Swann, the report was embargoed. Benenson, who was also in poor health, suspected government infiltration of Amnesty and had the report published outside of Britain without AI's official approval."[5] Benenson was also deeply concerned about Sean MacBride's role in the ICJ following exposure of that group's ties to the CIA.[6] Yet Benenson's singular achievement remains: he created an international organization that did not, like so many others, disintegrate or fade away when its founding figure or charismatic leader passed from the scene or when a core objective was achieved. Amnesty International was the first secular, cause-oriented nongovernmental organization operating worldwide that demonstrated a capacity to sustain itself through support from a large public constituency and to maintain its influence on what appears to be a permanent basis.[7] The significance of Amnesty's institutional development goes beyond the field of human rights. It is the pioneer and the model for the emergence of a distinctive phenomenon of our era: the formation of global civil society.

From the start, a crucial question for Amnesty has been its "mandate." At the outset, the organization limited itself to working on behalf of prisoners of conscience. Although he had founded the organization for that purpose, Peter Benenson soon proposed that it should also concern itself with torture. He encountered resistance from some who believed that the organization's success depended on the narrowness and singleness of its focus. Many of those incarcerated worldwide who suffered torture did not qualify as prisoners of conscience. They had advocated or engaged in violence. Yet Benenson prevailed and, as a consequence, the issue with which Amnesty International is most identified in the minds of many around the world is its campaigns against torture. Some years after it began documenting individual cases of torture, Amnesty began publishing global reports on the subject. As the author of a leading work on torture, Darius Rejali, pointed out in a 2007 book, "Comprehensive public auditing began in 1973 when Amnesty International issued its *Report on Torture*. . . . The report's impact was greatly facilitated by the military coup in Chile that year, which focused world attention on torture, and Amnesty used the new global attentiveness to broaden its antitorture campaign. Annual global audits now became a standard feature of Amnesty's efforts to move governments and the United Nations to enforce greater compliance with international human rights norms."[8]

One indication of the impact and significance of Amnesty's 1973 report on torture was, writes Edward Peters, "illustrated by a *New York Times* story dated 4 December 1973. The *Times* reported that UNESCO had denied Amnesty International use of UNESCO facilities in Paris for its planned conference on torture in the wake of the 1973 Report, because many countries represented in UNESCO were unfavorably mentioned in the Report, and UNESCO had a general rule that 'an outside conference at UNESCO can not use material unfavorable to any member state.' In fact, Amnesty had named more than sixty countries, from democracies to police states, that used torture systematically."[9]

In 1973, a decade or so after Amnesty took on the issue of torture, and the year that it published the report that helped focus world attention on the subject, the organization expanded its mandate once again to take on the issue of capital punishment. This aroused far more controversy within Amnesty. One of the Americans who resigned over this stand was conservative commentator William F. Buckley, Jr. In subsequent years, long debates—some of them lasting for years—took place over further extensions of the mandate.

The decision to take on the issue of capital punishment was only made after careful deliberation that reflected the concern about expansion of its mandate that had characterized Amnesty for most of its history. The group's deliberate approach was described in 1994 by Peter Baehr from the Netherlands, a long-time member of the organization's International Executive Committee:

> Political impartiality is seen as contributing to Amnesty's credibility and thus to its effectiveness. The need for maintaining its political impartiality as well as the wish to avoid even the *appearance* of such partiality, was the main reason why Amnesty has not found it possible to condemn the best known legally based system of human rights violations in the world: Apartheid in South Africa. It wanted to avoid having to take up all kinds of discriminatory legislation in other parts of the world as well and limited itself to ". . . condemning and opposing those laws and practices of Apartheid which permit the imprisonment of people on grounds of conscience or race; the denial of fair trial to political prisoners; torture; or the death penalty." This compromise text was arrived at with considerable difficulty. It has been challenged at regular intervals at meetings of the membership. Especially African members of the organization, but also members of other sections have found it difficult to accept that Amnesty did not outright condemn Apartheid.[10]

From time to time, questions arose within Amnesty about one of the central tenets of its mandate: its insistence that it would not include those who had advocated or condoned violence among persons it identified as prisoners of conscience. The issue periodically arose in connection with South Africa, and it came up at a conference at which some seventy writers from all over the world gathered in Toronto in October 1981 to discuss how they could aid the work of Amnesty International. The participants included such prominent authors as Margaret Atwood, Hans Magnus Enzensberger, Allen Ginsberg, Nadine Gordimer, and Susan Sontag. A question was placed to Nadine Gordimer from the floor:

> A couple of years ago, Amnesty International put out a report on South Africa, and as we all know Amnesty International always draws the line at violence. All its publications state that it is seeking to defend writers who are prisoners of conscience, people who have never at any time advocated violence. In its report on South Africa, Amnesty International describes the conditions for blacks. There is a detailed description of the arrests, the imprisonment, the banishment, the exiling: there are descriptions and photographs of torture and of the bodies of prisoners who have died in prison. And the report meditates that for a black South African living in these conditions, there is no alternative to advocating a revolutionary uprising. In fact, Miss Gordimer, you describe such an uprising in your latest novel. Now what I get from reading that report is that a black South African, to attain freedom, has in effect to advocate violence. So how can one draw the line at violence?

Several of the participants in the meeting attempted to respond to this question. One of them was Joshua Rubenstein, a long-time staff member of the U.S. section of Amnesty, known for his expertise on Soviet abuses of rights. Rubenstein said:

> I would like to clarify Amnesty's position on violence. Amnesty works for the release of prisoners of conscience, people who are in jail for their religious or political beliefs, who have not used or advocated the use of violence. Sometimes this issue becomes cloudy—for instance, when people are in a war and then years later get involved in this or that activity: their participation in violence in wartime does

not in any way disqualify them from becoming prisoners of conscience later, like General Grigorenko in the Soviet Union . . . . But if people are in what are sometimes dubbed revolutionary groups, and these groups are engaged in violence, if they're actual members, then Amnesty has to decide whether their arrest is associated with specific incidents of violence or advocacy of violence. We actually have a committee to clarify these borderline cases. Amnesty is not a pacifist organization. It doesn't demand anything of anyone, except that prisoners of conscience be released, that there be no torture, that there be no executions. We are not judging a revolutionary's use of violence; we're simply saying that our organization cannot adopt them as prisoners of conscience. And we don't mean to deprive anyone of the right to self-defense. It may be that blacks in South Africa have no choice but to engage in violent revolutionary activities; but if they're caught we can't define them as prisoners of conscience—they're something else. They may still deserve the support of many well-meaning people, but they're not prisoners of conscience by our definition.[11]

One debate over the mandate involved the question of whether to promote compliance with international humanitarian law. This was resisted by some of Amnesty's leaders, who believed that their efforts to address such issues as imprisonment for the peaceful expression of opinion and torture derived legitimacy from the prohibition of such practices by the Universal Declaration of Human Rights and by U.N.–sponsored treaties that followed and gave legal force to the Declaration. As international humanitarian law had developed outside the United Nations system, and as no U.N. body had responsibility for attempting to secure compliance, some in Amnesty apparently believed that efforts by their organization in this field would lack legitimacy.

Another factor may have played a comparable or perhaps even a larger role in the reluctance by many in Amnesty International to embrace a commitment to promoting compliance with international humanitarian law. Amnesty's ethos from the start was centered on close identification with the individual victims of human rights abuses on whom its work focused.[12] At the outset, these were the prisoners of conscience. Somewhat later on they were joined by torture victims, victims of disappearances and extrajudicial killings, political prisoners denied fair trials, and then by those sentenced to death and awaiting execution. A shift to deal with international humanitarian law, which regulates the practices that combatants may engage in during armed combat, would change that focus. In the circumstances of armed conflict, it is rarely possible to single out a particular individual and to campaign for the rights of that individual. Rather, the focus turns to such practices as indiscriminate bombardment or attacks on civilians en masse. For the most part, campaigners concerned with violations of the laws of armed conflict do not even discover the names of those whose rights they try to protect. Rarely are they able to identify with the individuals whose suffering they take up. Ultimately, after debating the question for a decade or so, Amnesty did decide to monitor violations of international humanitarian law. Arguably, the fact that it took so long contributed to the emergence of Human Rights Watch as an effective competitor in its capacity to influence public policy. When armed conflicts took place in the 1980s and in the early 1990s in such places as Central America, Afghanistan, Sri Lanka, Ethiopia, and Sudan, Human Rights Watch was alone in providing governments, journalists, and the general public with reliable reporting on violations of the laws of armed conflict by the combatants. Amnesty addressed matters that fell within its mandate that took place during these conflicts such as targeted disappearances; but only Human Rights Watch provided systematic reporting on such indiscriminate practices as bombings of villages as a counterinsurgency measure. If it had not had this field to itself in that era, it might have had far more difficulty building its rapidly growing reputation among those seriously concerned with international public affairs.

Another consequence of Amnesty International's lengthy debate over whether to extend its mandate to address violations of international humanitarian law is that it long considered that, because international human rights law only applies to governments, it did not have a legal basis for reporting on abuses by guerrilla organizations opposing governments. Though this probably did not damage the organization in most parts of the world, it did provide its antagonists in the Reagan administration in the United States an opportunity to criticize Amnesty for being one-sided in is reporting on countries such as El Salvador and Guatemala, where internal armed conflicts were underway. Later on, in 1991, even before embracing international humanitarian law, Amnesty adjusted its mandate to give it a basis for denouncing guerrilla organizations for such practices as torture, disappearances, and extrajudicial executions.

Amnesty International's historic focus on individual victims of abuse served the organization very well in another respect, however. It gave the organization a much higher level of popular support than was enjoyed by other organizations concerned with human rights or, for that matter, with almost any other secular cause. Unlike more recent entrants into the human rights field, Amnesty International derives by far the largest part of its income from contributions by its members. The members give to their national sections and, in turn, the national sections remit a portion of the contributions they collect to the International Secretariat in London. With those remittances, the International Secretariat serves as the research arm for the entire institution. It does not raise significant funds from other sources. Over time, the funds obtained primarily in this manner have greatly enhanced the capacity of the Secretariat also to launch and manage campaigns. For the most part, campaigning is conducted in collaboration with the national sections.

Early on, Amnesty International developed a rule that limited volunteers' campaigning on behalf of prisoners of conscience to cases outside their own countries. Over time, however, the organization has enlarged the role of national sections so that they address a range of issues in their own countries. The shift began in the 1970s, when the organization took on the question of capital punishment. National sections also address their own governments' policies in dealing with refugees and the right to asylum. Dealing with such questions in their own countries provides additional volunteer opportunities for many Amnesty members. As the number of prisoners of conscience worldwide has declined—due in part to the efforts of Amnesty International—it is useful to the organization to have other issues of concern that may be addressed by volunteers.

Aside from providing Amnesty with a dependable and substantial source of income, Amnesty's membership endows it with a certain legitimacy that other groups lack. The ability to speak on behalf of millions of dues paying members all over the world is a great asset. Also, Amnesty has made a point of not allowing contributions from other sources to "loom large in its finances." Groups that depend on financial support or contributions from foundations, wealthy individuals, and, in the case of some organizations, from governments, are unable to use this backing to establish their legitimacy. Instead, they point to the international legal norms with which they promote compliance. Amnesty does this, but it also cites its worldwide membership.

Amnesty International's greatest asset is its moral authority. That authority, which some critics would say has declined to an extent in the past two decades—though even most of those critical of particular actions would acknowledge Amnesty retains authority to a significant degree—derives in substantial part from the work of its researchers. The researchers at the International Secretariat, from an early point in the organization's history, tended to be highly qualified and well informed on the countries on which they reported, even though the rule is that, to avoid political bias, they do not report on their own countries. Also, the researchers have worked hard to ensure that the information they report is reliable. And, they generally have not had to meet the kinds of deadlines that are required of journalists. Reports are issued when they are ready and judged to meet the organization's standards.[13] Another factor also played an important role: the researchers deliberately avoid sensationalism. This has made the reports more authoritative. The awarding of the Nobel Peace Prize to Amnesty International in 1977 further enhanced the moral stature that derives from the organization's reporting.

Many of those with a long association with the organization particularly admired Thomas Hammarberg, a Swede who served for a number of years as head of the research office and was subsequently designated in 1980 as secretary general.[14] Hammarberg's farewell talk when he stepped down from that post in 1986 to return to Sweden reflects the understated professionalism that he brought to the post. It was a professionalism that did not conflict with the institution's volunteer character. Rather, he honored "amateurs" and the amateur spirit that played such an important role in shaping Amnesty's ethos. Hammarberg said:

We are growing, we are getting more money, we make many more travels than before, we are more important than ever. This is fine. But, let us not be carried away by that, and let's not be corrupted by it. Corruption is not a big nasty beast, sleeping outside the airlock here.[15] Something that you can readily identify and could protect yourself against—keep outside. Corruption is invisible, corruption is creepy, corruption is very contagious. It often starts with friendship relationships but it spreads easily. Money of course is one aspect but only one aspect. We work on money that people have given us on trust, those who give Amnesty International money, who finance our work, our salaries here, they give it because they believe that that very power is going to the business of release of prisoners. That means that we must maintain a moral here to be careful of money. . . . But there are other things than money. I don't think we should go to unnecessary conferences and mingle too much with the false diplomatic world. I don't think that we should allow ourselves to begin to personalize our work, because we are only representatives. We should stay amateurs, that's what it is about.[16]

Thomas Hammarberg's leadership of Amnesty International was complemented by the role played in the organization by José (Pepe) Zalaquett, a Chilean lawyer with a generous, spirited, outgoing personality and a passionate commitment to the arts, who had been forcibly exiled from his own country. Zalaquett had served as Legal Director of the Vicaría de la Solidaridad in Chile and was imprisoned there in 1975 and expelled from the country the following year. In exile, he was elected to serve on the international executive committee of Amnesty International and, in 1979, to serve as chair. He stepped down from that post to become deputy executive director from 1983 to 1985. In those posts, Zalaquett served as the organization's inspirational leader[17] and, with Hammarberg, contributed to the organization's fastest growth, both in membership and influence. When Amnesty was awarded the Nobel Peace Prize in December 1977, the organization reported that it had 168,000 members in 107 countries.[18] Five years later, by the beginning of 1983, Amnesty could claim about three times as many members, or more than 500,000 in over 160 countries.[19] No doubt, the publicity resulting from the Nobel Prize contributed to the rapid growth.

In 1986, with the assistance of the American ambassador to Chile, Harry Barnes, Zalaquett was permitted to return to his country after a decade in exile. In Chile, he remained active in Amnesty International, serving for a period as chair of the country's national section. He also played a leading role in the Truth and Reconciliation Commission established following the end of Pinochet's rule and the restoration of democracy; and later served as a member of the Organization of American States Inter-American Commission on Human Rights and, for a period, as the Commission's president. Many of those in different countries who became active in the human rights cause in the 1970s and the 1980s looked to Zalaquett as their movement's most charismatic leader, and also as one of its moral and intellectual architects.

Amnesty developed more rapidly in Europe than in the United States. When it did establish an American presence, however, its impact was substantial. Writing about its effect on America's policies towards Latin America in the 1970s in a book published in 1981, Lars Schoultz, a political scientist who studied the question closely, said:

It is difficult to overestimate the influence of the AI reports on U.S. human rights policy during the 1970s. With a Nobel Peace Prize added to its credits and a reputation for impartial documentation of human rights abuses around the globe, AI helped to create a receptive attitude among members of Congress to general human rights legislation and to country specific reductions in foreign assistance. In particular, AI publicity contributed significantly to a change in the nature of the debate over United States policy towards Argentina, Chile, and specifically Uruguay. Prior to the AI report on obscure Uruguay, the debate in the United States focused upon whether Uruguay deserved to be singled out as a gross violator; after the report, it centered on what the response should be to the accepted fact that the Uruguayan government was among the most repressive on earth.... In the 1970s, the debate over U.S. policy toward repressive governments was sometimes won or lost on the empirical question of the severity of human rights violations. This was the question AI could answer with authority.[20]

At least so far as its influence on American policy is concerned, the late 1970s and the early 1980s, when Amnesty International was led by Thomas Hammarberg and José Zalaquett, and when its efforts were recognized by the award of the Nobel Peace Prize, and while the groups that evolved into such organizations as Human Rights Watch and Human Rights First were still in their infancy, was probably the highest point. Those associated with Amnesty International during its period of greatest influence also tend to speak highly of the tenure of Hammarberg's successor, Ian Martin, who went on to a number of leading U.N. posts in the human rights field after serving as AI's Secretary General. Under his leadership, the organization maintained and even added to the moral authority that it had previously achieved. The organization has continued thereafter to play an influential role in American thinking and public policy, in part because the membership of the U.S. section is the most substantial body of those in the country who have organized to promote rights internationally. In addition, the influential role played by Amnesty International in the late 1970s and the early 1980s is of lasting significance in the United States because that was the era in which the principal American laws were adopted requiring the foreign policy practices designed to promote human rights internationally. It is also the period in which the different approaches of the Carter and Reagan administrations combined to make concern for human rights a long-term, or permanent, feature of America's approach to its role in world affairs.

Those who question whether the organization has lost some of its moral authority generally cite two developments. First, while the reporting by the researchers has not diminished in quality and is as unemotional in style as ever, the materials produced by Amnesty's campaign staff are replete with the adjectives avoided by the researchers. The campaigners sometimes seem to sensationalize the work of the researchers. A more important factor cited by critics is that two recent occupants of the post of secretary general of Amnesty International, Pierre Sané of Senegal and Irene Khan of Bangladesh, sometimes spoke out publicly in ways that seemed to some to politicize the organization. (In 2010, a new secretary general, Salil Shetty of India, was designated. Though his background is international development assistance rather than human rights, early assessments of Shetty by some of those committed to Amnesty's historic nonpolitical core mission are enthusiastic. In his first year, in contrast to the previous two decades, Amnesty's reports focusing on core human rights issues such as political imprisonment and torture were consistently cited in the press. It played an important role also in reporting on efforts by governments to crush the protests that marked the Arab revolutions of 2011.) Both Sané and Khan experienced internal dissension from members of the staff concerned that the contributions of the researchers were undervalued and that the focus on individual victims of abuses had diminished. The author of a book on Amnesty International, Stephen Hopgood, entitled it *Keepers of the Flame*, a reference to those within the organization who have struggled to maintain the organization's traditional values against what they see as tendencies that detract from its moral authority.[21]

Some of the criticism of Amnesty's purported politicization during the tenure of Irene Khan as secretary general seems excessive. An example involves attacks on the assertion in the organization's annual report for 2005 that the detention of prisoners at Guantanamo is "the gulag of our times." The reference to the gulag was not a good idea. However abusive it has been to detain several hundred men suspected of involvement in terrorism for extended periods without charges or trial, it does not warrant comparison to the detention of millions under appalling conditions, often resulting in their deaths, because they were suspected of political dissent. Like comparisons to Nazi crimes, references to the gulag should be avoided except in the most extreme cases. At the same time, the criticism of Amnesty published in an editorial in the *Washington Post* also seems hyperbolic. "It is always sad," the newspaper opined, "when a solid trustworthy institution loses its bearings and joins in the partisan fracas that nowadays passes for political discourse. It's particularly sad when the institution is Amnesty International, which for more than 40 years has been a tough, single-minded defender of political prisoners around the world and a scourge of left- and right-wing dictators alike."[22] Neither the claim that Amnesty had lost its bearings nor that it was partisan was warranted. The editorial exaggerated in denouncing Amnesty, just as Amnesty exaggerated in suggesting an analogy to the gulag.

The flurry of attention to Irene Khan's statement about the gulag probably contributed to a trend that had already been noted in prior years: namely, a decline in the organization's prestige in the United States to a level below its very high standing in Europe. A Harvard Business School case study of the Amnesty "brand" notes: "In a study conducted by Edelman PR in January 2003, Amnesty International ranked number one in terms of public trust among brands in Europe, above all other NGOs and major corporations such as Microsoft, Coca-Cola, Nike and McDonald's. In the United States, the Amnesty brand ranked 10th in brand trust, behind the major U.S. corporations and the World Wildlife Fund, and just behind Nike."[23]

More worrying than occasional rhetorical excess to some of those who have valued Amnesty International's powerful role in the promotion of human rights is the increasing emphasis the organization is placing on economic and social issues instead of its long-standing core concerns: imprisonment for reasons of conscience, unfair trials, torture, extrajudicial executions, disappearances, and the death penalty. The shift in the organization's focus was exemplified by the introduction written by outgoing secretary general Irene Khan for the "Amnesty International Report 2009: The State of the World's Human Rights." Khan's twelve-page essay entitled "It's Not Just the Economy, It's a Human Rights Crisis," barely mentioned Amnesty International's traditional concerns. Instead, its focus was on the shortages of food, jobs, clean water, land, and housing that it attributes to government abandonment of economic regulation in the interest of market forces. Though this may or may not be valid as social or economic analysis, it did raise questions about Amnesty International's special qualifications to address such issues and whether such a focus diverts energy and resources from the abuses of rights it was founded to address and that continue in widespread practice in much of the world. Khan's essay concludes:

It is to people power that we must now turn to bring pressure to bear on our political leaders. That is why, together with many local, national and international partners, Amnesty International is launching a new campaign in 2009. Under the banner of "Demand Dignity," we will mobilize people to seek accountability . . . for human rights abuses that drive and deepen poverty. We will challenge discriminatory laws, policies and practices, and demand concrete measures to overcome the factors that impoverish and keep people poor. We will bring the voices of the people living in poverty to the center of the debate to end poverty and insist that they are allowed to participate actively in decisions that affect their lives.

Almost 50 years ago, Amnesty International was created to demand the release of "prisoners of conscience." Today we also "demand dignity" for prisoners of poverty so that they can change their own lives. I am confident that with the help and support of our millions of members, supporters and partners around the world we will succeed.[24]

At this writing, Amnesty International is probably somewhat less influential, both in the United States and globally, than it was at its high point in the 1970s and the 1980s. Some would argue that this reflects the extension or dilution of its mandate to cover the full range of human rights issues, including economic and social rights. Many more would say it reflects the shortcomings of the leadership of the international secretariat during the last years of the twentieth century and the first decade of the twenty-first century, and they are optimistic that if the organization turns out to be fortunate in its current secretary general, as appears to be the case, it could readily recover much of its former prestige. That process may well be already underway. Others suggest that the decline in Amnesty's preeminence is based on the rise of newer human rights organizations and their closer identification with issues that have risen to the top of the international human rights agenda. Globally, the issues that have been most significant are violations of the laws of armed conflict, accountability for past gross abuses, and violations of human rights in the struggle against terrorism. In the United States and the United Kingdom, the latter of these issues has been the foremost concern for those addressing human rights issues since the September 11, 2001 terrorist attacks on New York and Washington, DC, and since President George W. Bush launched the global war on terror in response. Amnesty International has not been so prominent as Human

Rights Watch in dealing with violations of the laws of armed conflict; nor so significant as Human Rights Watch or a newer organization, the International Center for Transitional Justice, in struggles over accountability; nor as central to debates over counterterrorism policies as Human Rights First and domestic civil liberties bodies such as the American Civil Liberties Union and the Center for Constitutional Rights in the U.S. and Liberty in the U.K. Amnesty continues to be the foremost organization worldwide promoting the rights of individual victims of human rights abuse; and its country reporting and advocacy on abuses in particular countries are comparable to that of Human Rights Watch in significance. Though these remain crucial concerns of the international human rights agenda, they are not so dominant as once was the case. Concomitantly, Amnesty International no longer spearheads the international human rights movement as it did a generation earlier. It is indeed no longer possible for any single institution to do so. And though it may no longer be *the* lead player, Amnesty remains *a* leading player in the worldwide movement.

9

Human Rights Watch

AS OF OCTOBER 3, 2011

THOUGH HUMAN RIGHTS WATCH HAS BECOME ONE OF THE TWO most important institutions for the protection of human rights worldwide, its beginnings in the late 1970s did not seem to foreshadow its subsequent development. The organization is an outgrowth of the efforts of a handful of people to address one particular human rights problem of the era. They did not plan in advance its expansion to address a full range of issues worldwide. Nor did they begin with the intent to adopt the *modus operandi* that soon came to define the organization's character. Those developments were, to a large extent, accidents of history.

There were, of course, aspects of the development of Human Rights Watch that, at least in retrospect, seem inevitable. The organization was created in the late 1970s, at a moment of burgeoning public concern, particularly in the United States, with the cause of international human rights. As the major nongovernmental organization already active in the field, Amnesty International, was based outside the United States, was not the recipient of significant financial support from well-to-do U.S. donors and private philanthropies, and did not seek such support, there was an obvious opening for a new American organization. Moreover, in that period, Amnesty's definition of its own mandate was narrow. It did not include efforts to address violations of the laws of war and, from the standpoint of many Americans who were starting to become concerned with the protection and promotion of rights internationally, it had an even more important shortcoming. It did not then consider that it should devote itself to influencing the conduct of American foreign policy. Amnesty was so concerned to operate evenhandedly that it would only have turned its focus on American foreign policy if it could do the same with respect to the foreign policy of the Soviet Union, which was impossible. In combination, these factors assured that one or another of the several international human rights organizations that were formed in the United States in that period would become an important institution in the field and would have the potential to rival Amnesty International in the leadership it could provide worldwide. The accidental factors that worked in favor of the development of Human Rights Watch included the radical political shift in the United States in 1981 from the Carter administration that espoused the human rights cause to the Reagan administration that initially disdained it; the growing need to confront violations of the laws of war in the context of the Central American wars of the 1980s; and the organization's development of a style of reporting that equipped it well to enter into political combat with officials of the Reagan administration who were intent on co-opting the human rights cause for their own Cold War purposes, and who greatly resented reporting that portrayed American client states and military forces as culpable for serious abuses.

The first component of the organization that began using the name Human Rights Watch nearly a decade later was Helsinki Watch, established in 1978. Robert L. Bernstein, the chairman and C.E.O. of Random House, had become engaged in the human rights cause as a consequence of a visit to Moscow to sign a copyright agreement with Soviet publishers. While there, he met with Russian authors published by Random House and returned with greatly heightened awareness of the persecution that some had suffered and the resolve to assist them. Back in the United States, he enlisted a number of fellow American publishers, authors such as Toni Morrison, Kurt Vonnegut, and a few others to join him in launching an organization to defend the rights of such authors. It was called the Fund for Free Expression. Helsinki Watch was an outgrowth of the Fund.

Bernstein enlisted two others, a prominent New York lawyer, Orville Schell, Jr., and the present author, who was then winding up service as executive director of the American Civil Liberties Union, as his cofounders. They obtained initial funding from the Ford Foundation and, subsequently, from the MacArthur Foundation, and launched Helsinki Watch.

At the outset, the new group's main role was to issue a number of statements denouncing Soviet abuses of rights and similar abuses by a few other countries that had also signed the Helsinki Accords (see chapter 6), such as Czechoslovakia and Poland. In an effort to show that it was not aligned with either of the opposing sides in the Cold War struggle, the new organization also published a series of reports on human rights in the United States, making critical comments whenever they seemed appropriate. Helsinki Watch sent representatives to Madrid to serve as a citizens' lobby for human rights at the conference of the thirty-five signatory governments that took place there, starting in 1980, to review progress under the 1975 Helsinki Accords and to discuss the "confidence building" measures called for in the agreement.

Political developments in different parts of the world helped to transform Helsinki Watch into what became Human Rights Watch. These included the Soviet invasion of Afghanistan in December 1979; the emergence of Solidarity in Poland in August 1980, followed by a sixteen-month period in which it enlisted much of the Polish population as members before it was declared illegal in December 1981, most of its leaders were imprisoned, and martial law was imposed by the Polish government; and, most significant for the way that Human Rights Watch evolved, the election of Ronald Reagan as president of the United States in November 1980 and his inauguration as the country's fortieth president in January 1981.

The Reagan election made it plain to the Helsinki Watch leadership that they had to broaden their mandate. That was because the new administration came into office intent on repudiating the human rights policy of the previous president, Jimmy Carter. Reagan and leading members of his administration, such as Secretary of State Alexander Haig and U.N. Ambassador Jeane Kirkpatrick, would continue to denounce the Soviet Union and other antagonists of the United States for their abuses of human rights, they made clear. They would not do the same with respect to governments aligned with the United States, however. Military dictatorships in regions such as Latin America and East and Southeast Asia, along with client states of the United States in Africa and the Middle East, would no longer be subject to criticism. To the contrary, they could expect praise for (supposedly) making progress towards democracy. Leading officials of the Reagan administration were explicit in their intent to hold governments to different standards depending on their geopolitical alignments.

The leaders of Helsinki Watch were concerned that, in such circumstances, an American organization that denounced abuses of human rights by the Soviet Union and the states it controlled, but did not also deal with abuses of human rights by regimes aligned with Washington, would lose credibility. It would be seen simply as a mouthpiece for an administration that had made clear its intention to use accounts of human rights abuse as a stick to belabor its enemies while serving as an apologist for severe abuses by its friends.

Because it seemed evident that the battle lines would be drawn most sharply in Latin America, the leaders of Helsinki Watch decided to form an Americas Watch Committee under the same roof. The two groups were in fact one and were often referred to at the time as "the Watch Committees," a plural name for a single organization. They shared offices, finances, staff, lay leadership, and the same philosophy. Americas Watch began operating in the spring of 1981, a few months after the Reagan administration came into office.

Even before that, Helsinki Watch leaders came into sharp conflict with the Reagan administration over its choice for the post of Assistant Secretary of State for Human Rights. The individual selected, Ernest Lefever, represented a point of view that differed from most others in the new administration. Where many Reagan administration officials supported denunciations of abuses by governments that were considered to be antagonists of the United States, Lefever opposed all efforts to make human rights a concern of U.S. foreign policy. As his post existed to carry out laws adopted in the mid-1970s that required the promotion of human rights, he was a preposterous choice to fill it. The nomination of Lefever was especially galling to members of Congress who had taken part in the adoption of those laws and to those Americans who were beginning to mobilize around efforts to promote human rights internationally, because he was to succeed Patricia Derian who had proved such a stalwart proponent of human rights when she held that post in the Carter administration. Helsinki Watch took the lead in organizing opposition to Lefever. Although it was rare in that era for presidential nominees for executive office to be denied confirmation,[1] the Lefever candidacy was defeated in the Senate Foreign Relations Committee by a vote of 13–4, and the administration was then forced to withdraw his nomination. The remarkable success of the then tiny international human rights movement in the United States in securing the overwhelming defeat of a nominee put forward by a president whose party also controlled the U.S. Senate—and this at the beginning of his term, when he was at the peak of his popularity—gave the movement a great lift. Helsinki Watch's key role in leading the effort to defeat Lefever greatly enhanced its own standing within that nascent movement and also with others who followed the process, such as members of Congress and their staffs, and journalists who covered developments in Washington.

One reason that Helsinki Watch was able to play a key role in the defeat of Lefever is that Amnesty, by far the largest and most influential human rights group at the time, had a policy of not supporting or opposing candidates for elective or appointive office. It did not take a stand on the nomination of Lefever, and it played no role in his defeat. Amnesty's absence from the fray left a vacuum that was filled by Helsinki Watch. The fact that Helsinki Watch had been formed to denounce human rights abuses by the Soviet Union turned out to be a great advantage. It meant that the Reagan administration could not readily depict its most effective opponent in the struggle over Lefever as a group of leftists intent on undermining the U.S. side in the Cold War struggle, which was the approach it took in response to most other critics of its human rights policies. Among those who ultimately voted against Lefever in the Senate Foreign Relations Committee were a majority of its Republican members, including its chair, Senator Charles Percy of Illinois. They were far more ready to confer with the Helsinki Watch leaders and to rely on their arguments than they were to deal with organizations that devoted most of their efforts to criticizing the human rights practices of governments aligned with the United States.

The country that loomed largest in the Senate debate over the Lefever nomination was Argentina. Ruled by a military dictatorship since 1976, the crime for which it had become particularly known was "disappearances": kidnappings by groups of men in plain clothes, traveling in unmarked vehicles, followed by torture of the victims to obtain from them the names of others who might then be designated for similar treatment, and then their murder. The bodies were secretly disposed of, and the government disavowed any knowledge of what happened to them. Pioneered in Guatemala in 1966, disappearances had become a favored practice of a number of Latin American dictatorships. It was particularly common under the military regime that ruled Argentina from 1976 to 1983.

Even before his Senate confirmation hearings, Lefever moved into the State Department and played a role in determining the Reagan administration's stand on disappearances in Argentina at a meeting of the United Nations Human Rights Commission in Geneva. By chance, it happened that the hearings in the U.S. Senate on his confirmation coincided with the publication by Random House of a book by a rare survivor of a disappearance, Argentine newspaper publisher and editor Jacobo Timerman.[2] The night before the Senate Foreign Relations Committee hearing on Lefever,

Robert Bernstein gave a small publisher's dinner for Timerman in Washington. It was attended by several members of the Senate committee. The next day, Timerman attended the hearing on Lefever and was cheered both by the audience and by some of the senators as he entered the room. A few of them had met him over dinner the previous evening, including the ranking Democrat on the committee, Senator Claiborne Pell of Rhode Island. By the time the vote on Lefever took place, it was regarded by many as *Timerman v. Lefever*. Timerman won.

The episode helped to shape the agenda of the new Americas Watch. One of its earliest efforts involved a visit to the United States by the president of the military junta that ruled Argentina, General Jorge Videla, who denied that his government was responsible for disappearances. The method had been designed for purposes of deniability, and it was standard practice for the military government to claim that those who were missing had left the country or had joined a clandestine guerrilla group. Americas Watch assembled a number of survivors of disappearances for a press conference to refute Videla, and his visit to the United States became a public relations setback for the Argentine junta.

Another country that became a focus of the early efforts of Americas Watch was Chile. When several human rights leaders were seized by the Pinochet regime in December 1981 as they left a ceremony marking international Human Rights Day, an Americas Watch representative—the present author—immediately flew to Santiago and managed to get into a prison to see some of the detainees, including one who had been severely tortured with electric shocks. The Chilean public learned about the arrests and the torture when local media published articles about the press coverage in the United States that resulted from the visit.

The largest part of the work of Americas Watch from its start, and for more than a decade thereafter, focused on Central America. Throughout that period the organization was immersed in reporting on the conflicts underway in three countries of that region: El Salvador, Nicaragua, and Guatemala. The methods that Americas Watch learned to use in trying to mitigate the rights abuses committed during those conflicts have shaped the way that Human Rights Watch has operated ever since.

Americas Watch began its engagement in Central America by seizing an opportunity. Concerned by press reports of abuses committed by the armed forces of El Salvador, the U.S. Congress adopted legislation in late 1981 mandating that the president certify that certain human rights requirements were being met by those forces and by the government of El

Salvador as a condition of further U.S. military aid; and that additional presidential certifications of compliance with those requirements should be issued every 180 days thereafter in order for aid to continue. The first certification was required on January 28, 1982.

Quickly pulling together information that had been gathered over a period of several months by a number of researchers, Americas Watch published a book-length report on January 26, 1982 demonstrating that certification was not warranted.[3] The report attracted extensive attention both on its release and thereafter, when journalists contrasted it with the brief and perfunctory report published by the Reagan administration two days later. Though less than a year old, Americas Watch had put itself on the map and, from that moment on, was a leading voice internationally on human rights in Latin America and, especially, on the wars in Central America.

The methods used in Americas Watch's reporting on the Central American wars that became the distinguishing characteristics of the work of Human Rights Watch were:

- Frequent, lengthy, well-documented reports that discussed not only findings and conclusions—the style of many previous human rights reports—but also the evidentiary basis on which the organization relied for its conclusions. That is, the reports did not merely assert that certain events had taken place. Rather they set forth the basis for Americas Watch's belief that those events had transpired. In the case of El Salvador, Americas Watch published additional reports every 180 days, always just ahead of the required presidential certification. The organization sustained its focus on countries on which it reported, and made clear that this focus would be maintained until sufficient changes had been made in the country's human rights practices to warrant relaxed scrutiny.
- Reports timed to secure maximum public attention. Often this required intense effort in a short period to take advantage of an opportunity.[4] This contrasted with the practice of Amnesty International, which often spent an extended period vetting its reports and, in that era, did not try to time them for purposes of newsworthiness.
- Reporting on violations of international humanitarian law. The first Americas Watch report to do this was its initial report on Guatemala, published in 1982, a few months after its first report on El

Salvador. This was the organization's most significant innovation, as by far the largest number of severe human rights abuses take place in the context of armed conflict.

- Reporting on abuses committed by all parties to an armed conflict. Previously, it had been the practice of those issuing human rights reports to publish only abuses by governments, as governments were the parties to international human rights agreements. But as Americas Watch initiated reporting on violations of international humanitarian law, which applies to both sides in international armed conflicts, and to guerrilla forces as well as to government forces in internal armed conflicts, it soon began reporting on guerrilla abuses. This helped the organization make clear that it was not aligned with one side in such conflicts. It was a critic of abuses, regardless of who committed them.
- Assessment of the responsibility of those supporting the parties committing abuses as well as of those actually committing abuses. In the Central American context, this ensured that Americas Watch would come into sharp conflict with the Reagan administration and, subsequently, the administration of President George H. W. Bush, on account of their support of forces in all three conflicts in the region that were guilty of severe abuses. The steadfastness of Americas Watch/Human Rights Watch in its intense debates with the Reagan and Bush administrations—which did their utmost to discredit their critics, especially those who contradicted their claims that they were promoting human rights—was another important factor in enhancing the stature and influence of the organization. It provided public visibility that Americas Watch/Human Rights Watch could not have obtained in any other way.
- Scrupulous care in the compilation and publication of reports. Given its conflicts with the Reagan and George H. W. Bush administrations, it was essential to Americas Watch/Human Rights Watch that its reporting should stand up to exacting scrutiny. Any error would be seized upon by its antagonists to undermine its credibility. Accordingly, making certain that its reports were accurate, and balanced, and that they could be substantiated, became critical. On the infrequent occasions when it erred, the organization tried hard to acknowledge its own mistakes as soon as it became aware of them, and before they were pointed out by critics.

In the early 1980s, the controversies generated by the conflicts between Americas Watch and the Reagan administration ensured that it was the most visible component of the organization. Yet the Helsinki Watch Committee, through which the organization had been launched, also made significant strides and, in its own right, became a significant force. It took advantage of the brief period in which Solidarity had been free to operate in Poland to stimulate the establishment of a Polish Helsinki Committee. Though leaders of that group were imprisoned when martial law was imposed in December 1981 and the regime of President Wojciech Jaruzelski declared Solidarity to be illegal, the Polish Helsinki Committee continued to operate, though as a clandestine underground organization. Helsinki Watch maintained contact with it and published English-language versions of its reports, thereby establishing itself as a leading voice in the West for those struggling for rights in Poland.

The especially hostile relationship between the United States and the Soviet Union that developed in the period when Ronald Reagan was denouncing the "evil empire" led to another important initiative by Helsinki Watch. Concerned that criticism of Moscow emanating from the United States would have little impact, Helsinki Watch decided to enlist Europeans in denunciations of Soviet abuses in the hope that they might have more influence. This effort came at a time when the Soviets were engaged in a major push to win support in Western Europe by denouncing American efforts to place Pershing missiles in the region.

In September 1982, Helsinki Watch convened a meeting in Italy to launch a new organization, the International Helsinki Federation for Human Rights. Groups formed in Western countries to denounce Soviet violation of the Helsinki Accords already existed in the Netherlands and Norway, as well as the United States. In preparing for the meeting in Italy, Helsinki Watch encouraged the establishment of such organizations in several additional European countries. The meeting in Italy was attended by Westerners active in human rights efforts in their own countries, as well as by several individuals from the East. Some of the latter were exiles from their countries; others came to the meeting in Italy from countries like Hungary and Yugoslavia, where there was somewhat greater latitude for human rights activism than in more repressive communist countries such as the Soviet Union and Czechoslovakia.

The 1982 meeting in Italy gave birth to a sector of the international human rights movement that remains an important force three decades later. In the majority of countries of the former Soviet bloc, it is still the case that the leading human rights organizations include Helsinki Committees. Also, a few Western groups launched in connection with the creation of the International Helsinki Federation, especially the Swedish and Norwegian Helsinki Committees, continue to play important roles in supporting efforts to promote human rights in former communist countries.[5]

The Soviet Union's invasion of Afghanistan in December 1979 also had an important impact on the development of Helsinki Watch. Initially, the organization focused on the consequences for those in the Soviet Union who protested the invasion. Physicist Andrei Sakharov, for example, was exiled from Moscow to the industrial city Gorki (now again called Nizhny Novgorod, as in the pre-Soviet era), and cut off from his scientific work and from all contact with friends and colleagues other than his wife. Later on, however, taking a leaf from Americas Watch, which was monitoring all three armed conflicts in Central America, Helsinki Watch extended its reach and began monitoring the war in Afghanistan. As no other Western human rights organization was engaged in such an effort (in part because of the movement's failure at that point to accept that its mandate should include compliance with international humanitarian law, and also because of the difficulty and danger in obtaining access to Afghanistan), Helsinki Watch had the field to itself. The organization's researchers also lacked access to the country during the period of Soviet occupation and were required to gather most of the information they published by interviewing refugees crossing the border into Pakistan. At the height of the exodus, the number of those refugees was about five million, approximately a third of Afghanistan's entire population at the time. While obtaining refugee testimony was not wholly satisfactory as a method of research, it was the most that was feasible at the time, and it substantially enhanced the role of Helsinki Watch as a force for the promotion of human rights.

One of the issues that emerged in Helsinki Watch's work on Afghanistan was the widespread use of landmines by Soviet forces, many of them dropped from planes. Tens of thousands of Afghans were killed and many more were maimed by the use of these weapons in populated civilian areas. Landmines were also a factor in Central America, where they were used particularly by the Salvadoran guerrillas attempting to overthrow the military government and by the Nicaraguan Contras who were trying to topple the Sandinista regime. Reports on landmines published by both Watch Committees were the first human rights documents to address the issue. The organization then launched a campaign against the use of landmines and obtained funding from the Rockefeller Foundation to establish an Arms Project that made landmines its primary concern. The campaign began to attract significant public attention in 1991, when King Sihanouk of Cambodia visited New York to speak at the United Nations General Assembly. Human Rights Watch had just completed an investigation (conducted in collaboration with Physicians for Human Rights) on landmines in Cambodia, where they had been used as widely and as indiscriminately as in Afghanistan. On the eve of the king's talk, a copy of the report was sent to his hotel. The result was better than could be expected, as the king devoted his speech to the world body to the scourge of landmines. Wide attention to the talk was a factor in impelling Human Rights Watch to take the lead the following year in organizing an International Coalition to Ban Landmines in partnership with two other U.S.–based groups, Physicians for Human Rights and the Vietnam Veterans Foundation; a French-based organization, Handicap International; and a German group, Medico. (The latter two organizations had extensive experience in providing humanitarian assistance to landmine victims.) The Coalition promoted the adoption of an International Convention to Ban Landmines. With strong support from the Canadian government, this succeeded in Ottawa in 1997. The Coalition's campaign led to its selection to receive the Nobel Peace Prize.

Because Helsinki Watch's work focused on abuses by the communist dictatorships in its region, while Americas Watch addressed the violations of the right-wing military dictatorships in its territory, the two complemented each other and each also provided the other with a ready response to the charge that it was one-sided. Yet that was not enough in the charged political atmosphere of the Reagan years when it was commonplace for rights organizations to be labeled either Cold War pawns of the U.S. government or apologists for anti-American Marxist-Leninist guerrillas. As it happened, however, there was one right-wing military dictatorship in Helsinki Watch's territory: namely, Turkey. And there was one repressive communist regime in Americas Watch's region: Cuba. Both Watch Committees welcomed the opportunity to deal with these countries, not only because their abuses of human rights warranted such efforts, but also because it provided further evidence of their readiness to denounce repressive regimes regardless of their political character. Substantial efforts were devoted to Turkey and Cuba and, over time, had an impact on both countries. In the case of Turkey, Helsinki Watch helped attract international attention to a range of abuses: torture, denials of free expression, suppression of the Kurdish language and culture, and abusive counterinsurgency methods in the war with Kurdish guerrillas in the southeastern part of the country. Turkey had to curb such abuses in order to gain international acceptance and, years later, to become a credible candidate for accession to the European Union. In the case of Cuba, Americas Watch's efforts helped to reduce the number of dissenters confined in the country's prisons and to diminish abuses against prisoners who resisted the regime's reeducation programs. The deliberate effort by the Watch Committees to demonstrate their geopolitical evenhandedness resembled the manner in which Amnesty International had positioned itself when it was established in the 1960s.

The growing prominence of both Americas Watch and Helsinki Watch inevitably spurred efforts to extend the organization's reach to other parts of the world. Yet their leaders decided to proceed step by step rather than attempt too quickly to operate globally. They had learned that they could make a greater impact by concentrating sustained effort on particular countries, acquiring expertise on them, establishing close contacts with domestic human rights monitors, and publishing frequent reports; it was also essential to build relationships with the journalists who reported on those countries and with policy officials in the U.S. government, in international institutions, and in the countries suffering from human rights abuses. It would be a mistake, they believed, to spread the organization's efforts too thinly. In 1985, they launched an Asia Watch Committee and decided they would wait until it too was operating effectively before venturing further afield. Africa Watch was established in 1988, and Middle East Watch in 1989. The name Human Rights Watch, suggesting a global mandate, was adopted in 1987 when the last two regional Watch Committees were in the planning stage.

Each regional extension produced its own set of challenges. For Asia Watch, the most significant was, inevitably, China. At first, Asia Watch's efforts with respect to that country focused on Tibet. The mid-1980s was a period when access to the Tibetan region was extremely limited and open human rights monitoring impossible. The effort had to be conducted covertly, entailing difficulty and danger. Asia Watch did, however, manage to gather reliable information on Tibet by enlisting a Western scholar, fluent in both Tibetan and Chinese, who traveled to the region frequently and who was willing to gather human rights information while pursuing his academic research. Such a person is a rare find. Most scholars who specialize in a region that has a repressive government avoid human rights work because, if their engagement in such efforts is discovered, they may be denied further access and be forced to abandon the scholarly research on which their entire careers are based. Worse, some scholars whose academic work focuses on a country with a repressive regime become apologists for its abuses because this attitude enhances their access. Identifying a scholar whose work focused on Tibet and who was willing to put his future research at risk by gathering data on human rights abuses was an important asset for Asia Watch. Unquestionably, the Chinese authorities attempted to discover how Asia Watch was obtaining its information on Tibet, but, so far as is known, they did not succeed.

With the 1989 events in Tiananmen Square, Human Rights Watch widened its focus on China to deal with a range of human rights abuses throughout the country. It happened that a long-time student of human rights in China who had previously worked for Amnesty International, Robin Munro, was in the country when the Tiananmen demonstrations began. He was at the time writing a travel guide to the Yangtze River, but he dropped that assignment and went to Beijing to monitor developments. Human Rights Watch hired him and, on the basis of his close observation of the events there, was able to publish a reliable and comprehensive account of what happened.[6] Thereafter, Munro's efforts made it possible for Human Rights Watch to gather information on dissent in minority regions and to expose other abuses, among them the use of prison labor to manufacture goods sold in the West and the harvesting of the organs of executed prisoners for sale to institutions that used them for transplants.

Another country that proved a major challenge for the Asia division of Human Rights Watch was India. Given the organization's concern with violations of international humanitarian law, much of its early reporting focused on the long-standing conflict in Kashmir and on the war then under way in the Punjab. The Indian government greatly resented this reporting and tried to put a stop to it by declaring the organization's lead researcher on India *persona non grata*. Though India was the country on which she had built her professional career, she could no longer travel there. Over time, she transformed herself into a specialist on Afghanistan.

Among the countries on which Africa Watch focused in its early days were those of the Horn—Somalia, Sudan, and Ethiopia—where armed conflicts were causing much suffering. Its reporting examined in depth the methods used by the governments of these countries in conducting counterinsurgency campaigns, adding to international understanding of the human rights crisis in the region. One unanticipated consequence was a dispute within Human Rights Watch that became public. When President George H. W. Bush decided in November 1992, shortly after he lost his campaign for reelection, to send American troops into Somalia to relieve a reported humanitarian crisis, the move was publicly denounced by a Somali lawyer on the staff of Human Rights Watch. The comments of Rakiya Omaar drew wide press attention and made it appear that the organization had adopted this stand. As Omaar had previously served as director of Africa Watch and was publicly known in that role, this was understandable. When she declined to make it clear that she was speaking for herself, however, and not for the organization—which had taken no position on the military intervention—Human Rights Watch fired her.

Some of the most significant reporting by the Africa division of Human Rights Watch dealt with Rwanda. The organization had enlisted one of the few American scholars who specialized on Rwanda, Alison des Forges, as its lead researcher on the country. Her work was widely recognized for its important role in setting forth the background to Rwandan genocide and describing the manner in which it was carried out. Eventually, she too became *persona non grata* in the country on which her research focused because of her reporting on abuses by President Kagame's Rwanda Patriotic Front and by his government. Alison des Forges was killed in a plane crash in the United States in 2009. By the time of her death, she had become an icon in the human rights field, known—among other things—for her role in mentoring many of the young researchers gathering human rights information in Africa.[7]

The formation of its Middle East division plunged Human Rights Watch into the intricate and long-lived controversies of the region and soon engaged it in a project that required a larger effort than any it had undertaken up to that point. It remains the most ambitious in the organization's history. The focus was Iraq.

The Middle East division's first substantial publication was a report, issued in book form, that provided an overview of human rights in Iraq under Saddam Hussein.[8] Human Rights Watch put forward its greatest effort in documenting Saddam's onslaught against the country's Kurdish minority in 1988, the last year of the Iraq-Iran war. The effort grew out of an unusual opportunity that became available to the organization in 1991, following the Gulf War. The Kurds in the north and the Shiites in the South had attempted to exploit what they thought was Saddam's weakness in the immediate aftermath of the Gulf War by launching rebellions. Some of the rebels may also have believed that they would get assistance from the United States and its allies, which had so readily defeated Saddam after his invasion of Kuwait. That aid was not forthcoming, however, and

Saddam's forces readily put down the Kurdish and Shiite revolts, committing severe abuses in the process. Million of Kurds fled to neighboring Turkey and Iran—creating an immense refugee crisis—and only returned to northern Iraq after the United States had created a security zone for them and promised that it would protect them if Saddam's forces attempted to enter Iraqi Kurdistan. Before Saddam's forces crushed the revolt in the north, the Kurdish guerrillas had briefly overrun the regime's security offices in a number of cities in Iraqi Kurdistan and had seized large quantities of documents. It turned out that the security services—in accordance with the training they had obtained from East Germany's Stasi—had kept extensive and detailed records of the crimes they had committed against the Kurds during the "Anfal," the Iraqi regime's name for the campaign that slaughtered scores of thousands of Kurds in 1988. Saddam had launched the Anfal to punish the Kurds for what he apparently considered their treasonous behavior in trying to take advantage of the war with Iran to secure independence for Kurdistan.

Human Rights Watch's efforts to document the Anfal had several components. It collaborated with another organization, Physicians for Human Rights, in verifying that Saddam Hussein's forces had used chemical weapons against the Kurds at Halabja, killing about 5,000. This was done at a time when some spokespersons for the Reagan administration were trying to exculpate Saddam from the allegation that he had used poisonous gas. Human Rights Watch opened an office in Iraqi Kurdistan after the Kurds were repatriated under U.S. protection and sought out survivors of the Anfal to take testimony from them. Its researchers conducted more than 350 field interviews with witnesses and survivors. It sent forensic scientists to the area to exhume a mass gravesite. The most ambitious part of its effort, however, was to arrange for transportation to the United States of the documents the Kurds had seized from Iraqi security offices and to establish a team in Washington, where the documents were stored, that spent more than two years examining them (they were all in Arabic) and distilling from them a comprehensive account of the crimes that had been committed. The documents flown to the United States filled 847 cardboard boxes and weighed more than fourteen tons.[9]

One of the purposes of this effort was to assemble the evidentiary basis for a genocide suit that could be brought against Iraq in the International Court of Justice[10]. Such a suit must be filed by another government that is a party to the Genocide Convention. Most likely, the United States would have been willing to be a plaintiff in such a case, but Human Rights Watch judged that this would be a mistake. Not only would a suit by the United States have appeared simply as an extension of the Gulf War, but in addition, the reservations by the United States when it ratified the Genocide Convention (see chapter 4), including a prohibition on a suit against the United States without its agreement, would detract from its ability to serve as an effective plaintiff.

Although a number of other governments expressed some interest in serving as the plaintiff, ultimately none agreed to do so. In one case a government that seemed ready to file suit backed away when two of its citizens strayed into Iraqi territory from Kuwait and were captured. Freeing them took precedence. Up to that point there had only been one suit for genocide in the International Court of Justice filed in 1993 while Human Rights Watch's research on the Anfal was underway.[11] The findings about what took place in the Anfal were not used in a court until criminal prosecutions took place in Baghdad following the U.S. invasion. Saddam Hussein himself was scheduled to be tried for the Anfal, but was executed for other crimes for which he had been convicted before that trial could begin. Prosecution, conviction, and punishment of some of Saddam's top associates for the crimes against the Kurds eventually took place in Iraq in 2007.

Though efforts related to Iraq consumed more of the energy and resources of the Middle East division of Human Rights Watch than any other country between the division's establishment in 1988 and the Arab revolutions of 2011, the work that attracted by far the greatest controversy was that involving Israel's relationship to the Palestinians within its own borders and in the Occupied Territories; and also Israel's engagement in Lebanon. The organization followed the same procedures as in other conflicts, examining abuses committed by all sides—Israeli forces and groups like Hamas and Hezbollah that organized Palestinian suicide bombers and launched other attacks against Jewish Israelis—and assessing them in accordance with the standards of international humanitarian law. Though it reported serious abuses by all parties, it was its findings critical of Israeli government practices that became the target of widespread denunciations. The only comparable assault against the organization had been the criticism of Americas Watch in the early 1980s for its reporting on the wars in Central America by the Reagan administration and its media allies on the editorial page of the *Wall Street Journal*.

Perhaps the fiercest attack ever experienced by Human Rights Watch took place in connection with its reporting on abuses by the Israel Defense Forces during the war against Hezbollah in July and August 2006.

The director of Human Rights Watch, Kenneth Roth, was accused of bias against Israel and of being an anti-Semite by a number of critics, including the editorial page of a now defunct newspaper, the *New York Sun*,[12] and by the national director of the Anti-Defamation League, Abraham Foxman.[13] Other such attacks appeared in the *New Republic*, the *Weekly Standard*, and the *Jerusalem Post*. Writing in the *Jerusalem Post*, for example, Harvard law professor Alan Dershowitz claimed that, "When it comes to Israel and its enemies, Human Rights Watch cooks the books about facts, cheats on interviews, and puts out predetermined conclusions that are driven more by their ideology than by evidence."[14]

These denunciations were inspired by a report published by Human Rights Watch on August 3, 2006, three weeks after a Hezbollah raid into Israel set off the conflict that lasted until August 14. Entitled "Fatal Strikes: Israel's Indiscriminate Attacks against Civilians in Lebanon," the report documented aerial attacks that killed 153 civilians, about a third of the number reported killed in Lebanon during the first two weeks of the war. There were a number of things wrong with this report, according to the critics. It did not label Hezbollah as the aggressor in the conflict. In addition, although Human Rights Watch also published reports documenting indiscriminate attacks by Hezbollah—mainly its rocket attacks against Israel—the organization did not use statements by Hezbollah's leader expressing a desire to kill Jews as a basis for accusing Hezbollah of genocide. As for Alan Dershowitz's charge that Human Rights Watch "cooks the books," this rested on the claim that the organization "ignored credible news sources" which pointed out that Hezbollah fighters had a practice of mingling with civilians. On those grounds, Dershowitz and others charged, the civilian deaths recorded by Human Rights Watch were the fault of Hezbollah, not of indiscriminate attacks by Israel.

As for not labeling Hezbollah as the aggressor, Human Rights Watch responded that it had never labeled any party to any conflict as an aggressor. Kenneth Roth wrote: "The question of who started any given conflict or who is most at fault leads to lengthy historical digressions that are antithetical to the careful, objective investigation into the contemporary conduct of warring parties in which [Human Rights Watch] specializes."[15] It could be added that if Human Rights Watch made pronouncements as to who was the aggressor in a particular conflict, it would not be able to conduct investigations on the territory of parties to a conflict, and it would lose credibility in speaking out on abuses. Also, it should be noted that both

Israel and the United States had opposed giving the International Criminal Court jurisdiction over aggression on the basis that it is virtually impossible to come up with both a definition and a factual account of the events leading up to armed conflict in such a way as to avoid politicization.[16]

As to genocide, like other responsible groups in the field, Human Rights Watch uses the term sparingly. Among the factors it takes into account are the scale and systematic nature of the killing. On the three occasions in its history when it has used the term—in Bosnia, in Rwanda, and in the case of Saddam Hussein's slaughter of the Iraqi Kurds in 1988—the number of those killed ranged from several scores of thousands to several hundreds of thousands. Human Rights Watch described the killings of Israeli civilians by Hezbollah rockets as war crimes. The number of Israeli civilians killed during the entire conflict was forty-three, eighteen of them Israeli Arabs.

To prove that Human Rights Watch ignored credible news sources showing that Hezbollah fighters deliberately mingled with Lebanese civilians, Alan Dershowitz cited eight such press accounts. Commenting on them at the time, the present author wrote: "[T]he eight press accounts cited by Dershowitz prove less than he suggests. Two of them refer to quotations in Canadian publications from a retired Canadian military officer, General Lewis MacKenzie, who was apparently nowhere near Lebanon when the conflict took place but speculated about Hezbollah's practices. As Dershowitz may not have known but should have found out before citing the general twice, this is characteristic of MacKenzie. When he was commander in 1992 of U.N. peacekeepers in Sarajevo, he became notorious for accusing Bosnia's Muslims of attacking themselves. In his memoir, *Peacekeeper*, he recalled that he told President François Mitterrand of France that 'there is strong but circumstantial evidence that some really horrifying acts of cruelty attributed to the Serbs were actually orchestrated by the Muslims against their own people, for the benefit of an international audience.' As National Public Radio reporter Tom Gjelten pointed out:

> MacKenzie took Serb army commanders at their word when they said they were not responsible for the bombing of the breadline on Vaso Miskin Street in May [1992]. He accepted their claim that the Bosnian army had laid a ground mine at the site and staged the massacre to win international sympathy. . . . The "evidence" that it was a Muslim-laid mine came entirely from Serb military sources, and all of it eventually proved bogus.

As a frequent visitor to Sarajevo during the war, I went to the site and saw the distinctive flower-like splash of a mortar shell on the pavement, which looks nothing like the damage done by a mine. The journalist David Rieff pointed out that MacKenzie 'never actually visited the site.'"

The remainder of Dershowitz's press citations were similarly flawed or irrelevant to Human Rights Watch's report.[17] Dershowitz did not respond to the criticism.

The attack on Human Rights Watch failed for three reasons. First, and most important, the organization's reporting, and its application of international humanitarian law, were solid and, therefore, could be readily defended. Second, the reputation the organization had established on the basis of its worldwide reporting helped it to counter charges of bias against Israel. Third, at the very end of the conflict, after the critiques of Human Rights Watch cited here, Israel engaged in a practice that undermined the efforts of those who had defended its practices. Following an agreement to end the conflict, in the seventy-two hours that remained before a cease-fire went into effect, Israel dropped large quantities of cluster bombs over southern Lebanon. These left millions of unexploded bomblets in place to maim and kill civilians returning to the region after fleeing the conflict. Even the staunchest supporters of the Israeli cause had difficulty finding ways to justify this action. Denunciations of Human Rights Watch subsided. Two years later, the United Nations Mine Action Center reported that twenty-seven civilians had been killed and 234 wounded in southern Lebanon by unexploded munitions and that an additional thirteen bomb disposal experts had been killed and thirty-nine wounded.[18]

Although Human Rights Watch was not damaged by attacks against its reporting on Israel's conflict with Hezbollah, its critics did not give up. Similar criticism was leveled against it in 2009, following its reporting on another Israeli war, "Operation Cast Lead" against Gaza, which began in late 2008. In its reporting on Gaza, Human Rights Watch cooperated with two Israeli human rights groups, Breaking the Silence, an organization of former Israeli Defense Forces' soldiers that collected soldiers' testimony about Gaza; and B'Tselem, an organization that has documented abuses in the Israeli-Palestinian conflict for an extended period.

In 2009, one of those who criticized Human Rights Watch for its reporting on Israel was its founding chair, Robert L. Bernstein. Insiders at Human Rights Watch had long known that Bernstein, who stepped down as chair eleven years earlier, was unhappy about the organization's attention to Israeli abuses of human rights. He frequently complained about such reporting and had been given opportunities to speak on the subject to the organization's Board of Directors. In October 2009, for the first time, Bernstein made his views public, publishing an op-ed piece in the *New York Times*.[19] He made several points: HRW should focus on closed societies, whereas Israel is an open society; HRW has focused far more on Israel than on the "brutal, closed and autocratic" regimes of the region; HRW errs by differentiating "wrongs committed in self-defense and those perpetrated intentionally"; and he questioned reporting on "Gaza and elsewhere where there is no access to the battlefield" and where "[r]eporting often relies on witnesses whose stories cannot be verified . . . ."

In a rejoinder, the present author, who had collaborated closely with Bernstein in establishing Human Rights Watch, pointed out that while Bernstein was "right to differentiate between closed and open societies, he is wrong to suggest that open societies should be spared criticism for human rights abuses." The response noted the history of abuses in the United States, including slavery, racial segregation, the internment of Japanese-Americans, and, in our time, torture at Abu Ghraib. Though the U.S. is an open society, no human rights group could be silent about such abuses. The response also said that Bernstein's allegation of a disproportionate focus on Israel was mistaken. HRW has reported extensively on Iraq, Iran, Saudi Arabia, Syria, Egypt, and other countries of the region. About 15 percent of HRW's reporting on the Middle East had dealt with Israel. It was that high because of Israel's engagement in armed conflicts, on which HRW specializes. (The Arab revolutions of 2011 have required Human Rights Watch to devote far greater resources to the region than ever previously, and the proportion of reporting devoted to Israel has declined accordingly.) The response also noted that Bernstein's differentiation of abuses committed in self-defense is not a distinction made by the laws of war, and one that is dangerous. Those purportedly acting in defense of Iraq after the U.S. invasion of 2003 murdered tens of thousands of civilians. In many conflicts, as in the Israel-Gaza conflict, both sides claim self-defense, and it is often those who portray themselves as victims who commit horrendous abuses. Finally, with respect to access to Gaza, the response points out that it was the policy of the Israeli government to deny access during the war. If such policies were accepted, HRW would never have been able to report on Saddam Hussein's Iraq. As it happens, HRW had a consultant in Gaza throughout the conflict and sent in a research team three days after hostilities ended. Though witness testimony is often self-serving, it plays a crucial role in judicial determinations of guilt beyond a reasonable doubt when followed by crosschecking and through examination of its consistency with other evidence. HRW's reporting matters because its experience and fastidious care with fact gathering has built its reputation for getting the story right.[20]

The movement, again with Human Rights Watch in the forefront, was also tested in yet another part of the world in August 2008, when Georgian troops moved into the secessionist province of South Ossetia to assert control. The region has a mixed population of ethnic Ossetians, Russians, and Georgians. Though within the internationally recognized borders of Georgia, South Ossetia and another breakaway region, Abkhazia, had maintained *de facto* independence from Georgia since the breakup of the Soviet Union in 1991. That independence was made possible by Russia's support and military might. South Ossetia was known as a base for criminal enterprises that were active in both Russia and Georgia.

Just how the military confrontation in South Ossetia started is sharply disputed. The controversy includes charges of human rights abuses. Russia relied principally on a claim that Georgian troops had engaged in extensive human rights abuses in South Ossetia to justify its strong military response, which included the invasion of Georgia, occupation of a major Georgian city, the seizure of Georgian military bases where a great deal of equipment was destroyed, the occupation of Georgia's major port on the Black Sea, the taking of Georgian prisoners, and the formal recognition of the independence of South Ossetia and Abkhazia, effectively ending Georgian sovereignty over these territories. According to the Russian authorities, when Georgian troops entered South Ossetia on August 7, 2008 and invaded its capital, Tskhinvali, they ethnically cleansed Russian and Ossetian villages and neighborhoods, killing some 2,000 civilians. Russia had recently granted ethnic Russians in South Ossetia Russian citizenship and was coming to the defense of its citizens, according to Prime Minister Vladimir Putin and his associates. Some Russian officials also proposed international criminal prosecution of Georgia's president, Mikhail Saakashvili, for the attack on the civilians.

Human Rights Watch responded quickly by deploying five of its researchers to the region, two on the Russian side and three on the Georgian side. Overnight, its reporting became a factor in the conflict. Its researchers on the Russian side went to the only hospital in South Ossetia and to the morgue to try to find out how many persons had been killed, and reported that doctors at the hospital counted forty-four bodies, some of them clearly members of the military. In addition, Human Rights Watch was able to establish that 273 persons had been wounded. Russian authorities responded that many civilians in South Ossetian villages had buried relatives in backyards because they were unable to take the bodies anywhere else. That may indeed have happened in one or two cases, but the discrepancy between Russian claims and the number of deaths that could be verified seems far too great to be explained away by backyard burials. Two weeks after the Georgian military attacks, Russian authorities said that they had confirmed 133 deaths of civilians due to Georgian attacks. Eventually, the number they settled on was 162 South Ossetian civilians killed by Georgian forces.[21] This figure is more plausible than the previous Russian claim of 2,000 deaths, as the number of those killed in such circumstances is ordinarily about one third of the number wounded. Human Rights Watch was able to establish that many of the civilian deaths were due to indiscriminate shelling by Georgian forces. While it is not possible to establish exactly how all the deaths took place, it is clear that Georgian troops did commit war crimes in South Ossetia and also that Russian troops committed war crimes on undisputed Georgian territory. The Georgian government said that 228 civilians had been killed on its side.[22] Some of the most severe abuses were committed by Ossetian militias operating under the protection of regular Russian troops against residents of ethnic Georgian villages within South Ossetia. Also, Human Rights Watch reported evidence that both sides used cluster bombs. Though their use was not then a war crime in and of itself, the organization made clear that it saw no justification for the deployment of such indiscriminate weapons. Earlier in 2008, ninety-four countries had agreed to ban cluster bombs at an intergovernmental meeting organized to draw up a treaty against them.[23]

Though Russia is not a party to the International Criminal Court, Georgia has ratified the Rome treaty. Accordingly, war crimes committed by Georgian troops and war crimes committed on Georgian territory by Russian troops or by Ossetian militias are subject to the Court's jurisdiction. Whether the office of the prosecutor for the ICC should have taken action on Georgia is a difficult question. The crucial issue the prosecutor was required to examine was whether the scale of the abuses met the "gravity test" required by the treaty for cases brought before the ICC. The treaty itself does not define "gravity," but only cites a number of factors to be considered. If the prosecutor had sought indictments, it would have been the first time that any international criminal tribunal took on one of the five permanent members of the United Nations Security Council. The Russian authorities called for prosecution of Georgian president Saakashvili, and it is possible that this could have taken place. If it had, it would have increased pressure on the prosecutor to proceed against the Russians as well. It is possible that he was reluctant to prosecute because he did not want so momentous a step against a permanent member of the Security Council to turn on the question of whether or not it met the gravity test. Although no prosecution was brought before the ICC, it seems evident that the human rights aspects of the war between Russia and Georgia will continue to be an important part of the story of the war.

. . .

Aside from Human Rights Watch's focus on abuses in the context of armed conflict, the most significant innovation in international human rights work that grew out of the early efforts of Americas Watch consists in its effort to secure accountability for past abuses. This was an outgrowth of the organization's concern with Argentina. In 1983, the military junta that ruled the country could no longer govern. The economy was a shambles and the armed forces had disgraced themselves the previous year by launching and losing a war with Britain over the Falkland Islands (known to Argentines as the Malvinas). The poor performance of the military hierarchy in that struggle, including episodes of cowardice, forced the junta to allow elections to restore democratic government. Before leaving office, however, the Argentine military issued what it called its "Final Document on the Struggle Against Subversion and Terrorism," in which it denied responsibility for the disappearances that the military had committed. This was followed by a decree by the armed forces granting itself amnesty for the crimes that it continued to deny.

Collaborating closely with an Argentine human rights organization, the Center for Legal and Social Studies (CELS, the acronym for its Spanish-language name), Americas Watch documented many of the disappearances and condemned the denial and the amnesty. The democratically elected president who took office in Argentina on December 10, 1983 (international Human Rights Day), Raúl Alfonsín, also rejected the amnesty and established a commission to investigate the disappearances (popularly known as the "truth commission," the origin of that term[24]) and ordered prosecutions of those responsible. Americas Watch's support for these efforts put the accountability issue on the international human rights agenda where it has held a prominent place ever since.

In subsequent years, Human Rights Watch engaged in efforts to promote accountability in many countries. In 1992, the organization initiated the effort to establish the International Criminal Tribunal for the Former Yugoslavia.[25] It also played an important role in establishing the other ad hoc international criminal tribunals and in creating the permanent International Criminal Court. An important part of the work of Human Rights Watch in recent years has been its efforts to ensure that accountability mechanisms work effectively (see chapter 11).

Yet another expansion of Human Rights Watch's definition of its mandate also grew out of the early efforts of its Americas Watch division. This was a decision not to restrict its work to abuses that were politically motivated, but also to address law enforcement misconduct in dealing with ordinary crimes. The two countries that figured most prominently in this decision in the mid-1980s were Jamaica and Brazil. In both countries unusually large numbers of suspects in criminal cases were shot and killed by the police. The standard explanation for these deaths—that criminals engaged in frequent shoot-outs with the police—was not convincing. If the deaths had occurred in shoot-outs, one would expect that a large number of police would also be wounded and killed, but there were few such casualties. Also, when police elsewhere shoot criminal suspects, many more are wounded than killed. The statistics are typically the same as in armed conflicts, where the number of wounded is generally at least three times as high as the number killed.[26] In Jamaica and Brazil, however, the great majority of those shot by the police were killed. This suggested that the victims were not hit by bullets while engaged in gun battles, or while trying to escape the police. Rather, it indicated that they were probably shot at a point when the police had sufficient control over them so as to be able to execute them. By themselves, the numbers did not prove that the police had a policy of summarily executing criminal suspects, but they were sufficiently suspicious to warrant a case-by-case examination of whether executions were practiced.

Brazil was a country where there was much evidence that the police routinely tortured suspects in ordinary criminal cases. Americas Watch's investigations confirmed this practice. It appeared that many Brazilians did not trust the country's courts to prosecute and punish criminals. In comparison to its high crime rate, the level of incarceration in Brazil was low,[27] and crime victims apparently looked to the police to dispense summary justice. The police acted accordingly. The same situation prevailed in a number of other countries where Human Rights Watch conducted investigations.

Human Rights Watch also focused attention on prisons. Again, it diverged from what had been standard practice in the human rights field and examined abuses against common prisoners as well as against those detained for political offenses. This required the organization to look into prisons in the United States, as the U.S. incarcerates a far larger number of prisoners in proportion to population, in relation to its crime rate, and also in absolute numbers, than any other country in the world.[28] HRW's reports on American prisons led to a general increase in its efforts to address rights abuses in the United States.[29]

In 1989, Human Rights Watch established a Women's Rights Project. At the time, this was controversial both within the human rights field generally and within the organization itself. Critics complained that much of the agenda of such a project would focus on abuses by private persons—as in cases of domestic violence—rather than on the violations of rights by states, which are the customary concern of the international human rights movement. Proponents responded that, in such circumstances, it is the responsibility of the state to protect the victims of violence. Systematic failure to do so in many countries constitutes state denial of equal rights under law.

Within just a few years, it became widely accepted that protecting women's rights should be an important part of the mandate of human rights organizations. This was manifest at the world conference on human rights that the United Nations convened in Vienna in 1993. Two years later, however, it was apparent that this was still a novelty. Hillary Clinton electrified the delegates to the U.N. world conference on women's rights in Beijing by declaring, "If there is one message that echoes forth from this conference, let it be that human rights are women's rights and women's rights are human rights, once and for all." Yet at the moment that Human Rights Watch created its Women's Rights Project in the late 1980s, the organization's longest-term supporter, the Ford Foundation, made the displeasure of its human rights program officers known by reducing the funding it provided to Human Rights Watch.[30] At this writing, the Women's Rights Project continues as an important component of Human Rights Watch, addressing such issues as trafficking, "honor" crimes (in which men murder women in their families for supposedly violating the honor of their husbands or fathers, and are customarily not prosecuted), rape prosecutions in war crimes trials, abuses against migrant domestic workers, and discrimination under the "Family Codes" of various countries involving such matters as divorce and child custody. (A shift in personnel at the Ford

Foundation in the mid1990s ended that institution's opposition to the notion that women's rights are an essential component of human rights.)

In the 1990s, Human Rights Watch established a special project to address human rights issues related to HIV/AIDS. As the organization pointed out, "HIV/AIDS is commonly thought to be related to 'economic, social and cultural rights' (such as the right to health care), as opposed to 'civil and political rights,' such as freedom of expression and association and due process of law. However, many of the human rights abuses that most increase HIV risk—violence and discrimination against women and marginalized populations as well as people living with HIV/AIDS, harassment and imprisonment of outreach workers and at-risk populations seeking HIV/AIDS information or services, and censorship of health information—are abuses of civil and political rights."[31] Human Rights Watch addressed such issues as restrictions on AIDS activists in China, discrimination against HIV-positive mothers and their children in Russia, governmental neglect of education for children who are HIV-positive, and human rights abuses in the fight against HIV/AIDS in Zimbabwe.

During the present author's tenure as executive director of Human Rights Watch, the organization did not deal with questions of economic and social rights. That changed slowly and gradually following the appointment of a successor, Kenneth Roth, who took office in 1993 and continues to hold the post at this writing. Human Rights Watch amended its policies to accept the concept of economic and social rights, but Roth applied the new policy only in limited circumstances. As noted in chapter 3, he took the position that a human rights organization could only address such issues in a meaningful way in circumstances in which it is possible to identify a specific violation, a perpetrator, and a victim. This can be done, he has argued, where it is possible to point to state action that is either arbitrary or discriminatory.

Of course, when there is discriminatory state action, a violation of civil or political rights is implied. And to the degree that there is an economic dimension to the violation, what is involved is the economic consequence of discrimination rather than economic rights as such. In recent years, Human Rights Watch has also addressed economic rights in cases of such arbitrary abuses as the exploitation of migrant construction workers in the United Arab Emirates, abuses against domestic workers worldwide, the situation of street children in the Democratic Republic of the Congo, and the abuse and exploitation of child domestic workers in Indonesia.

At least one major shift took place in the *modus operandi* of Human Rights Watch during the first decade of the twenty-first century. In the organization's early days, an important focus of its work was the effort to bring as much influence as possible to bear on the foreign policy of the United States because of the potential that U.S. policies had for promoting Human Rights Watch's agenda in other countries. Even in the case of repressive governments for which the United States was an apologist, such as the 1980s military regimes that were politically aligned with the United States in the Cold War struggle with the Soviet Union, bringing pressure to bear on Washington was often the most effective way to secure advances of rights. Public arguments with Reagan administration officials over what was going on in such countries attracted attention to abuses of human rights and, that attention often put pressure on the governments directly responsible to curb abuses. The Reagan administration—and subsequently that of President George H. W. Bush—became what was referred to at Human Rights Watch as a "surrogate villain." Debates with the surrogate were frequently effective in turning a spotlight on violations of rights that would otherwise have been ignored. In that respect, Human Rights Watch came to regard some officials of those administrations—U.N. Ambassador Jeane Kirkpatrick, Assistant Secretary of State for Human Rights Elliott Abrams and Abrams's successor in that post, Richard Schifter, among them—as its inadvertent allies. The more they explained away abuses of rights, the more those abuses became a focus of pressure from many quarters.

That changed during the Clinton administration in the last years of the twentieth century. While that administration used its power and purse to promote human rights only sparingly, it refrained from acting as an apologist for governments committing abuses. In contrast to common practice during the Reagan and George H. W. Bush presidencies, the State Department's annual *Country Reports* on human rights worldwide no longer included distorted accounts of conditions in certain countries. They acquired an ever more professional quality and, having retained that character during the subsequent administrations of Presidents George W. Bush and Barack Obama, are now regarded as among the most comprehensive and reliable sources of human rights data available anywhere.

The main reason that Human Rights Watch shifted from a major focus on U.S. government policy, however, is that Washington has declining influence internationally to promote human rights. It is not completely lacking in such influence. American foreign policy is still a factor to be reckoned with in some parts of the world. But the readiness of the Bush administration to abandon crucial protections of human rights in the context of its "war on terror" following September 11, 2001 diminished the frequency of admonitions from Washington to other states for such abuses as torture, prolonged arbitrary detention, and trials without due process in military tribunals. In cases where Washington continued to raise such issues, other governments have felt less urgency than before to take seriously the concerns expressed by the United States. At this writing, after nearly three years of the Obama administration, it is still unclear whether and to what degree U.S. global influence will recover, or even how much the administration will use its influence to promote the cause of international human rights. As time passes, the Obama administration has become somewhat more willing to denounce abuses than it was at the outset when it sought "engagement" with such governments as that of President Ahmadinejad of Iran. Yet it is still more reticent than its predecessors when it comes to denunciations.

Human Rights Watch has not succeeded in identifying an effective substitute for the United States in efforts to influence other governments. Though it has increased its efforts to influence the actions of the European Union and of various United Nations bodies such as the Human Rights Council, these have not proven to be adequate substitutes. It is difficult to persuade the twenty-seven governments that make up the European Union at this writing to speak with one voice on global issues, and the Human Rights Council has proven only a little more effective a body in its early years than the discredited Human Rights Commission that it replaced. As in the case of the previous United Nations body, regional solidarity— that is, the reluctance of an African or Middle Eastern state to criticize another country in its regional bloc (at least in the period prior to the Arab revolutions of 2011)—has generally trumped concern for human rights in decision-making. Also, the economic power of China has helped to immunize it against criticism by most countries. At present, Human Rights Watch is taking steps to put itself in a position to influence the foreign policies of governments such as those of Brazil, India, Indonesia, Japan, and South Africa to promote human rights internationally. It is too soon to tell how effective this effort will prove.

In the first decade of the twenty-first century, Human Rights Watch was not able to gain much traction in dealing with abusive governments through intergovernmental bodies, nor did it have much success in influencing them through other governments. It did, however, demonstrate increased ability to exercise direct influence through its own activities.

The organization has substantially internationalized its operations. While about two thirds of its funds are still raised in the United States as of 2011, and while more of its operations are still based in New York and Washington than elsewhere, it now has established a presence in many other countries. That is, it not only conducts research in other countries worldwide but also has established many locally supported offices to act as pressure groups within those countries. In contrast to its first quarter of a century, it now credibly presents itself as a global organization. Most important, it is taken seriously by governments today not because of its capacity to be an influential voice in Washington but principally in its own right. In this respect, its role has become more analogous to that of Amnesty International. Though it lacks a large global membership like that which gives Amnesty enhanced legitimacy, yet to a significant extent, Human Rights Watch speaks for informed public opinion worldwide when it publishes its reports. While some, such as the Israeli and Lebanese governments and their partisans following the 2006 war, still make accusations of bias, these have little impact. The media in many countries and a substantial share of world public opinion accept the *bona fides* of Human Rights Watch. Internationally, civil society has greater standing than ever before and few organizations, if any, have greater credibility, prestige, or influence as a voice of international civil society than Human Rights Watch.

10

The Worldwide Movement

AS OF OCTOBER 3, 2011

THOUGH AMNESTY INTERNATIONAL AND HUMAN RIGHTS WATCH are the largest, best known, and most influential human rights groups operating worldwide, literally thousands of other organizations are also active in the field. Many of them make distinctive contributions by focusing on abuses of rights in a particular country or locality; by addressing violations of rights suffered by discrete segments of the population such as gays and lesbians, indigenous peoples, women, members of racial, religious or ethnic minorities, or persons suffering from mental or physical disabilities; by dealing with a particular form of abuse, such as torture or the denial of freedom of expression; by using a particular method to promote human rights, such as litigation or the rehabilitation of torture victims; or by enlisting members of a certain profession, such as lawyers, physicians or journalists, in the struggle for human rights.[1]

As noted in chapter 1, the American-based human rights movement came into its own in the late 1970s as a result of U.S. dominance of the Cold War struggle against the Soviet empire, and especially U.S support for many anticommunist tyrannies that regularly abused rights. A subsidiary factor was the relatively greater availability of private philanthropy in the United States than elsewhere to support organizations at home and abroad that were promoting human rights. Small donations from Amnesty International's global membership, the largest part of it in Europe, continued to make that organization dominant financially and in other ways.

But the total volume of funding from the United States, mainly from large private foundations, but also from wealthy individuals, exceeded what could be obtained elsewhere. Most U.S.-based human rights organizations, like Amnesty International, adopted policies against accepting funds from any government or intergovernmental body so as to make it clear that they were not accessories to the policies of such donors. Human rights organizations in other parts of the world, however, did accept government funds. Among them were a large number that accepted funding from government or government-supported bodies, such as those in the Scandinavian countries or the Netherlands, that were not prominently engaged in geopolitical struggles, while disdaining support from U.S.-government-related bodies such as the National Endowment for Democracy and Freedom House. A smaller number placed no such restrictions on their acceptance of funding.

Though U.S.-based human rights organizations continue to have a leading role in the worldwide human rights movement at this writing, it seems likely that their relative prominence will decline in the years ahead. The increasing vigor and significance of many human rights organizations based in parts of the world other than Europe and the United States suggest that they will play an increasingly important role in public affairs internationally. This seemed evident during the Arab revolutions of 2011. Though not leaders in those revolutions, local organizations' documentation of abuses was critical in setting the agenda of the protestors. In addition, locally based organizations played a crucial role in providing information on the protests.

An example is Syria. Throughout the protests, the Syrian government attempted to create a news blackout by excluding all foreign journalists and representatives of foreign human rights organizations. Yet the world's press was able to report on the demonstrations in various provincial cities and towns of Syria, and on the rising death toll due to military assaults on the unarmed demonstrators. The reporting was based on the work of Syrian human rights organizations that were able to monitor developments. The arrests and other forms of harassment against leaders of those organizations did not suffice to suppress their monitoring, though such practices effectively cut off almost all other communications from the country.

As indicated, one of the important ways that the international human rights movement has developed has been along professional lines. One of the organizations in the United States that started out as a group based in a profession has evolved to play a broader role and has acquired a reputation and an operational capacity that places is in the same company as the two larger bodies in terms of its influence on certain aspects of American public policy. Though it lacks the global reach or standing of either Amnesty International or Human Rights Watch, the organization currently known as Human Rights First is an important participant in debates in Washington over such questions as American counterterrorism policies. In addition, it has long had an important role in the field of refugee rights.

Established in 1978 as the Lawyers Committee for International Human Rights, an offshoot of the World War II era International League for Human Rights, it soon abbreviated its name by dropping the word "International" and, more than two decades later, changed its name to Human Rights First. One of those who joined its Board of Directors at its founding was Louis Henkin, a professor of law at Columbia University, who was long regarded as the preeminent American scholar in the human rights field. The course he began teaching on human rights at Columbia Law School in 1971 may have been the first anywhere with such a focus. In its early years, "The Lawyers Committee"—as it was widely known—enlisted hundreds of American lawyers to provide free legal representation to applicants for asylum in the United States in immigration proceedings. Many of the lawyers volunteering to take on such matters were young associates at major law firms, especially New York City firms. Their participation helped to establish strong ties between the American legal profession and the Lawyers Committee. In addition to calling on the professional skills of lawyers in its asylum work, the Lawyers Committee campaigned on behalf of lawyers in other countries who were persecuted for defending human rights and, in one notable case, provided legal representation for the families of four American churchwomen murdered by the armed forces of El Salvador in December 1980. The murders of the churchwomen, and the court cases arising from it, figured prominently for a number of years in policy debates about American government support for the Salvadoran military in their civil war against leftist guerrillas.

Though the Lawyers Committee sustained its representation of asylum applicants and its campaigns on behalf of persecuted lawyers, it discontinued the use of litigation to promote human rights. A handful of other organizations have since emerged as leaders in such efforts (see below). Instead the Lawyers Committee, from time to time, shifted its focus. In its early years, it sometimes conducted investigations of human rights abuses in countries outside the United States, publishing reports that resembled those of Amnesty International or Human Rights Watch, though they were not as focused on individual victims as were Amnesty's reports or concerned with violations of the laws of war as were the reports of Human Rights Watch. Two countries on which the Lawyers Committee focused were El Salvador (up to the end of the war there in 1992) and the Philippines (up to the end of the dictatorship of Ferdinand Marcos in 1986). In other cases, however, the country reporting by the Lawyers Committee lacked the systematic follow-up of Amnesty or Human Rights Watch.

In its early years, the Lawyers Committee also monitored the American government's policies towards other countries in which rights were abused and joined Human Rights Watch (when its components were still known as "the Watch Committees") in publishing critiques of those policies and also of the U.S. State Department's annual *Country Reports on Human Rights Practices Worldwide*. During the eight years of President Ronald Reagan's presidency and the subsequent four years of President George H. W. Bush, the *Country Reports* often contained significant distortions calculated to portray client states of the United States in Third World countries in a better light than they deserved. Such politicized reporting ended with the advent of the Clinton administration in 1993, and it has not reappeared since. As a consequence, the critiques were discontinued.

While the Lawyers Committee appeared to flounder for a period—except in its asylum work, which continued to provide an important and distinctive service—it acquired a new sense of mission about the time of its name change to Human Rights First and, more important, with the beginning of the Bush administration's "global war on terror." Its most notable contribution was to build a network of retired generals and admirals from all four branches of the United States military to speak out against Bush administration policies and practices that involved the use of torture and the cruel, inhuman, and degrading treatment of detainees. The senior officers, including such notable figures as General Charles Krulak, former commandant of the United States Marine Corps,[2] met with public officials and candidates for office, published op-ed articles, testified at Congressional hearings, and issued repeated public statements. They became among the most effective opponents of the policies promoted by Vice President Richard Cheney, Secretary of Defense Donald Rumsfeld, and various officials of the United States Department of Justice (see chapter 12) who espoused practices—in Cheney's words—"on the dark side."

The leader of Human Rights First's work with the generals and admirals was the organization's long-time Washington director, Elisa Massimino. Herself the daughter of a submarine commander, Massimino apparently understood how to communicate with military officials and established credibility with them. In 2008, she took over the leadership of Human Rights First as its executive director. Her standing in the human rights community and the respect she enjoys in U.S. government circles suggests that the organization will continue to play an influential role in shaping American policies on human rights in the years ahead.

Two other American organizations based in professions, Physicians for Human Rights (PHR) and the Committee to Protect Journalists (CPJ), have also played prominent roles in U.S.–based efforts to promote human rights. For the most part, the work of PHR, which was established in 1985, has focused on investigations and campaigns that draw upon the skills of physicians and other scientists. One of its early investigations looked into beatings of Palestinians by Israeli soldiers during the first intifada. PHR doctors pointed out that many of the Palestinians had suffered broken bones on the insides of their forearms. If they had been injured in a confrontation in which they tried to ward off blows, the bones on the outside of their forearms might have been broken. To have bones broken on the inside of their forearms, the doctors pointed out, required that someone hold down their arms while blows were administered. Another early investigation involved refugees from Halabja who had crossed into Turkey in 1988 following Iraqi dictator Saddam Hussein's reported use of chemical weapons to attack the town predominantly populated by Iraq's Kurdish minority. At the time, the Reagan administration, which had sided with Saddam in the prolonged war that he launched against America's enemy, Iran, cast doubt on reports of his use of chemical weapons. The investigation by PHR played an important role in verifying that the allegations by the Kurdish refugees were justified. Subsequent investigations by Human Rights Watch, following the establishment of an autonomous Iraqi Kurdistan after the 1991 Gulf War, indicated that Saddam's chemical weapons in Halabja had killed about 5,000 persons. The 1988 attack had been part of the Iraqi leader's genocidal "Anfal" campaign meant to punish the Kurds for trying to exploit Iraq's war with Iran as an opportunity to create an independent Kurdistan.

One of the important contributions by Physicians for Human Rights has been its sponsorship of investigations by forensic anthropologists in which mass grave sites are exhumed to identify the victims of human rights abuses and to determine how and when they died. This method of conducting human rights investigations had been pioneered by Eric Stover, a veteran human rights researcher, who served as executive director of PHR in the late 1980s and the early 1990s. Stover had been director of the human rights program at the American Association for the Advancement of Science when the transition from military dictatorship to democracy took place in Argentina in 1983.

In his AAAS post, Stover sought ways to use science to aid the human rights cause and enlisted a prominent forensic anthropologist, Clyde Snow, to go to Argentina to exhume the graves of victims of the Argentine military's "disappearances." The testimony that Snow provided at the trial of members of the military junta that ruled Argentina from 1976 to 1983 played a dramatic and important role in obtaining convictions. For many in Argentina and elsewhere, Snow's testimony about one of the disappeared came to epitomize the cruelty of the dictatorship. The forensic anthropologist identified a young woman and demonstrated to the court that the position of her pelvic bones showed that she had been executed immediately after giving birth.[3]

At Physicians for Human Rights, Stover enlisted Clyde Snow in conducting forensic investigations in many places, including Iraqi Kurdistan and, beginning while the wars in the ex-Yugoslavia were still underway in the early 1990s, in Bosnia and Croatia. One of the investigations conducted by Snow and Stover for PHR supplied proof that more than two hundred men taken from a hospital in 1991 in the Croatian town of Vukovar had been executed by Serb soldiers a few miles away. PHR's evidence played a crucial role years later in trials conducted by the International Criminal Tribunal for the former Yugoslavia.

Physicians for Human Rights has played an important investigative role throughout its history. One of its noteworthy efforts involved the discovery of a mass execution of prisoners in Afghanistan and a subsequent cover-up of the slaughter by the Bush administration. PHR has also conducted campaigns on behalf of physicians who have been victims of human rights abuses, and it has attempted to ensure that members of the medical profession do not themselves take part in abuses of human rights. An example of its efforts on behalf of persecuted physicians is its campaign to secure the release of two Iranian physicians imprisoned in 2008 in connection with their treatment of drug addicts. The doctors, brothers named Alaei, were charged with conspiring against the Iranian state, apparently because of their contacts with physicians in other countries engaged in similar drug treatment programs. (The younger brother was released in late 2010 and was able to emigrate to the United States, and the older brother was released the following summer and also emigrated.) One of PHR's campaigns against medical participation in human rights abuses focused on physician participation in executions in the United States.

The Committee to Protect Journalists, founded in 1981, has a narrower focus than PHR. It does only what its name says: protects journalists when they suffer reprisals for their work. The organization deals with abductions, assaults, expulsions, exclusions, libel suits, harassment, imprisonment, disappearances, and murders of journalists. The organization's significance in the human rights field derives in part from the important role that journalists play in reporting on abuses against others and from the fact that reprisals against them often take place to discourage such reporting. In addition, because the constituency of CPJ is largely made up of journalists, and individuals and institutions associated with the media provide a large part of the organization's financial support, it has contributed substantially to knowledge and appreciation of the human rights cause by members of the profession. Since its founding—principally by Michael Massing, an editor of the *Columbia Journalism Review* and a freelance journalist—CPJ has enlisted the best-known journalists in the United States in its activities. They have included prominent media personalities: Walter Cronkite, Dan Rather, Christiane Amanpour, Tom Brokaw, Peter Jennings, Gwen Ifill, Brian Williams, and many more.

Yet another organization based in a profession, Global Rights, started as the International Human Rights Law Group in 1979. Initially, it was a Washington, DC counterpart of the New York–based Lawyers Committee for International Human Rights, without the emphasis on asylum cases but with a comparable association with leading law firms. Over time, its focus became the establishment of legal programs to protect human rights in countries around the world that had not previously established such efforts indigenously. It established programs in such countries as Nicaragua, Bosnia, Nigeria, Burundi, and Afghanistan. A main role of Global Rights is the training l of local lawyers and others in documenting and exposing violations of rights, advocating reform, and bringing litigation in local courts on behalf of victims of abuses. Unlike the other principal U.S.–based human rights groups, Global Rights seeks and accepts government funds.[4]

An organization with a regional focus, the Washington Office on Latin America (WOLA) was established in1974, somewhat earlier than most other U.S.–based human rights groups. Its principal organizer and long-time executive director, Joseph Eldridge, had been a Methodist minister in Chile until the Pinochet coup the previous year. Forced to leave the country following the coup, Eldridge established WOLA in the Methodist building in Washington, DC, across the street from the Capitol, with support from his own church and from other religious groups. An influential group in its first several years, WOLA came under severe attack from the Reagan administration when it entered office in 1981 for the organization's mildly left of center stand. Less combative in style than Americas Watch (one of the forerunners of Human Rights Watch), which thrived on conflict with the Reagan administration, WOLA lost ground to the newer group as the leading advocate in the United States of human rights in Latin America.

In subsequent years, while WOLA has continued to play a role in promoting human rights in Latin America, much of its focus is on supporting public policies that are conducive to democratic development in the hemisphere. These include promoting civilian control of the military and more enlightened approaches to combating drug trafficking than those that rely on military solutions.

Other U.S.–based human rights groups operating internationally include Mental Disability Rights International, which conducts investigations and exposés of the institutions where the mentally ill and the intellectually disabled are confined, mainly in Europe and Latin America; Cultural Survival, which campaigns on behalf of indigenous peoples worldwide; the Center for Justice and Accountability, which specializes in litigation, principally in the United States, against the perpetrators of gross abuses of human rights in other countries; PEN, the writers' association that campaigns on behalf of persecuted writers worldwide; human rights programs at a number of universities, including Harvard, Yale, Columbia, American, Berkeley, and Georgetown—often, but not always or not exclusively, at their law schools; and human rights programs associated with a few scientific organizations. The involvement of the scientific groups is a legacy of the prominent role of scientists in the human rights movement in the Soviet Union during the Cold War era. In addition, there are a number of U.S.–based groups that focus on a particular country or territory, such as Tibet, China, Burma, Sudan (Darfur), Iran, and Haiti. Some of the latter are led by expatriates or exiles from the regions on which they focus.

Probably the oldest U.S.–based organization that might be considered a part of the international human rights movement is Freedom House, established in 1941, a year prior to the International League for the Rights of Man. Whether it should be considered part of the movement is questioned by some because of its close relationship to the United States government, which provides most of its funding.

Freedom House was formed at the behest of President Franklin D. Roosevelt who wanted to enlist prominent citizens in promoting support for the Allies against the Axis powers in the period before the United States entered World War II. From the start, Eleanor Roosevelt served as the organization's honorary chair. After the war, Freedom House became a valued ally of the U.S. government in Cold War denunciations of Soviet tyranny. It did not conduct investigations of human rights abuses in the manner that became characteristic of Amnesty International and Human Rights Watch. Rather, the organization made its mark primarily by publishing an annual survey of freedom around the world in which it gave numerical rankings to countries for their practices with respect to civil liberties and democracy. In the early years, these rankings were somewhat skewed to present countries aligned with the United States in the Cold War struggle in a more favorable light. Over time, however, the surveys have become more reliable.

Although Freedom House's annual surveys have achieved a high standard of objectivity, the organization continued as late as the 1990s to associate itself with ideologically driven reports of human rights abuses that were not substantiated. It promoted the work of a former Chinese dissident, Harry Wu, who published greatly exaggerated reports on the number of political prisoners in China. And it absorbed a small organization, the Puebla Institute, and gave a platform to that organization's director, Nina Shea, who issued comparably exaggerated accounts of persecutions of Christians in China and elsewhere. In both cases, Freedom House dealt with issues of genuine significance to those concerned with human rights but alienated some of those associated with the cause through its failure to adhere to the standards that others in the field imposed on themselves.[5]

In the first decade of the twenty-first century, while continuing to derive most of its funding from the U.S. government, Freedom House gained more acceptance from the mainstream of the human rights movement because its work improved in objectivity. Some observers of the organization give credit to a new director who assumed charge during that period, Jennifer Windsor. Despite its financial dependence on government support, Windsor demonstrated a readiness to criticize policies of the George W. Bush administration that violated civil liberties. In 2010, Windsor was succeeded as the organization's director by David Kramer, a former State Department official. It is not yet known at this writing how the organization will perform under his leadership.

The newest U.S.–based group to become a significant factor in international human rights is the International Center for Transitional Justice. Like a small number of other organizations in the field, the impetus for the establishment of ICTJ, which began operations in 2001, came from a philanthropic foundation, in this case the Ford Foundation. An important source of financing for human rights organizations in many parts of the world since the 1970s, the Foundation seemed eager to make an additional mark in the field. Initially, ICTJ focused on providing a source of expert support for truth commissions, which were in vogue at the time on account of what was widely regarded as the successful experience of the South African Truth and Reconciliation Commission (TRC).

Ford chose Alex Boraine, the one-time head of the Methodist Church in Southern Africa, who had served as deputy chair of the TRC in South Africa, to serve as president of the ICTJ. He recruited a distinguished board of directors for the new organization and, with the help of substantial funding provided by the Ford Foundation and a few other foundations, attracted a high-quality staff. Though many in human rights were skeptical that there was a need for a new player in the field, the organization won respect relatively quickly. Its success reflected its decision not to limit its efforts to truth commissions but to employ the full range of remedies that might assist countries in repairing the damage done by governments that committed gross abuses of human rights. These included the prosecution of perpetrators, institutional reforms, and efforts to obtain reparations for those who had suffered specific harms under repressive regimes.

In 2009, ICTJ underwent a financial crisis brought about by a combination of its own rapid expansion and the global recession. Many of its staff left the organization during this upheaval. With new leadership provided by David Tolbert, former deputy chief prosecutor of the International Criminal Tribunal for the Former Yugoslavia, the organization later regained its momentum.

The number and significance of the human rights organizations operating internationally that are based in the United Kingdom, in addition to Amnesty International, is not substantially below than that of U.S.–based groups. One leading organization is Interights—as it is generally known—or, to give it its full name, the International Centre for the Protection of Human Rights. Established in 1982, it plays a prominent role in sponsoring litigation internationally to protect rights.

The key figure in the establishment of Interights was Anthony Lester—subsequently, Lord Lester of Herne Hill—a barrister and a leading litigator in human rights cases in the British courts; in the courts of Commonwealth countries in which a Queen's Counsel is entitled to practice; in the European Court of Human Rights, the Court associated with the Council of Europe, that enforces the European Convention on Human Rights; and in the European Court of Justice, the Court associated with the European Union that enforces the laws adopted by that body. Trained in American law (Lester is a graduate of Harvard Law School), as well as British law, he brought to the creation of Interights an understanding of the central and strategic place that litigation has occupied in the advancement of rights in the United States. In addition to bringing litigation before domestic and international courts—especially the European Court of Human Rights, which has become the world's most significant judicial body in the protection of rights internationally—Interights has organized many judicial colloquies in different parts of the world. These have contributed significantly to the reliance by judges on international human rights standards in their decision-making. The organization's training programs for young lawyers have also helped to advance the invocation of those standards in domestic courts, as well as in cases that are brought before international tribunals.

Other important organizations sponsoring international human rights litigation include the Washington, DC–based Center for Justice and International Law (CEJIL); and another London-based organization, the Kurdish Human Rights Project. CEJIL focuses on litigation before the Inter-American Commission and the Inter-American Court of Human Rights. Those western hemisphere bodies were established more recently than their European counterparts and deal with a smaller number of cases from fewer countries. Over time, however, the Inter-American Court has grown in significance and CEJIL, which operates as a kind of Western-hemisphere counterpart to Interights in Europe, is an increasingly significant body in promoting the international protection of rights through litigation.

An especially large number of the cases brought before the European Court of Human Rights involve the Kurdish minority in southeastern Turkey. The Kurdish Human Rights Project, often calling upon the services of British barristers who volunteer to assist in such matters under its auspices, participates in many such cases. As a consequence of the frequency with which it appears before the European Court, the Kurdish group has become a center of expertise on the jurisprudence of the Strasbourg-based tribunal. In addition to cases emanating from Turkey, the Kurdish Human Rights Project also assists in litigation from Armenia and Azerbaijan as these two states also are subject to the jurisdiction of the European Court of Human Rights and have Kurdish minority populations.

Groups based in the United Kingdom include two that oppose censorship. *Index on Censorship* is a bimonthly journal, published since 1972, that chronicles attacks on freedom of expression worldwide. Its founding editor, Michael Scammell, is a scholar of Russian literature and, in its early years, *Index* often published works that were banned in the Soviet Union and other communist countries. Its founding board members included David Astor, the editor of the *Observer* whose publication of Peter Benenson's "Appeal for Amnesty" launched Amnesty International. The poet Stephen Spender was also instrumental in establishing *Index* and, over the years, such literary figures as Tom Stoppard and Philip Roth have been associated with the journal. Although its circulation has never been higher than several thousand, *Index* is widely known and respected in the international human rights movement. Under the leadership of its director, John Kampfner, it has also played an important role in free speech issues in the United Kingdom. In 2010 and 2011, *Index* was at the forefront of efforts to revise British libel laws, which have encouraged individuals in many countries to bring lawsuits in the courts of the United Kingdom to suppress critical writings about them published anywhere in the world.

The group Article 19, established in 1986, is named for the provision of the Universal Declaration of Human Rights that protects freedom of expression. Though based in London, its founder and main supporter during its first several years was an American philanthropy, the J. Roderick MacArthur Foundation, which wanted to create a counterpart to Amnesty International that would have as its mission opposing censorship. Amnesty's location made London the foundation's choice. Article 19's primary method has been investigation and documentation. For a number of years following the Ayatollah Khomeini's issuance of his 1988 *fatwa* against author Salman Rushdie, in which he called for Rushdie's murder and the murder of others associated with the publication of his novel *The Satanic Verses*, Article 19, led by its executive director, Frances D'Souza (now Baroness D'Souza), spearheaded the worldwide campaign on behalf of Rushdie. Though merger between Article 19 and *Index on Censorship* was discussed from time to time by the boards of the two organizations, arrangements always fell through. They exist side by side in the same city and, at times, have even shared office space, but have maintained their separate identity. The American foundation that created Article 19 discontinued support after about a decade, and the organization currently derives most of its support from European donors.

At this writing, a third organization with the mission to defend freedom of expression has been established in London: the Media Legal Defence Initiative. Its role, as its name indicates, is to provide legal representation to journalists whose rights are in jeopardy. MLDI's creation was inspired by a number of lawsuits for libel brought against journalists in Asian countries, such as Indonesia and Thailand, whose primary aim seemed to be to silence critical voices. In one such case, the then prime minister of Thailand, Thaksin Shinawatra, sued a young journalist who had published information about his business affairs. MLDI is too new as yet to have been able to prove its effectiveness, but potentially it could meet an important need.

Other prominent London-based organizations promoting human rights internationally include Penal Reform International, which does not rely on investigation and documentation but instead works with prison authorities worldwide to seek improvements in the conditions of confinement; the Minority Rights Group, which publishes investigative reports and conducts training programs for representatives of such neglected minorities as the Pygmies in Central Africa and sponsors a range of educational and public awareness campaigns; and a relatively recently established organization, the Business and Human Rights Resource Centre. Too small to conduct extensive investigations on its own, the latter group has proved effective in helping to persuade corporations to respect rights by gleaning information on their practices from investigations conducted by such organizations as Amnesty International and Human Rights Watch and by seeking responses from businesses to allegations of misconduct. In essence the organization leverages the efforts of much larger organizations to achieve additional impact. At this writing, the Business and Human Rights Resource Center says that its website provides information on the practices of over 4,000 companies in more than 180 countries. That website has become the first place to check for those seeking information on a corporation's human rights practices.

Global Witness is an organization established in London in 1993. It could just as easily be classified as a human rights organization, an anti-corruption group, an anti-conflict group, or as an environmental organization. It brings together all those concerns in the interests of investigating and documenting the links between the exploitation of natural resources and a range of abuses. Global Witness began its operations by demonstrating the manner in which the Khmer Rouge in Cambodia sustained itself through the timber trade in collaboration with Thai logging companies and corrupt officers of the Thai military. The organization's work in Africa led to the establishment of the Kimberley Process Certification Scheme to curb the trade in conflict diamonds. Other investigations have focused on such countries as Angola, Burma, the Democratic Republic of the Congo, Liberia, and Sierra Leone. It took the lead in organizing the "Publish What You Pay" campaign, a coalition of more than 300 nongovernmental organizations worldwide that has pressed corporations to disclose their payments to the governments of countries where the natural resources that they extract are located. This effort was instrumental in persuading the government of the United Kingdom to establish the Extractive Industries Transparency Initiative, launched by then prime minister Tony Blair in a speech at Johannesburg in 2002. In essence, Global Witness created the movement, since joined by a number of other organizations, to disclose publicly the vast sums involved in the extraction of natural resources and the frequent misuse of those funds. Because Global Witness also promotes other interests, it is not regularly thought of as a human rights organization, and even some of those associated with it may not think of themselves in that way. Yet its impact in the human rights field in demonstrating how the Khmer Rouge financed itself, or in exposing the role of the Liberian dictator Charles Taylor in the ghastly conflict in Sierra Leone, has been substantial.

Another organization that does not see itself as a human rights organization, and is not seen that way by most knowledgeable observers of the movement, nevertheless frequently plays an important part in debates over human rights issues. The International Crisis Group, founded in 1995 with headquarters in Brussels, has a global research capacity that puts it in the same category as Amnesty International and Human Rights Watch. It defines its primary mission as conflict prevention. It seems appropriate to mention the group in a discussion of human rights organizations, because there is frequently a significant rights component to its efforts to prevent conflict. Gareth Evans, the former foreign minister of Australia, who served as the organization's president for about a decade and was instrumental in establishing its reputation and influence, was also a major player in developing the concept of a "responsibility to protect" (see chapter 12) and used his ICG post to build support for the concept.

At times, ICG has taken stands contrary to those of many advocates of human rights. An example is its position on Burma. ICG has criticized those who have advocated isolation of Burma because of its gross abuses.

The organization attacked the Global Fund to Fight AIDS, Tuberculosis and Malaria for revoking a grant to the Burmese military government. The Fund said that it revoked the grant because the Burmese regime refused to honor its commitment to allow the Fund to monitor administration of the grant according to its standard procedures. Many in the human rights movement had sought such monitoring to ensure that assistance was provided fairly in parts of the country where many Burmese are opposed to the regime. ICG argued that cancellation of the grant did harm to Burmese who needed the care that would be available under the grant.

In 2008, former United Nations High Commissioner for Human Rights Louise Arbour succeeded Gareth Evans as president of the International Crisis Group. It seems likely that her appointment will lead to heightened collaboration between ICG and human rights groups. When riots took place in southern Kyrgyzstan in spring 2010, following the ouster of President Bakiyev, and many thousands of ethnic Uzbeks living in the vicinity of the major city of the region, Osh, were driven from their homes or killed, the International Crisis Group and Human Rights Watch issued a joint report and coordinated their advocacy.

A handful of international human rights groups are based in Paris and Geneva. Of these, the most prominent are the Fédération Internationale des ligues des droits de l'Homme (FIDH) in Paris and the International Commission of Jurists in Geneva. A predecessor of FIDH, the Ligue Internationale pour droits de L'Homme, was established in 1902 as an outgrowth of the Dreyfus case, and after maintaining a presence in Paris for many years, migrated to New York in the early 1940s at the time of the Nazi occupation and helped give birth to the U.S.–based International League for the Rights of Man (later, the International League for Human Rights).

FIDH sponsors investigations and documentation and establishes affiliations with many national human rights groups, especially in Francophone countries. At this writing, FIDH reports that 164 organizations around the world have affiliations with it. The organization dates its founding to 1922 and, in the period between the two world wars, enlisted a number of prominent persons in Germany and France in efforts to promote both peace and human rights. One of the Germans associated with the organization was Karl von Ossietzky, a journalist known for his exposé of secret German rearmament in violation of the Versailles peace accord. In 1936, Ossietzky was chosen as the recipient of the Nobel Peace Prize, but as he was then in prison in Germany, he was unable to travel to Oslo to collect the prize. Hitler was so infuriated by the award to Ossietzky that he prohibited Germans from ever accepting any Nobel Prize. Ossietzky died before the beginning of World War II, from tuberculosis, which he may have contracted while in prison. Among the French members of FIDH during the inter-war period were René Cassin, subsequently an important figure in the Resistance as legal advisor to General DeGaulle, an author of the Universal Declaration of Human Rights after the war, and himself a recipient of the Nobel Peace Prize; and Victor Basch, the organization's president, who was murdered during the war by French collaborators with the Nazis. The organization disappeared during the war years but was revived in the 1950s. Some of FIDH's current efforts focus on getting French courts to exercise universal jurisdiction to try those alleged to have committed severe abuses of human rights in countries in which there are affiliates of the Federation. As in some other civil law countries, criminal trials in France may take place in the absence of the defendant. FIDH obtained one conviction in absentia by a French court in 2005 in a case involving a Mauritanian officer accused of torture. It obtained another such conviction of a Tunisian in 2010, also for torture. In the Tunisian case, defendant Khaled Ben Said had been a police superintendent in 1991 when the torture took place. A decade later, a woman he had tortured learned that he had become the Tunisian vice consul in Strasbourg. On the basis of her complaint FIDH initiated proceedings, which eventually led a French court to impose a twelve-year prison sentence on Ben Said. He evaded imprisonment by returning to Tunisia, where he was employed by the Interior Ministry prior to the January 2011 revolution. Whether he will ultimately be brought to justice is not known.

The International Commission of Jurists, an organization of lawyers, was established in Geneva in 1952. An influential body in its early years before the emergence of the international human rights movement, it was damaged in 1967 by a report in an American magazine of the era, *Ramparts*, that it was funded by the CIA; and again in 1975 when former CIA agent Philip Agee alleged that it was a front for the CIA (as noted in chapter 8.) Though it was funded by the CIA in its early years, that was almost certainly no longer the case by 1975. Yet the organization was never severely discredited by the revelations of its covert funding. ICJ still has a sufficiently good name internationally that beleaguered human rights organizations in some countries—for example a West Bank Palestinian human rights group, Al-Haq, which itself has a good reputation—have found it advantageous to affiliate with the ICJ. Some of ICJ's most significant work in recent years has focused on documenting interference with the independence of judges and lawyers. The organization has also periodically enlisted "eminent jurists" to issue substantial reports on important questions. An example is a book length-study it published in 2009 on counterterrorism policies and human rights that was written by a panel chaired by the former chief justice of the Constitutional Court of South Africa, Arthur Chaskalson.[6]

A few organizations that promote human rights internationally are located in other parts of the world. The Commonwealth Human Rights Initiative is based in New Delhi, India. Originally established in 1987 by five Commonwealth professional bodies in the fields of journalism, law, legal education, organized labor, and medicine, the organization's headquarters was in London until 1993 when it relocated to India. Currently the largest part of its work focuses on Commonwealth countries in South Asia, particularly India; and on a few Commonwealth countries in Africa, including Ghana, Kenya, Uganda, and Tanzania. The organization engages in more modest efforts in some other parts of the world, most notably the Caribbean. In addition to its main office in New Delhi, it has offices in Accra, Ghana and in London. CHRI's projects in India makes up so large a part of its efforts that it could readily be described as an Indian human rights group. Much of its work involves advocacy for reform of institutions, such as the police and the prisons. A major concern everywhere that CHRI operates has been adopting and implementing legislation on the right to information. In India, a particular focus for several years was on the 2002 riots in the state of Gujarat in which about two thousand Muslims were killed in communal violence that was justified and even promoted by the state's political leaders, and in trying to end impunity for those responsible for the murders.

Though the Commonwealth Human Rights Initiative is based in New Delhi, only a small part of its funding comes from India. The remainder is provided by government-connected agencies in a few other Commonwealth countries, and by donors in Europe and the United States.

Another international organization based in Asia is Forum Asia. With headquarters in Bangkok, it is active in several countries of Southeast Asia, where it has been instrumental in persuading ASEAN (the Association of Southeast Asian Nations) to initiate an effort to establish a regional human rights agreement and a regional body to promote compliance.

Budapest, Hungary is also the site of at least two human rights groups operating internationally. The older of the two is the European Roma Rights Center, established in 1996. It conducts investigations, sponsors litigation, and engages in advocacy on behalf of an oppressed minority that is primarily concentrated in Romania, Bulgaria, the Czech Republic, and Slovakia, as well as in Hungary, and also has significant numbers in the former communist countries of Macedonia, Serbia, Kosovo, Albania, Ukraine, and Russia. At times, the ERRC has also extended its work to Western European countries to counter discrimination. When the government of Italian Prime Minister Silvio Berlusconi provoked racist attacks against the country's Roma minority in 2010, ERRC sought condemnation by the European Union and also legal remedies. The organization has also challenged French President Nicolas Sarkozy's summary deportations of Roma to Bulgaria and Romania.

Another Budapest-based group is the Mental Disability Advocacy Center, which relies primarily on litigation to protect the rights of those institutionalized for mental illness or intellectual disability in the former communist countries. Its work complements that of the U.S.–based Mental Disability Rights International, which relies on investigations and exposés in confronting the same issues.

By far the largest number of organizations worldwide that attempt to promote human rights are organized nationally or locally and limit their efforts to causes within their own territory. No other country has organizations in this field with the longevity and wide public support of such American groups as the NAACP (established in 1909) or the American Civil Liberties Union (established in 1920). Liberty, in the United Kingdom, established as the National Council of Civil Liberties in 1934, comes closest in durability and in the manner of its operation to the American organizations, and, in recent years, has been particularly effective in limiting rights violations arising from concerns about terrorism. Yet, as of 2011, it had no more than ten thousand members, while its American counterpart had more than a half million.

The overwhelming majority of the world's national and local organizations promoting human rights have been established since the last half of the 1970s. The remainder of this chapter will furnish brief descriptions of a half dozen organizations in different parts of the world that are emblematic of the worldwide human rights movement: the Moscow Helsinki Group (established in 1976); the Fund for Humanitarian Law in Serbia (1992); the Legal Resources Center in South Africa (1979); the Center for Legal and Social Studies in Argentina (1979); the Asociación Pro Derechos Humanos in Peru (1983); and the Human Rights Commission of Pakistan (1987). These are not the only human rights groups in their respective countries. In each case, they play an important, but by no means an exclusive role in protecting the rights of citizens.

As described in chapter 6, the Moscow Helsinki Group (MHG) was established in early 1976 to promote compliance by the Soviet Union with the human rights provisions that Leonid Brezhnev committed his country to respecting by signing the Helsinki Accords in August 1975. By 1982, however, the MHG was forced to announce that it had suspended operations because virtually all of its members had been imprisoned or forced into exile. The organization reconstituted itself at the beginning of the 1990s as the Soviet Union collapsed and those imprisoned in labor camps for peaceful dissent were released and, in many cases, resumed their efforts to promote human rights. One of the founders of the Moscow Helsinki Group, historian Ludmilla Alexeyeva, who had lived in exile in the United States since the late 1970s played a prominent role from afar in chronicling Soviet repression and campaigning for victims, returned to Moscow and took over the organization's leadership. Though in her 80s at this writing, Alexeyeva continues in that role. As leader of the Moscow Helsinki Group, she has frequently been critical of the actions of Vladimir Putin during his tenure as president of Russia and, subsequently, as prime minister. Another Russian organization, Memorial, founded as communism was collapsing in 1989 with the original purpose of preserving a record of the crimes of the Stalin era and of subsequent repression, has been even more outspoken. It has been in the forefront of efforts to document repression in Chechnya and, as a consequence, its leaders have themselves suffered attacks. In 2009, one of its principal investigators, Natalya Estemirova, was kidnapped and murdered in Chechnya (see chapter 1). Alexeyeva's age and her long and distinguished record of struggle for human rights during the Soviet era have provided her with a certain protection against the kinds of reprisals that might be used against comparably forthright critics of the Russian regime who lack her credentials. While he was president, Putin held an annual hour-long meeting with representatives of the country's leading human rights groups. One such meeting coincided with Alexeyeva's birthday and, though she has been one of his most consistent critics, Putin showed up with a bouquet of flowers to present to her.

A principal role of the Moscow Helsinki Group in recent years has been to encourage and support the development of local human rights groups across Russia. In documenting violations of human rights, it has included reports on economic and social rights as well. While that is a common practice in other parts of the world, it is not generally done in former

Soviet bloc countries. Human rights activists in that region recall that, during the Soviet period, their governments regularly countered Western denunciations of their civil and political rights records by pointing to economic inequalities in the West and labeling these as violations of economic and social rights. That history has tended to discredit the concept of economic and social rights in former communist countries. When asked why the Moscow Helsinki Group does not follow the general practice in the region, Alexeyeva's response tends to be tactical. She points out that many in Russia are deeply unhappy about practical problems—poor quality health care, for example, and the state's failure to pay promised pensions. Their motivation for joining or supporting local human rights groups is often concern about such matters. Through their involvement in such groups, according to Alexeyeva, they also become aware of civil and political rights. In this way, the Moscow Helsinki Group strives to use public concern about economic and social issues to strengthen the Russian human rights movement.

The formation of the Moscow Helsinki Group during the Soviet era was the inspiration for the formation of other organizations bearing "Helsinki" in their names in other countries of the region. Among those that currently play leading roles are the Bulgarian Helsinki Committee, the Czech Helsinki Committee, the Hungarian Helsinki Committee, the Polish Helsinki Foundation for Human Rights, and the Romanian Helsinki Committee. Less well developed are Helsinki organizations in several other area countries, including Serbia, Croatia, Belarus, Ukraine, and Montenegro. Some of the funding for Helsinki organizations in former communist countries is provided by counterparts in such countries as Sweden, Norway, and the Netherlands, which obtain support from government aid agencies in their own countries to be used for this purpose.

Throughout the conflicts of the 1990s, the Fund for Humanitarian Law in Serbia was the leading organization in the countries of the former Yugoslavia monitoring violations of the laws of war. In the years since those wars ended it has continued to document the crimes that were committed during that era and has been an important source of information for prosecutors at the International Criminal Tribunal for the Former Yugoslavia and for the courts established in Serbia, Croatia, and Bosnia that have also brought prosecutions for war crimes.

For more than two decades, the organization has been led by Natasa Kandic, a lawyer, well known in the region for her determination and her fearlessness. During the war in Kosovo, she regularly crossed military lines to gather information on abuses. Those aware of her work were astonished that the only physical attack she suffered during the conflict took place when a Serb policeman slammed her car door on her legs. After the war, when Albanian Kosovars took reprisals against many Serbs, she had no hesitation in traveling around Kosovo, speaking Serbian. For a time, she may have been the only person without armed protection who was able to do so without coming to harm.

The Fund for Humanitarian Law has established an important archive in Belgrade on the wars in ex-Yugoslavia. At this writing, Natasa Kandic is attempting to persuade the governments of the region to join together in creating an investigative commission to thoroughly document the wars and assess culpability. If this plan were realized the result would be in effect a multi-state truth commission, the first of its kind. Kandic does not seem to be succeeding in this effort.

Just as the Moscow Helsinki Group was born at a time of severe repression in the Soviet Union, and the Fund for Humanitarian Law was founded during the ethnic cleansing and slaughter that marked the break-up of Yugoslavia, so the Center for Legal and Social Studies (CELS, the acronym for Centro de Estudios Legales y Sociales) in Argentina was established in 1979, at roughly at the mid-point in the period of oppressive military dictatorship that lasted from 1976 to 1983. As discussed in chapter 7, military rule in Argentina was marked by close to nine thousand officially documented "disappearances." The actual number may be twice that.

The principal founder of CELS and the organization's leader until his death in 1998 was a lawyer and former university rector, Emilio Mignone. He was propelled into human rights activity when one of his daughters became a disappeared person. Many of those who knew him at the time said that after his daughter's disappearance there was nothing more the military could do to him that would deter him from pursuing investigations of their crimes. While the military dictatorship held power, the main role of CELS was to document disappearances and such abuses as the long-term imprisonment of many thousands of Argentines without charges or trial.

As recounted in chapter 9, the brief disappearance of Emilio Mignone himself in 1981, and the role of the United States in that episode, had significant consequences for the human rights policies and practices that the newly installed Reagan administration was required to adopt. The international reaction focused attention on the threat to the organization and its leadership and probably helped to enable CELS to continue its operations until the armed forces yielded power to a democratically elected government in December 1983. Following the transition, CELS played an important public advocacy role in efforts to ensure that those responsible for abuses would be held accountable. The documentation that it had collected during military rule was an essential resource for the national commission that investigated the disappearances and for the prosecutions that took place. Three decades after its establishment, CELS still deals with issues of accountability and historical preservation related to the years of military dictatorship. In the present day, its major focus is on such issues as abuse by the police, prison conditions, and the mistreatment of vulnerable minorities, including the mentally ill and the intellectually disabled. The organization has extended its work to economic and social rights as well. In 2009, CELS reported that it was litigating about a hundred cases before Argentine courts and, in the process, attempting to introduce international human rights norms in domestic jurisprudence. The organization also said that it was pursuing more than thirty cases internationally through bodies of the Organization of American States and the United Nations. At this writing, CELS is in the process of establishing offices in Brussels and New York to enhance its capacity to influence the European Union and the United Nations on issues of concern to the organization, and also to bolster its international fundraising.

APRODEH, the Association for Human Rights in Peru, was established at a time of severe human rights abuses related to the guerrilla war launched in 1980 by the messianic Maoist movement, Sendero Luminoso (Shining Path). The organization's main work during its early years was documenting abuses in the conflict zones in the Andes that particularly victimized the region's indigenous population. Like many other human rights groups created to deal with severe abuses during a time of crisis, it maintained its operations after the conflict came to an end and today is one of the leading organizations in Peru dealing with a broad range of issues. It documents violations, provides legal representation to victims, and, like CELS in Argentina, takes some cases to the Inter-American Court of Human Rights. APRODEH has also extended its work to address questions of economic and social rights.

Yet another organization established while a repressive system was in place is the Legal Resources Center in South Africa. It began operations in 1979 under the leadership of Arthur Chaskalson, a leading advocate of the South African bar. (In South Africa, an advocate is the equivalent of a British barrister: that is, she argues cases in court.) From the start, the work of the Legal Resources Center has focused on bringing strategic litigation. In its early years, its efforts addressed the injustices resulting from the apartheid system. Since the transition to majority rule democracy in 1994 and an end to legally mandated racial subjugation, its work has covered a wide range of issues involving both civil and political rights and economic and social rights. Its most prominent case in the latter category involved representation of the Treatment Action Campaign in its successful effort to require the ministry of health to distribute Nevirapene to pregnant women so as to prevent transmission of HIV to their children (see chapter 3). That case was decided by the Constitutional Court of which Chaskalson was appointed chief justice in 1994, following Nelson Mandela's election as president of South Africa.

The Human Rights Commission of Pakistan is well known internationally in part because of two remarkable women in the organization, Asma Jahangir and Hina Jilani. Sisters, in their fifties at this writing, both lawyers, they are the daughters of a man who was a political prisoner when Ali Bhutto was prime minister of Pakistan. They became known in the 1980s for leading the struggle against what were called the "Hudood Ordinances" of President Zia-ul-Haq, who seized power from Bhutto in 1977. Under these laws, which were part of Zia's drive to Islamicize the country's political and cultural life, women who complained they had been raped could prevail in court only if they could obtain testimony from four male witnesses. A woman who claimed rape but failed to produce such testimony could herself be prosecuted for fornication or adultery. Ever since they began their battle against the Hudood Ordinances—which have been modified and are not vigorously enforced because the campaign against them stigmatized their use—Asma Jahangir and Hina Jilani have been at the forefront of the struggles for women's rights, and for human rights generally in Pakistan. Much of their work, and the work of other lawyers engaged in the rights cause, has taken place through the Human Rights Commission of Pakistan. Asma Jahangir and Hina Jilani have also played significant roles internationally. Hina Jilani has served as the U.N. Special Rapporteur on the Protection of Human Rights Defenders, and at this writing Asma Jahangir is the U.N. Special Rapporteur on Freedom of Religion. Though they frequently come under various forms of attack in Pakistan, Asma Jahangir, Hina Jilani, and their colleagues in the Human Rights Commission of Pakistan remain active and prominent in the struggle for human rights in their country.

There are other human rights organizations not mentioned here that have at times been comparably important in the same countries. These were chosen for mention here not so much because they are representative of the worldwide human rights movement as because they are indicative of it. By now, most of them have been in operation for more than a quarter of a century, and the likelihood is that they will continue to play an important role in their countries for the foreseeable future.

For the most part, the human rights groups operating internationally and those working nationally lack formal ties to one another. The exceptions include affiliations by some national organizations with the Paris-based FIDH and the Geneva-based International Commission of Jurists. In those cases, however, the main function of affiliation is to enhance the status, and in some cases the security, of the national bodies. It does not extend to the coordination of policy or sharing of funds. Another body, the Vienna-based International Helsinki Federation for Human Rights, operated from 1982 to 2007, and, during its quarter of a century, played a significant role in launching human rights organizations in many of the countries that signed the 1975 Helsinki Accords and in providing them an opportunity to act jointly on issues of common concern. It had to close its doors in 2007 because financial irregularities were discovered (involving a bookkeeper who was stealing money from the organization) that reflected weak management. By the time it ceased operating, the importance of the Federation's role had declined greatly as many of the national groups affiliated with it had become substantial organizations in their own right and no longer needed the support of the Federation. Moreover, joint action by groups in the region had declined as the importance of their common roots in combating communist-era repression faded into the past, and they were largely unaffected by the Federation's demise.

The Coalition for the International Criminal Court, another federation, tallies its membership as including more than 2,500 civil society organizations in more than 150 countries. Many of its members are not human rights organizations, however. They have joined the CICC merely as a means of expressing support for a particular institution that promotes rights. As noted in chapter 11, a newer global group has been formed, the International Network of Civil Liberties Organizations, but it is too soon to tell whether it will become a significant body. It does not aspire to co-ordinate activities or to distribute funds. Rather, its main purposes are to share information and to facilitate efforts by its members to assist one another in periods when they come under attack or when they confront an opportunity that allows them to draw on common experience. An example of the latter situation took place in early 2011. A member of the new association, the Egyptian Initiative for Personal Rights, sought guidance from CELS in Argentina on how to deal with a transition from authoritarian rule.

Despite the scarcity of formal ties, or of ties that involve coordination of activities, the international human rights movement maintains a high level of coherence based on its commitment to certain core principles; its belief that it is the responsibility of citizens to join together in nongovernmental organizations to defend those principles; and its insistence that government officials should be held accountable for their failure to implement those principles. Those active in the international human rights movement in countries governed by repressive regimes run substantial risks on account of their adherence to the movement's principles, but they know that those risks are mitigated to some degree by the fact that others all over the world who share their commitments are watching. Even if that will not suffice to protect them, the sacrifices they make for allegiance to their principles will not go unnoticed. The growth of a worldwide secular movement committed to certain principles, and to efforts to see those principles implemented in practice, has created a sense of global solidarity in recent decades among those struggling to promote human rights. It is a development that has no historical precedent.

11

Accountability

AS OF OCTOBER 3, 2011

FOR ABOUT A QUARTER OF A CENTURY, A MAJOR GOAL OF THE international human rights movement has been to secure accountability for especially grave abuses. This focus has led to the so-called "truth commissions" in many countries, principally in Latin America and Sub-Saharan Africa, but also in several countries of Asia and in Morocco; prosecutions of literally scores of former heads of state or government before national courts in various parts of the world; increased use of the principle of universal jurisdiction in prosecutions, mainly in Europe, against those accused of gross abuses committed in other countries; and, what is likely to be the most lasting and significant means of securing accountability, the establishment of several international criminal tribunals to prosecute and punish those accused of war crimes, crimes against humanity, and genocide. In 2002, a permanent International Criminal Court (ICC) was established in The Hague. While it got off to a slow start, at this writing 120 countries are parties to the Court and it is bringing prosecutions involving the Democratic Republic of Congo, Uganda (for crimes committed by a guerrilla group, the Lord's Resistance Army), Sudan (Darfur), the Central African Republic, and Kenya. In March 2011, the United Nations Security Council adopted a unanimous resolution referring to the ICC crimes committed in Libya in connection with Colonel Muammar Qaddafi's efforts to crush a rebellion against his forty-one-year dictatorship. Two months later, prosecution began of Quaddafi himself, one of his sons, and another official of his government. Over time, the ICC has the potential to develop into the main instrument able to persuade governments to take responsibility themselves for accountability and, if they do not meet that responsibility, to deal with the question internationally.

Accountability has become a central concern of the international human rights movement for several reasons. It means recognition, or official acknowledgment, of the suffering of victims of human rights abuses. As there is, in most cases, little more that can be done to alleviate the pain caused to those whose rights have been severely violated, and to their families and their communities, such acknowledgment has great significance. Accountability also means identification of those responsible for abuses, stigmatizing them and, where criminal prosecution and punishment are possible, imposing penalties on them. Another reason that accountability matters greatly is that it makes clear that the actions of those who commit violent abuses of rights are crimes and that they warrant condemnation and, where possible, punishment. Accountability also helps to prevent history from being rewritten by those who committed abuses or who were bystanders or the beneficiaries of abuses. And, of course, provided that accountability is regularly enforced and there is, consequently, some likelihood that it will continue in effect, it may deter the commission of further abuses.

Accountability became a focus of the human rights movement starting in 1983. As discussed in chapter 7, the military dictatorship, infamous for disappearances, that had ruled Argentina for seven and a half years (since 1976) was then losing its grip on the country. Before leaving power, the junta issued what it called a "final report" on disappearances, denying responsibility, and decreed an amnesty for its own crimes. The truth commission established by President Raúl Alfonsín after he took office in December 1983 demonstrated the falsity of the junta's denials and documented 8,960 disappearances committed by the armed forces. (Some Argentines estimated that the actual total was more than double the number of those whom the commission was able to identify.) Following the issuance of the commission's report,[1] prosecutions began of nine former members of the military juntas, including three former presidents of Argentina: Eduardo Viola, Jorge Videla, and Leopoldo Galtieri. Five of the nine were convicted and sentenced to prison, including former presidents Viola and Videla.

In addition to the former junta members, a few other top military officers responsible for disappearances, torture, and other crimes were tried and convicted in Argentina. But when it came time for prosecutions against middle-level officers responsible for such crimes, they rebelled. They had only been following orders, they claimed, and demanded that prosecutions should end. Though the democratic government in Argentina put down the officers' rebellions without great difficulty, it also backed down under the pressure. President Alfonsín halted prosecutions and his successor, President Carlos Saœl Meném, pardoned those who had been convicted.

Developments in Argentina seemed to persuade democratic governments in other Latin American countries that came into office in the aftermath of military dictatorships that trials were too risky. Prosecutions and punishment might evoke a backlash from the armed forces and, after all, the military still had its guns and could threaten the survival of a nascent democratic government. In Uruguay, a law was adopted in 1986 barring prosecutions of the military for human rights abuses, and it was upheld in a popular referendum in 1989.[2] Truth commissions on the other hand, such as the body that investigated and documented the disappearances in Argentina, were feasible. In Chile, Pinochet's democratic successors made it clear that they would not challenge an amnesty that the dictator had decreed for crimes by the military. Instead, they made do with what they called a "Truth and Reconciliation Commission" that declined even to publish the names of the military officers who committed the crimes it documented, though it did make clear Pinochet's own culpability.[3] In El Salvador, a U.N.–sponsored truth commission documented crimes by both sides in the civil war that lasted from 1980 to 1992, and it named names, but the members of the commission themselves acknowledged that the Salvadoran courts were incapable of conducting trials.[4] In addition, an amnesty law hastily enacted immediately after the truth commission issued its report—one of several adopted from time to time in that country—barred prosecutions. Another Salvadoran commission was more effective. It also named names and forced the dismissal of more than a hundred military officers who had committed abuses.[5]

Though mere documentation of crimes such as torture, murder, and disappearances committed on a large scale does not seem commensurate with the gravity of those crimes, the significance of the work of truth commissions in Latin America was not negligible. Of course, the victims, and the families and friends of victims who did not survive, knew all along that the armed forces were the authors of the abuses they suffered, but official acknowledgment of the crimes and identification of the criminals (where this took place) was nevertheless important to many of them. Such acknowledgment had heightened meaning in countries where a characteristic of abuses was that they were designed to be deniable. And disappearances epitomized the concern for deniability. In the case of Argentina, after being tortured to extract the names of others who might be marked for similar treatment, many of the victims were taken aboard planes, drugged, and then pushed out over the South Atlantic so that no bodies would ever be found.[6]

The purpose of deniability was to make it possible for the military regimes in Latin America that committed such abuses to maintain a facade of legality. An important factor was their relationship to the United States. It had been the policy of the United States to foster the development in the region of counterinsurgency measures, especially after Fidel Castro seized power in Cuba in 1959, and Castro's associate, Che Guevara, set out to foment revolutions in other Latin American countries. The emergence of left-wing rebel groups such as the Tupamaros in Uruguay and the Monteneros in Argentina heightened U.S. apprehension that its Cold War enemies would gain a foothold on the Latin American mainland as they had done in the Caribbean.

While promoting counterinsurgency strategies, American officials were aware that many of their own citizens would not stand for their government's involvement in such practices as torture and murder. Crimes that were deniable—as when the Argentine government said that those who had disappeared had either left the country or joined the Monteneros—served the purposes not only of those committing and authorizing such crimes, but also of the American officials who were intent on providing them with support.

The advent of the Carter administration in 1977 disrupted many of the understandings that had previously prevailed between military dictatorships in Latin America and officials in Washington who promoted counterinsurgency and, simultaneously, publicly accepted denials of responsibility for crimes such as disappearances. Little wonder, then, that some Latin American officials and their friends in Washington were outraged by the activities of Assistant Secretary of State for Human Rights Patricia Derian. Their outrage was reflected in the famous attack on Carter's human rights policy by Jeane Kirkpatrick that earned her a prominent place in the successor Reagan administration (see chapter 9).

Another government that sought to preserve a facade of legality while committing gross abuses of human rights was that of South Africa. Apartheid itself was of course not clandestine. It was the declared policy of the government in Pretoria.[7] What was not acknowledged is that the regime tortured and sometimes murdered its critics—including some who were killed after they had fled its territory and while they were living in other countries. At a later point, its security services also secretly fomented violence between different groups of black South Africans as a means to discredit them. When a transition took place in 1994 in which South Africans of all races were permitted to vote and Nelson Mandela was elected president, one of the questions that had to be faced by the new government was how to deal with past abuses.

Mandela's administration was constrained in its ability to enforce accountability, because it had come into office under a temporary constitution that required amnesty for crimes committed under apartheid. The all-white government of President F. W. de Klerk that negotiated the transition with Mandela and the African National Congress had made clear that it would not agree to a peaceful end to apartheid and transfer of power unless its officials were guaranteed amnesty.

Barred from prosecuting those covered by the amnesty, Mandela's government instead established a Truth and Reconciliation Commission (TRC)—adopting the name of the body created in Chile after the end of Pinochet's dictatorship—to investigate and report publicly on the crimes committed under apartheid. This TRC had far more power and significance than its Chilean predecessor, for two reasons. First, whereas the Chilean body had investigated the crimes of the Pinochet era in closed proceedings, as had been the practice for all such bodies up to that point, and then published a report, the South Africans decided that their Commission's inquiries should take place in public. Witnesses would appear before the TRC in open hearings that could be attended by the public, broadcast on the radio, televised, and reported freely.[8] The ability of the South African TRC to conduct its proceedings in public reflected the fact that with the transition much of the power of the previous regime was effectively terminated. By contrast, the truth commissions in various Latin American countries that had been military dictatorships were hampered because the armed forces retained considerable power after transitions to democracy, enough to prevent public hearings. Second, and even more important, in accordance with a proposal by South Africa's minister of justice, Dullah Omar, amnesty as required by the temporary constitution would not be collective. It would be granted individually by the TRC only to those who acknowledged and fully disclosed their crimes. Those who did not do so would remain subject to prosecution.

This innovation dramatically increased the significance of the TRC. Apartheid-era officials had to choose between remaining silent and covering up their crimes on the one hand, thereby risking prosecution; or acknowledging and fully disclosing them, thereby facing public obloquy and disgrace, but obtaining amnesty. Many chose the latter course. Accordingly, the South African TRC was able to do what previous truth commissions had not done. It obtained testimony from the authors of crimes describing their crimes as well as testimony from victims and survivors. Also, the testimony obtained by the TRC was delivered in public hearings. Watching a former torturer come forward to identify his victims and demonstrate the techniques he had used to inflict pain on them proved a riveting spectacle.[9]

Subsequent to the work of the TRC in South Africa, there have been truth commissions in a number of other countries. As in South Africa, some have conducted their work through public hearings. Several, such as the commissions in Peru and Sierra Leone, are generally considered to have done important work. Yet none has seemed to match the significance of the TRC in South Africa, no doubt because the latter body operated in a context in which it penetrated the facade of legality that the apartheid regime had sought to maintain; and because of the distinctive means used by the TRC to obtain public testimony from perpetrators as well as victims. In such countries as Liberia and Sierra Leone, there was nothing secretive about the gross abuses that took place. Deniability was not a major concern of the perpetrators while they were committing their crimes. The principal value of the truth commissions in those countries has been in compiling a comprehensive record of abuses. As noted, such a record is important to victims, provides a measure of accountability by pinpointing responsibility, and makes it more difficult to rewrite history.

Priscilla Hayner, author of the leading articles and books on truth commissions, has identified some forty such bodies that have operated worldwide and calls five of them "the strongest." They are those of South Africa, Peru, Guatemala, Timor-Leste, and Morocco.[10] The reasons for selecting South Africa and Peru are self-evident. Peru was, among other things, the first Latin American commission to hold public hearings. The case for Guatemala also seems persuasive. Though the commission there did not hold public hearings and was barred from naming perpetrators by the terms of the agreement that established it, the commission's documentation of abuses was so systematic and powerful that it fundamentally shifted public understanding both in Guatemala and internationally of the crimes committed in that country. The commission labeled what had happened in Guatemala, especially in the early 1980s, as genocide. That term had not previously been widely used about Guatemala, but, since publication of the commission's report in 1999, its finding has been generally accepted. Timor-Leste is a much more surprising choice, as the country's government suppressed publication of the commission's report. Though it was subsequently published by the International Center for Transitional Justice, it is not widely known in the country that it covers. Morocco is also somewhat surprising as the commission there had limited investigative authority and was also barred from naming perpetrators. On the other hand, its report did result in the swift payment of reparations to the families of many victims.

Though truth commissions were the preferred means of securing accountability for roughly a decade following the transition in Argentina in 1983, some in the nongovernmental human rights movement continued to espouse prosecutions and criminal sanctions against those principally responsible for the most egregious abuses. Criminal sanctions seemed especially appropriate as a means to hold accountable the perpetrators of the crimes committed in connection with the "ethnic cleansing"—a term coined by the Serb forces, who were the primary authors of the practice, as a euphemism for their forced expulsions and murders—that characterized the wars of the 1990s in the former Yugoslavia.

Those wars began in June 1991 with the break-up of what had been a united Yugoslavia, followed by atrocious crimes committed along ethnic lines in Croatia after its declaration of independence. The following year, Bosnia and Herzegovina also declared independence, and the crimes committed there reached even greater extremes of ferocity. Many of the most serious were committed by Bosnian Serb forces who were equipped, financed, and largely controlled by the Serb government in Belgrade—then called the Federal Republic of Yugoslavia—against Muslims who were the largest population group in Bosnia.[11] Croatian and Bosnian forces also committed many crimes.

A call for criminal sanctions seemed appropriate to many in the human rights movement on two grounds. First, the ethnic basis for "cleansing" made what had taken place in Croatia and, to an even greater degree, what was taking place in Bosnia, reminiscent of the crimes committed a half century earlier by the Nazis. As Nuremberg had been the principal means used by the international community to hold the Nazis accountable, so a tribunal modeled after Nuremberg seemed appropriate in ex-Yugoslavia. Second, from the standpoint of international law, many of the acts committed in the cause of ethnic cleansing met the definition of war crimes.

In addition, the scale of the criminality warranted labeling these as crimes against humanity and, because of their ethnic character, even as genocide.

It had not been customary up to that point for the human rights movement to invoke the concept of war crimes. Human Rights Watch had chosen nearly a decade earlier to monitor violations of international humanitarian law, but most other nongovernmental human rights groups had not yet made the shift or were just beginning to make it when the wars of the 1990s in ex-Yugoslavia got underway. So far as Human Rights Watch was concerned, most of the conflicts it had monitored—those in Central America and in various countries in Asia and Africa, for example—were internal armed conflicts where the concept of war crimes did not seem to apply. The Geneva Conventions of 1949 and the Additional Protocols of 1977 refer to "grave breaches"—or war crimes—only in the sections of those treaties dealing with international armed conflicts. There is no reference to grave breaches in Common Article 3 of the 1949 Conventions, or in Additional Protocol II of 1977, the sections dealing with non-international conflicts. Accordingly, the prevailing view in that era among students of international humanitarian law was that the concept of war crimes was not applicable to internal armed conflicts. As almost all of the wars monitored by Human Rights Watch were not international armed conflicts, the organization had not previously labeled acts committed in the course of such conflicts as war crimes.

On the other hand, the wars in ex-Yugoslavia were clearly international armed conflicts. Three internationally recognized states—Croatia, Bosnia & Herzegovina, and the Federal Republic of Yugoslavia—were involved. The crimes that were committed met the definition of war crimes. In July 1992, Human Rights Watch issued a public call for the establishment of an international criminal tribunal to punish war crimes committed in Bosnia and Croatia.

By chance, that call for an international war crimes tribunal coincided with the publication of a story in *Newsday*, a New York area newspaper, by journalist Roy Gutman, describing two Serb-run death camps in northern Bosnia.[12] Gutman's account caused a sensation that was heightened when a U.S. State Department spokesperson who was asked about the story at a regular press briefing the day it appeared essentially confirmed it. At that point, many saw the parallels to the Nazis. Human Rights Watch's call for an international war crimes tribunal quickly gained supporters among other nongovernmental organizations, some in the media, and a number of diplomats eager to find a way to respond to the terrible crimes that were being reported by the press. By October, the United Nations Security Council had established a War Crimes Commission; by December, U.S. Secretary of State Lawrence Eagleburger had endorsed the establishment of a U.N. War Crimes Tribunal; by February 1993, a unanimous Security Council had directed the secretary general of the U.N. to prepare a specific plan for such a tribunal; and in May of 1993, the Security Council unanimously endorsed the secretary general's plan and directed the establishment of the International Criminal Tribunal for the former Yugoslavia (ICTY), the first such body since the Nuremberg and Tokyo war crimes tribunals in the immediate aftermath of World War II, and the first created under the auspices of the United Nations.

Then the pace slowed. It took fourteen months for the Security Council to endorse a choice for chief prosecutor. In the interim, the war in Bosnia continued, and large numbers of additional atrocities took place. Those whose crimes made them likely targets of the tribunal probably saw the possibility that they might some day be held to account as more and more remote. The impasse that had developed over the choice of a chief prosecutor was finally broken in July 1994 when the secretary general of the U.N. presented the name of Richard Goldstone to the Security Council. A white South African judge, Goldstone had played a crucial role in his own country in the transition from apartheid. His selection had the endorsement of Nelson Mandela, just elected as president of South Africa, who gave Goldstone a leave from his place on the country's newly established Constitutional Court to accept the U.N. appointment. Russia, an ally of the Federal Republic of Yugoslavia, had blocked other nominees but did not want a conflict with Mandela whose cause the Soviet Union had championed during his long incarceration. Goldstone was appointed and took up his new duties in August of 1994.

At the outset, it seemed that the ICTY would have little to do. For a significant period, it had only one defendant in custody: Dusko Tadic, a low-ranking guard at one of the death camps identified in Roy Gutman's reporting. To evade conscription into the Bosnian Serb army, Tadic had left Bosnia and migrated to Germany. There he was recognized on the streets of Munich by camp survivors who identified him to the German authorities. They arrested Tadic and turned him over to the ICTY, which had no means of its own to make arrests. U.N. troops stationed in Bosnia did not help. They were lightly armed and their role was limited to helping in the delivery of humanitarian assistance. They were intent on not antagonizing the Bosnian Serbs, for that might lead to reprisals that would make it impossible for them to carry out their mission. There seemed little prospect of further arrests other than through such fortuitous accidents as those that led to the apprehension of Dusko Tadic.

Despite the seeming impotence of the ICTY, Goldstone gave it credibility by his stellar reputation in South Africa and by the force of his personality. He traveled extensively to world capitals, calling on governments to support the ICTY, and, by projecting bulldog tenacity, persuaded many he encountered to take the tribunal seriously. In July 1995, he indicted Radovan Karadzic, the "president" of the Bosnian Serbs, and General Ratko Mladic, their military leader. Those indictments bolstered his effort to make the ICTY seem credible.

The previous year, from April to June 1994, during the period when there was an impasse at the U.N. over the designation of a chief prosecutor for the ICTY, the Rwandan genocide took place. As it was underway, the U.N. Security Council and the Secretariat took no action to try to halt it. Worse, the Security Council, led by the United States, fearing entanglement in an African conflict it did not understand, withdrew U.N. troops from Rwanda who might have stopped the slaughter. Eighteen Americans soldiers had been killed in a battle on the streets of Mogadishu, Somalia in October 1993, six months before the start of the genocide in Rwanda, and the Clinton administration did not want to risk involvement in another such episode in Africa. In November 1994, having done virtually nothing else about Rwanda, the Security Council created an International Criminal Tribunal for Rwanda (ICTR) as a parallel to the ICTY and designated Goldstone to be its chief prosecutor as well.

In Bosnia, the worst crime of the war, the massacre of about eight thousand Muslim men and boys at the besieged town of Srebrenica, took place in July 1995, about two weeks before the ICTY announced its indictments of Karadzic and Mladic. The murders were personally directed by Mladic. At the moment the indictments were issued, however, the massacre was not yet known. It was revealed to the world about two weeks later through a combination of investigative reporting by a young journalist for the *Christian Science Monitor*, David Rohde[13]; and then through the release of aerial reconnaissance photos of mass grave sites displayed by the United States at a hearing of the U.N. Security Council. Goldstone issued additional indictments against Karadzic and Mladic later in 1995 for the Srebrenica massacre. The two sets of indictments made it impossible for either man to take part in the peace negotiations at Dayton, Ohio in November and December of 1995 for fear of being arrested. The president of the Federal Republic of Yugoslavia, Slobodan Milosevic, who had not yet been indicted, represented Serb interests and agreed to an end to the war.

The Dayton agreement provided for the deployment of NATO troops in Bosnia and parts of Croatia to maintain peace. At the outset, those troops did not attempt to enforce indictments handed down by the ICTY by making arrests. An exception was one arrest made by troops acting under the direction of an American general, Jacques Klein, serving with the United Nations, who administered a part of Croatia known as Eastern Slavonia. It had been predicted that if such arrests were made, Serb forces would take reprisals against peacekeepers, but the arrest in Eastern Slavonia took place without incident.

Thereafter, other arrests were made. Tony Blair became prime minister of England in 1997 and his foreign secretary, Robin Cook, a strong human rights advocate, was intent on cooperation with the ICTY. British troops in Bosnia began arresting indictees in the territory that they patrolled, and their actions persuaded (or embarrassed) troops from other NATO countries, among them the United States and France, also to make arrests. With its credibility greatly enhanced by these moves, the ICTY was able to make demands on all three parties to the conflict—Croatia, the Federal Republic of Yugoslavia, and Bosnia—that they themselves turn over those who had been indicted. When yet another war was launched in Kosovo in 1998 by Yugoslav forces under the direction of Slobodan Milosevic, and NATO intervened in 1999 against the Federal Republic of Yugoslavia, additional indictments were handed down pertaining to violations in that conflict. Demands by the ICTY itself that defendants should be turned over for trial began to be heeded. Milosevic himself was sent to The Hague by Serb authorities in 2000 after losing his hold on power. Radovan Karadzic and General Ratko Mladic, on the other hand, continued to evade arrest. Karadzic devised a rather unusual but effective means of keeping himself concealed. A trained psychiatrist, he masqueraded as a practitioner of alternative medicine, disguised by a full white beard and minus the distinctive hairdo that had made him instantly recognizable. He was eventually turned over to the ICTY by the Serb government in July 2008. As for Mladic, he was reportedly protected by the Serb military. Although the question of Mladic's arrest became an important obstacle to Serbia's ambitions to draw closer to the European Union and, ultimately, to become a member, Serb civilian officials seemed to lack either the will or the capacity to persuade the military to surrender the general for trial. The arrest of Karadzic, however, signaled that Mladic's turn to face justice might not be postponed indefinitely. It was not. In May 2011, Mladic was apprehended. He had been living quietly, without disguise, at the home of a relative in a village in the Vojvodina region. He put up no resistance.

Like the ICTY, the International Criminal Tribunal for Rwanda (ICTR) got off to a slow start. The difficulty had less to do with the apprehension of defendants than with incompetence and even corruption in the organization of the tribunal. Eventually, however, the ICTR straightened itself out (or was straightened out by the United Nations) and began to function effectively. It had somewhat less difficulty in obtaining custody of those who were indicted than had the ICTY. Defeated by the Rwandan Patriotic Front whose forces took over the country, those who had directed the genocide no longer had a country of their own. Over time, governments elsewhere in Africa and in other parts of the world turned over to the tribunal many of those who were indicted. A number of those tried were convicted of genocide, the first such convictions ever to take place before an international tribunal. Among those convicted of that crime and sentenced to life imprisonment—the most severe punishment that could be imposed—was Jean Kambanda, who was prime minister of Rwanda when the genocide took place.

Establishment of ad hoc tribunals for ex-Yugoslavia and Rwanda inevitably spurred many advocates of international human rights to envision a permanent international criminal court with worldwide jurisdiction. A proposal to create such a court had been made many years earlier by the American judge at the post–World War II Nuremberg tribunal, Francis Biddle, but it went nowhere. It was impossible during the Cold War era to obtain the international consensus needed to create such an institution. In the aftermath of the great crimes in ex-Yugoslavia and Rwanda, however, and with U.N.–created tribunals that dealt with those crimes beginning to function effectively, there seemed a great need for a permanent court, and there were no longer any insuperable obstacles to its creation. In 1998, just five years after the establishment of the Yugoslav tribunal and four years after the Rwanda tribunal was launched, representatives of 148 governments assembled in Rome and adopted a treaty to create a permanent International Criminal Court. Nongovernmental organizations played an essential role. In advance of the Rome meeting, a few NGOs had lobbied governments in various parts of the world—especially in Europe, Africa, and Latin America—in support of the establishment of the International Criminal Court. An especially important role was played by an Italian organization, No Peace Without Justice (NPWJ), which convened conferences in several parts of the world that brought together government officials to learn about the proposed court. NPWJ had been founded by the Italian political leader Emma Bonino, a veteran of many campaigns for civil liberties in her own country and of struggles to promote human rights internationally. In the period in which the ICC was being established, Bonino was a member of the European Commission, the agency that directs the operations of the European Union, and she took advantage of her post and her contacts with heads of state to ensure the participation of high-level officials from many countries in NPWJ's conferences, such as the one in Dakar, Senegal that was hosted by the country's president. The result was that by the time the conference took place in Rome—Bonino's city—many governments were ready to support establishment of the ICC. One hundred and twenty approved the treaty drafted in Rome, twenty-one abstained, and seven—the United States, Iraq (still ruled by Saddam Hussein), Sudan, China, Israel, Qatar, and Yemen—voted in opposition.

Following adoption of the treaty at Rome, sixty countries were required to ratify it before it could take effect. It was widely predicted that this would take at least five years. Many countries had to change their constitutions in order to ratify the treaty, and this could not be done quickly. In some countries, for example, certain national officials enjoyed immunity from criminal prosecution under the constitution. These included monarchies, such as Thailand's, in which the king is exempt from the possibility of prosecution. Under the treaty establishing the ICC, however, everyone is potentially subject to criminal sanction. Other constitutional provisions that conflicted with the treaty were those limiting criminal sentences in certain countries to no more than thirty years, while the ICC treaty required potential sentences of up to life in prison, and provisions prohibiting the transfer of citizens for trial in foreign courts.

Despite such difficulties, the necessary sixty ratifications were obtained by April 11, 2002, less than four years after adoption of the Rome treaty. Here too, lobbying by a number of nongovernmental organizations—including the Coalition for an International Criminal Court that is made up of many hundreds of organizations worldwide and was established for this purpose—played an important part. Ten countries ratified on that April 11, each apparently hoping to provide the necessary sixtieth ratification to bring the treaty into effect. By the end of that day, sixty-six countries had ratified.

One of the ten that ratified on April 11, 2001 was the Democratic Republic of the Congo, and it became the first beneficiary of the International Criminal Court's establishment. At the moment of ratification, the armies of five other African governments—Angola, Namibia, and Zimbabwe on one side of the conflict, and Rwanda and Uganda on the other—had armies in the DRC. In addition to combating one another, and committing great crimes against noncombatants, they were harvesting the rich natural resources of the impoverished country and sending home the spoils. Following ratification, the treaty was scheduled to go into effect on July 1, 2002. The International Criminal Court would only have jurisdiction over war crimes, crimes against humanity, and genocides committed after that date. This left less than three months between the DRC's ratification of the treaty and the date when the commission of continuing war crimes in the DRC by the armed forces of other African states could result in the prosecution of their military chiefs or their heads of state.[14] All five African governments withdrew their forces from the DRC within that brief period. While conflict continued between local warlords who had been allied with the invading armies, and between forces still supported by the Rwandan government and, perhaps, by other governments that had intervened directly in the Congo, there was some reduction in the overall level of suffering and in the despoliation of the country. Apparently, some officials of the DRC had pressed for ratification of the ICC treaty because they hoped to achieve just this result.

With ratification, the state parties to the Rome treaty proceeded with establishment of the court, choosing judges and appointing a chief prosecutor. The first person chosen as prosecutor to serve the non-renewable nine-year term provided in the treaty was Luis Moreno Ocampo, an Argentine who had previously served as a prosecutor of members of the military juntas responsible for the disappearances and other crimes committed when his country suffered under military dictatorship a quarter of a century earlier.

As chief prosecutor, Moreno Ocampo seemed particularly concerned at the outset of his term to allay the fears expressed by the governments that had opposed establishment of the ICC, especially the United States. Washington's major complaint was that the prosecutor would make his own determination as to which prosecutions to initiate. This would make American troops and American officials especially vulnerable, according to Washington, because the United States deploys troops in many countries to maintain international peace and security. Though the ICC's primary jurisdiction derives from state ratifications of the Rome treaty, and the United States could exempt itself with respect to crimes committed on its own territory by not ratifying the treaty, Americans could be prosecuted for crimes committed on the territory of another country that did ratify. Washington argued that prosecutions should only be initiated with the approval of the U.N. Security Council. This would permit the United States as well as the other four permanent members of the Council—the United Kingdom, France, Russia, and China—to veto prosecutions. Proponents of the ICC said that this would largely nullify its value. It was rejection of such a role for the Security Council that led the Clinton administration to oppose the treaty when it was voted on at the Rome conference in 1998; and that motivated the administration of President George W. Bush, at least during its first several years in office, to do everything in its power to undermine the ICC. Members of the Bush administration, led by John Bolton, who served as undersecretary of state and subsequently as U.S. ambassador to the United Nations—until refusal of the U.S. Senate to confirm his appointment forced him to step down—attacked the ICC as a threat to members of the American military serving in other countries. This covered up what was probably the administration's main concern: that high officials, such as Secretary of Defense Donald Rumsfeld, might be subject to prosecution for crimes committed under their direction in countries that were parties to the treaty. Rumsfeld and many other officials and former officials, including former president George W. Bush and former vice president Dick Cheney, who may believe themselves vulnerable to prosecutions, either before the ICC or before national courts exercising universal jurisdiction, have probably had to consider with care where they travel to avoid the possibility of arrest and prosecution. Holidays in the south of France, the British countryside, or on the coast of Spain are not on their agendas. The example of what happened to General Pinochet in London in 1998 is undoubtedly a factor in their thinking.[15]

In practice, of course, it seems highly unlikely that the ICC would bring such a prosecution. To the degree that any charges against a high level U.S. official might involve the war in Iraq, the ICC lacks jurisdiction because neither Iraq nor the United States is a party to the treaty for the Court. Also, of course, even if it could be shown that such an official was responsible for war crimes in circumstances in which the ICC has jurisdiction, the prosecutor would be wary of bringing a case. Almost certainly, he would recognize that the Court needs to make great gains in international acceptance before it can take on Chinese, Russian, or U.S. targets. The fact that even officials of the great powers cannot be guaranteed immunity helps to legitimize the role of the Court in dealing with crimes attributable to officials of less powerful states. Realistically, however, the indictment against a former secretary of defense of the United States seems a long way off.

Moreno Ocampo dealt with the objections of Washington and other critics of the ICC by limiting the prosecutions that he brought—at least at the outset—to cases referred to the ICC by the governments of countries where crimes had been committed and to cases referred by the U.N. Security Council. He did not initiate any prosecutions without such a referral. Three African governments—the Democratic Republic of the Congo, Uganda, and the Central African Republic—asked the ICC to bring prosecutions for crimes committed on their territory. In addition, the Security Council in 2005 referred the case of Darfur to the ICC, leading to a prosecution of Sudanese officials and, in 2011, adopted a unanimous resolution referring Libya to the Court. The Darfur referral was especially notable because it could have been blocked by a Bush administration veto. That the United States instead abstained on the vote reflected in part Moreno Ocampo's success in securing an abatement of Bush administration hostility toward the ICC. Another factor was the departure of John Bolton from the administration following the U.S. Senate's rejection of his appointment as ambassador to the U.N. Bolton has made opposition to the ICC a personal crusade.

The ICC's role in bringing indictments in Kenya arose out of the efforts by former U.N. secretary general Kofi Annan to negotiate a peaceful settlement of the ethnically charged violence that followed the disputed outcome of national elections in December 2007. One element of the settlement worked out by Annan was the appointment of a commission to investigate the violence. Though that commission produced a report identifying (but not publicly naming) those principally responsible for crimes in which about 1,500 persons were killed during the first two months of 2008, Kenyan authorities failed to bring prosecutions. Accordingly, Annan turned over the findings of the commission to the ICC prosecutor, initially with the backing of both the president and the prime minister of Kenya, the opposing candidates in the contested election. Subsequently, however, President Kibaki led an effort to block prosecutions before the ICC, claiming that the Kenyan courts were capable of dealing with the matter.

Moreno Ocampo's decision to limit prosecutions at the outset to those referred to the Court by the governments on whose territory crimes were committed or by the U.N. Security Council, and in the Kenyan case by Kofi Annan, contributed to what has been portrayed as a significant imbalance:

that is, all those indicted in the Court's start-up years were Africans who had committed crimes in Africa. Inevitably, this provoked concern by some Africans that the ICC is a Western institution established to punish African criminality. One of those espousing this view was Mahmood Mamdani, a well-known scholar of Ugandan origin who teaches African studies at Columbia University. Mamdani, who has often seen Western conspiracies at the heart of political developments, published an article alleging that the International Criminal Court is a component of a new "international humanitarian order" and argued that its selection of cases has been essentially dictated by the United States. "Its name notwithstanding," according to Mamdani, "the ICC is rapidly turning into a Western court to try African crimes against humanity. It has targeted governments that are U.S. adversaries and ignored actions the United States doesn't oppose like those of Uganda and Rwanda in eastern Congo, effectively conferring impunity on them."[16] The fact that this would have required the ICC prosecutor to obtain proof that the leaders of those countries directed the commission of war crimes in the DRC after they withdrew their own troops from the country—which may have been the case, though evidence usable in court was difficult to obtain—when the Court obtained jurisdiction, was not mentioned by Mamdani. Nor did he take note of the Bush administration's hostility to the ICC, which made it unlikely that it would try to influence its choice of cases. Moreno Ocampo did his best to counter such criticism by pointing to the role of African governments themselves in initiating the prosecutions that he did bring; but, at this writing, it is evident that he has not succeeded in dissipating such concerns. Accordingly, he has found himself in something of a dilemma. By bringing a prosecution elsewhere he might reinvigorate the antagonism of those critical of the latitude granted him under the treaty establishing the Court to initiate a prosecution solely on his own motion. Also, such a prosecution might be of questionable appropriateness, because the most abusive governments in other parts of the world—such as those in Burma, North Korea, Iran, and Uzbekistan—have not ratified the ICC treaty. Absent Security Council referral, the prosecutor lacks jurisdiction over their crimes. (This problem was partially solved in 2011 by the unanimous decision of the Security Council to refer Libya to the ICC. Though Libya is in Africa and a member of the African Union, it is widely regarded as a Middle Eastern state more than an African state.) In contrast, a number of African countries that have ratified or have referred cases to the ICC have either committed severe abuses or have been the sites of significant abuses by other forces. All the same, by not initiating prosecutions elsewhere during the Court's early years, Moreno Ocampo provided inadvertent ballast to those Africans intent on provoking resentment against an institution they perceive as focusing disproportionately on African malfeasance. This seems the most critical issue confronting the International Criminal Court in its early years.

A particularly serious challenge to the operation of the International Criminal Court was touched off by the prosecutor's announcement in July 2008 that he was asking a pretrial panel of judges to issue an arrest warrant against President Omar Hassan Al Bashir of Sudan for the commission of war crimes, crimes against humanity, and genocide in Darfur. Predictably, the request was denounced by the Arab League and the Organization of the Islamic Conference. More surprisingly, however, it also became the target of strenuous criticism by the African Union, even though the crimes in Darfur had been carried out by Sudanese militias of mainly Arab stock (the Janjaweed) and the Sudanese armed forces, also predominantly of Arab stock, against somewhat darker-skinned tribespeople in Darfur. (Whether and to what degree ethnicity was a factor in these crimes is a complex and disputed question, but it was enough of an issue that the African Union might have been expected not to ally itself with the Arab League in defending Bashir.[17]) By the time of the issuance of the request for an arrest warrant against Bashir, the U.N. estimated that Sudanese forces had killed some 300,000 Darfurians since 2003 and had forcibly displaced another 2,700,000. Prior to acting against Bashir, the prosecutor had indicted two others—Ali Kushayb, leader of the Janjaweed, and Ahmed Harun, former minister of state for the Interior—for the crimes in Darfur. Many in the international human rights community had been disappointed that only those two men were indicted, as it seemed unlikely that such extensive slaughter over a period of several years could take place without the direct engagement of higher-ranking officials. The indictments of Kushayb and Harun had attracted little international attention. In contrast, the request for an arrest warrant against President Bashir precipitated a storm. Hardly any critics of the action claimed that Bashir was innocent. Rather, they suggested that the prosecutor for the International Criminal Court had made it more difficult to achieve a peace settlement that would resolve the conflict in Darfur. Variations on this theme in some of the critical response included a suggestion that Bashir would take revenge against African Union peacekeepers in Darfur and that the request for an arrest warrant would jeopardize the North-South peace agreement that had settled a protracted conflict in Sudan that had taken an even larger death toll than that in

Darfur. (The latter prediction did not come to pass; in 2011, South Sudan achieved independence through a peaceful process.) Some also suggested that the prosecution would strengthen Islamist forces in Sudan with which Bashir had formerly been allied. The action Bashir did take when a panel of judges of the ICC upheld the arrest warrant in March 2009[18] was to expel international humanitarian groups providing services to those forcibly displaced in Darfur. His action seemed to confirm his disregard for the lives of Darfurians. Bashir's regime also intensified repression against Sudanese lawyers and others active in efforts to promote human rights, apparently in the belief that some of them may have cooperated with the prosecutor of the ICC in compiling evidence against him. During 2009 much of the leadership of Sudan's nongovernmental human rights community, some of them lawyers affiliated with the Sudan Organization Against Torture (SOAT), fled into exile in Uganda, Egypt, and other countries.

In late 2008, Libya and South Africa introduced a resolution in the U.N. Security Council to invoke Article 16 of the treaty establishing the International Criminal Court to delay the prosecution of Bashir. Under Article 16, the Security Council may act in the interest of promoting peace, delaying a prosecution for up to a year, and such postponements may be renewed indefinitely. The proposal to invoke Article 16 was supported by Russia and China, the latter being the major customer for Sudanese oil, but did not come to a vote in the Security Council. Though the resolution was ostensibly intended to serve the interests of peace, no peace negotiations involving Darfur were underway when it was proposed. Britain and France indicated that they would make substantial demands on Sudan before agreeing to the resolution, including surrender of Ali Kushayb and Ahmed Harun to the ICC; and the United States, formerly the principal antagonist of the ICC, held out the possibility of a veto. The transition from the Bush administration to the Obama administration in January 2009, and the appointment of Susan Rice as Obama's ambassador to the United Nations, put in place an official far more friendly to the International Criminal Court and highly critical of Bashir's role in Darfur. Though close to three years have elapsed by this writing since the introduction of the resolution to invoke Article 16, and the African Union has repeatedly complained of inaction on it by the U.N. Security Council, there is no sign of movement. Most likely, it will continue to languish.

The Darfur case highlighted an issue that has arisen repeatedly in the course of efforts to secure accountability through criminal prosecutions. Namely, whether there is a conflict between doing justice and achieving peace? As noted, the ICC seems to have contributed to peace, or reduced conflict, in the Democratic Republic of the Congo in 2002 just by coming into existence. The issue has also arisen in a number of cases involving international tribunals when specific prosecutions were pursued. It arose first in connection with the indictment for the massacre at Srebrenica of Radovan Karadzic and General Ratko Mladic in November 1995, just as the talks were getting underway at Dayton to try to end the war in Bosnia. Those indictments, following indictments of the same two individuals the previous July, made it impossible for Karadzic and Mladic to go to Dayton for fear they would be arrested. In their absence, however, leaders of Bosnia, Croatia, and the Federal Republic of Yugoslavia reached an agreement that ended the war in Bosnia. In fact, the absence of the Bosnian Serb leaders may well have facilitated the peace process.

The issue arose again in May 1999 during the Kosovo war when the prosecutor of the International Criminal Tribunal for the former Yugoslavia indicted President Slobodan Milosevic of Yugoslavia for crimes committed during that war. One of those who denounced the indictment was former Russian prime minister Victor Chernomyrdin, who was then collaborating with Finland's former president, Martti Ahtisaari, in attempting to mediate an end to the conflict. Chernomyrdin claimed that the indictment would prevent a settlement. Yet, a week later, Milosevic capitulated and the war in Kosovo ended. The issue came up again in 2003 when the Special Court for Sierra Leone indicted President Charles Taylor of Liberia. The indictment was initially handed down that March but remained sealed until June, when Taylor traveled outside his country to a peace conference in Ghana that was intended to try to achieve a settlement of the civil war in his own country. Though the indictment was then made public, the Ghanaians were angry that they had not been consulted in advance and refused to arrest Taylor. He was able to return to Liberia, but he fled the country two months later and took refuge in Nigeria. Taylor's departure brought an end to the conflict in Liberia. Though Nigeria gave him asylum, international pressure eventually made it necessary to turn him over for trial by the Special Court for Sierra Leone. For reasons of safety, the trial was held in the facilities of the International Criminal Court in The Hague, where it was still underway in 2011. With Taylor out of the picture, both Liberia and Sierra Leone have been at peace for several years and have democratic governments that are rebuilding their devastated countries.

Kenya and Lebanon could provide additional tests. Though Kofi Annan's mediation efforts in Kenya in 2008 halted most of the ethnic violence that followed the elections in December 2007, the country remains tense. As national elections approach again in 2012, a further outbreak of violence is possible. If prosecutions are then underway in the ICC, will fear of accountability prevent leaders from whipping up further violence? Or will prosecutions intensify ethnic tensions and thereby contribute to violence? As to Lebanon, expected indictments of individuals connected to Hezbollah led to a crisis in early 2011 and to the installation of a new government. It is not yet known what will happen when indictments are announced.

Though it is possible that there could be a conflict between efforts to do justice and to achieve peace in Kenya, Lebanon, and elsewhere, the record since 1993 when the International Criminal Tribunal for the Former Yugoslavia was established suggests that fears of such a conflict are greatly exaggerated. Over close to two decades, doing justice internationally has contributed to peace. This does not preclude the possibility that a conflict may arise in the future. If it should, the challenge will be to try to achieve both justice and peace. They are independent values and should not be subordinated one to the other. Some accommodation may be necessary, however, in order to achieve both. It is difficult to foretell what will be required in advance.[19]

At the time that the International Criminal Tribunal for the Former Yugoslavia was being proposed and established in 1992 and 1993, those seeking its creation—the present author among them—claimed that it would serve a number of purposes in addition to the establishment of accountability. It would contribute to the restoration of a sense of justice in a society devastated by horrendous crimes. It would demonstrate respect for the victims and thereby help the survivors to resume their lives. It would individualize criminal guilt and, at the same time, foster a sense of collective political responsibility among those who helped actively and passively to make it possible for the perpetrators to commit their crimes. It would interrupt cycles of revenge in which those who see themselves as victims of crimes become the perpetrators of the next set of crimes. And, over time, it could deter the commission of such crimes. (Subsequently, some have assessed the ICTY and other such tribunals on the basis of whether they have contributed to peace, to democracy, and to reconciliation. These were not among the goals articulated by the tribunals' early proponents.")

Are the international criminal tribunals achieving the purposes of their early advocates? We have no means of objectively answering this question. Yet, as nearly two decades have elapsed since it was first raised in conjunction with the attempt to establish the Yugoslav tribunal, it seems appropriate to reflect on what appear to be the successes and failures so far. Most of the observations that are possible are based upon the work of the tribunals for ex-Yugoslavia and Rwanda, because they have been underway for the longest period.

Reverting first to the question of accountability, it is worth noting that, at this writing, more than 250 persons have been indicted by the tribunals for ex-Yugoslavia, Rwanda, Sierra Leone, Cambodia, and the International Criminal Court. They are from thirteen countries: four in Europe (all countries that were previously part of a united Yugoslavia: Serbia, Croatia, Bosnia-Herzegovina and Kosovo); one in Asia (Cambodia); eight in Africa (Rwanda, Sierra Leone, Liberia, the Democratic Republic of the Congo, Uganda, Sudan, the Central African Republic, and Kenya); and one in the Middle East (Libya). A tribunal for Lebanon, based in The Hague, focusing on the assassination of former Prime Minister Rafik Hariri is underway at this writing. It has reportedly decided on indictments, but it has not yet issued them publicly.[20] With the exception of a few low-level defendants indicted in the early days of the Yugoslav tribunal because they were the only individuals accused of major crimes who could be apprehended at that time and brought to trial, all the others were high-ranking—heads of state, government ministers, military commanders, political leaders, and guerrilla leaders. They include six heads of state or government (Slobodan Milosevic of Yugoslavia, Jean Kambanda of Rwanda, Charles Taylor of Liberia, Khieu Samphan of the Khmer Rouge in Cambodia, Omar Hassan al Bashir of Sudan, and Muammar Qaddafi of Libya) and two heads of a statelet (Radovan Karadzic and Biljana Plavsic of the Bosnian Serb Republic). Of those eight, six were apprehended. Only Bashir and Qaddafi remain free at this writing. In general, the tribunals have fared well in getting custody of their indictees despite lacking the means to make their own arrests.[21]

In addition, there are indications that the example of international justice has inspired national justice systems to take on matters that previously seemed beyond their reach.[22] Latin America is a case in point. In recent years, national prosecutions for gross human rights abuses have been brought against former heads of state in four countries: Chile, where Augusto Pinochet was prosecuted after he was returned to the country from the United Kingdom, but was ultimately spared a trial due to age and infirmity; Argentina, where former President Jorge Videla, who had been pardoned many years earlier by President Meném, was arrested again, tried and convicted; Uruguay, where former President Juan Bordaberry was convicted for crimes under his dictatorial rule in the 1970s; and Peru, where former President Alberto Fujimori was convicted by a national court in 2008 for human rights abuses and sentenced to twenty-five years in prison. Perhaps the best known case outside of Latin America is the execution of Saddam Hussein in 2006, after he was convicted of ordering the massacre of the residents of the town of Dujail after a failed assassination attempt apparently committed by a resident of that town. There was a mass of evidence that Saddam had also perpetrated many additional crimes that victimized hundreds of thousands of other Iraqis, but he was executed before he could be tried for those crimes.[23]

Another significant consequence of international justice is that judicial systems in Serbia, Croatia, and Bosnia-Herzegovina are now conducting large numbers of trials of their own nationals for the crimes committed in ex-Yugoslavia in the wars of the 1990s. In some instances, these cases were referred to national courts by the International Criminal Tribunal for the Former Yugoslavia, because they involved lower-ranking defendants than those whose cases were being pursued in The Hague. In other cases, national courts themselves initiated the cases. In general, high standards are being maintained in the conduct of these trials. The important precedent for the influence of international tribunals on national courts is the more than five thousand prosecutions of Nazi war criminals by German courts in the years following international trials at Nuremberg. Those trials made a crucial contribution to widespread German acceptance of political responsibility for Nazi crimes. In contrast, there were no trials before Japanese courts of Japanese war criminals following the international prosecutions at Tokyo. As discussed previously, that may be one of the factors behind the unwillingness of many Japanese to accept their country's responsibility for crimes during World War II that led to the deaths of approximately ten million civilians and that contributed to lingering hostility toward Japan in countries that particularly suffered from those crimes, such as China, Korea, and the Philippines.

With the exception of Rwanda—which has tried tens of thousands of "genocidaires" before so-called *gachacha* courts, a traditional communal justice mechanism, national justice systems in African countries and Cambodia have not so far followed international justice by bringing prosecutions in domestic courts. On the other hand, the increasing willingness of national courts elsewhere to deal with serious human rights crimes is an important development. It means that the International Criminal Court may become what it was intended to be: a court of last resort to deal with war crimes, crimes against humanity, and genocide worldwide when other bodies fail to address these issues or to deal with them appropriately. International accountability for atrocious crimes appears to be among the most significant achievements of the international criminal tribunals and of the international human rights movement.

As to the tribunals' success in restoring a sense of justice in devastated countries, it is very difficult to make a judgment. One positive sign is that in most of ex-Yugoslavia, and in Rwanda, there have been hardly any cases of revenge killings. Yet these are countries in which a defining characteristic of the horrifying violence of the early 1990s was that neighbors—people who had lived together, worked together, and played together all their lives, and had even married each other—murdered their neighbors. The lack of revenge killings may be contrasted to France at the time of the liberation from Nazi rule in 1944, when there were thousands of murders and summary executions of persons accused of collaborating with the Nazis.[24] The killing period in France was known as the *épuration*, and it was not an exclusively French phenomenon. Reprisal killings took place in a number of European countries at the end of World War II. Indeed, taking revenge may be considered a natural instinct. A fourteenth-century writer, Paolo da Certaldo, in his *Book of Manners*, wrote: "The first grief is to receive an injury; the second pleasure to wreak vengeance."[25] An exception to the general absence of incidents of vengeance in ex-Yugoslavia was Kosovo—a territory known for vendettas—where there were some dozens of revenge killings following NATO's defeat of Serbia in 1999, though they took place before international justice began to be felt in that territory. Most of the murders in Kosovo did not involve individuals accused of specific crimes. Rather, the victims were targeted because of their ethnicity.

It is also difficult to say whether the international tribunals are achieving the goal espoused by some of their partisans of demonstrating respect for the victims and helping the survivors to resume their lives. One indication may be whether a society is able to confront openly the crimes that it has suffered and the survivors are able to build lives that are not wholly tied to the fact that they are survivors. Here the picture seems mixed. In Bosnia, there is considerable openness about the crimes that took place. Little is covered up. The gachacha courts in Rwanda are seriously flawed from the standpoint of due process, but because they involve whole communities, they have ensured that almost everyone takes part in thinking seriously about what took place. (The government's refusal to acknowledge crimes by the Rwandan Patriotic Front when it liberated the country from the *genocidaires* detracts from the atmosphere of openness.) Yet in the case of Bosnia, there are some, including many of the wives and mothers of the 8,000 or so Muslim men and boys murdered at Srebrenica in 1995, whose lives still seem to be focused, even many years later, on that awful period. Up to 2011, about thirty of the Bosnian Serb military officers, many high-ranking, who committed the massacre have been tried and convicted, or are under arrest and being tried or facing trial for what happened in Srebrenica. This is, in comparison to other great crimes, a rather high level of accountability. The main factor preventing the families from deriving satisfaction from the prosecutions that have taken place and are continuing to take place seems to be that General Mladic, who ordered and supervised those killings, long remained at large. His arrest in May 2011 could have a significant impact. It is possible that his trial, conviction, and punishment could release the widows and mothers from the anger and depression into which many have fallen.

There is one respect in which international justice has proven a great disappointment, and that is in its failure thus far to persuade the great majority of those who facilitated the commission of severe crimes to acknowledge their responsibility. The obvious example is Serbia. Although it was Serb political leaders, the Serb media, and the Serb military that launched the Croatian war in 1991, the Bosnian war in 1992, and the Kosovan war in 1998, and though there were a few in Serbia who spoke out clearly and forcefully against those wars and against the manner in which they were conducted, it still seems at this writing that only a small minority of Serbs accept political responsibility for the crimes committed by Serb military and paramilitary forces. It is possible that, over time, the trials conducted before national courts in Serbia of Serbian war criminals will foster a sense of such responsibility, but the signs that this is happening remain scarce.[26] For the most part, political leaders in Serbia who have espoused cooperation with the International Criminal Tribunal for the former Yugoslavia have done so, at least publicly, on pragmatic grounds, because that is what is required to achieve the country's goals in Europe and in relations with the United States. They have rarely supported the ICTY on the basis that it is morally just that those who are criminally responsible should be punished. Many Serbs seem to think of themselves as victims rather than as either perpetrators or accomplices who facilitated the actions of perpetrators, because they resent that Serb leaders have been held accountable for the crimes committed in other countries of ex-Yugoslavia; because NATO bombed Serbia in 1999 after Serb forces drove a majority of the ethnic

Albanian citizens of Kosovo out of their homes, communities, and their country, killing thousands of them in the process; and because, in 2008, the United States, the United Kingdom, and many other leading Western countries recognized the independence of Kosovo, which many Serbs regard as the historic heartland of their country. Similarly, many of those in other parts of ex-Yugoslavia who also facilitated crimes as accomplices and bystanders show little sense of political responsibility for those crimes.

It is too soon to tell whether the evolution of international justice has interrupted the cycles of revenge in which victims or their compatriots become perpetrators. Demands for vengeance often seem to lie dormant for extended periods and then to emerge as powerful forces long after the initial victims have passed from the scene. The fact that demagogues can exploit historical grievances, real or alleged, is often a contributing factor. When the war between Serbs and Croats broke out in 1991, some Serbs apparently saw themselves as avenging crimes committed during World War II by the Croatian fascist Ustashe half a century earlier. Even more remarkable, some Serbs seemed to think that their wars of the 1990s against Muslims in Bosnia and Kosovo were opportunities to avenge offenses allegedly committed against their Christian ancestors over the course of several centuries by the Ottoman Empire. Visitors to the region have often been amazed at recitations of grievances that hark back to the fourteenth century. Similarly, in Rwanda the Hutu militias who perpetrated the 1994 genocide apparently considered that they were avenging crimes committed against their ancestors over a number of generations by the Tutsis who had, at one time, lorded it over them. The fact that Tutsi forces from Rwanda or supported by Rwanda have over many years continued to pursue Hutu genocidaires who fled to the Democratic Republic of the Congo does not encourage confidence that cycles of revenge have been interrupted in Rwanda or in neighboring countries where there are both Hutus and Tutsis. It will take much longer before it is possible to offer a judgment on what impact international justice will have in ex-Yugoslavia and other parts of the world where there are periodic attempts to avenge what some in those regions consider their ancestral grievances.

There is also the question of whether the advances that have been made in accountability are having a deterrent impact; that is, whether they are diminishing the frequency and the severity of the crimes committed by governments and guerrilla forces, especially in situations of armed conflict. Of course, deterrence is not the only criterion for assessing the value of accountability. Doing justice is of intrinsic value. Yet it is very important to know whether accountability also has the instrumental effect of deterring future crimes.

It is widely thought that deterrence works best in the case of ordinary crime when punishment is both swift and sure. Certainly, we have not yet reached the point where it is possible to laud the swiftness and sureness of punishment for the kinds of crimes that have motivated the international human rights movement to devote a substantial portion of its attention to accountability since the 1980s. It is, however, possible to cite such developments as the withdrawal of the armed forces of other African countries from the Democratic Republic of the Congo in 2002 to support the contention that the prospect of accountability is having deterrent impact. It remains to be seen, of course, whether there will be a wider reduction in war crimes, crimes against humanity, or genocide. An attempt to secure such a reduction could be seen as a central purpose, along with the overriding purpose of doing justice for its own sake, of the drive for accountability. It will take a good many years before it is possible to make an assessment of whether the mechanisms for promoting accountability that are now in place are also achieving that deterrent purpose. In the interim, what can be said now is that they are contributing to a recognition that even those who seem all powerful as they commit atrocious crimes face a growing prospect of someday having to answer for their deeds.

Though most of those in the international human rights movement who have played leading roles in the promotion of accountability over the past quarter of a century would be cautious about making claims for the results they have achieved, it seems fair to say that the belief that they are on the right track is widely shared within the movement. Much more has been accomplished in a relatively short period than most could have imagined. It will take longer to determine whether and to what degree other benefits are realized. But the increased awareness of the importance of accountability is in itself already one of the principal accomplishments of the international human rights movement since the end of the Cold War.

12

Rights after 9/11

AS OF OCTOBER 3, 2011

IN THE AFTERMATH OF THE SEPTEMBER 11, 2001 TERRORIST ATTACKS on the United States, some of those active in efforts to promote human rights feared that the era in which their cause held a prominent place on the world stage could be over. That era began about a quarter of a century earlier as an outgrowth of the Cold War, and it had a part in bringing the Cold War to an end. Dictatorships of the Right and the Left had fallen—with help from those denouncing their abuses of human rights—yet those who hoped that there would be a substantial decline in gross abuses worldwide had been disappointed.

The 1990s, the decade that followed the fall of the Berlin Wall, the collapse of communist regimes in the former Soviet bloc, the end to almost all the military dictatorships in Latin America as well as some in Asia, and that saw the establishment of a multiracial democracy in South Africa, was indelibly scarred by ethnically based genocidal conflicts in ex-Yugoslavia and Rwanda and by conflicts increasingly centered on the control of natural resources in various parts of Asia, Africa, and the Middle East. Yet the human rights movement continued as a major force in the 1990s. It promoted truth-telling and accountability in countries that had suffered from severe repression. It led the way in establishing international criminal tribunals to prosecute and punish the gravest crimes committed in the conflicts of that decade and secured the adoption of a treaty establishing a permanent International Criminal Court. It focused international public attention on attacks on noncombatants in the many conflicts underway worldwide and made compliance with the laws of war an important focus of its work and a criterion for assessing the governments and guerrilla forces engaged in those conflicts. It persuaded most governments worldwide to adopt and ratify a treaty, the Landmines Convention, outlawing a particularly pernicious and indiscriminate weapon and, at this writing, it is pursuing ratification of another such treaty involving cluster munitions.

Whether the human rights movement would be capable of playing such a significant role after September 11, 2001, however, was not self-evident. At least two factors made the challenge different, and greater, than any it had faced before.

The first difference was that it was apparent that one side in the new worldwide international conflict—that is, the side responsible for the September 11 attacks—was not susceptible to the human rights movement's main weapon: embarrassment. Al-Qaeda made no claim to respect rights. Documenting and publicizing the abuses of al-Qaeda would therefore have little or no effect. This was not a body that sought to prevail internationally by establishing its legitimacy or by winning hearts and minds. Its imperviousness to the methods used by the human rights movement was symbolized by the readiness of those who actually carried out the September 11 attacks to commit suicide in the process. They accomplished their mission by hurting the United States and its citizens to the maximum extent possible and did not even demonstrate a need to live to see the result of their efforts. The harm they did was not only a means to an end. Proving America's vulnerability was an end in itself. If anything, al-Qaeda's apparent fragmentation into autonomous terrorist groups made it even more difficult to shame those engaged in its deadly assaults. After September 11, the human rights movement could embarrass the United States and governments allied with it for the way they conducted themselves in responding to terrorism. But its efforts would inevitably suffer from the perception that they were one-sided. The human rights movement had come to the fore and established its *bona fides* during the Cold War because it denounced abuses of rights by all sides and made rights a central issue in the struggle between East and West. It undermined the legitimacy of communist regimes by documenting their abuses and demonstrating the ways in which they crushed the human spirit; and, simultaneously, it embarrassed the United States and its allies over their support for anticommunist dictatorships that also engaged in systematic gross abuses of rights. After September 11, no such even-handed strategy could be pursued effectively.

Another major difference involved the role of the United States. Americans were the victims of the September 11 attacks. The loss of life, the damage to property, and the blow to the American psyche—creating both the unprecedented sense of vulnerability sought by the terrorists and a powerful urge in some quarters to demonstrate that the country could and would crush its foes—changed the landscape. During the Cold War, and to a lesser extent thereafter, the United States had played a crucial role in the promotion of human rights worldwide. This was the case even though America's actual policies and practices with respect to human rights were mixed. At times, as when it demonstrated respect for civil liberties at home and denounced Soviet bloc abuses of human rights, the United States led by embodying virtue. At other times, when it diverged from its own commitments to rights at home and when it backed military dictatorships in such countries as Argentina, Chile, Indonesia and the Philippines, and a racist regime in South Africa, the U.S. was criticized most severely by Americans for its failings and made culpable by the American human rights movement for abuses of rights by client states. The fact that domestic critics of American government shortcomings took the lead in documenting and publicizing such abuses was crucial. Embarrassing the United States government was a particularly effective means for the American nongovernmental movement to put pressure on Washington to rein in its client governments, and, ultimately, to help bring an end to their dictatorships. Also, to a degree, the United States redeemed itself and its international standing by its openness to intense domestic criticism. The shared perception by many Americans that they and their government were, or should be, champions of rights played a crucial role. Now the severity and impact of the September 11 attacks on the United States made it possible that maintaining this stance would no longer matter so much to most Americans. Protecting themselves against the perpetrators of September 11 and against those who applauded the events of that day would take precedence. If the United States would no longer take the lead in addressing human rights violations, or if its credibility in that role were diminished because Americans trampled on rights in their pursuit of their enemies, who could take its place? It was apparent, too, that defection from the rights cause by the United States would be seized upon by many other governments to justify their own violations of rights. Prior to September 11, many other countries had suffered more grievously than the United States from terrorism, and their resort to prolonged detention without charges, coercive interrogation, torture, and trials before military tribunals had been criticized by Washington in the State Department's annual *Country Reports on Human Rights Practices* and in other government pronouncements. With Washington adopting such practices, many of those protecting national security in other countries considered themselves vindicated. They too could respond to terrorism—or, in some cases, what they chose to label as terrorism—by employing extraordinary measures. September 11, it was plain to see, set back the human rights cause worldwide.

A third major difference was that the United States government made the decision early on that securing criminal convictions of those who took part in terrorist attacks or conspired to engage in such attacks, was not its primary goal. A more important concern was preventing further attacks. As U.S. Attorney General John Ashcroft told a New York audience in early 2003, "In order to fight and to defeat terrorism, the Department of Justice has added a new paradigm to that of prosecution—a paradigm of prevention."[1] The focus on prevention was, of course, understandable. At the time, the administration of President George W. Bush was undergoing strenuous criticism for missing signs that the September 11 attacks were going to take place. The former national coordinator for counterterrorism in the National Security Council, Richard Clarke, repeatedly criticized President Bush himself and National Security Advisor Condoleezza Rice for ignoring various warnings.[2] Congressional hearings focused on Rice's failure to respond in a significant way to a briefing paper headed "Bin Laden determined to strike in U.S."[3] Even aside from such criticism, there were clearly good grounds for the administration to consider that one of its primary responsibilities, and perhaps its responsibility of greatest importance, was to prevent additional attacks. September 11 caused great loss of life and suffering, as well as enormous damage to property. Making sure that nothing of the sort could happen again had to be a priority.

Despite the immense harm done to the United States by the attacks of September 11, and despite what those attacks revealed about the prospects of further harm, it seems nonetheless amazing that the reaction to them has been comparable in scale and intensity to U.S. reaction to the two greatest twentieth-century threats to national security: those posed by World War II and by the Cold War with the Soviet empire. Yet the actual and potential damage done by those earlier crises was incomparably greater. In the case of World War II, there seemed for a period a genuine possibility that the Axis powers could achieve their goal of global conquest. Even if the outcome of the war seems inevitable in retrospect, perhaps as many as fifty million persons worldwide were killed in the conflict. Many countries experienced large-scale destruction. To prevail in the war required all out mobilization of the population and resources of the United States, and hundreds of thousands of Americans were killed in combat in Europe, Asia, and other parts of the world. Coming hard on the heels of World War II, the Cold War threatened the entire world with nuclear annihilation. It caused terrible suffering in many countries under communist rule and in other countries where right-wing dictatorships justified abuses because of the communist threat. A great number of armed conflicts took place in different parts of the world between forces supported by and, in some cases, operating at the behest of the principal Cold War antagonists, the Soviet Union and the United States. Scores of thousands of Americans died in two of those conflicts: the war in Korea in the 1950s and the war in Vietnam in the 1960s and 1970s. Unless the terrorists of the twenty-first century acquire quantities of weapons of mass destruction *and* the capacity to deliver them, there seems little prospect that terrorism will become the same kind of existential threat to the United States that the Axis powers were during World War II or the Soviet empire during the Cold War. Yet the readiness of the U.S. government to violate rights in reaction to terrorism, though lesser in some respects, has been greater in others than in earlier periods when the actual danger to the country and its citizens was far graver.

The decision to make prevention the defining concern of U.S. government policy in responding to the threat of terrorism had fateful consequences for human rights. Because prosecution and punishment in accordance with law were not considered of primary importance, the Department of Justice and other branches of the Bush administration did not focus on making certain that evidence against suspected terrorists and plotters of terrorism would stand up in court. It was not crucial to avoid means of coercion that could taint evidence. The admissibility of information extracted from detainees was of secondary significance. Accordingly, the use of coercive methods to acquire information was not offset by concern that a prosecution might founder if a judge excluded that information because improper means had been used to procure it.

One of the consequences, therefore, of the primacy given to prevention is that it removed one of the restraints on the use of torture or cruel, inhuman, and degrading treatment. A second consequence was that it fostered the use of indefinite detention without charges or trial. As the Bush administration gave up on the possibility of securing criminal convictions, either because it lacked evidence that would prove guilt or because much of the evidence it obtained against terrorist suspects could not be put before a court, it needed a means other than a trial for continuing to hold them in custody indefinitely so as to prevent their involvement in future terrorist acts. Confining foreigners without charges at Guantanamo, at Bagram in Afghanistan, and at other detention centers at undisclosed locations outside the United States, or holding those who were American citizens as "enemy combatants" at military prisons in the United States without bringing charges against them, were the Bush administration's preferred alternatives.[4] Though that administration has passed into history, and Bush's successor, President Barack Obama came into office apparently eager to make major changes, many of the policies and practices of the Bush are still in place.

By and large, the European response to terrorism has differed from the American reaction because Europeans see the threat as emanating primarily from the Muslim communities in their midst. This has helped to ensure that prosecuting and punishing criminally those engaged in terrorism remains the primary response of European governments. It does not seem that most European governments see a conflict between prevention on the one hand and prosecution and punishment on the other. Though there have been a substantial number of domestic prosecutions for terrorism of homegrown suspects in American courts, and most of these have resulted in convictions and prison sentences, most Americans, including most American officials addressing terrorism, see the principal threat as external. It is the foreign enemies of the United States seeking to do harm to the country who are considered to pose the most pressing threat of severe harm. This perception, strongly shaped by the events of September 11, 2001, in which it was nineteen Muslim terrorists from other countries who had gained entry to the United States and perpetrated the attacks, has persuaded a large number of Americans that the most effective means of combating terrorism are prevention and fighting wars.

It did not take long after September 11 for the United States to determine that previous restrictions on the manner in which it dealt with those it considered its enemies would no longer apply. Five days after the attack, Vice President Dick Cheney appeared on "Meet the Press" and told interviewer Tim Russert that the U.S. would have to "work . . . sort of the dark side, if you will." He added, "It is a mean, nasty, dangerous, dirty business out there, and we have to operate in that arena."[5] In January 2002, Alberto Gonzales, White House Counsel before he was appointed attorney general by President Bush, sent a memorandum to the president advising him that he should not make available the protections of the Third Geneva Convention—which regulates the treatment of prisoners taken in the course of an armed conflict—to al-Qaeda and Taliban prisoners captured in Afghanistan. Excluding the protections of the Geneva Conventions would "preserve flexibility." It would also "reduce the threat," in Gonzales's strained reading of the law, that those dealing with these prisoners in a harsh manner would ultimately be prosecuted for war crimes. In Gonzales's view, the terrorist attacks on New York and Washington had made the restrictions required by the Geneva Conventions "obsolete."[6] Two weeks after receiving this memo, on February 7, 2002, President Bush formally endorsed its recommendations, stating that the events of September 11 had created "a new paradigm."[7] The consequences of that decision are summarized by two lawyers for the American Civil Liberties Union who, through litigation under the Freedom of Information Act, succeeded in securing public release of more than a hundred thousand pages of documents dealing with the Bush administration's torture policies and practices. In an introduction to a volume that includes a selection of those documents, they write:

> [T]he abuse captured in the Abu Ghraib photographs was far from isolated. The same kind of abuse, and indeed much worse, was inflicted on prisoners at detention facilities throughout Afghanistan and Iraq. The documents supply countless examples—far too many to catalogue here. One navy document describes a "substantiated" incident in which marines in Al Mahmudiyah, Iraq, electrocuted one prisoner and set another's hands on fire. Another document—the report of a soldier recently returned from Samarra, Iraq—describes incidents in which soldiers strangled prisoners and placed lit cigarettes in their ears. In a sworn statement, a private contractor who worked with military intelligence in Iraq states that there were approximately ninety incidents of abuse at Al Asmiya Palace, another detention facility in Baghdad. According to the contractor, some of the prisoners "were abused with cigarettes burns and electric shocks." A report issued in February 2006 by Human Rights First found that nearly one hundred prisoners had died in U.S. custody since August 2002 and that of these deaths, thirty-four had been classified by military investigators as suspected or confirmed homicides. Autopsy reports obtained by the ACLU attribute numerous deaths to "strangulation," "asphyxia," and "blunt force injuries." ... Incidents of this kind cannot be traced directly to publicly available interrogation orders

issued by senior civilian or military officials. So far as we know, no senior official directed soldiers to electrocute prisoners, to strangle them, to beat them, to hang them by their arms, or to burn them with cigarettes. But though the interrogation directives issued by [Secretary of Defense Donald] Rumsfeld and [General Ricardo] Sanchez authorized only certain kinds of abuse, they conveyed the message that abuse was acceptable, and they created a climate in which more extreme abuse was foreseeable.[8]

It is difficult to say whether other countries also brushed aside what had been well-established restrictions on the use of torture in the aftermath of September 11. What can be said, of course, is that countries where torture was commonplace prior to September 11—such as Egypt and Saudi Arabia—continued to engage in torture against terrorism suspects. There has not been a showing that Western countries that suffered from terrorism both before and after September 11, 2001, such as Spain and the United Kingdom, have resorted to torture in dealing with suspects.

On the other hand, there has been an upsurge in other restraints on rights in all parts of the world. Governments have collaborated in creating "blacklists" to restrict the travel of large numbers of persons. Many countries have cooperated with the United States in transferring individuals to U.S. custody without legal process and, in turn, have taken custody of persons turned over to them by the United States, also without legal process, through the practice of "extraordinary rendition." In the post-9/11 period, among the leading collaborators with the United States in counterterrorism practices were Afghanistan, Jordan, and Pakistan. Egypt, Morocco, and Thailand also cooperated extensively in abusive interrogations, as did some European countries, including Poland and Romania.[9] New counterterrorism laws have been adopted in many countries, often lengthening the periods in which suspects can be detained without charges. One such effort in the United Kingdom in 2008 was defeated when the House of Lords refused to go along with Prime Minister Gordon Brown's proposal that such detentions should be permissible for periods up to forty-two days. A decision by France's highest court, the Court of Cassation, in October 2010, is likely to bring about a similar result in that country. The Court held that police may no longer interrogate a terrorism suspect without a lawyer present except when there are "imperious reasons." That phrase is thought to refer to a ticking bomb scenario. The police incentive to detain suspects without charges for long periods will be greatly reduced if they cannot conduct interrogations of detainees who do not have a law-yer.[10] On the other hand, in Thailand, an emergency decree was enacted in 2005 allowing preventive detention for up to thirty days in the country's southern provinces, where there has been conflict with a Muslim group and, in 2008, an Internal Security Act was adopted allowing the military to detain individuals without charges for six months of "reeducation." A far more draconian measure has been in place in Malaysia since 1960. That country's Internal Security Act provides indefinite detention without trial on national security grounds. Long used abusively, it has been invoked with increasing frequency since 2001. Elsewhere, measures that have been adopted in various countries include laws that use overbroad and vague criteria to define "membership" in a terrorist organization, "glorification" of terrorist activities, and possession of terrorist materials. In other cases, new laws have not been adopted but laws already on the books—such as "control orders," which provide a form of house arrest—are being applied more broadly than was the case previously.

The United Kingdom, where control orders are used, is an example of the latter trend. Its Terrorism Act of 2000, adopted during the year prior to September 11, provides that: "A person commits an offense if he possesses an article in circumstances which give rise to a reasonable suspicion that his possession is for a purpose connected with the commission, preparation or instigation of an act of terrorism" (Section 57). The law also criminal-izes possession of materials "likely to be useful to a person committing or preparing an act of terrorism" (Section 58). As criminality is determined on the basis of such vague criteria as "reasonable suspicion" and "likely to be useful," the potential for abuse is apparent. With intense public pressure on the authorities to prevent terrorist incidents, it is hardly surprising that abuses have taken place since September 11.

•   •   •

A sign that not all has been lost, however, was the way that Americans and others concerned about rights rallied to the support of the nongovern-mental human rights movement following September 11. On that date, the American Civil Liberties Union had about 275,000 members nationwide, roughly the same number as a quarter of a century earlier. Five years after September 11, the organization's membership had doubled and its income had quadrupled. Human Rights Watch, which does not have the mem-bership structure of the ACLU, also secured a major increase in donor support. Many smaller rights groups also prospered. Increased willingness to support the rights cause was not confined to the United States, making it possible for Human Rights Watch to increase the number of its locally supported branches in other countries and spurring the growth of indigenous rights groups. In the United Kingdom, Liberty, which led the fight against Prime Minister Gordon Brown's proposal to extend detention without charges to forty-two days, has experienced a significant growth in public support. At this writing, though it is not possible to provide exact figures, it is evident that a great many more persons, both in the United States and worldwide, support the human rights cause and identify with it than was the case on September 11, 2001, or ever previously. In a period of crisis, they have rallied to the cause.

The rights issue that has been at the forefront of concern in the United States as in much of the rest of the world, has not been abuses by other governments, whether friends or foes, but America's treatment of those who were identified by the Bush administration as "enemy combatants" or "unlawful combatants." President Bush contended that the Geneva Conventions did not apply to America's conflict in Afghanistan with al-Qaeda and the Taliban (see chapter 5) on such grounds as the lack of international recognition of a "Taliban state," and the fact that neither al-Qaeda nor Taliban fighters wore uniforms. In addition, officials of the Bush administration invented new labels—most notably "unlawful combatants"— that are not recognized in international humanitarian law but that were intended to apply to those it considered ineligible for Geneva Convention rights. Also, Bush insisted that U.S. constitutional law does not protect those detained at Guantanamo Bay, because the territory belongs to Cuba even though it is under the permanent control of the United States and U.S. personnel stationed there are subject to American law exclusively. The Bush administration also used detention facilities at the Air Force base at Bagram, Afghanistan to detain prisoners from many countries, including such distant places as Algeria and Kenya, as well as those it had captured fighting for the Taliban in Afghanistan and Pakistan. Bagram continued to be used for such purposes by the Obama administration after it took office, with a substantial number of new detainees, though there have been indications that greater efforts were made to diminish the arbitrariness of detentions and mistreatment.

A fundamental question of constitutional theory also played a large role in determining the policies of the Bush administration. The issue concerns the powers of the president. Vice President Richard Cheney, who served on the White House staff during the Nixon administration when it was under fire for Watergate-related abuses, and was a member of Congress during the Reagan years when debate took place in that body over the "Iran-Contra" affair, had long been a partisan of the view that the president has essentially unchecked powers under the Constitution to deal with matters involving war policies, foreign policy, and national security. The approach favored by Cheney and his long-time counsel David Addington, is known as the theory of the "unitary executive." It purports to derive from the approach promoted by Alexander Hamilton at the time the Constitution was adopted, and its partisans selectively quote some passages in the Federalist Papers that were written by Hamilton.

From the standpoint of those favoring this theory of presidential power, the metaphor of "the war on terror" is very useful. If it is a "war," it implicates the president's powers as commander-in-chief.[11] Accordingly, they contend, any attempt to limit the power of the president when he exercises that power is an improper intrusion on his authority under the Constitution. For example, when it comes to torture, proponents of rights may point out that it is forbidden by customary international law as well as by a host of international agreements to which the United States is a party, including the United Nations Convention Against Torture, which also forbids cruel, inhuman, and degrading treatment; in circumstances of armed conflict it is forbidden by the Geneva Conventions; and, under domestic law, it is barred by statute as well as by the Eighth Amendment to the United States Constitution prohibiting cruel and unusual punishment. All these requirements of national and international law are overridden by the president's plenary powers as commander-in-chief, according to at least some of those who subscribe to the concept of the unitary executive. One of those identified with this view has been John Yoo, a Professor of Law at the University of California at Berkeley who served in the Office of Legal Counsel of the Department of Justice during the early years of the Bush administration and who was an author of some of the legal memos that appear to justify torture. Professor Yoo's views on presidential power are set forth in a memo he sent to Pentagon General Counsel William Haynes on December 28, 2001 (written with Patrick Philbin), dealing with detention at Guantanamo. Yoo and Philbin argued that those held at Guantanamo were not entitled to habeas corpus and that, if Congress tried to extend that right to them, it "would represent a possible infringement on presidential discretion to direct the military."[12]

As noted, foremost among those holding this view, and asserting the importance of not restraining presidential power, was Vice President Dick Cheney who had served on the White House staff under President Richard Nixon. Nixon himself expressed the essence of the theory in a crude way when he famously responded to a question from television interviewer David Frost by saying, "Well, when the president does it, that means that it is not illegal." Frost responded, "By definition?" to which Nixon answered, "Exactly. Exactly. If the president determines that a specific action is necessary to protect national security, then the action is lawful, even if it is prohibited by a federal statute."[13] Americans who regarded it as an attempt by Nixon to argue that the president is above the law had overwhelmingly rejected that view more than a generation ago. The rejection manifested itself in the decision of the Judiciary Committee of the House of Representatives, in hearings in 1974 that were televised and that riveted the attention of the country, to vote by a large margin with bipartisan support to recommend to the full House that Nixon should be impeached on three counts of high crimes and misdemeanors. It was those hearings by the House Judiciary Committee and its subsequent call for impeachment that forced Nixon to resign.

The theory that what the president does on a matter of national security is legal even if it violates a specific federal statute was revived during the second term of the Reagan administration under the leadership of Reagan's attorney general at that time, Edwin Meese III. One of the young attorneys in the U.S. Department of Justice who was assigned by Meese to help develop the theory was Samuel Alito, Jr., appointed to the U.S. Supreme Court two decades later by President George W. Bush. There he joined Justice Antonin Scalia, who had written a lone and lengthy dissent in a Supreme Court case decided during Reagan's second term that was the first substantial articulation of the theory in any proceeding of the high court.[14] Before Alito joined Scalia on the Supreme Court, Clarence Thomas, appointed by the first President Bush, made clear that he too subscribed to the theory. Accordingly, with Alito's appointment, the theory of the unitary executive enjoys support from at least three U.S. Supreme Court justices. (Whether a fourth, Chief Justice John Roberts, also subscribes to the theory is not yet clear at this writing.)

The most significant controversy that arose during Reagan's second term concerned Iran-Contra: that is, the covert activities of the Reagan administration in financing the contra rebels in Nicaragua in spite of a federal statute specifically prohibiting such support. The Reagan administration had secured the funds for this purpose by such practices as selling weapons to America's enemy, the Khomeini regime in Iran. Some officials of the Reagan administration, including Elliott Abrams, who previously served as assistant secretary of state for human rights in Reagan's first term, were criminally convicted for their part in Iran-Contra. In Abrams's case, his conviction was for lying to Congress. Yet those convicted for offenses related to Iran-Contra were spared prison terms through pardons issued by Reagan's successor, President George H. W. Bush. Abrams was subsequently appointed by the second President Bush to a key position overseeing Middle East policy on the National Security Council, where Senate confirmation was not required. (Very likely, someone convicted of lying to Congress could not have obtained Senate confirmation even during a period when the Senate was controlled by the president's own party. Putting Abrams on the staff of the National Security Council, where confirmation hearings are not required, was a way to give him a high-ranking post while avoiding Senate scrutiny.)

During the period of the Iran-Contra investigation, as a newly elected member of the House of Representatives from Wyoming, Dick Cheney was in the forefront of those defending Reagan's actions on the basis of presidential power. In recent years, Cheney has made it clear that he takes considerable pride in his role in producing a minority report in connection with the House investigation and, from time to time, he makes public references to it. For example, in a press interview in December 2005, Cheney was quoted as saying:

> Over the years there had been an erosion of presidential power and authority . . . a lot of the things around Watergate and Vietnam, both, in the 70s served to erode the authority. I think the President needs to be effective especially in a national security area. If you want references to an obscure text, go look at the minority views that were filed with the Iran-Contra Committee; the Iran-Contra Report in about 1987. . . . [T]hey were actually authored by a guy working for me, for my staff, that I think are very good in laying out a robust view of the President's prerogatives with respect to the conduct of especially foreign policy and national security matters . . . . I do believe that, especially in the day and age we live in, the nature of the threats we face—it was true during the Cold War, as well as what I think what is

true now—the President of the United States needs to have his constitutional powers unimpaired, if you will, in terms of the conduct of national security policy. That's my personal view.[15]

With the advent of Barack Obama as president of the United States, the theory of the unitary executive suffered a substantial setback. It is highly unlikely that Obama would appoint to the U.S. Supreme Court anyone who subscribes to this theory. Accordingly, it appears improbable that the concept will soon command a majority on the Court. Yet what would have been a radical revision in the high court's jurisprudence on a range of issues involving questions of national security, as espoused by the likes of John Yoo and David Addington, came very close. If a new President who shares the general views on such matters of Cheney and Bush takes office in 2013, it is possible that the theory of the unitary executive could command a majority of the U.S. Supreme Court in a few years time.

In the Bush administration, the theory was championed forcefully by Yoo, Addington, and Vice President Cheney; accepted by Alberto Gonzales during his tenure as White House counsel and, subsequently, as attorney general; vigorously promoted by some lawyers active in the Federalist Society—so named because of a reading of the Federalist Papers that favors this theory—and by individuals who held important legal positions in the Bush administration such as William Haynes III (general counsel of the Department of Defense), Stephen Jay Bybee (director of the Office of Legal Counsel of the Department of Justice and subsequently an appointee of President Bush to the Ninth Circuit U.S. Court of Appeals), and John Bolton (undersecretary of state and subsequently a recess appointment of President Bush to serve as ambassador to the United Nations, a post he had to vacate when he was denied confirmation by the U.S. Senate) and endorsed in deed, if not articulated in theoretical terms, by President Bush. The theory of the unitary executive was the main philosophic rationale for the Bush administration's violations of rights both domestically and internationally that were manifest at Guantanamo, Abu Ghraib, Bagram, and other such places; and in such practices as extraordinary renditions; indefinite detention without charges; disregard of legal prohibitions on torture and cruel, inhuman, and degrading treatment; and the use of military commissions lacking protections for the rights of defendants. The theory also provided the philosophic basis for President Bush to ignore the Foreign Intelligence Surveillance Act (FISA) and to claim that he could order wiretapping in national security investigations without complying with the procedures required by law. According to many proponents of the unitary executive, all these measures taken in the conduct of the global war on terror are prerogatives of the unitary executive as commander-in-chief and as the individual who is vested with the constitutional responsibility for conducting the foreign policy of the United States and who, therefore, should be immune from interference by the other branches of government. The extent to which this theory pervaded the thinking of the Bush administration was made manifest a few months after the end of President Bush's second term when his secretary of state, Condoleezza Rice, spoke at Stanford University, where she had been provost years earlier and to which she returned after completing her service in government. Responding to a question from a grade-school student, she said: "The President instructed us that nothing we would do would be outside of our obligations, under the Convention Against Torture." Rice then added, "And so, by definition, if it was authorized by the president it did not violate our obligation under the Convention Against Torture."[16] Inevitably, press reports evoked comparisons to Nixon's famous interview with David Frost.

As noted, the theory has failed up to now to secure support from a majority of the justices of the United States Supreme Court. Instead, in June 2004, taking the side of the human rights movement, the Court decided two cases in which it made clear that it intended to exercise jurisdiction over violations of rights committed by the United States in conducting the war on terror. In subsequent cases, the Court has continued to place restrictions on the way that war is conducted that are based both on American constitutional law and, in an important precedent, also on international humanitarian law. Those decisions demonstrate that the human rights cause remained resilient, even under Bush, after September 11. For the time being, it continues to be an important factor in shaping domestic public policy in the United States. The nongovernmental organizations that have been in the forefront of litigation in such cases include the American Civil Liberties Union, the Center for Constitutional Rights and, unusually, an organization based in the United Kingdom, Reprieve. A number of the prisoners detained at Guantanamo were represented by the British organization, which had gained experience in American courts through previous participation in death penalty litigation.

One of the two cases decided by the U.S. Supreme Court in June 2004 was *Rasul v. Bush*.[17] In *Rasul*, in a 6–3 decision, the Court reversed a lower court that dismissed the case on the grounds that the naval station at Guantanamo is outside American sovereign territory. The Court held that a statutory requirement of habeas corpus applies to Guantanamo. In the other case decided at the same time, *Hamdi v. Rumsfeld*,[18] the Supreme Court decided that the United States may not hold American citizens as prisoners indefinitely without charges. They are entitled to such elements of due process of law as representation by counsel and the right to challenge their detention before a "neutral decision-maker." Justice Sandra Day O'Connor pointed out in the majority opinion that "A state of war is no blank check" for the president in exercising his powers to detain suspected terrorists. In an important development, one of the founding fathers of the theory of the unitary executive, Justice Scalia, sided with the majority in holding that citizens detained as enemy combatants must be charged with a crime or released unless Congress had suspended the right to habeas corpus. Hamdi, who was born in the United States, had been held in custody for more than two years prior to the Supreme Court's ruling. During that period, he was allowed no contact with anyone other than his jailers, because, the Bush administration argued, he was so dangerous. Soon after the Supreme Court decision, however, he was released and allowed to return to his home in Saudi Arabia, where he was freed.

Two years later, in 2006, the Supreme Court decided another case involving the global war on terror. In *Hamdan v. Rumsfeld*,[19] the Supreme Court reviewed a case that involved a Yemeni, Salim Ahmed Hamdan, who had been the driver for Osama Bin Laden in Afghanistan. Hamdan's case involved a law adopted by the United States Congress in 2005, the Detainee Treatment Act (DTA), that authorized President Bush to go forward with his plan to use military commissions to try those it designated as unlawful combatants. The DTA stated that "no court, justice, or judge shall have jurisdiction to hear or consider . . . an application for a writ of habeas corpus filed by or on behalf of an alien detained at Guantanamo Bay, Cuba." Writing for the majority in the Supreme Court's 5–3 decision, Justice John Paul Stevens did not directly confront the question of whether Congress had the authority under the United States Constitution to suspend habeas corpus in the circumstances that prevailed after September 11, 2001. Instead he held that Congress had not intended to deal with pending cases, such as that of Hamdan, when it passed the DTA. Also, crucially, he found that Bush's military commissions did not meet the requirements of Common Article 3 of the Geneva Conventions, which guarantees rights to combatants that may not be violated even if a war does not rise to the level of international armed conflict. Under Common Article 3, those taken prisoner in noninternational combat, though lacking the protections provided to prisoners of war in international armed conflicts, may only be tried by a "regularly constituted court affording all the judicial guarantees recognized as indispensable by civilized peoples." Bush's military commissions, limiting the right to counsel, the right to examine evidence, the right to be judged by a court independent of the executive branch of government, and the right to appeal to an independent court, did not meet that standard. The military commissions violated a host of the judicial guarantees recognized as indispensable by civilized peoples.

Following the decision in *Hamdan*, Congress acted again, adopting the Military Commissions Act of 2006 (MCA). It attempted to close the loophole the Supreme Court had found in the DTA by denying habeas corpus to an alien determined by the United States to be an enemy combatant or one who "is awaiting such determination." Also, it purported to strip the courts of "jurisdiction to hear or consider any other action against the United States or its agents relating to any aspect of the detention, transfer, treatment or trial, or conditions of confinement of an alien who is or was detained by the United States . . . ." In June 2008, however, the Supreme Court decided *Boumediene v. Rumsfeld* 5–4, holding that the Military Commissions Act was an unconstitutional suspension of the writ of habeas corpus.[20]

Justice Anthony Kennedy wrote the majority opinion in *Boumediene*. He traced the history of habeas corpus back to the Magna Carta and also explored such aspects of the struggle for the great writ as those that took place in seventeenth-century England. In addition, he cited Lord Chief Justice Mansfield's decision of 1772 in the *Somerset* case prohibiting slavery in England. Kennedy's opinion is a short history of the struggle for rights and points to the central significance of habeas corpus in that struggle. In response, Justice Antonin Scalia filed a dissent, justifying the denial of habeas corpus on the basis that "America is at war with radical Islamists." Scalia began his history of that war with the incident in 1983 in which "the enemy began by killing Americans and America's allies abroad: 241 died at the Marine barracks in Lebanon," thereby suggesting that the global war against terrorism had been underway for at least twenty-five years and that, therefore, certain violations of rights during that entire period were justified. The quarter of a century encompassed in Scalia's chronology emphasized the endlessness of the war on terror. Scalia went on to say that the Supreme Court's majority opinion "will make the war harder on us. It will certainly cause more Americans to be killed."

Justice Scalia's assertion that the majority of the Supreme Court would have blood on its hands for upholding constitutional rights may be without precedent in the history of American jurisprudence. It indicates the depth of feeling aroused by the detentions at Guantanamo. Worldwide, these detentions became a symbol of American readiness to abandon its commitment to rights as soon as the country and its citizens themselves became the objects of attack. The readiness of a majority of the justices of the United States Supreme Court to stand firm for rights in such circumstances reflects an ingrained culture of rights. On the other hand, the denunciations of those justices from within the Supreme Court itself, as well as from others active in the political process, reveal deep fissures in American society. In the wake of September 11, 2001, a significant part of the country is not ready to accept restraints on the power of the executive to restrict rights in the name of security. The congressional majorities that supported enactment of the Detainee Treatment Act and the Military Commissions Act are indicative of a substantial body of public sentiment.

In his first week in office, President Barack Obama ordered that Guantanamo should be closed within a year[21] and that the operation of President Bush's military commissions should cease. By then, only one trial had been held before one of those military commissions.[22] Bin Laden's driver, Salim Ahmed Hamdan, the subject of the 2007 decision by the Supreme Court, was tried at Guantanamo in the summer of 2008 on two charges and convicted only on the more minor charge. Having been held in detention for sixty-one months prior to his trial, the military commission gave him credit for that time and sentenced him to sixty-six months imprisonment. That meant that his sentence was due to expire just five months after his trial, before the end of the Bush administration. In November 2008, he was put on a military plane that carried him back to Yemen to serve the last month of his sentence in prison there before being set free. In May 2009, Boumediene, the plaintiff in the challenge to the Military Commissions Act, was deported to France.

Boumediene's story is emblematic of the kinds of situations that inspire doubts about many of the long-term detentions at Guantanamo. He had been arrested in Sarajevo in October 2001, along with five other Algerians, on charges of plotting to blow up the American and British embassies in Bosnia. At the time, Boumediene was a humanitarian worker employed in Sarajevo by the Red Crescent Society. The charges in that case, which were brought in the immediate aftermath of September 11, were subsequently withdrawn. Yet in January 2002, without judicial approval,

American officials in Bosnia took the six into custody and flew them to Guantanamo.

One of the other Algerians taken from Bosnia to Guantanamo, Belkacem Bensayah, was accused by American investigators of being an al-Qaeda operative. Reportedly, Bosnian police had found a piece of paper in Bensayah's home with the name and phone number of a senior leader of al-Qaeda in Afghanistan. The questioning of Boumediene at Guantanamo apparently focused on Bensayah and also on the fact that Boumediene had been in Pakistan in the early 1990s. According to Boumediene, he did not know his fellow Algerian well, but had come in contact with him through the Red Crescent Society; and his sojourn in Pakistan was as a proctor in a school for Afghan orphans financed by Kuwaitis. During his stay in Pakistan, he renewed his passport at the Algerian embassy in Islamabad. As a number of Algerians had also gone to Pakistan during this period to aid the Afghan resistance to the Soviet military occupation of their country, Boumediene's presence there marked him as a possible Islamist fighter.

According to Boumediene, he was interrogated more than 120 times during the seven and a half years he spent in Guantanamo. Though he did not allege that he was tortured, he says he was treated roughly during a sixteen-day period in 2003 and that he was interrogated day and night. When he started a hunger strike in 2006, he reports that he was force-fed through a tube in his nose that reached into his stomach.

When Boumediene was released on May 15, 2009, he was flown from Guantanamo to Paris in shackles and set free by the French authorities. At the time he was forty-three years old and was able to join his wife and two daughters.[23] It is, of course, impossible to know whether Boumediene was innocent of all involvement in terrorist acts or conspiracies. As no charges were ever brought against him, much less a judicial determination of guilt following a trial, he is entitled to the presumption of innocence.

The reluctance of both the Bush administration and the Obama administration to bring those detained at Guantanamo to trial before regular federal courts has created the impression in some quarters that those courts are incapable of conducting the trials of alleged terrorists. According to a study conducted by two former federal prosecutors under the auspices of Human Rights First, that impression is not warranted.

The former prosecutors examined 119 federal court prosecutions conducted since September 2001 against 289 defendants charged with crimes involving terrorism that were associated with al-Qaeda or other Islamic groups. The defendants whose cases were resolved during that period number 214; 195 of those, or 91 percent, were convicted. Some of those who were acquitted were held to face additional charges or detained for immigration violations. The former prosecutors also found that 171 of the convicted defendants had been sentenced by the time of their study. Twenty were sentenced to time served or placed on probation. Of the 151 who received prison terms, eleven received life sentences, the rest sentences averaging 8.4 years. The authors of the study also found that the availability of a federal statute, the Classified Information Procedures Act, had helped to prevent the disclosure of significant sensitive information as a result of any of the prosecutions.[24]

Given these findings, it is difficult to avoid the conclusion that a significant factor in the effort since September 2001 by both the Bush and Obama administrations to avoid trying alleged terrorists in regular federal courts is that they lack evidence—or evidence that could be presented in court—that many of those held at Guantanamo and other detention centers committed any crime. If they had such evidence, there would be no reason to avoid trials at which all the rights of the defendants would be fully respected.

While constitutional litigation arising from the global war on terror focused mainly on the avoidance of federal court trials, prolonged detentions at Guantanamo, and the use of military commissions, public debate centered on coercive interrogation. Very soon after September 11, the Bush administration decided that its main interest in detainees was not in bringing them to trial. Rather, as noted, its principal concern was prevention of future incidents. A main focus, therefore, was obtaining information from detainees that would be useful in preventing additional terrorist attacks and in pursuing the struggle against al-Qaeda.

From the start, the Bush administration insisted that it did not engage in torture to get that information. On the other hand, it authorized many practices—waterboarding, sleep deprivation, the use of extremes of temperature, forced standing for prolonged periods, "wall slamming," various forms of sensory deprivation, sexual humiliation, and the use of dogs to menace prisoners—that the State Department had frequently labeled as torture in its annual *Country Reports on Human Rights Practices* on other countries. These were not designated as alternative methods; they could be used, and were used, in combination with each other. Nor were they used just once; detainees who were waterboarded were subjected to the practice scores of times. Some Bush administration officials made no effort to distinguish such practices from torture. Richard Cheney, David Addington, and John Yoo, as discussed, espoused the view that any attempt by Congress or anyone else to impose limits on the treatment of detainees was an unconstitutional restraint on the powers of the president as commander-in-chief of the armed forces.[25] In April 2009, acting in a case in which the American Civil Liberties Union had secured a decision from the Second Circuit Court of Appeals under the Freedom of Information Act, the Obama administration released a set of memos written by John Yoo, Jay Bybee, and others at the Justice Department, to John Rizzo, general counsel of the CIA, assuring him that agents who used these methods had not violated any laws.

Starting with the scandal in 2004 over the treatment of prisoners at Abu Ghraib, and continuing with additional revelations of the treatment of detainees at Guantanamo and other locations, public condemnation of the Bush administration's practices grew steadily louder. Alberto Gonzales was forced to resign as attorney general over an unrelated scandal but, by the time he stepped down, he was a reviled figure on a number of grounds, including his role in authorizing the abuse of detainees. William Haynes III was denied U.S. Senate confirmation as a United States Court of Appeals judge because of his role in providing a legal justification for the mistreatment of detainees. Several other Bush administration nominees for federal judgeships and other posts requiring confirmation by the U.S. Senate were rejected on similar grounds. Defense Secretary Robert Gates made clear that he would not permit use of the interrogation methods authorized by former Pentagon chief Donald Rumsfeld on the advice of Haynes. Even so, the Bush administration successfully resisted efforts to impose limits on the CIA comparable to those accepted by the Department of Defense. Proponents of human rights in organizations such as the American Civil Liberties Union, Human Rights First, and Human Rights Watch nonetheless made steady headway in gaining support for their condemnation of the mistreatment of detainees that had been authorized by President Bush and his administration.

A factor in the debate over these abuses was the widespread recognition by Americans that they were damaging American prestige internationally. Ordinarily, world opinion does not play a significant part in shaping American public policy. In fact, in that respect, the United States may be more insular than almost any other country, claiming an "American exceptionalism" that is a matter of pride to many Americans. That exceptionalism (or insularity) has been manifest when it comes to human rights issues, as in such other public policy decisions as America's rejection some years earlier of the Kyoto Treaty on climate change. The Bush administration's policies and practices with respect to torture, however, were a different matter. Many Americans realized that this lowered the standing of the United States in the eyes of the rest of the world. The fact that on the international stage U.S. use of torture was being denounced as a human rights violation became one of the reasons often cited as grounds for ending the abuse of detainees.

In addition to ordering the closing of Guantanamo, President Barack Obama also issued an order during his first week in office effectively prohibiting torture by limiting the conduct of interrogations by any U.S. government agency to the methods set forth in the U.S. Army Field Manual. Though this order was denounced by former Vice President Cheney, who claimed that the interrogation methods used by the Bush administration had maintained American safety during the years following September 11, few others in the United States, outside the precincts of Fox News, responded critically. It appeared that most Americans were relieved that their government had gotten out of the business of torture. Yet President Obama did not abandon all the practices of the Bush administration that abridged civil liberties in the interests of preventing future terrorist attacks. In an address to the nation on May 21, 2009 delivered from the National Archives, where the Declaration of Independence and the United States Constitution and its Bill of Rights are displayed and celebrated, Obama said that he would resume the use of military commissions to try some of those accused of terrorism, but that he would expand the due process protections for defendants; and that he would not release additional photos showing the abuse of detainees. As in the case of the torture memos released the previous month, the photos were the subject of a court order obtained by the ACLU under the Freedom of Information Act. Obama said publication of the photos would endanger American troops in Iraq, Afghanistan, and Pakistan. His decision indicated that the struggle over the photos would go to the U.S. Supreme Court, where refusal to release the photos was upheld.[26] Obama also reiterated his previous refusal to appoint a presidential commission to look into abuses of the Bush era. Most troubling from the standpoint of human rights advocates, he indicated that his administration would devise a system of preventive detention for suspects in terrorism cases who could not be brought to trial. As time passed, however, plans to adopt new legislation for this purpose were shelved. Instead, the Obama administration maintained the practice with respect to some

Bush-era detainees without attempting to incorporate its codification in U.S. law.

Looking back on the way that the U.S. has set aside civil liberties during periods of crisis and perceived crisis over the past century, the response to September 11 is not altogether surprising. Literally thousands of prosecutions of peaceful dissenters took place in state and federal courts during World War I; and in the immediate postwar period, when the country suffered a number of anarchist bombings and when a red scare was touched off by the Russian Revolution. During World War II, more than 110,000 Japanese-Americans, most of them citizens, were forcibly relocated from the West Coast on racial grounds and confined in internment camps. The start of the Cold War was accompanied by national hysteria about communist subversion, and many thousands were persecuted for their peaceful opinions and associations. Protests against the Vietnam War led to a great increase in domestic political surveillance by a host of federal government agencies, including even the United States Army.

Each time, of course, as the sense of crisis passed, there was a period of substantial restoration of civil liberties. President Calvin Coolidge and his attorney general, Harlan Fiske Stone, freed those still held in federal prisons for their opposition to U.S. entry into World War I. The country eventually apologized more than four decades later to the Japanese-Americans who had been interned during World War II and paid modest damages to the survivors. The United States Supreme Court, over time, struck down loyalty oaths and most other remnants of the post–World War II hunt for subversives. Lower federal courts in the late 1970s and the early 1980s dismantled a large part of the country's political surveillance machinery.

At this writing, the crisis that started on September 11 is a decade old. There is no sign, however, that it is over. For the time being, with the important exception of torture, there is little to indicate that the country is ready to get beyond Bush-era practices. Indeed, anti-Muslim sentiment, manifested in some instances by strenuous opposition to the construction of mosques, seems to have risen. In the immediate aftermath of September 11, President Bush made a number of efforts to counter bias against Muslims. His actions in that period may have prevented earlier manifestations of prejudice.

In June 2010, the U.S. Supreme Court handed down its first decision in a case that seemed to involve a clash between the First Amendment rights to speak and associate and the country's struggle against terrorism. In *Holder v. Humanitarian Law Project*,[27] the Court upheld federal legislation that permits the imprisonment of Americans for up to fifteen years if they provide material support to a terrorist organization, even if that support is not in the form of weapons or finances but in the form of speech. The material support law was originally enacted by Congress in 1996 as part of the Antiterrorism and Effective Death Penalty Act and was subsequently revised in The Patriot Act of 2001, adopted in the immediate aftermath of September 11. It specifies that material support may take place through such forms of speech as "expert advice," "training," and "services." Even if "expert advice" consisted of efforts to persuade a group such as the Kurdistan Workers Party, the organization that the State Department designated as "terrorist" in the case, to abandon violence and use peaceful methods, it could constitute "material support" under the law as upheld by the Supreme Court.

A few weeks after the Supreme Court decision in *Humanitarian Law Project*, there was another judicial decision dealing with abusive government conduct in battling terrorism that alarmed proponents of civil liberties. It was a case involving "extraordinary rendition," the transfer of foreign nationals seized by the CIA at various locations around the world to the custody of governments such as Egypt and Morocco, where they were allegedly tortured while being interrogated. One of the plaintiffs in the case (*Mohamed v. Jeppesen*), a young Ethiopian named Binyan Mohamed who was a legal resident of the United Kingdom said he had been seized in Pakistan and flown to Morocco. In separate proceedings in a British court after he was released from five years detention at Guantanamo following a year-and-a-half in Morocco, his claim of torture had been upheld.

The American decision in the case of Binyan Mohamed and four other plaintiffs was *en banc* (that is, a decision of all the judges of the court) by the United States Court of Appeals for the Ninth Circuit, holding 6–5 that the case should be dismissed because it involved state secrets. Binyan Mohamed and the others were thus denied the opportunity to prove in an American court that the CIA had arranged their torture and to get any compensation or any ruling prohibiting further conduct of the same sort.[28] In May 2011, the U.S. Supreme Court declined to review the decision, leaving it in place. If it had been accepted for review by the Supreme Court, there seems little likelihood that it would have been overturned. Justice Elena Kagan would probably have had to disqualify herself because the case was litigated by the U.S. Department of Justice while she served as solicitor general. Even if the swing member of the Supreme Court, Justice Anthony Kennedy, had ruled in favor of consideration of the case on its merits—by no means an assured result—it seems likely that the four right-wing justices—Alito, Roberts, Scalia and Thomas—would have prevented Mohamed and the others from securing more than a 4–4 decision by the high court. Though such an outcome would not establish a binding precedent, it would uphold the decision of the Ninth Circuit. As the Ninth Circuit is usually considered to be a court that is protective of civil liberties, its ruling that an inquiry into extraordinary rendition and torture can be derailed because of the possibility of revealing state secrets was dismaying to rights advocates. Some probably breathed a sigh of relief when the Supreme Court declined to review the case, as they feared an adverse decision.

It is too soon, at this writing, to tell whether the rulings in *Humanitarian Law Project* and *Mohamed v. Jeppesen* are a sign of things to come. Yet these decisions are a disturbing indication that even battles that seemed to have been won long ago may be refought when the country considers that it is under threat, and that, a decade after September 11, far from having abated, the sense of threat may be greater than ever.

■   ■   ■

Though its own practices in the wake of September 11 limited the readiness and ability of the Bush administration to speak out about many abuses of human rights by other governments, it was forcefully outspoken—more so than any other government—in denouncing Sudanese oppression in Darfur.[29] Not long after the most significant attacks on civilian residents of the vast territory began in 2003, U.S. Secretary of State Colin Powell applied the term "genocide" to the killings of members of indigenous tribes by Arab militias, the Janjaweed, aided and abetted by the Sudanese armed forces. Though references to genocide were avoided by groups such as Human Rights Watch—which used the term "crimes against humanity" because it was not convinced that the intent was ethnic destruction rather than the destruction of civilians who were regarded as supporters of insurgent groups—there was broad agreement between the Bush administration and nongovernmental human rights groups on the extent of the human rights abuses committed in the region and on the identity of the perpetrators. By June 2005, when the question of referral of Darfur to the International Criminal Court came before the United Nations Security Council (see chapter 11), as many as 200,000 persons had been killed in attacks on civilians in Darfur. Many hundreds of thousands more had been forcibly displaced.

As noted in chapter 11, the question of how to vote on the Security Council resolution referring Darfur to the ICC created a quandary for the Bush administration. Up to that moment, it had displayed unrelieved hostility to the Court. Diplomats often expressed amazement at how high noncooperation with the Court was on the administration's agenda, particularly during President Bush's first term, in its relations with their governments. On the other hand, having labeled the crimes in Darfur as genocide, the Bush administration was not eager to cast a veto in 2005 that would obstruct one of the few significant measures that the international community was prepared to take to deal with the slaughter. China, which had become the main financial backer of Sudan through its purchases of that country's oil, was also reluctant to veto the resolution because it was preparing to hold the Olympics three years later and did not want to make itself the target of protests over Darfur by the substantial international movement that had developed to denounce abuses there. Russia preferred not to stand alone in casting a veto. The other two permanent members of the United Nations Security Council, France and Britain, strongly supported referral to the ICC. Initially, France was the sponsor of the resolution on Darfur, but it yielded to Britain because it would be more difficult for President Bush to authorize a veto of a resolution identified with his closest ally and a crucial supporter of his invasion of Iraq, Prime Minister Tony Blair. An accident of timing was also helpful in avoiding an American veto. The most vehement antagonist of the ICC in the Bush administration was John Bolton. At the time, he was the president's nominee to serve as ambassador to the United Nations. When the vote over Darfur came before the Security Council, Bolton was sidelined by a battle in the United States Senate over his confirmation that he eventually lost. With the post of U.N. ambassador temporarily vacant, Secretary of State Condoleezza Rice made the decision to abstain rather than veto. Though three permanent members of the Security Council with veto power—China, Russia, and the United States—were not parties to the International Criminal Court, and each had its own reasons for being hostile to the referral, the human rights movement prevailed. Subsequently, after a three-judge panel of the ICC upheld a request by the Court's prosecutor for an arrest warrant against Sudanese President Omar al Bashir in March 2009 for war crimes and crimes against humanity committed under his leadership in Darfur,[30] China and Russia joined Arab and African governments in denouncing the action. By this time, with the Obama administration in office, the U.S. became one of the Court's few public defenders. The development highlighted the importance to the human rights movement of reestablishing a *de facto* alliance with the government of the United States on such matters.

• • •

Four years after the terrorist attacks of September 11, 2001, a World Summit convened by the United Nations unanimously endorsed the principle that there is an international "responsibility to protect" those who may be the targets of crimes against humanity, ethnic cleansing, or genocide. Despite the unanimity, the responsibility to protect—widely know as "R2P"—is deeply controversial. Many governments, especially those in Africa, Asia, and the Middle East, fear that it is a license for Western governments to intervene militarily in their countries. (The action of the Arab League in March 2011 in unanimously endorsing the imposition of a "no-fly zone" over Libya to prevent Colonel Qaddafi's forces from massacring rebels was a significant departure from what had been hostility to such intervention by governments in the region.) While the concept seemed to enjoy strong support from the international human rights movement, leading organizations in the field have been hesitant to invoke it. They are concerned about appearing to support interventions such as that of the United States in Iraq, which the Bush administration sometimes attempted to justify on the basis of Saddam Hussein's gross abuses of human rights. Also, they are sensitive to their own role as institutions based in Western countries and financed by Western donors, whereas interventions are most likely to take place in third-world countries. They wish to avoid taking positions that seem to evoke a "white man's burden" approach to countries populated by persons of other races.

Before the term "responsibility to protect" was coined at the beginning of the twenty-first century, the concept was referred to as "humanitarian intervention." Bernard Kouchner, foreign minister of France until 2010, was an early proponent in the contemporary period. In 1986, he convened a large gathering in Paris under the auspices of an organization he then headed, Médecins du Monde (which Kouchner formed in 1980 when he broke with Médecins Sans Frontières, which he also founded) to discuss "le devoir d'ingerence" (the duty of intervention).[31]

It is possible to cite much earlier examples of actions by Western governments, particularly Britain, to intervene in conflicts elsewhere on behalf of oppressed peoples. Gary Bass, a political scientist at Princeton University, has pointed to the British role in supporting Greece's struggle for independence from the Ottoman Empire in the 1820s as an early example of humanitarian intervention. Today, we recall the British role primarily because of the leading part played in it by the most famous poet of his era, Lord Byron, who died of a fever in Mesologgi, Greece in 1824 at the age of thirty-six. Byron and many others in Britain were attracted to the struggle because they saw the Greeks of their era as heirs of the classical civilization of ancient Greece. "Philhellenism," as some referred to it, was a cause worth dying for.[32] Later in the decade, a few years after Byron's death, Russia and France joined England in intervening in Greece to end reported Ottoman atrocities and to secure Greek independence.

Gary Bass also cites the 1869 intervention of the French under Napoleon III in Syria in response to a massacre of Maronite Christians; and Russia's intervention in Bulgaria in 1877 in response to the atrocities there that also inspired Gladstone's denunciations of Disraeli for failing to respond appropriately (see chapter 2). In both these cases, as in the case of the war for Greek independence of the 1820s, the fact that it was the Ottoman authorities—that is, Muslims—who were accused of grave crimes against Christians within their empire, may have played a part in the readiness of other European powers to intervene.

Closer to our time and in a different part of the world, we have the example of Tanzania's intervention in Uganda in 1979 to end the murderous rule of Idi Amin. Yet this was not portrayed by Julius Nyerere, Tanzania's president at the time, as a case of humanitarian intervention, even though that was probably the prime motive. In that era, humanitarian grounds were not recognized as an acceptable basis for entering into a military conflict. The concept was particularly unwelcome in Africa where many states were still governed by elites that had taken part in the struggle to end colonial rule and who knew that their former masters had often justified their actions on humanitarian grounds. Rather, the invasion by Tanzanian forces was said to be in self-defense, because Amin was threatening to send troops into a region that bordered on Tanzania to quash opposition to his rule.

The concept of humanitarian intervention gained support in the 1990s with many proponents of human rights criticizing the failure of Western governments to intervene in Bosnia and Rwanda to stop genocidal slaughter. Support for humanitarian intervention reached its peak in 1999 when NATO—led by British Prime Minister Tony Blair and his foreign secretary, Robin Cook, and followed by President Bill Clinton of the United States and his secretary of state, Madeleine Albright—intervened in Kosovo to stop Serbian attacks on the province's ethnic Albanian majority.

NATO's intervention in Kosovo was highly controversial at the time, mainly because it bypassed the United Nations Security Council, which is given exclusive power under the United Nations Charter to authorize military action against a sovereign state for any motive other than self-defense. Blair and Clinton chose to call on NATO because they knew that Serbia's ally, Russia, would veto a resolution in the Security Council to authorize military action.

Later in the same year as NATO's war in Kosovo, a crisis in East Timor caused by widespread attacks on civilians by pro-Indonesia militias following a landslide vote in favor of independence again raised the question of international intervention. In that instance, Security Council authorization of military force was facilitated by Indonesia's agreement, under pressure, to allow an international force led by Australian troops to occupy the territory. Coming hard on the heels of the intervention in Kosovo, East Timor seemed to add to the urgency of securing international agreement on interventions for humanitarian purposes.

The International Commission on Intervention and State Sovereignty, a panel convened by the Canadian government, proposed the shift in terminology in 2001.[33] It proposed that the focus should be on the protection of victims by the state concerned. Only when the state is unwilling or unable to fulfill that responsibility, or itself is the perpetrator of abuses, is it the responsibility of the international community to protect. The purpose of action is not to attack the state engaged in crimes but only to do as much as is needed to protect the victims. The ICISS approach was, in essence, endorsed by United Nations Secretary General Kofi Annan. Prior to his designation as secretary general, Annan had headed the Department of Peacekeeping at the United Nations. In that role, he was implicated in the failure to prevent genocide in Rwanda by rejecting efforts by the Canadian commander of U.N. forces in that country, General Romeo Dallaire, to use his troops against the Hutu militias at the outset of the genocide to stop the killing. Annan subsequently authorized a U.N. investigation of events in Rwanda that was highly critical of his own role. His sense of personal responsibility for not doing all he could have done to try to stop the genocide clearly affected him deeply, so much so that his personal efforts were a leading factor in the adoption of the principle of "responsibility to protect" by the member states of the United Nations at the 2005 U.N. world summit.

There are clear parallels between the establishment of the International Criminal Court and adoption of the responsibility to protect. In both cases, the intent is to address mass atrocities—through prosecution and punishment of the perpetrators in the case of the ICC; and through intervention to protect the victims in the case of R2P. Also, both place the primary responsibility on the state that is directly concerned. Under the treaty establishing the ICC, the Court may only exercise jurisdiction when the state is unable or unwilling to conduct good faith investigations and prosecutions. Similarly, in the case of R2P, the state must prove unable or unwilling to protect its nationals against atrocities before international action is warranted.

An important difference, however, is that in the case of prosecutions, a permanent institution has been established to take the actions needed to bring perpetrators to justice. There is no counterpart in the case of R2P, unless it is considered that this is a responsibility of the U.N. Security Council. The actions of that body of course reflect the political agendas of its members and especially those of the five permanent members with veto power. Accordingly, while the ICC is able to carry out its responsibilities in a depoliticized and professional manner, R2P may only be implemented through a political process.

In the period subsequent to the 2005 world summit, a number of situations arose that potentially could have been addressed through the invocation of R2P. Foremost among these is Darfur. Whether or not the crimes committed there constituted "genocide," as they have been labeled by the United States government and by some others, they certainly involved mass atrocities against a civilian population perpetrated by their own government. Though the Security Council referred Darfur to the ICC, it did not seriously consider whether to invoke R2P. Other cases in which there was talk of R2P include Zimbabwe, where there was extensive violence by supporters of President Robert Mugabe during the 2008 elections and, subsequently, a humanitarian disaster that included a cholera epidemic; and Burma, where the military regime violently suppressed peaceful protests led by Buddhist monks in 2007 and, not long after, blocked international humanitarian assistance to hundreds of thousands of victims of a devastating cyclone. Even before the cyclone, Burma might have justified invocation of R2P because of its refusal to spend its own resources on combating the diseases prevalent in the country—including HIV-AIDS, tuberculosis, and malaria—and because of the difficulties it created for international humanitarian groups trying to compensate for the regime's neglect. Yet R2P was never seriously considered by the United Nations in the case of either Zimbabwe or Burma.[34]

Though R2P was not invoked, to a limited extent an effort was made to protect Darfurians subject to violence from the Janjaweed militias and the Sudanese armed forces. An inadequate force of African Union peacekeepers was sent to the region with backing from the United Nations under a Resolution of the Security Council. Poorly armed, the peacekeepers were not able to furnish much protection, and some of them became victims of Janjaweed abuses themselves. Rebel forces in Darfur opposing the Sudanese government also seem to have targeted the peacekeepers, leading the prosecutor of the International Criminal Court to issue an indictment in November 2008 against three leaders of those rebel groups for war crimes that involved the killing of peacekeepers. One of those indicted turned himself in to the Court in order to stand trial. As to Zimbabwe and Burma, no substantial discussion of protection took place in the U.N. Security Council despite the immense suffering to which the general population was subjected in recent years in both countries.

Some would argue that despite the suffering, neither Burma nor Zimbabwe fit the criteria contemplated for the invocation of R2P, though a credible argument could be made in each case that the government's actions constituted crimes against humanity. The decision by the U.N. Security Council in March 2011 to establish a "no-fly zone" in Libya, and to take other military action to stop the forces of Colonel Qaddafi from attacking rebel-held cities, was in essence the first international action since adoption of R2P to put the concept into practice. Yet, there was no reference to R2P in the Security Council resolution, and the concept was infrequently mentioned in the public debate over Libya. It was as if the U.N.'s 2005 resolution did not exist.[35]

If and when another situation develops along the lines of the mass killings on ethnic or religious grounds in Rwanda and Bosnia, the leading organizations in the human rights field will have to determine whether they are prepared to call on the United Nations Security Council to invoke the responsibility to protect and authorize military intervention.[36] Unquestionably, they will be hesitant to do so, as Darfur has demonstrated. Until the situation arises, however, it is not possible to know how they will act. Much will depend on the particular circumstances, as was manifest in the intervention in Libya. What can be predicted is that, unless the human rights movement provides the impetus, the concept of the responsibility to protect will fade away even though, from time to time, situations such as Libya may arise in which something analogous to R2P needs to be put into practice.

. . .

Today, more than ten years after September 11, 2001, it is clear that the era of human rights has not ended. The Arab revolutions of 2011 were not only about human rights; anger over corruption was probably of comparable significance. Yet concerns about rights were a significant enough factor to make it apparent that the rights issue is as important as it was at any time in the previous three-and-a-half decades.

In certain respects, the Arab revolutions are an even greater manifestation of the importance of the rights cause than the East European revolutions two decades earlier. That is because those who overthrew the communist regimes of Eastern Europe in 1989 were rebelling against imperial control by the Soviet Union at the same time as they were seeking rights within their own societies. Also, in 1989, the West—and, in particular, the United States—had succeeded in persuading East Europeans and others all over the world that enhancement of political freedom would also lead to greater economic prosperity. In contrast, the participants in the Arab revolutions were not struggling to free their countries from subjugation to a foreign power. They were attempting to end abuses of rights by their own governments. Moreover, the belief that political freedom is the only path to material prosperity has been severely undercut by the spectacular economic rise of China despite its authoritarian system of government. The claim of a supposed link between democracy and material well-being is also hard to reconcile with the difficulty that some Western democracies have had recovering from the economic crisis of 2008. Indeed, in some quarters, the idea has taken hold that authoritarian systems have an advantage in dealing with economic crises.

An essential characteristic of the Arab revolutions is that they were home grown. No outside force, governmental or nongovernmental, had a role in fomenting them. A few partisans of George W. Bush claimed that they were a legacy of his efforts to promote democracy in the region by invading Iraq and removing Saddam Hussein. But the suggestion that what has transpired in Iraq since 2003 was an inspiration to the demonstrators in Tunisia, Egypt, and other Arab countries in 2011 seems nonsensical.[37] The Arab revolutions owe their legitimacy to their indigenous origins, leadership, and support. To the extent that the international human rights movement had a role, it was because some of its ideas have taken hold in the Arab countries, as elsewhere.

Most of the time, in contemporary circumstances, it is up to the human rights movement itself to ensure that its concerns figure significantly in thinking about public issues and in disputes over public policy. No government, and no intergovernmental body—whether it is the United Nations, the European Union, the African Union, or any other—now plays a role comparable to that of the United States in the quarter-century prior to the terrorist attacks on New York and Washington. Without foreclosing the possibility that the United States under President Obama or a successor will reclaim its international leadership, or that another body will come to occupy that role, the prospect is that the nongovernmental movement must largely rely on itself to push human rights concerns to the forefront of public policy. The movement succeeded to some extent in placing restraints on the manner in which the Bush administration conducted its global war on terror and in securing a small measure of accountability for the grave crimes committed in Darfur by making it an issue for the International Criminal Court. It also made anger over abuses of human rights an important element in the international reaction to armed conflicts such as those involving Israel and Hezbollah and Georgia and Russia. On the other hand, its own ambivalence has prevented it from providing leadership with respect to the responsibility to protect. For the time being, lacking an effective champion, it appears that the R2P concept will languish.

In an earlier period, an important focus of the work of leading human rights groups was persuading others to speak out on abuses. In the years after World War II, a group such as the International League for Human Rights focused on getting U.N. bodies to take stands on human rights. Leadership in such efforts was then taken over by Amnesty International, which also promoted efforts to get national governments and other intergovernmental bodies to support human rights. With the emergence of organizations such as Human Rights Watch and the Lawyers Committee for International Human Rights (now, Human Rights First) in the late 1970s, a major focus became enlisting the United States to take strong stands on human rights. Though human rights activists have persisted in these efforts, their usefulness has declined. In the twenty-first century, it is the capacity of the international human rights movement itself to inform and to mobilize global public opinion that is its foremost means of promoting its cause.

13

Going Forward

AS OF OCTOBER 3, 2011

IT IS TOO SOON AT THIS WRITING TO KNOW HOW THE ARAB revolutions of 2011 will turn out. Will one or more of the Arab states become liberal democracies? Will they become military dictatorships? Is it possible that Islamists will take power? Or will the new regimes that emerge largely replicate those that were overthrown, combining corrupt oligarchical rule with special privileges for the military and the security forces so as to ensure their backing?

Though it does not seem possible to predict the outcome of these revolutions, the fact that they have taken place is, in significant part, a tribute to the success of the human rights movement in spreading its ideas. A desire for an end to such abuses of rights as emergency rule, imprisonment for peaceful dissent, gross mistreatment of detainees, and rigid control of the media were high on the list of the issues that led millions to take to the streets in Tunis, Cairo, and many other cities to demand change. Of course, increased political freedom was not their only concern. Repugnance at the flagrant corruption of the ruling families in Tunisia, Libya, Egypt, and Syria probably played an equally significant role. As in the case of the revolutions in Eastern Europe in 1989, it is impossible to quantify the part played by concern for human rights. It is only possible to say that it had a leading role.

The differences between 1989 and 2011 are important. From a geopolitical standpoint, 1989 was of far greater significance because it brought an end to the Cold War and the threat of mutual nuclear destruction. In other respects, however, the Arab revolutions of 2011 seem just as momentous.

Most of the Europeans who rebelled in 1989 were seeking independence from the Soviet empire as well as rights within their own countries. In that sense, they were engaged in an anti-colonial struggle as well as a struggle for human rights. Probably, many of them did not distinguish between the two. They associated the subjugation of their countries to the Soviet Union with denial of their individual rights. In the Arab states, on the other hand, there was no imperial power. In demanding rights, the participants in the vast demonstrations that toppled some governments and shook others were clear that it was their own rulers from their own countries who had abused them.

Another difference is that, by 1989, the West—led by the United States—had successfully spread the view that respect for rights and economic prosperity went hand in hand, and that political repression was a cause of economic backwardness. Accordingly, in seeking political freedom, many in Eastern Europe also thought this was a path to a more affluent style of life. More than two decades later, however, by the time the Arab revolutions took place, the link between human rights and economic prosperity no longer seemed so close. Everyone knew that China had achieved immense economic success while maintaining authoritarian control. Also, many Western states were having more difficulty recovering from the economic crisis of 2008 than a number of countries where rights were less respected. By 2011, some in the Arab states, as elsewhere, probably believed that states with authoritarian regimes had an economic advantage over those where political freedom is vigorously protected. The Arab revolutions of 2011 took place despite doubts about whether greater respect for rights would lead to prosperity and not because that link seemed assured.

Arab human rights organizations like the Cairo-based Egyptian Initiative for Personal Rights, the Cairo Institute for Human Rights, the Tunis-based Tunisian League for Human Rights, and the Arab Institute for Human Rights were not the organizers or the leaders of the demonstrations that forced President Ben Ali of Tunisia to flee the country in January 2011 and brought down the government of President Hosni Mubarak of Egypt the following month. But their roles in documenting and protesting abuses of rights by their governments significantly influenced the thinking of those who did organize and lead those demonstrations, as well as the large numbers who responded to their initiatives. They are also playing an important role in efforts to ensure that rights-respecting governments emerge as a result of the revolutions to which they contributed. This is their greatest challenge.

A significant part of the early success of the Arab revolutions is attributable to the fact that no one could effectively question their indigenous character. Outsiders did not organize them. Ideas about rights and in opposition to corruption that circulated internationally had a central role, but the revolutions did not take place as a result of foreign organizing or foreign exhortation or foreign financing. When the Bush administration's other rationales for going to war in Iraq were discredited, it fell back on the claim that it was motivated by an interest in removing a tyrant and promoting democracy. Yet no one could credibly claim that what took place in 2011 was a consequence of the military attack that Bush, Cheney, and Rumsfeld, aided and abetted by Tony Blair, launched in 2003. Democracy in Iraq, such as it is, did not inspire the Arab revolutions of 2011.

The reaction of the Obama administration to the revolutions of 2011 has reflected ambivalence. At the outset, the administration seemed intent on supporting Mubarak in Egypt, stressing his important role in regional stability. Washington shifted its position only after it became clear that it would be impossible for the long-time Egyptian ruler to hold on to his office. Similarly, the Obama administration did not take the lead in restraining Muammar Qaddafi's use of armed force to try to suppress the Libyan rebellion. It only joined in endorsing forceful intervention under the authority of the United Nations after the Arab League unanimously called for such action. (Probably, the unanimity of the Arab states was made possible by the reporting from Libya by al-Jazeera—the Qatar-based satellite network—and, to a much lesser extent, by al-Jazeera's Saudi counterpart, al-Arabiya. They turned Arab public opinion strongly against Qaddafi.)

A factor in the uncertain stand by the Obama administration was probably its eagerness not to do anything that would destabilize important U.S. allies in the region, such as the monarchies in Jordan, Bahrain, and Saudi Arabia. Thus, the role of the United States in the Arab revolutions of 2011 stands in sharp contrast to its role in the East European revolutions of 1989, which it took pride in having helped to bring about and whose leaders it supported.

Whether or not the United States government resumes its role as an outspoken public advocate of human rights, it is unlikely that it will again play as significant a role internationally as it did when it started speaking out on such matters during Jimmy Carter's presidency three-and-a-half decades ago. That is because of the steep decline in American influence on other governments that has been most evident since about the time of the invasion of Iraq in 2003. It is reflected as well in such developments as former Brazilian President Lula da Silva's ostentatious flaunting of comradeship with President Ahmadinejad of Iran; in the perfunctory (and infrequent) way that the United States says anything about human rights abuses in China or Russia; and in the way that several Latin American leaders have gone out of their way to establish warm ties to Venezuela's Hugo Chavez. The main incentive in the case of the Latin Americans seems to be to demonstrate the ability of some leaders to thumb their noses at the United States. The fact that Ahmadinejad and Chavez have committed severe violations of human rights has not stood in the way of their ability to travel to many foreign capitals where they are received as honored guests. Unfortunately, no other government or association of governments (such as the European Union or the United Nations) has shown the capacity and the will to provide the leadership on international human rights issues that was sometimes provided by the United States.

In the second decade of the twenty-first century, and for the foreseeable future, it is the nongovernmental movement that has assumed and must assume leadership as the voice of human rights. Its own actions, rather than those of any government or intergovernmental body will largely determine how well it advances its cause. Of course, the movement must proceed by constant interaction with governments and intergovernmental agencies. Prodding them to act has to be a major part of its *modus operandi*, for moral pressure is its most effective means of attracting public attention to its cause. But the impetus will most often have to come from the movement itself.

Though the international human rights movement plainly has much to do in the years ahead if it is to make significant headway in addressing the issues with which it is now preoccupied, it is probably also necessary for its leaders to consider a certain number of questions it has not yet addressed, or has barely addressed. Up to now, the human rights movement has advanced not by expanding the definition of rights to embrace so-called second and third generation rights, but by applying the civil and political rights with which it has been concerned from the start of its emergence as a movement in circumstances on which it had not previously focused. This has included, of course, the extension of its work to address the severe abuses of rights commonly committed in armed conflicts; the rights abuses that take place outside the context of political struggles, as in the routine operations of the criminal justice system; and rights abuses that particularly victimize marginalized sectors of the population.

One issue that is certain to continue to require intensive concern is terrorism. Though the human rights movement contributed to the rejection of the war metaphor as the appropriate basis for dealing with terrorism, or at least rejected the implication that use of this metaphor legitimizes the exercise of unrestricted authority by the commander-in-chief in dealing with suspected terrorists, most would agree that a criminal justice approach by itself will not suffice. To cite an obvious example, it does not make sense to suggest that the only appropriate way to deal with Osama bin Laden was to try to apprehend him and bring him to trial. Given the acts in which he engaged, using military force to kill him and others who have committed such crimes is unquestionably legitimate.[1] Accordingly, a war-fighting approach has to be part of the way that the United States or other governments deal with terrorism. It is the extension of war powers beyond what is required to engage in military conflict that is objectionable from a human rights standpoint.

There is also the question of prevention. The criminal law approach relies on punishment to do justice and to deter crime. Yet that is plainly insufficient in dealing with terrorism. The prospect of punishment is probably not a deterrent to a suicide bomber. As it is clearly as legitimate and appropriate for governments to try to prevent terrorist acts as to punish those who commit them, some means of prevention that go beyond deterrence have to be accepted. The use of incapacitating prison sentences—that is, very long terms—for those convicted of terrorism is one obvious means to promote prevention. But what procedures can be devised that will make it possible to gather the information that is needed for prevention without authorizing such repugnant and impermissible practices as the cruel, inhuman, and degrading treatment of detainees and torture? How can terrorism be prevented without resorting to preventive detention which, in practice, will necessarily be prolonged and which will vest government officials with arbitrary authority to deprive individuals of freedom without proof of their criminal behavior? One approach to the problem is that adopted by an "eminent jurists panel" established by the International Commission of Jurists (ICJ) to consider the problem of terrorism, counterterrorism, and human rights. The ICJ's report, published early in 2009, has the endorsement of such prominent proponents of human rights as Arthur Chaskalson, former chief justice of the Constitutional Court of South Africa, who chaired the eminent jurists group.[2] They accepted administrative detention for terrorism suspects but attempted to surround it with safe-guards, asserting that:

> The Panel thought it vital to reiterate that administrative detention must be limited to genuine declared states of emergency threatening the life of the nation. Even in a *bona fide* emergency, administrative detention must be strictly necessary, proportionate to the threat and non-discriminatory; it must allow for prompt legal advice of one's choosing; effective *habeas corpus*; provision must be made for the courts to decide on the lawfulness of detention; judicial review must allow for both substantive and procedural challenges; detention must be time-limited; and all individuals subject to administrative deten-tion should as a rule be allowed treatment of the same standards as that accorded to prisoners accused of criminal offenses.[3]

Though the safeguards proposed by the panel sound substantial, it is not easy to imagine how they would operate in practice. What is the signifi-cance of habeas corpus in circumstances where detention may take place and may be sustained without charges? On what grounds may a court de-cide that the detention of a person not accused of a specific crime is law-ful? How does one secure judicial review of a substantive legal challenge by a detainee who need not be told the basis for his or her detention? Ul-timately, although authorizing preventive detention with such supposed safeguards may appear to make the practice more palatable, it may not make a substantial difference. The challenge remains that of engaging in prevention without resorting to preventive detention, even of the sort that is purportedly made less repellent by safeguards like those advocated by the eminent jurists.

It will not do, of course, simply to suggest that better public policies will reduce the incentive to terrorism. If that were the case—and one hopes that it is—it would take a very long time to secure general recognition that such policy shifts have taken place and a substantial amount of time would be required for them to have an impact. How, then, does one prevent ter-rorist attacks in the short term? That question still requires attention.

In the seven-and-a-half years that elapsed from the attacks of September 11, 2001 until the end of the Bush administration, the human rights move-ment devoted much of its thought and its efforts in regard to terrorism to combating what it considered policies that led to severe violations of human rights. The advent of the Obama administration made two principal changes for the better. First, as discussed, President Obama made it unmistakably clear that torture and cruel, inhuman, and degrading treatment are prohibited. Second, and as important, the president renounced any claim that his office has exclusive power to deal with such questions on the theory that sole authority flows from his powers as commander-in-chief. He explicitly acknowledged that the Congress and the courts also have significant powers in this area. Yet President Obama made clear that, in other respects, he would follow the path charted by the Bush administration. He is using military commissions to conduct trials of some of those accused of terrorist acts or conspiracies. And, though he recognizes the weight of the constitutional issues at stake, he has not been persuaded by the civil liberties and human rights movements to abandon preventive detention for those already detained when he assumed office.

The human rights movement must think through and address the boundaries and relationships between war-fighting, prevention, and criminal punishment. Difficult as it may be, it is important for the movement to develop a comprehensive approach to terrorism. It may be, for example, that human rights proponents should focus on some of the innovations that were made in American criminal law to fight organized crime and consider their utility in combating terrorism. Also, some of the theories that have been put into practice in the prosecution of war criminals by various international criminal tribunals, such as the concept of "joint criminal enterprise," could be applied in cases involving terrorist conspiracies. It should be possible to prosecute successfully on such a basis any suspect about whom enough is known to warrant long-term detention. On the other hand, if such a prosecution is not possible, it seems appropriate to conclude that preventive detention is also not warranted. An approach of this nature respects established principles of due process while recognizing the need for enhanced prosecutorial capacity to deal with novel forms of crime, and it may make possible prevention without resort to the abusive forms practiced by the Bush administration and also endorsed in practice by President Obama.

. . .

The international human rights movement has also faced significant challenges in its efforts to minimize harm to noncombatants in the armed conflicts that have taken place in the period subsequent to September 11. Previously, most of the armed conflicts on which the movement focused since it began, in the early 1980s, to apply the principles of international humanitarian law were internal. The main exceptions were the wars in ex-Yugoslavia, where the breakup of that country produced a number of independent states, thus rendering the conflicts international. After September 11, there was an increase in the number of international armed conflicts. They included, of course, such long-lasting wars as those in Afghanistan and Iraq, as well as conflicts of much shorter duration—the war in 2006 between Israel and Hezbollah, for example; and the war in 2008 between Russia and Georgia. (The conflict that began in the last days of 2008 when Israeli forces launched Operation Cast Lead against Hamas in Gaza, is probably best characterized as non-international.) Reporting on these conflicts, as discussed in chapter 9, has become especially challenging to the human rights movement, because the parties are aware of the important role such reporting played in the conflicts of the 1980s and the 1990s. This has made the opposing forces all the more intent on delegitimizing human rights monitors critical of their conduct. It seems likely that governments will step up their efforts to exclude human rights monitors from conflict zones—as the Israelis did while their bombardment of Gaza was underway—and will take other measures to limit efforts to monitor their military practices. Devising ways to cope with such challenges is already a significant concern for human rights groups.

■　■　■

Another important question that the international human rights movement has yet to confront in a substantial way, but that arguably should be high on its agenda, is how to address the problems created by the increasing dispersion of cultural minorities worldwide. The issue is particularly acute in a number of Western European countries where there has been a significant increase in the numbers of persons whose racial, linguistic, and religious backgrounds are different from those that had long characterized the population. In 2009, the Italian government of Prime Minister Silvio Berlusconi launched a series of attacks on Roma communities in the country, some of them made up of recent immigrants from Romania and Bulgaria, while others included Roma who had resided in Italy for generations. In 2010, a campaign against Roma migrants in his country was also launched by French President Nicolas Sarkozy. A divisive issue in several countries of Europe has been what policies to follow with respect to the Muslim minorities that make up an increasingly significant percentage of their population. It is an issue that has been of great significance in such countries as Denmark, France, the Netherlands, Spain, and the United Kingdom and, in 2010, it also became an issue in the United States when the construction of mosques became a heated political controversy in a number of communities in different parts of the country.

To the extent that the human rights movement has played a part in such matters, it has been mainly by calling on the authorities in these countries to stop deportations of Roma and other attacks on their communities and to treat Muslims equitably. In a few cases, rights organizations have also pursued litigation to address such issues.

At the same time that human rights organizations defend the rights of Muslims, they must also protect rights that are threatened because of concern about offending Muslims. Organizations concerned with free expression have spoken out in defense of the right to publish and exhibit works that many Muslims find insulting, such as Salman Rushdie's *Satanic Verses*, the Danish cartoons of the Prophet Muhammad, and the film about Islam by the Dutch provocateur, Theo Van Gogh, that led to his assassination. Claims by those who are offended by such forms of expression cannot be the basis for legitimizing censorship, even when those taking offense threaten, and engage in, violence. Rather it is the violence that must be prevented and punished.

Debates over such matters may obscure the fact that the human rights movement has largely refrained from participating in serious thought and discussion of the relative merits of the multicultural policies pursued by the United Kingdom and the Netherlands, on the one hand, and the more assimilationist policies of a country such as France, on the other hand. International human rights law does not provide a basis for suggesting that either approach is preferable and leaders of human rights organizations may well believe that they lack a basis for intervening in debates over such issues.

Yet a case can be made that this is an appropriate set of issues to be considered by the human rights movement. In the United States, most of those concerned with domestic human rights came to believe that it was not possible to secure equal protection under the law for racial minorities in the absence of racial integration. This required going beyond desegregation to advocate affirmative policies that would promote integration. The same may well be true with respect to the Muslim minorities, often separated from the majority by both race and religion, sometimes by their own initiative, in the countries of Western Europe. Integration—or social inclusion as it is generally called in Europe—is also an important issue that should be addressed in dealing with Roma minorities in both Eastern and Western Europe.

As the debate over such questions as multiculturalism, assimilation, and social inclusion now stands, the primary question of most of those involved in Western Europe, at least in dealing with Muslim minorities, is which approach is likely to be most successful in preventing terrorism.[4] Indeed, it seems possible that policies designed to promote integration or inclusion would simultaneously reduce the likelihood of violence. Whether or not that is the case, it seems an issue worthy of serious examination by human rights proponents. The American experience is that integration is of intrinsic value in securing equality before the law. That is the main reason why it should be of concern to the human rights movement. If it also serves the instrumental purpose of helping to prevent terrorism, as seems to be the case in the U.S., so much the better.

The human rights movement also has a responsibility to clarify the basis on which it defends free expression in circumstances in which Muslims or members of other religions object to statements or materials that they consider defamatory to their religion. In doing so, it is important to differentiate such expression from what is commonly referred to as "hate speech."

The United States provides greater legal protection for hate speech than any European country, or in fact just about any other country on earth. In Europe, hate speech is subject to sanctions when a speaker incites violence or other unlawful action against others on the basis of race, religion, or certain other personal characteristics. In the United States, on the other hand, such incitement, by itself, is not sufficient to justify sanctions. It is only when incitement takes place in circumstances where violence or other unlawful behavior is imminent that the state may take action against those engaged in the provocation.[5] In Europe, the crucial question with respect to the incitement of racial hatred is the *content* of speech. In the United States it is the *context* in which hate speech takes place. To cite an example with which all are familiar, shouting "fire" falsely in a crowded theatre may be made punishable in the United States. Shouting "fire" falsely in an empty theater, on the other hand, is no offense. The difference is the context.

Provocation in and of itself should not be the basis for state sanctions. If it were, it would, for example, be up to those who say they are provoked by a certain piece of writing to determine what may—or may not—be published.[6] They may have a right in certain circumstances to invoke the powers of the state to stop a speaker from inciting others to attack them.

On the other hand, they should not have the right to obtain assistance from the state in silencing a speaker on the basis that they may attack the speaker because of a provocation. Their own propensity to engage in violence should not be a basis for deploying the powers of the state against those who have offended them. The distinction between hate speech and religious defamation, or blasphemy, may not be easy for some to grasp. Yet it is essential to try to get across the basis on which proponents of human rights uphold the rights of those who engage in group defamation, however much they may disapprove of such slurs, rather than of those who consider themselves victims of such defamation.

■ ■ ■

Another of the great challenges confronting the international human rights movement is how to have an impact on both the domestic and the international practices of oil- and gas-rich states such as Russia, Iran, and Venezuela. The vast revenues secured by these states in the first decade of the twenty-first century during periods when energy prices soared made them seem more or less immune to external pressure. And indeed these three governments did become more repressive, to varying degrees, during exactly the period when they were accumulating giant treasuries. It is unfortunately the case that many countries that are largely dependent on revenue from natural resources tend to have repressive governments. One factor may be that lack of reliance on tax revenues contributes to a lack of accountability. Another factor seems to be that there are great opportunities for corruption in countries dependent on natural resources, and repression is a means to avoid exposure of that corruption. Norway may be the only fully democratic, rights-respecting country where income from oil makes up the bulk of the country's revenues. Its democracy had developed and matured before it began deriving significant revenue from the exploitation of its natural resources. Equally worrying from the standpoint of the human rights movement, Russia, Iran, and Venezuela are also significant backers of repressive tendencies in other countries. Though the international human rights movement supports the efforts of those within such countries who struggle for rights, there is often little it can do to protect them against reprisals by their governments because external economic pressures are not effective.

China is, of course, also a long-term challenge for the international human rights movement, perhaps its greatest challenge. Though a consumer of energy produced by others rather than an energy exporter, China has used its vast purchasing power to fend off efforts by others to try to modify its human rights practices. In addition, China has used its policy of noninterference in the affairs of other governments as a competitive advantage in purchasing energy and other natural resources from countries that practice significant abuses of human rights. Its policy of noninterference is actually, in practice, a policy of interference, for it results in making China a supporter of many repressive governments. The effect has often been to negate efforts emanating from Europe and the United States to bring pressure on resource-rich governments in Africa, Central Asia, and Southeast Asia to modify their human rights abuses because those governments are no longer so dependent on the West to assist in the development of their natural resources and to purchase what they produce.

So far as rights within China are concerned, the situation is bleak to be sure, but it does not seem hopeless. The movement's efforts over an extended period are paying dividends in the form of increased human rights consciousness within China. Though it is not possible at this writing for Chinese citizens to join together to form organizations to promote political freedom, it is possible for members of certain professions—such as journalists and lawyers—to conduct themselves in ways that promote human rights. Some journalists report stories of abusive behavior by officials, thereby curbing such conduct. Some lawyers try to make sure that the rights of criminal defendants and others who come into conflict with the state or with powerful interests are protected, pressing for the reduced use of pre-trial detention and the death penalty. The impact on China is slow—often, painfully slow—but it is not insignificant. At times, of course, the journalists, lawyers and others who call attention to rights abuses, or exercise their professional skills to protect rights, themselves become the targets of reprisals. China seems to take two steps backwards for every three steps forward. Yet overall, the trend is slow movement in a positive direction. The best strategy to counter the extreme repression of the government would seem to be gradually increasing adherence to the rule of law. The Communist Party leadership is clearly apprehensive about providing greater scope for rights because of vast popular discontent over such questions as the country's multiple environmental disasters, land seizures for urban expansion and for increased manufacturing capacity, dangerous working conditions, severe exploitation of the country's 130 million or so migrant workers and their families, the rapidly increasing disparity between those who have quickly become rich and the much larger numbers left behind and, above all, the endemic corruption of local public officials and their frequent arbitrary and abusive behavior. The country's political leaders do seem to realize, however, that they cannot suppress all dissent. They must provide some greater scope for the exercise of rights if they are to avoid an explosion.

Another factor plays a role in fostering increased respect for rights in a country like China. Though the country's vast economic power makes it largely immune to economic pressure from other governments or intergovernmental bodies, it is impossible for the Chinese authorities to ignore public opinion worldwide. It is here that the international human rights movement is able to have its greatest impact on China in the present day. Because it is a worldwide movement that enjoys substantial legitimacy almost everywhere, it is an important force in shaping public opinion. Even a country so little dependent on other governments as China is constrained by concerns about its public reputation. If the stakes are high enough, as they were so far as the Chinese authorities were concerned at the time of the 1989 demonstrations in Tiananmen Square, the government is probably ready again to crack down hard on those proclaiming their rights. Certainly, they have reacted harshly when faced with protests by the Tibetan and Uighur ethnic minorities. Indeed, it appears that China deliberately publicized those protests, their violent aspects, and the reprisals by the authorities as a means of whipping up nationalist sentiment in support of the government. On the other hand, where they feel less threatened, or where they do not see opportunities for mobilizing support for their own actions, the Chinese authorities seem not inclined to antagonize international public opinion. For example, the sentencing of Liu Xiaobo in 2009 for his role in promulgating Charter 08 was timed so that the harsh eleven-year prison term imposed on him was announced on Christmas Day. The obvious intent was to ensure that a sentence designed to intimidate other Chinese from following in Liu's footsteps would attract as little reaction as possible in Europe and the United States. (As made clear by the award of the Nobel Peace Prize to Liu in 2010, this ploy did not succeed.) Similar attempts to conceal repressive practices and to minimize international denunciations of those practices are also characteristic of many other governments worldwide. This reflects their awareness that the capacity of the international human rights movement to influence public opinion worldwide is its most powerful asset.

. . .

At this writing, the future of international justice is uncertain. After making great headway since the establishment of the International Criminal Tribunal for the former Yugoslavia in 1993, it has now run into severe difficulty in the form of the strenuous opposition by Arab governments and, less predictably, many African governments, to the indictment of President Omar al Bashir by the International Criminal Court for his crimes against humanity and for genocide in Darfur. The backlash against the Bashir indictment is likely to make the United Nation more reluctant to establish additional ad hoc tribunals.[7] Yet that backlash did not prevent the Security Council of the United Nations in March 2011 from acting unanimously in referring Colonel Qaddafi's crimes in Libya to the ICC. That action had the effect of greatly enhancing the status of the Court.

From the standpoint of the international human rights movement, the best short-term means of dealing with the ICC's difficulties in Africa seems to be to try to alter the stand of a number of key African governments with respect to the Bashir indictment. Such an effort, led by African rights organizations—has made some headway—but its outcome is not yet clear. The African governments are particularly important because more than thirty of them are among the state parties to the International Criminal Court and because, up to this writing, all of the Court's prosecutions are for crimes committed in Africa (including the prosecutions involving Libya, an African state generally looked on as part of the Middle East). Withdrawal of African support would do great damage to the ICC and to the cause of international justice.

At the same time that it attempts to prevent regression in international justice, it is important to the human rights movement to sustain the trend for national judicial systems to hold accountable heads of state and other officials responsible for gross abuses. As that trend seems attributable to heightened awareness of the importance of accountability, which stems from advances in international justice, reverses internationally could also have a negative impact on efforts to do justice in national courts. It seems evident that struggles over impunity will continue to be in the forefront of the human rights movement's concerns for a good many years to come. Yet no long-term strategy has been developed by the movement to promote its concern for accountability. It may be that such a strategy can only emerge as the movement attempts to work its way through the difficulty caused by the solidarity that African and Arab leaders have manifested with their fellow head of state in Sudan.

■ ■ ■

Though the international human rights movement will undoubtedly suffer significant setbacks as it attempts to address issues that matter to it greatly, it seems safe to say that it will maintain its importance in public affairs for the long term. It has taken hold almost every place on earth and would readily establish itself in many of the places where it has been suppressed, such as China, Burma, or Iran, if state restrictions were relaxed. While particular institutions and, to a far lesser extent, certain leaders and some financial donors play an important role, the movement is not dependent on them. It can be said with confidence that certain achievements of the international human rights movement during the last three-and-a-half decades will endure and will help make it possible for the movement to continue to play an influential role. These include:

- Strong identification with the human rights cause by millions of persons almost everywhere in the world;
- The development of a large body of persons in most parts of the world who have acquired the professional know-how to promote human rights and who have chosen this as their career. By now, they number in the thousands;
- Greatly enhanced public recognition that armed conflict should be conducted in accordance with the laws of war which are designed, among other goals, to minimize harm to civilians. When President Barack Obama pledged in his Nobel Peace Prize address in December 2009 to abide by the Geneva Conventions, many more persons worldwide than at any earlier time knew what he was talking about and considered it important to meet such obligations;
- Substantial development of international law for the protection of rights, as in the determination that certain abuses committed during internal armed conflicts constitute war crimes and are punishable in trials before international criminal tribunals;
- The establishment of new institutions, particularly the International Criminal Court, to enforce the protection of human rights;
- The increasing frequency and significance of litigation before regional courts, such as the European Court of Human Rights and the Inter-American Court of Human Rights, and the growing acceptance of the jurisprudence of such bodies in the domestic courts of the countries within those regions;

- The development of a large number of local, national, and international nongovernmental organizations, including many with specialized mandates, to protect and promote human rights on an ongoing basis. These include organizations focusing on the rights of marginalized and stigmatized sectors of the population such as drug addicts, persons suffering from HIV-AIDS, sexual minorities, prisoners, and the developmentally disabled;
- An increasing emphasis on education about human rights in secondary schools, colleges, and graduate schools—especially law schools—in many countries, and an increase in public education in the field through the media. In particular, the proliferation of documentary films dealing with human rights issues has played an important part in public education.

The most widely used method for promoting human rights—collecting and disseminating detailed and reliable information on rights abuses and assessing the findings against the requirements of international law—is not difficult to master. The main requirements are a commitment to fairness and accuracy, care in taking and crosschecking testimony from those with first-hand knowledge, and a grasp of the principal provisions of international law protecting rights. Ensuring that the information gets to the places where it can have an impact in a timely fashion is easier than ever in an era in which information technology has advanced with such astonishing rapidity. Though repressive regimes from Burma to Iran to Cuba to Uzbekistan make strenuous efforts to control the flow of information about their abuses of rights, and are assisted in such efforts by their access to the technology that China has developed for its own use in controlling electronic communications, the human rights movement usually manages to collect the information on which its activities and its impact depend. In the nearly four centuries since John Lilburne and his fellow Levellers fought for their own rights, and in the two and a half centuries since the beginning of the antislavery struggle in England, the citizen movement for human rights has achieved a great deal. Though it is impossible to predict the outcome of the particular struggles in which it is now engaged, it is certain that many of the movement's achievements lie ahead.

The Arab revolutions of 2011 made clear that human rights issues will continue to loom as large in relations between states, as well as within states, as during the period from the 1970s to the present. A thesis of this book is that the movement came to the fore and emerged as an ongoing significant factor in world affairs as a result of the Cold War. Its greatest achievement may indeed have been the part it played in the 1980s in delegitimizing the Soviet system and simultaneously delegitimizing some of the practices of states that claimed they were combating communist subversion. In the process, it played a part that cannot be measured but that was significant in bringing the Cold War to an end. After the Cold War, the international human rights movement maintained its own important role in international relations by focusing its attention on violations of the laws of war, by insisting that officials should be held accountable for atrocities committed by them or under their directions, and by resisting efforts by governments to ride roughshod over rights in combating terrorism. Its engagement in those struggles is likely to continue for a long time to come. The movement came again to the forefront of international public policy in connection with the Arab revolutions. While it is impossible to predict what struggles lie ahead, it appears that the movement has the creativity, the energy, and the intensity of commitment to its fundamental principles to be able to meet the challenges that it will face.

Notes

CHAPTER 1

1. C. J. Chivers, "A Fearless Activist in a Land of Thugs," *New York Times*, July 18, 2009.

2. Samuel Moyn, *The Last Utopia: Human Rights in History* (Cambridge, MA: Harvard University Press), p.7.

3. The concept of independent journalism during wartime was much less well established on the other side of the conflict. As Phillip Knightley has reported, "Goebbels had decided early on that there would be no German war correspondent as such. Instead, journalists, writers, poets, photographers, cameramen, film and radio producers, publishers, printers, painters, and commercial artists—the whole range of occupations belonging to what is now described as the media industry—were simply conscripted into the Propaganda Division of the army." *The First Casualty* (New York: Harcourt Brace Jovanovich, 1975), pp. 220–21.

4. Robert Gates, *From the Shadows* (New York: Simon & Schuster, 1996), p. 89.

5. Jeane Kirkpatrick, "Dictatorships and Double Standards," *Commentary* 68–5 (November 1979).

6. A factor in Washington's decision was the emergence of a human rights movement made up of evangelical Christians in the United States. The persecution of Christians in southern Sudan had been important in the development of that movement. The Bush administration's strong stand on Darfur, where the Sudanese government was also seen as the villain, reflected the influence of that movement, which focused much of its energy on Darfur even though it was a case of Muslims persecuting other Muslims.

CHAPTER 2

1. Lynn Hunt, *Inventing Human Rights: A History* (New York: W.W. Norton, 2007), p. 27.

2. Paul Gordon Lauren, *The Evolution of International Human Rights* (Philadelphia, PA: University of Pennsylvania Press, 2003), p. 17.

3. Christopher Hill, *The World Turned Upside Down: Radical Ideas during the English Revolution* (New York: Viking, 1972), pp. 292–93.

4. Cited in David Zaret, "Tradition, Human Rights and the English Revolution," *Human Rights and Revolutions*, Jeffrey N. Wasserstrom, Greg Grandin, Lynn Hunt and Marilyn B. Young, eds. (Lanham, MD: Rowman and Littlefield, 2007), p. 61.

5. See Christopher Hill, *Milton and the English Revolutions* (New York: Viking, 1977), pp.149–60.

6. Craft unions, some of which have sustained themselves continuously until the present, had begun to appear by the beginning of the nineteenth century in England and the United States. As their focus was higher wages, shorter hours, and improved working conditions, it seems appropriate to think of them as mutual benefit societies rather than as rights movements. See Foster Rhea Dulles, *Labor in America: A History* (New York: Crowell, 1949), pp 1–34, for an account of early unions.

7. As early as the sixteenth century, the Spanish missionary Bartolomé de Las Casas denounced the destruction of the Indian civilizations of the new world and the colonial oppression in which Indians were held in servitude. Unfortunately, one of his proposed solutions was the importation of African slaves to take the place of the Indians on whose behalf he struggled.

8. See *Social Contract: Essays by Locke, Hume and Rousseau* (London: Oxford University Press, 1953), pp. 5–8.

9. Ibid., p. 206.

10. Bentham wrote that "natural rights is simple nonsense: natural and imprescriptible rights, rhetorical nonsense, nonsense upon stilts," in *Anarchical Fallacies: Being an Examination of the Declaration of Rights Issues during the French Revolution*, 1792.

11. Steven M. Wise, *Though the Heavens May Fall: The Landmark Trial that Led to the End of Human Slavery* (Cambridge, MA: Da Capo Press, Perseus Books, 2005), p. 173. Another version of the Latin phrase used by Mansfield is the one cited by Immanuel Kant in his essay, "Perpetual Peace." In Kant's version, it is *fiat justitia, et pereat mundus* [let justice be done, though the world perish]. That version is attributed to the Holy Roman Emperor Ferdinand I, 1503–1564.

12. Ibid., 191.

13. David Brion Davis, *Inhuman Bondage: The Rise and Fall of Slavery in the New World* (New York: Oxford University Press, 2006), p. 159.

14. Henry Mayer, *All on Fire: William Lloyd Garrison and the Abolition of Slavery* (New York: St. Martin's Griffin, 1998), p. 52.

15. David King, *Vienna 1814: How the Conquerors of Napoleon Made Love, War and Peace at the Congress of Vienna* (New York: Random House, 2008), p. 217.

16. In the first issue of *The Liberator*, published January 1, 1831, Garrison wrote: "I shall strenuously contend for the immediate enfranchisement of our slave population. In Park Street Church, on the Fourth of July, 1829, in an ad-

dress on slavery, I unreflectingly assented to the popular but pernicious doctrine of *gradual* abolition. I seize this opportunity to make a full and unequivocal recantation, and thus publicly to ask pardon of my God, of my country, and of my brethren the poor slaves, for having uttered a sentiment so full of timidity, injustice and absurdity."

17. Davis, op. cit., p. 326.

18. The preamble to the resolutions adopted at Seneca Falls cites Blackstone for the proposition that the "law of Nature . . . is binding over all the globe, in all countries at all times . . . ." The first resolution then provides, "That all laws which prevent woman from occupying such a station in society as her conscience shall dictate, or which place her in a position inferior to that of man, are contrary to the great precept of nature, and therefore of no force or authority."

19. See Margaret E. Keck and Kathryn Sikkink, *Activists beyond Borders: Advocacy Networks in International Politics* (Ithaca, NY: Cornell University Press, 1998), pp. 60–66. It is difficult to assess membership figures in circumstances in which it would have been complicated to rely on such mechanisms as the regular payment of dues to ascertain the intentions of those associated with an organization.

20. See Ellen Chesler, *Woman of Valor: Margaret Sanger and the Birth Control Movement in America* (New York: Simon & Schuster, 1992).

21. See Edmund Wilson, *Patriotic Gore* (New York: Farrar, Straus & Giroux, 1965), pp. 535–37 for an account of Tourgée.

22. For an account of Tourgée's efforts in Plessy's case, see Otto H. Olsen, *The Thin Disguise* (New York: Humanities Press, 1967).

23. *Plessy v. Ferguson*, 163 U.S. 537 (1896).

24. Ibid., at 551.

25. Ibid., at 559.

26. See Charles Black, "The Lawfulness of the Segregation Decisions," (*Yale Law Journal* 69 [1960], p. 421) for a more extended comment along these lines.

27. See Samuel Walker, *In Defense of American Liberties: A History of the ACLU* (New York: Oxford University Press, 1990), p. 22.

28. See Roy Jenkins, *Gladstone: A Biography* (New York: Random House, 1997), pp. 121–26 for an account of his efforts dealing with prison conditions in Naples; and pp. 399–414 for his denunciation of the "Bulgarian horrors".

29. John Fabian Witt, *Patriots and Cosmopolitans: Hidden Histories of American Law* (Cambridge, MA: Harvard University Press, 2007), pp. 174–75.

30. Adam Hochschild, *King Leopold's Ghost: A Story of Greed, Terror, and Heroism in Colonial Africa* (Boston: Houghton Mifflin, 1998).

31. Ibid., p. 213.

32. Ibid., p. 242.

33. 245 U.S. 60 (1917).

34. Ibid. at 82.

35. See Zechariah Chafee, Jr., *Free Speech in the United States* (Cambridge, MA: Harvard University Press, 1941), for the classic account of the suppression of dissent during the World War I era.

36. John Fabian Witt, op. cit., p. 158

37. *Colyer v. Skeffington* 265 Fed 17 (D. Mass 1920). The two lawyers were Felix Frankfurter, subsequently a justice of the United States Supreme Court, and Zechariah Chafee, Jr., who was long regarded as the country's leading First Amendment scholar.

38. For Gandhi's own account of these experiences, see *Gandhi: An Autobiography* (London: Jonathan Cape, 1949).

39. See Gary Bass, *Stay the Hand of Vengeance: The Politics of War Crimes Tribunals* (Princeton, NJ: Princeton University Press, 2000), p. 117.

40. See Robert C. Cottrell, *Roger Nash Baldwin and the American Civil Liberties Union* (New York: Columbia University Press, 2000), p. 178.

41. See Emma Goldman, *Living My Life*, vol. 2 (New York: Dover, 1970 [originally published in 1931]), pp. 765–66. She writes that when she and Alexander Berkman met with the leader of the new Soviet state, Berkman asked, "[W]hy were anarchists in Soviet prisons? 'Anarchists?' Ilich interrupted; 'nonsense! Who told you such yarns, and how could you believe them? We do have bandits in prisons and Makhnovtsy, but no *ideiny* anarchists.' 'Imagine,' I broke in, 'capitalist America also divides the anarchists into two categories, philosophic and criminal. The first are accepted in the highest circles; one of them is even high in the councils of the Wilson Administration. The second category, to which we have the honour of belonging, is persecuted and often imprisoned. Yours also seems a distinction without a difference. Don't you think so?'"

42. Cottrell, op. cit., p. 180.

43. Interview with Justice Tarkunde by author, New Delhi, India, 1980.

44. Lauren, op. cit., p. 106.

45. An organization with the same name was established in England during World War I but did not last long. Among those who were in contact with the group were Bertrand Russell and George Bernard Shaw, though it is not clear whether they were members, or why the organization expired. It appears that this short-lived organization played a role in popularizing the term "civil liberties" and influenced its adoption in the United States.

46. See *The Collected Essays, Journalism and Letters of George Orwell*, Sonia Orwell and Ian Angus, eds., vols. 3 and 4 (New York: Harcourt, Brace and World, 1968).

47. Lauren, op, cit., pp.147–48.

48. The historian Samuel Moyn has argued that the events of World War II and the adoption of human rights declarations in the aftermath of the war had little to do with the emergence of the contemporary international human rights movement in the 1970s. While Moyn is probably right in arguing that a separate

set of developments in the 1970s played a crucial role in the emergence of the contemporary movement, he goes much too far in contending that what happened earlier is disconnected from what has taken place in the past three and a half decades. Without the philosophical, legal, and institutional foundations established previously, it is difficult to imagine that the present-day structure could have been built. See Samuel Moyn, *The Last Utopia: Human Rights in History* (Cambridge, MA: Harvard University Press, 2010).

49. See Peggy Lamson, *Roger Baldwin: Founder of the American Civil Liberties Union* (Boston: Houghton Mifflin, 1976), pp. 272–73.

CHAPTER 3

1. See "Two Concepts of Liberty," reprinted in Isaiah Berlin, *Four Essays on Liberty* (Oxford: Oxford University Press, 1969), pp. 118–72. Berlin discusses "self realization" as an aspect of positive liberty, which seems comparable to the pursuit of happiness.

2. Mary Ann Glendon, *A World Made New! Eleanor Roosevelt and the Universal Declaration of Human Rights* (New York: Random House, 2001), p. xx.

3. Lynn Hunt, *Inventing Human Rights: A History* (New York: W.W. Norton, 2007), pp. 196–97.

4. Pierre-Joseph Proudhon, "What is Property? Or, an Inquiry Into the Principle of Right and of Government," 1840. Reprinted in Micheline R. Ishay, *The Human Rights Reader* (New York: Routledge, 2007), p. 211.

5. See Cass R. Sunstein, *The Second Bill of Rights: FDR's Unfinished Revolution and Why We Need It More than Ever* (New York: Basic Books, 2004). Roosevelt's State of the Union Address of January 11, 1944 is reprinted as Appendix I, pp. 235–44.

6. Statement of Essential Human Rights, U.N. Doc. 1148 (1947).

7. See Philip Alston, "Making Space for New Human Rights: The Case of the Right to Development," *Harvard Human Rights Yearbook*, Spring 1988, pp. 3–40. Alston, a prominent advocate of economic and social rights, makes a somewhat half-hearted case for expanding the list of rights to include this right. His failure to advocate it more forcefully seems to reflect recognition that there is no institution that could compel global redistribution as a matter of right.

8. Department of State Bulletin, December 8, 1952.

9. See *Taking Rights Seriously* (Cambridge, MA: Harvard University Press, 1977).

10. For an argument that the right to environment can be judicially enforced, see Alexandre Kiss, "Concept and Possible Implications of the Right to Environment" in *Human Rights in the Twenty-first Century: A Global Challenge*, Kathleen Mahoney and Paul Mahoney, eds. (Dordrecht: Martinus Nijhoff, 1993), pp. 551–60.

11. See Shylashri Shankar and Pratap Bhanu Mehta, "Courts and Socioeconomic Rights in India," in *Courting Social Justice: Judicial Enforcement of Social and Economic Rights in the Developing World*, Varun Gauri and Daniel M. Brinks, eds. (New York: Cambridge University Press, 2008), p. 177.

12. Ronald Dworkin, *Taking Rights Seriously*, op cit.

13. *I.CON* vol. 1, no. 4 (New York: Oxford University Press and New York University School of Law, 2003), pp. 600–601.

14. *Soobramoney v. Minister of Health, Kwazulu-Natal*, 1998 (1) SALR 765 (cc).

15. Ibid., at para. 31.

16. *Grootboom*, 2001 (1) SALR 46 (cc).

17. Ibid., at para. 99.

18. *TAC*, 2002 (5) 721 (cc).

19. Chaskalson, op. cit., p. 607.

20. Varun Gauri and Daniel M. Brinks, eds. (New York: Cambridge University Press, 2008).

21. Ibid., p. 95.

22. Amartya Sen, *The Idea of Justice* (Cambridge, MA: Harvard University Press, 2009).

23. Ibid., pp. 382–84.

24. Ibid., pp. 360–61.

25. See Sunstein, *The Second Bill of Rights*, op.cit.

26. Ibid., pp. 106–107.

27. See Kenneth Roth, "Defending Economic, Social and Cultural Rights: Practical Issues Faced by an International Human Rights Organization," *Human Rights Quarterly* 26 (2004), pp. 63–73.

28. Ibid., p. 69.

29. Idem.

30. *The Federalist*, no. 78.

31. See Bilahari Kausikan, "Asia's Different Standard," *Foreign Policy*, Fall 1993, pp. 24–41.

32. Ibid., pp. 34–35

33. Ibid., p. 40.

34. Ibid., pp. 35–36

35. Ibid., p. 40

36. Idem.

37. See Amartya Sen, *Development as Freedom* (New York: Knopf, 1999).

38. See David Bandurski and Martin Hala, *Investigative Journalism in China: Eight Cases in Chinese Watchdog Journalism* (Hong Kong: Hong Kong University Press, 2010).

CHAPTER 4

1. *175 U.S. 677 (1900).

2. See Mary Ann Glendon, *A World Made New: Eleanor Roosevelt and the Universal Declaration of Human Rights* (New York: Random House, 2001). See also Paul Gordon Lauren, *The Evolution of International Human Rights* (Philadelphia, PA: University of Pennsylvania Press, 2003), for a detailed discussion of the adoption of the provisions of the U.N. Charter dealing with human rights, the Universal Declaration, and subsequent efforts at the U.N. to implement the Declaration.

3. There had been periodic conflict between the Rwandan government and the Uganda-based Rwandan Patriotic Front since October 1, 1990. The war was in abeyance, however, when the genocide began. "The organizers [of the genocide] used the slaughter of Tutsi to draw the RPF into renewed combat. Later, in the face of RPF advances, they demanded a cease-fire as a prerequisite for ending the genocide. The RPF resumed the war in part to stop the massacres and insisted on an end to the genocide as a condition for a cease-fire." Alison Des Forges, *Leave None to Tell the Story: Genocide in Rwanda* (Human Rights Watch, 1999), p. 20.

4. See Theodor Meron, *Human Rights and Humanitarian Norms as Customary Law* (Oxford: Clarendon Press, 1989).

CHAPTER 5

1. Robert C. Stacey, "The Age of Chivalry," in Michael Howard, George Andreopoulos, and Mark Shulman, eds., *The Laws of War: Constraints on Warfare in the Western World* (New Haven, CT: Yale University Press, 1994), p. 30.

2. Hugo Grotius, *De Jure Belli Ac Pacis Libre Tres*, 1625.

3. Jean Jacques Rousseau, *The Social Contract*, Book I, Chapter IV.

4. See Caroline Moorehead, *Dunant's Dream: War, Switzerland and the History of the Red Cross* (New York: Carroll & Graf, 1999), for a comprehensive history of Dunant and the institution he founded, the International Committee of the Red Cross.

5. Cited in Cecil Woodham-Smith, *Florence Nightingale* (London: Constable), p. 134.

6. This provision of the Constitution appears in Article 1, Section 9. While the Constitution does not specify who should have the power to suspend habeas corpus, most legal scholars agree that it is a power of Congress because Article 1 generally deals with congressional power. Speaking to Congress three months later, after a court had ruled against the suspension, Lincoln attempting to justify

his action, asked, "Are all the laws *but one* to go unexecuted, and the government itself go to pieces, lest that one be violated?" See Ronald C. White, Jr., *A. Lincoln: A Biography* (New York: Random House, 2009), pp. 416–26.

7. Adam Roberts and Richard Guelff, *Documents on the Laws of War* (Oxford: Clarendon Press, 1989), p. 7.

8. Theodor Meron, *International Law in the Age of Human Rights* (Leiden and Boston: Martinus Nijhoff, 2004), p. 43, fn. 56.

9. Adam Roberts, "Land Warfare From Hague to Nuremberg," in Michael Howard, George Andreopoulos, and Mark Shulman, eds., op cit., p. 130.

10. 333 House of Commons Debates (March 23, 1938).

11. 337 House of Commons Debates (June 21, 1938).

12. See Telford Taylor, *The Anatomy of the Nuremberg Trials* (New York: Knopf, 1992), for a first-hand account by an attorney who became chief prosecutor at Nuremberg after Justice Robert Jackson returned to his place on the U.S. Supreme Court.

13. To the ICRC's credit, it has been a leading sponsor and publisher of scholarship critical of its own role during World War II. See Arieh Ben-Tov, *Facing the Holocaust in Budapest: The International Committee of the Red Cross and the Jews in Hungary, 1943–1945* (Dordrecht: Martinus Nijhoff, 1988).

14. See Moorehead, op. cit., pp. 624–6, for a discussion of the role of Bernard Kouchner in leading the formation of Médecins Sans Frontières as a result of his experience in the Biafran conflict.

15. See Peter Bergen, *The Longest War: The Enduring Conflict between America and Al-Qaeda* (New York: Free Press, 2011), pp. 95–120, for a discussion of the Bush administration's decision to jettison application of the Geneva Conventions to the war in Afghanistan.

16. Gabor Rona, "International Law Under Fire—Interesting Times for International Humanitarian Law: Challenges from the War on Terror," *The Fletcher Forum of World Affairs* 27/2 (Summer/Fall 2003).

17. In August 2009, Holder authorized a preliminary investigation to determine whether CIA agents who went beyond the practices that were justified in legal opinions from the Justice Department in their mistreatment of detainees should be prosecuted. The results of that investigation are not known at this writing.

18. Theodor Meron, op. cit., pp. 27–30.

Chapter 6

1. Ludmilla Alexeyeva, *Soviet Dissent: Contemporary Movements for National, Religious and Human Rights* (Middletown, CT: Wesleyan University Press, 1985), pp. 275–76.

2. After Yuli Daniel's death, Larissa Bogoraz married Marchenko. He became the second husband she lost whose death was probably hastened by imprisonment.

3. In Israel he modified his name and became Natan Sharansky.

4. The treaty that concluded the Congress of Vienna 160 years earlier had been called the "Final Act." Apparently, history-minded diplomats who took part in the Helsinki meeting chose that name for the accords that concluded their peace conference. The Congress of Vienna had been a focus of the scholarship of one of those diplomats, Henry Kissinger, before he became a government official.

5. Alexeyva, op. cit., p. 338.

6. See Timothy Garton Ash, *The Polish Revolution: Solidarity* (New York: Scribner, 1984).

7. This number sometimes appears as "241" because one of the signatories withdrew soon after the manifesto was published.

8. See Vaclav Havel, *Disturbing the Peace* (New York: Knopf, 1990).

9. Wei Jingsheng, *The Courage to Stand Alone: Letters from Prison and Other Writings* (New York: Viking, 1997), p. 253.

10. Ian Buruma, *Bad Elements: Chinese Rebels from Los Angeles to Beijing* (New York: Random House, 2001), p. 101

11. See Elizabeth Becker, *When the War Was Over: The Voices of Cambodia's Revolution and Its People* (New York: Simon & Schuster, 1986).

12. Hugh Thomas, *The Cuban Revolution* (New York: Harper Torchbooks, 1971), p. 684.

13. See Aryeh Neier, *Taking Liberties: Four Decades in the Struggle for Rights* (New York: Public Affairs, 2003), pp. 256–70.

14. See George Black and Robin Munro, *The Black Hands of Beijing: Lives of Defiance in China's Democracy Movement* (New York: Wiley, 1993), pp. 139–52.

15. It was widely rumored at the time that the military units sent into Beijing were drawn from distant parts of the country and spoke dialects that would have made it difficult to communicate with the Mandarin-speaking residents of the capital. Reportedly, the delay in sending in the troops was attributable, at least in part, to the need to assemble such units for the June 3–4 crackdown.

16. Letter of January 23, 1996, published in *Izvestia* on January 24, 1996, and in a translation by Catherine A. Fitzpatrick in the *New York Review of Books*, February 29, 1996.

17. "The Putin Put-On," translated by Jamey Gambrell, *New York Review of Books*, August 9, 2001.

18. An account of Kovalev's struggle for human rights during both the Soviet era and in post-Soviet Russia appears in Emma Gilligan, *Defending Human Rights in Russia: Sergei Kovalev, Dissident and Human Rights Commissioner, 1969–2003* (London: Routledge Curzon, 2004).

19. The Central Asian countries that were formerly part of the Soviet Union—Kazakhstan, Kyrgyzstan, Tajikistan, Turkmenistan, and Uzbekistan—are not

members of the Council of Europe and, therefore, not subject to the jurisdiction of the European Court of Human Rights. This is one of the reasons why human rights are poorly protected in these countries. The record is particularly poor in Turkmenistan and Uzbekistan, which are among the most repressive countries in the world.

CHAPTER 7

1. *New York Times*, September 11, 1974. Quoted by Seymour Hersh.

2. See Peter Kornbluh, *The Pinochet File: A Declassified Dossier on Atrocity and Accountability* (A National Security Archive Book. New York: The New Press, 2003).

3. Pamela Constable and Arturo Valenzuela, *A Nation of Enemies: Chile under Pinochet* (New York: W.W. Norton, 1991), p. 120.

4. Castillo's forced exile in 1981 drew attention in the United States to the role of Jeane Kirkpatrick, who had become President Ronald Reagan's Ambassador to the U.N. She had visited Chile to convey to Pinochet Reagan's eagerness to break with the policies of the Carter administration, which had condemned the Chilean military dictatorship on human rights grounds. While she was in Chile, Castillo sought to meet with Kirkpatrick, but she declined. His forced exile followed soon after Kirkpatrick's departure from the country. See Americas Watch, "Chile Since the Coup: Ten Years of Repression," August 25, 1983, p. 110.

5. For a valuable account of this period, see Lars Schoultz, *Human Rights and United States Policy toward Latin America* (Princeton, NJ: Princeton University Press, 1981).

6. Starting in 1967, Senator William Proxmire, a Democrat from Wisconsin, had begun a practice of speaking every day that the Senate was in session about the importance of U.S. ratification of the Genocide Convention. Proxmire often spoke to an empty chamber. He also used his statements about the Genocide Convention to call attention to such great crimes against human rights as the massacres committed in the Biafran war in Nigeria in the late 1960s. Proxmire's principal ally in the Senate on such matters was another Democrat, Claiborne Pell of Rhode Island. Senator Pell took pride in the role of his father, Herbert Pell, during World War II, as one of the few advocates in the U.S. Government of efforts to save the Jews of Europe. Pell saw his own commitment to promote human rights as a way of carrying on his father's work. See Samantha Power, *A Problem from Hell: America and the Age of Genocide* (New York: Basic Books, 2002), pp. 78–85. In that era, many Americans considered Proxmire an eccentric for his unrelenting insistence on calling attention to U.S. failure to ratify the Genocide Convention.

7. See Emilio F. Mignone, *Witness to the Truth: The Complicity of Church and Dictatorship in Argentina* (Maryknoll, NY: Orbis Books, 1988).

8. The principal reason for the Church's silence in Cuba has been a shortage of priests. This makes it necessary for the Church to import priests from other countries, making it very vulnerable to visa restrictions. In 2010, however, with Raœl Castro having replaced his brother Fidel as head of state, the Cuban church did play a leading role in securing the release from prison and the emigration of more than fifty dissenters who had been arrested several years earlier and sentenced to long prison terms. Additional releases in which the Church played a leading role took place in 2011. This was the first occasion on which the Cuban church is known to have played an important role in human rights protection since Fidel Castro seized power in 1959. It seems possible that the Cuban church was able to play this role because it recognized that Raúl Castro is less vindictive against those taking a stand on human rights than his older brother.

9. Derian had two aides who greatly helped her to succeed. One was Mark Schneider, a former aide to Senator Edward Kennedy, whose knowledge of the Congress played an important role. The other was Roberta Cohen, the former director of the International League for Human Rights, who was then probably the country's most experienced human rights professional.

10. Jeane J. Kirkpatrick, "Dictatorships and Double Standards," *Commentary* (November 1979).

11. See Mark Danner, *The Massacre at El Mozote* (New York: Vintage Books, 1994).

12. Text of President Reagan's Address to Parliament on Promoting Democracy," *New York Times*, June 9, 1982.

13. See Lawyers Committee for Human Rights and The Watch Committees, "The Reagan Administration's Record on Human Rights in 1985," (1986), pp. 65–66.

14. Duvalier returned to the country twenty-five years later, in January 2011, about the time of the first anniversary of an earthquake that had resulted in more than two hundred thousand deaths.

15. See Americas Watch, *El Salvador's Decade of Terror* (New Haven, CT: Yale University Press, 1991), p. 133.

16. See Aryeh Neier, "Economic Sanctions and Human Rights," in Samantha Power and Graham Allison, eds., *Realizing Human Rights: Moving from Inspiration to Impact* (New York: St. Martin's Press, 2000), p. 299.

CHAPTER 8

1. See Linda Rabben, *Fierce Legion of Friends: A History of Human Rights Campaigns and Campaigners* (Brentwood, MD: The Quixote Center, 2002), p. 182.

2. See Jonathan Power, *Amnesty International: The Human Rights Story* (New York: McGraw Hill, 1981), pp. 13–14, for an account of the way that Amnesty dealt with the Mandela case.

3. *The Amnesty International Handbook* (Claremont, CA: Hunter House, 1991), p. 140.

4. Power, op. cit., back cover.

5. Ann Marie Clark, *Diplomacy of Conscience, Amnesty International and Changing Human Rights Norms* (Princeton, NJ: Princeton University Press, 2001), p. 15.

6. Whether MacBride knew about the funding by the CIA prior to its public exposure is unknown. The statement he issued said that the ICJ had received funds, without conditions, from a little-known American organization called the American Fund for Free Jurists. In that era, the CIA used a number of funds and foundations as conduits for support of nongovernmental organizations that it considered to be helpful in the global struggle against communism. Many of the leaders of those organizations did not know that the CIA was the ultimate source of the funds. In 1975, when former CIA agent Philip Agee identified the ICJ as one of many organizations he said were controlled by the CIA, the organization issued another statement saying that the ICJ "is not controlled, financed or influenced by the CIA in any way, and has no connection whatsoever with the CIA." That statement, phrased in the present tense, was almost certainly accurate when it was issued. In the previous year, the ICJ had published two particularly damning reports on human rights abuses by the Pinochet regime in Chile, which had seized power the previous year in a coup that the CIA had helped to make possible. The statement left open the question of whether the ICJ had been previously financed by the CIA. See Lars Schoultz, *Human Rights and United States Policy toward Latin America* (Princeton, NJ: Princeton University Press, 1981), p.85.

7. Greenpeace, a large membership organization in the environmental field also characterized by a high level of volunteer activity, was founded in Vancouver in 1971, a decade after Amnesty.

8. Darius Rejali, *Torture and Democracy* (Princeton, NJ: Princeton University Press, 2007), pp. 42–43.

9. Edward Peters, *Torture* (Oxford: Basil Blackwell, 1985), p. 160.

10. See Peter Baehr, "Amnesty International and its Self-Imposed Limited Mandate," in Neths Q.H.R. 5 (1994). Reprinted in Henry J. Steiner and Philip Alston, *International Human Rights in Context* (Oxford: Clarendon Press, 1996), p. 483.

11. *The Writer and Human Rights*, edited by the Toronto Arts Group for Human Rights (Garden City, NY: Anchor Press/Doubleday,1983), pp. 237–40.

12. See Stephen Hopgood, *Keepers of the Flame: Understanding Amnesty International* (Ithaca, NY: Cornell University Press, 2006).

13. The question of when information has been sufficiently verified to make it public often raises difficult questions. Jonathan Power discussed this issue in his

1981 book, published when the organization was only twenty years old. Power wrote: "The dilemma is obvious: is it better to keep quiet and wait until absolutely incontrovertible evidence arrives by which time hundreds more may be tortured or dead, or is not the more responsible course to come out with the reasonably watertight, but not perfect, case one has and take the risk? The dialectic between the two approaches is continuous among Amnesty's staff and members. The fact that so rarely has Amnesty had to issue corrections or apologies is proof of their good judgment." Power, op. cit., p. 121.

14. In subsequent years, Hammarberg held other posts in which he played an important role in the promotion of human rights. At this writing, he is Commissioner of Human Rights for the Council of Europe.

15. This is a reference to the double set of security doors through which one passes in entering the headquarters of Amnesty International in London. The story is told that on one occasion the electronic system failed and some visitors were stuck in the airlock. They were freed by the son of one of the researchers who was expert in electronics. Thereafter, he went about the building saying he had freed more prisoners that day than anyone else in Amnesty.

16. Quoted in Hopgood, op cit., pp. 101–102

17. See Margaret Keck and Kathryn Sikkink, *Activists beyond Borders* (Ithaca, NY: Cornell University Press, 1998). They write, "Zalaquett inspired a generation of new activists, many of whom mention him as one of the individuals they most admired" (p. 91).

18. William Korey, *NGOs and the Universal Declaration of Human Rights* (New York: St. Martin's Press, 1998), p. 160.

19. *Amnesty International Report 1983* (London 1983), p. 351.

20. See Schoultz, op. cit., pp. 84–85.

21. Hopgood, op. cit.

22. *Washington Post*, "American Gulag," May 26, 2005.

23. Harvard Business School, "Amnesty International," John Quelch and Nathalie Laidler, August 7, 2003, p. 8.

24. *Amnesty International Report 2009: The State of the World's Human Rights* (New York: Amnesty International, U.S.A., 2009), p. 17.

CHAPTER 9

1. The last time the Senate had rejected presidential nominees was about a decade earlier when President Nixon's nominations of two candidates for the U.S. Supreme Court, Clement Haynsworth and Harold Carswell, were turned down. No nominee by either President Ford or President Carter was defeated in a Senate vote.

2. Jacobo Timerman, *Prisoner Without a Name, Cell Without a Number* (New York: Knopf, 1981). Knopf is a division of Random House.

3. The report was subsequently published in book form as *Report on Human Rights in El Salvador*, compiled by Americas Watch Committee (New York: Vintage Books, 1982).

4. Two examples might be cited of this opportunistic approach. To call attention to a report on Paraguay, a representative of Human Rights Watch traveled to that country to release it publicly two days in advance of a visit by the Pope. Journalists who had gone to Paraguay in advance to do background stories on the country were an eager audience for the report. On another occasion, President Ronald Reagan arranged a one-day visit to Indonesia in connection with an Asian trip. HRW completed a report on that country in time to hand it out to journalists as they boarded the press plane that accompanied the President. The long flight provided ample time to read the report.

5. The International Helsinki Federation for Human Rights (IHF) was forced to close its doors in 2007, twenty-five years after its establishment, due to financial mismanagement. National Helsinki Committees that were formerly affiliated with IHF were not affected. By then, they no longer needed the international body to operate effectively in their own countries.

6. See George Black and Robin Munro, *Black Hands of Beijing: Lives of Defiance in China's Democracy Movement* (New York: John Wiley, 1993). Munro's account of Tiananmen Square differs from some contemporaneous press accounts. As one of the last Westerners to leave Tiananmen Square on the night of June 3 and 4, 1989, he did not witness mass killings in the Square. By the time the Chinese tanks moved in, almost all the student demonstrators had left the Square. On the other hand, he reported many killings of ordinary Chinese citizens who tried to block the military on their way to the Square. See pp. 234–48.

7. Alison des Forges's major work is *Leave None to Tell the Story: Genocide in Rwanda* (New York: Human Rights Watch, 1999).

8. Middle East Watch, *Human Rights in Iraq* (New Haven, CT: Yale University Press, 1990).

9. The products of this research are summarized in Human Rights Watch, *Iraq's Crime of Genocide: The Anfal Campaign against the Kurds* (New Haven, CT: Yale University Press, 1995).

10. See Human Rights Watch, "Genocide in Iraq: The Anfal Campaign against the Kurds" (1993).

11. The first such case was brought by Bosnia against Serbia. After thirteen years of litigation, it ended in 2006 with a judgment that essentially vindicated Serbia of the most serious charges.

12. "Roth's Supersessionism," editorial in the *New York Sun*, July 31, 2006.

13. *New York Sun*, August 2, 2007.

14. Alan Dershowitz, "What is 'Human Rights Watch' Watching?" *Jerusalem Post*, August 24, 2006.

15. *New York Sun*, July 31, 2006.

16. At a meeting in Kampala, Uganda in 2010, the Assembly of State Parties to the International Criminal Court considered a proposal to define the crime of aggression, thereby giving the Court jurisdiction to bring prosecutions for this crime. The proposal was defeated because of the inability of the state parties to agree on how prosecutions would be initiated. A proposal that such prosecutions should be launched on the basis of resolutions by the U.N. Security Council contributed to concerns about politicization.

17. Aryeh Neier, "The Attack on Human Rights Watch," *New York Review of Books*, November 2, 2006, p. 41.

18. Robert F. Worth, "Lebanon: Low Funds Imperil Bomb Removal," *New York Times*, August 23, 2008.

19. Robert L. Bernstein, "Rights Watchdog, Lost in the Mideast," *New York Times*, October 20, 2009. See also NGO Monitor, "Experts or Ideologues," Jerusalem, September 2009, for a more extended critique along similar lines to Bernstein's essay.

20. Aryeh Neier, "Human Rights Watch Should Not Be Criticized for Doing Its Job," *Huffington Post*, November 2, 2009.

21. Clifford J. Levy, "Defining Genocide Down," *New York Times*, August 9, 2009.

22. Ibid.

23. Human Rights Watch, "Up In Flames: Humanitarian Law Violations in the Conflict over South Ossetia," January 2009.

24. Relatives of the disappeared, known as the "Mothers of the Plaza de Mayo" after the location in front of the presidential palace in Buenos Aires where they conducted weekly demonstrations, had demanded the "truth" about what happened to their missing children. Establishment of the commission was a response to that demand.

25. See Aryeh Neier, *Taking Liberties: Four Decades in the Struggle for Rights* (New York: Public Affairs, 2003), pp. 230–31 for a more detailed account.

26. In the war in Iraq, those figures changed. By ensuring that wounded American soldiers got immediate high quality medical care, the proportion of those killed dropped to one of nine or one of ten.

27. In recent years, the number of those confined in Brazil's prisons has shot up. As of early 2011, it was in the vicinity of 300 prisoners per 100,000 of population—less than half the ratio of prisoners to population in the United States, but two or three times the ratio in Western Europe. Unfortunately, the rise in imprisonment has not been accompanied by a significant decline in police killings.

28. The two principal factors contributing to the high rate of incarceration in the United States are "the war on drugs" launched under President Ronald Reagan; and sentencing laws, such as those requiring mandatory minimum sentences, which deny judges flexibility in imposing sentences.

29. Though Human Rights Watch had reported on violations of rights in the U.S. from the earliest days of Helsinki Watch, the volume of such reporting had not been great out of a belief that many organizations in the U.S. with a domestic focus, including the American Civil Liberties Union, had greater capacity to monitor abuses in the U.S. and that it would be a mistake for HRW to devote substantial resources to matters that others could better address. The main reason that early reporting by HRW did include work on the U.S. was to make clear that the organization insisted that the country where it was based should be held to the same standards it applied to others. The increase in HRW reporting on the U.S. at a later period reflected the organization's recognition that no other organization regularly published carefully documented investigative reports of the sort for which it had become known, and that producing such reports on U.S. violations would be a valuable supplement to the work of U.S.–based organizations with a domestic focus that concentrated on litigation, lobbying, and other methods of promoting their cause.

30. The Ford Foundation program staff at that time also disagreed with Human Rights Watch's focus on promoting compliance with international humanitarian law, and that was probably also a factor in their decision to cut back on funding.

31. Joseph Amon, "Preventing the Further Spread of HIV/AIDS: The Essential Role of Human Rights," in Human Rights Watch, *World Report 2006*, pp.53–54.

Chapter 10

1. The institution headed by the author, the Open Society Foundations, is a donor to most, but not all, of the organizations mentioned in this chapter. In no case does support from the Open Society Foundations constitute more than one third of any organization's revenue. In most cases, it is a great deal less. For many of the organizations cited in this chapter, it is between 5 and 10 percent of their income.

2. In a letter to the editor published in the *Washington Post* (June 13, 2010), Krulak wrote that "the greatest cost of Guantanamo has been to American global leadership and credibility that respects the rule of law."

3. See Christopher Joyce and Eric Stover, *Witnesses from the Grave: The Stories Bones Tell* (Boston: Little, Brown, 1991), Stover's co-authored book about the forensic investigations carried out by Clyde Snow.

4. Physicians for Human Rights has also obtained a limited amount of U.S. government funding through such bodies as the National Endowment for Democracy. Amnesty International and Human Rights Watch accept no government support.

5. See William Korey, *NGOs and the Universal Declaration of Human Rights* (New York: St. Martin's Press, 1998), pp. 443–67, for a discussion of Freedom House and its espousal of the work of Harry Wu and Nina Shea.

6. International Commission of Jurists, *Assessing Damage, Urging Action" Report of the Eminent Jurists Panel on Terrorism, Counter-terrorism and Human Rights* (Geneva, 2009).

CHAPTER 11

1. *Nunca Mas* (Never Again). An English-language version was published in the United States as *Nunca Mas: The Report of the Argentine National Commission of the Disappeared* (New York: Farrar, Straus & Giroux, 1986).

2. See Lawrence Weschler, *A Miracle, A Universe: Settling Accounts with Torturers* (New York: Pantheon, 1990), for the story of the struggle in Uruguay.

3. See José Zalaquett, "Confronting Human Rights Violations Committed by Former Governments: Principles Applicable and Political Constraints," in *Transitional Justice: How Emerging Democracies Reckon with Former Regimes*, Neil J. Kritz, ed., vol. 1 (Washington, DC: United States Institute of Peace, 1995), p. 3. Zalaquett was an architect of Chile's Truth and Reconciliation Commission and served as one of the members.

4. See Thomas Buergenthal, "The United Nations Truth Commission For El Salvador," in Kritz, op.cit., vol. 1, p. 292. Buergenthal was a member of the Commission for El Salvador.

5. "El Salvador: Mexico Peace Agreement—Provisions on Purging of the Armed Forces," in Kritz, op. cit., vol. 3, p. 386. The text of the agreement under which the dismissals took place.

6. See Horacio Verbitsky, *The Flight: Confessions of a Dirty Warrior* (New York: The New Press, 1996). Verbitsky, a well-known Argentine journalist, based the book in part on interviews with Lieutenant Commander Adolfo Francisco Scilingo of the Argentine Navy, who participated in flights in which "subversives" were drugged, stripped naked, and thrown out of aerial transports.

7. To an extent, the South African government tried to conceal apartheid itself from foreigners. As an example, bathrooms and water fountains were segregated in the domestic section of the Johannesburg airport, but not in the international section. Five star hotels were the only accommodations that were not racially segregated. Certain luxury restaurants were also exempted from prohibitions on racial mixing. These exemptions made no difference in the lives of the overwhelming majority of South African blacks, but they gave international business visitors, who used such facilities, a grossly distorted impression of race relations in the country.

8. See Antije Krog, *Country of My Skull* (Cape Town: Random House, 1998), for an account of the work of the South Africa Truth and Reconciliation Commission by a journalist who covered its proceedings for the South African Broadcasting Company.

9. See Alex Boraine, *A Country Unmasked: Inside South Africa's Truth and Reconciliation Commission* (Oxford: Oxford University Press, 2000). Boraine served as deputy chair of the South African Commission.

10. See Hayner's book, *Unspeakable Truths: Transitional Justice and the Challenge of Truth Commissions*, 2nd edition (New York: Routledge, 2011), pp. 27–44.

11. Historically, Muslims in Bosnia had been identified that way because their religion differed from those of the Catholic Croats and the Orthodox Serbs. In the post–World War II era, under the Communist dictatorship of Marshall Tito, efforts were made by the state to reduce or eliminate the significance of religion, and Muslims came to be seen as a separate ethnic group.

12. Roy Gutman, "Death Camps: Survivors Tell of Captivity, Mass Slaughters in Bosnia," *Newsday* (Long Island, New York), August 2, 1992. Reprinted in Roy Gutman, *A Witness to Genocide* (New York: Macmillan, 1993), p. 44.

13. See David Rohde, *Endgame: The Betrayal and Fall of Srebrenica: Europe's Worst Massacre since World War II* (New York: Farrar, Straus and Giroux, 1997).

14. In 2010, a 545-page report was prepared by the office of the United Nations High Commissioner for Human Rights describing some 600 episodes in which Rwandan and Ugandan forces pursuing the genocidaires in the DRC themselves committed gross abuses against noncombatants before their withdrawal in 2002. The report characterized the attacks on Hutus in the DRC as genocide, infuriating the government of President Paul Kagame of Rwanda. Neil MacFarquhar, "Angry Rwandan Reaction Leads U.N. to Delay Report on Possible Congo Genocide," *New York Times*, September 3, 2010.

15. In February 2011, former president George W. Bush cancelled a planned visit to Switzerland in the face of threats by some legal groups, including an American organization, the Center for Constitutional Rights, that they would try to use principles of universal jurisdiction to bring a prosecution against him during his visit.

16. Mahmood Mamdani, "The New Humanitarian Order," *The Nation*, New York, September 29, 2008.

17. It should be noted, however, that three of the five governments that pay the lion's share of the costs of the African Union are those of Arab states: Algeria, Egypt, and Libya. The other two are Nigeria and South Africa.

18. The judges upheld the charges of war crimes and crimes against humanity but said that the facts alleged in the indictment did not warrant the charge of genocide. They did not rule out efforts by the prosecutor to bring a new indictment alleging genocide, and he did so more than a year later.

19. For a detailed study of the relationship between accountability and peace, see Human Rights Watch, "Selling Justice Short: Why Accountability Matters for Peace," 2009.

20. As elsewhere, the question of whether doing justice is consistent with peace has arisen in Lebanon. Leaders of Hezbollah have said that they expect to be targets of indictments and have threatened violence if that happens. Also, late in the day, they presented a dossier to the prosecutor of the Lebanon tribunal purporting to show Israeli culpability for the assassination of Hariri.

21. A valuable account of one of those cases appears in Judith Armatta, *Twilight of Impunity: The War Crimes Trial of Slobodan Milosevic* (Durham, NC: Duke University Press, 2010).

22. See Ellen Lutz and Caitlin Rieger, *Prosecuting Heads of State* (Cambridge: Cambridge University Press, 2009), for a discussion of the upsurge in such prosecutions for human rights abuses and for corruption during the last decade of the twentieth century and the first decade of the twenty-first century. Lutz and Rieger cite sixty-seven such prosecutions worldwide in that period.

23. See Michael A. Newton and Michael P. Scharf, *Enemy of State: The Trial and Excution of Saddam Hussein* (New York: St. Martin's Press, 2008).

24. "Highly exaggerated figures placed the total of Frenchmen killed by Frenchmen during the Liberation as high as 120,000, though the total was probably closer to 4,500. Over 100,000 Frenchmen were jailed, facing trial, confiscation of property, or loss of jobs, if not death." Robert O. Paxton, *Vichy France: Old Guard and New Order, 1940–1944* (New York: Norton, 1972), p. 331.

25. Iris Origo, *The Merchant of Prato* (Boston: Godine, 1986), p.348.

26. In a notable development, President Boris Tadic of Serbia visited the site near Vukovar, Croatia, where Serb forces murdered some two hundred men seized at a hospital when they captured the city in 1991. This visit in November 2010 was the most significant acknowledgment of collective political responsibility for great crimes by a Serb political leader. Tadic's gesture inspired President Ivo Josipovic of Croatia to reciprocate. He placed a wreath at the grave of eighteen Serbs killed by Croatian forces at Paulin Dvor, a village near Vukovar, and offered an apology to the families of the victims. See "Croatia: Apologies at Sites of '91 Killings," *New York Times*, November 5, 2010.

CHAPTER 12

1. Address to the Council on Foreign Relations, New York, February 10, 2003.

2. See Richard Clarke, *Against All Enemies: America's War on Terror* (New York: Free Press, 2004).

3. See *The 9/11 Commission Report* (New York: W.W. Norton, 2004), pp. 261-21, for a redacted version of the presidential Daily Brief received by President George W. Bush on August 6, 2001.

4. See David Cole and Jules Lobel, *Less Safe, Less Free: Why America is Losing the War on Terror* (New York: The New Press, 2007), for an extended discussion of the influence and significance of the preventive approach on the Bush administration's terrorism policies.

5. Transcript, *Meet the Press*, September 16, 2002.

6. Memorandum to President George W. Bush from Alberto Gonzales, January 25, 2002.

7. Memorandum from President George W. Bush to the Vice President et al., February 7, 2002.

8. Jameel Jaffer and Amrit Singh, *Administration of Torture* (New York: Columbia University Press, 2008), pp. 29–30.

9. See U.S. State Department, Office of the Coordinator for Counterterrorism, "Patterns of Global Terrorism 2003 (2004)." Though this report does not identify abuses, it does indicate which governments cooperated in counterterrorism efforts.

10. Edward Cody, "French Court Expands Terrorism Suspects' Right to a Lawyer," *Washington Post*, October 20, 2010.

11. A secondary value of the war metaphor from the standpoint of the Bush administration was that it provided a rationale for the detention of "enemy combatants" until the conclusion of the war. As the war on terror may never end, this provides a justification, in the eyes of some, for indefinite detention.

12. *The Unitary Executive Theory in Undermining the Constitution*, A Century Foundation Report, 2008, p. 38. John Yoo also invoked other grounds as justifications for violations of rights. In one memorandum, he wrote: "If a government defendant were to harm an enemy combatant in a manner that might arguably violate a criminal prohibition, he would be doing so to prevent further attacks on the United States by the al-Qaeda terrorist network. In that case, we believe that he could argue that the executive branch's constitutional authority to protect the nation from attack justified his actions. This national and international version of the right to self-defense could supplement and bolster the government defendant's individual right." "Memorandum Re: Military Interrogation of Alien Unlawful Combatants Held Outside the United States" for William J. Haynes III, General Counsel of the Department of Defense," 2003.

13. Cited in Frederick A. O. Schwarz, Jr. and Aziz Huq, *Unchecked and Unbalanced: Presidential Power in a Time of Terror* (New York: The New Press, 2007), p. 156. This episode figures centrally in the 2008 film, "Frost/Nixon."

14. *Morrison v. Olson*, 487 U.S. 654 (1988).

15. See Frederick A. O. Schwarz, Jr. and Aziz Huq, op. cit., pp. 152–53.

16. Alex MacGillis, "4th Grader Questions Rice on Waterboarding," *Washington Post*, May 4, 2009.

17. 542 U.S. 466 (2004).

18. 542 U.S. 507 (2004).

19. 548 U.S. 557 (2006). Also, for an account of the case, see Jonathan Mahler, *The Challenge:* Hamdan v. Rumsfeld *and the Fight over Presidential Power* (New York: Farrar, Straus and Giroux, 2008).

20. 553 U.S. 723 (2008).

21. At this writing, close to three years have expired since that assertion by President Obama. Congressional resistance suggests that the president will have difficulty carrying out his plans. Most observers believe that the president may be unable to make good on his commitment.

22. President Obama subsequently said that the use of military commissions would continue, but that more due process protections would be provided than under President Bush's order initially establishing them.

23. Edward Cody, "Ex-Detainee Describes Struggle for Exoneration," *Washington Post*, May 26, 2009.

24. Richard Zabel and James J. Benjamin, Jr., "In Pursuit of Justice: Prosecuting Terrorism Cases in the Federal Courts: 2009 Update and Recent Developments," (New York: Human Rights First, July 2009).

25. See generally, Jane Mayer, *The Dark Side: The Inside Story of How the War on Terror Turned into a War on American Ideals* (New York: Doubleday, 2008).

26. See Peter Bergen, *The Longest War: The Enduring Conflict between America and Al-Qaeda* (New York: Simon & Schuster, 2011), pp. 95–120.

27. *Holder v. Humanitarian Law Project*, 130 S. Ct. 2705 (2010).

28. *Mohammed v. Jeppesen*, U.S. Court of Appeals for the Ninth Circuit, No. 8–15693, September 8, 2010.

29. The Bush administration's outspokenness on Sudan has puzzled some observers. One factor that may explain it is that a human rights movement has developed among Christian evangelicals in the United States. The two countries that have been the principal focus of denunciations by this movement have been China and Sudan. In the case of Sudan, it is based on the persecution of Christians in the south during the long north-south struggle. Though both victims and persecutors in Darfur are Muslims, the evangelical human rights movement responded to another case of persecution by the Sudanese government by taking up the cause of the victims. Its concern with Darfur influenced the policies of the Bush administration.

30. The judges subsequently upheld an expansion of the indictment to include the crime of genocide.

31. Some accounts of this effort refer to *le droit d'ingerence* [the right of intervention]. Kouchner's word was *devoir* [duty].

32. See Gary J. Bass, *Freedom's Battle: The Origins of Humanitarian Intervention* (New York: Knopf, 2008).

33. "The Responsibility to Protect," Report of the International Commission on Intervention and State Sovereignty, International Development Research

Center, Ottawa, 2001. See also Gareth Evans, *The Responsibility to Protect: Ending Mass Atrocity Crimes Once and For All*, (Washington, DC: Brookings Institution Press, 2008). Evans, who served as co-chair of the International Commission, has been a leading proponent of R2P. After serving as foreign minister of Australia, he was president of the International Crisis Group.

34. In January 2007, China and Russia vetoed a resolution to place the situation in Burma on the Security Council's agenda, arguing that Burma did not pose a threat to peace and security in the region.

35. See John Harwood, "Opportunity and Perils for Obama in Military Action in Libya," *New York Times*, March 28, 2011, for a rare example of a news story that mentioned R2P in discussing the intervention in Libya.

36. For a time, it appeared that killings by different militias in the eastern part of the Democratic Republic of the Congo might prove to be such a situation. Though details are murky, an agreement between the governments of Rwanda and the DRC in early 2009 reduced the ongoing violence and diminished the likelihood that there would be serious calls for international intervention. Another situation that might have been considered is the situation in Cote d'Ivoire following the election in 2010 in which a northern Muslim, Alassane Ouattara prevailed, but his opponent, a Christian southerner, Laurent Gbagbo, held on to power. Killings by Gbagbo's forces threatened to plunge the country into what could become a disastrous communal conflict. Eventually, with the assistance of French forces, Ouattara assumed the presidency.

37. It is possible that the turmoil and carnage in Iraq following the 2003 invasion acted as a deterrent against the country's participation in the Arab revolutions of 2011. Observers of developments in Syria have noted that residents of Damascus largely refrained from participating in demonstrations against the Assad regime. One reason may be that there are hundreds of thousands of Iraqi refugees in Damascus, making that city's residents especially wary of upheaval. Another Middle Eastern city, Amman, Jordan, which is also a refuge for a great number of Iraqis, also was largely free of the demonstrations that were pervasive in other cities of the region.

CHAPTER 13

1. If Osama bin Laden had surrendered, of course, it would not be legitimate to kill him. On the other hand, the fact that he was unarmed when he was killed does not make the killing illegitimate. Bin Laden had engaged in sustained combat against the United States and was responsible for killing thousands. It was, therefore, reasonable to attack him as an enemy combatant.

2. Other members included Hina Jilani, a well-known Pakistani human rights lawyer (see chapter 10); Georges Abi Saab, a leading Egyptian scholar of international humanitarian law, who served as a judge on the International Criminal

Tribunal for the Former Yugoslavia; and Robert Goldman, another leading expert on international humanitarian law who served as president of the Inter-American Commission on Human Rights.

3. International Commission of Jurists, "Assessing Damage, Urging Action: Report of the Eminent Jurists Panel on Terrorism, Counter-terrorism and Human Rights," (Geneva, 2009), p. 110.

4. In the Netherlands, some of those who have manifested intolerance against Muslims justify their activities on the ground that Muslims are intolerant. On such grounds, gays—such as the late Pim Fortuyn—have been outspoken antagonists of Islam in Dutch society.

5. The leading U. S. Supreme Court case in this area is *Brandenburg v. Ohio*, 395 U.S. 444 (1969).

6. In the United States, this is often referred to by free speech proponents as a "heckler's veto." The term was coined by a prominent First Amendment scholar at the University of Chicago Law School, Philip Kurland.

7. In August 2010, U.N. Secretary General Ban Ki-moon proposed to the Security Council that it should establish a new tribunal to prosecute pirates operating off the Somali coast. Presumably, such a tribunal would not arouse political controversy of the sort provoked by the ICC indictment of President Bashir.

Index

AAAS. *See* American Association for the
Advancement of Science (AAAS)
abolition movement (United States):
advocates of, 35–36; after abolition,
39–40; and "Declaration of Sentiments," 37; generally, 10; gradual
abolition, 337n16; and Seneca Falls,
New York convention, 37–38, 337n18;
women involved in, 36–37
Abrams, Elliott, 172–73, 297
Abu Ghraib Prison, 133, 291, 298
accountability, 19, 258–84; and Argentina, 259–61, 264; and Democratic
Republic of the Congo, 271, 273–74,
277, 284; and deniability, 261; and
Guatemala, 263–64;and International
Criminal Court (ICC), 269–79;
and International Criminal Tribunal
for the Former Yugoslavia (ICTY),
266–69, 282; and Kenya, 277–78;
and Lebanon, 277–78; and Peru, 263;
and Serbia, 281–83; and South Africa,
261–63; and Sudan (Darfur), 317; and
"truth commissions," 258, 260; and
Yugoslavia, 264–65
ACLU. *See* American Civil Liberties
Union (ACLU)
Addams, Jane, 46, 50
Addington, David, 295, 298, 304–5
Afghanistan: Soviet Union invasion of,
213–14; United States invasion of,
132–33
Africa, Human Rights Watch, 216
African Americans: voting, exclusion
from, 45
African Union, 65, 109, 275
Agee, Philip, 248, 346n6
Ahmadinejad, President Mahmoud, 321

Ahtisaari, Martti, 277
AIDS. *See* HIV/AIDS
Alaei brothers, 238–39
Al Asmiya Palace, 291
Albright, Madeleine, 313
Alexeyeva, Ludmilla, 139, 144–45,
251–52
Alfonsín, Raúl, 171, 226, 259–61
Al-Haq, 248
Alito, Samuel, Jr., 296, 309
Allende, Salvador, 162–63
al-Qaeda, 133, 286, 354n12
Amanpour, Christiane, 239
American Association for the Advance-
ment of Science (AAAS), 238
American Civil Liberties Union (ACLU):
director of, 205; establishment of,
10, 250; and international law, 104;
membership recruitment of, 41; moni-
toring abuses of, 350n29; and post-
September 11 detainees, 291, 293–94,
305; and role of courts, 46–47
American Fund for Free Jurists, 346n6
American Law Institute, 61
American League for India's Freedom, 50
American National Red Cross, 120
American Women Suffrage Association,
38
Americas Watch, 207, 209–12; in Brazil,
227; in Cuba, 215; in El Salvador, 174;
focus of, 214; in Jamaica, 227
Amis des Noirs (France), 34
Amnesty International, 186–203;
attention to, 102; "brand," study of,
201; on capital punishment, 196;
claims against, 12; and Communism,
138; establishment of, 8–10; Europe,
development in, 161, 198–99;

Amnesty International *(cont)*
founders of, 186–92; global membership of, 233–34; growth of, 190; and Human Rights Watch, 205; impartiality of, 192; individual victims of abuse, focus on, 195–96; and International Executive Committee, 164, 192; launching of, 55; mandate of, 191, 195; monitoring by, 114–15; moral authority of, 196–97; Nobel Peace Prize awarded by, 4, 8, 198–99; *Report on Torture*, 191–92; strategy of, 188–89; and Toronto conference (1981), 193

Amnesty USA, Bureau of Human Rights, relationship, 172

Anarchical and Revolutionary Crimes Act, 49

Anglo Armenian Association, 49

Annan, Kofi, 112, 273, 277–78, 313

Anthony, Susan B., 38

Anti-Defamation League, 220

Anti-Footbinding Society, 37

Anti-Saloon League, 39

anti-Semitism, 48, 111–12

Anti-Slavery International, 8, 34

antislavery movement: in England (eighteenth century), 7–10, 33–35, 42; in France, 34–35; in United States (*see* abolition movement [United States])

Anti-Slavery Society: American, 36; London, 8

Antiterrorism and Effective Death Penalty Act, 308

apartheid: and denial of rights, 3–4, 13–14, 184; in South Africa, 262–63, 351n7

"Appeal for Amnesty" (Benenson), 244

April 5th Incident (China), 148

APRODEH. *See* Association for Human Rights in Peru (APRODEH)

Aquino, Benigno, 178

Arab Institute for Human Rights, 319

Arab League, 275, 311, 320

Arab revolutions of 2011: and Amnesty International, 200; characteristics of, 316; and Human Rights Watch, 219, 223; and Iraq invasion, 356n37; outcome, predicting, 319, 333–34; role of organizations in, 24; and U.S.-based human rights organizations, 234

Arbour, Louise, 112, 247

Arbourezk, James, 164

Arendt, Hannah, 13

Areopagitica (Milton), 28

Argentina: and accountability, 259–61, 264; disappearances in, 208, 238, 259–60; and "Final Document on the Struggle Against Subversion and Terrorism, 226; human rights groups in, 250; military coup in, 171; and torture, 259–60

Aristotle, 30

Armenians, massacre of, 49–50

Arms, Cardinal Paulo Evaristo, 167

Aron, Raymond, 13

Article 19, 244

Articles and Ordinance of War (Scotland), 123

ASEAN. *See* Association of Southeast Asian Nations (ASEAN)

Ashcroft, John, 288

Asia: universality of rights in, 90–91; wealth, 88

Asia Watch, 215–16

Asociación Pro Dechos Humanos, 250

Assistant Secretary of State for Human Rights, 94

Association for Human Rights in Peru (APRODEH), 254

Association of Southeast Asian Nations (ASEAN), 109, 113

Astor, David, 187, 244

atomic bombs, 127–28, 142

Atwood, Margaret, 193

Augustine, 118

Baehr, Peter, 192

Bagram, 298

Baldwin, Roger: and ACLU, 50–51; and Civil Liberties Bureau, 46; in Japan, 53–55; *Letters from Russian Prisons*, 51

Ban Ki-moon, 112, 357n7
Barcelona, bombing of, 126–27
Barnes, Harry, 15, 179, 198
Basch, Victor, 52, 248
Bashir, Omar Hassan al, 275–76, 279, 310, 331, 357n7
Bass, Gary, 312
Beijing: military units in, 343n15; and Tiananmen Square (see Tiananmen Square)
Ben Ali, President Zine al-Abidine, 319
Benenson, Peter, 187–91, 244
Ben Said, Khaled, 248
Bensayah, Belkacem, 303
Berger, Jonathan, 74
Berkman, Alexander, 51
Berlin, Isaiah: influence of, 13; and rights definition, 58
Berlin Wall: construction of, 13; fall of, 14, 16, 153–54, 285
Berlusconi, Silvio, 250, 325
Bernstein, Robert L., 205, 209, 222–23
Betancourt, Romulo, 55
Bhutto, Ali, 255
Biddle, Francis, 269
Biko, Steve, 3, 150, 168–69
Bill of Rights (American): adoption of, 58–59; display of, 306; first words of, 68; and property rights, 105
Bin Laden, Osama, 300, 322, 356n1
Black, Charles, 41
Black Consciousness, 168–69
"blacklists," 292
Blackstone, William, 337n18; Commentaries, 33
Blackwell, Henry, 38
Blair, Tony: attacks launched by, 320; and Extractive Industries Transparency Initiative, 246; and free speech, 52; and humanitarian intervention concept, 312–13; and International Criminal Tribunal for the Former Yugoslavia (ICTY), 268; and Sudan (Darfur), 310
Blom-Cooper, Louis, 188
Board of Education, Brown v., 161

Bogoraz, Larissa, 141
Bolton, John, 272–73, 298, 310
Bonino, Emma, 270
Bonner, Elena, 143–44
Bonnet, Henri, 54
Book of Manners (Certaldo), 281
Boraine, Alex, 242
Bordaberry, Juan, 279–80
Bosnia: Muslims, 221, 352n11; Special Rapporteur, 110–11
Botswana, marketable resources of, 89
Boumediene v. Rumsfeld, 301–3
Brazil: and Americas Watch, 227; prisons in, 349n27
Breaking the Silence, 222
Brezhnev, Leonid, 14, 143
Britain: libel laws of, 244; suffragist movement in, 38–39. See also England
British Armenia Committee, 49
British Union of Fascists, 52
Brodsky, Joseph, 140
Brokaw, Tom, 239
Brown, Gordon, 292, 294; and free speech, 52
Brown v. Board of Education, 161
Bryce, Viscount James, 49
Buchanan v. Warley, 45
Buckley, William F., Jr., 192
Budapest, human rights groups in, 249–50
Bukovsky, Vladimir, 139
"Bulgarian Horrors and the Question of the East" (Gladstone), 42
Bureau of Human Rights, 172
Burma: HIV/AIDS, 314; and International Crisis Group (ICG), 246–47; R2P, 314–15
Bush administration: cover-ups by, 238; and detainees ("war on terror"), 135–36; and Guantanamo, 294–95, 303; and human rights, 323; September 11, 2001, rights after, 288–90, 294, 304–5; and Sudan, 355n29; Sudan (Darfur), 273; torture, policies on, 291–92, 306; and unitary executive, theory of, 298–99. See also Bush, George W.

Bush, George H. W.: and Americas
Watch, 211; appointments by, 296;
and Argentina, 171; and distortions in
reporting, 236; and El Salvador, 183–
84; and Human Rights Watch, 216–17,
230; pardons by, 297; and Sudan
(Darfur), 310
Bush, George W.: and accountability,
272; and Afghanistan invasion, 132;
appointments by, 136; and human
rights movement, 21; and Human
Rights Watch, 230; and international
human rights law, 110; legacy of, 316;
and legal threats, 352n15; on national
security, 296; Secretary of Defense
post, appointment of, 14; and Sudan
(Darfur), 19, 335n6; "war on terror,"
launching of, 202–3. See also Bush
administration
Bush, Rasul v., 299–300
Business and Human Rights Center, 245
Bybee, Stephen Jay, 136, 298, 305
Byron, Lord, 312
"Bystander" (Tourgée), 40

Cairo Institute for Human Rights, 319
Cambodia: Communism, 151; and
Global Witness, 245–46
capital punishment, 196
Carmichael, Stokely, 37
Carswell, Harold, 347n1
Carter administration: as advocate for
human rights, 320; and Country Re-
ports, 169; criticisms of, 182–83; and
Human Rights Watch, 205; Kirkpat-
rick, Jeane, attacks by, 171; and Latin
America, 261. See also Carter, Jimmy
Carter, Jimmy: appointments by, 170–71;
and Country Reports, 168–69; and
Helsinki Watch, 206; and human
rights policy, 15; Supreme Court
nominees of, 347n1. See also Carter
administration
Casas, Bartolomé de Las, 336n7
Cassin, René, 97–99, 248
Castillo, Jaime, 164, 344n4
Castlereagh, Lord, 35

Castro, Fidel, 151–52, 162–63, 261
Castro, Raúl, 345n8
CAT. See Convention Against Torture
and Other Cruel, Inhuman or Degrad-
ing Treatment or Punishment (CAT)
Cathleen ni Houlihan (Yeats), 188
Catholic Church, influence of in Latin
America, 109, 345n8
CEDAW. See Convention on the Elimi-
nation of All Forms of Discrimination
Against Women (CEDAW)
CEJIL. See Center for Justice and Interna-
tional Law (CEJIL)
CELS. See Center for Legal and Social
Studies (CELS)
Center for Constitutional Rights, 203,
352n15
Center for Justice and Accountability,
240
Center for Justice and International Law
(CEJIL), 243
Center for Legal and Social Studies
(CELS), 226, 250, 253–54
Central Africa, Pygmies, 245
Central Intelligence Agency (CIA): and
Chile, 163; funding of, 176, 248,
346n6
CERD. See Convention on the Elimina-
tion of All Forms of Racial Discrimi-
nation (CERD)
Cerezo, Vinicio, 180
Certaldo, Paolo da, 281
Chafee, Zechariah, Jr., 338n37
Chalidze, Valery, 141–42
Chamberlain, Neville, 126–27
Charles I (king of England), 31–32
Charter 08, 155–56
Charter 77, 13, 146–47, 155
Charter of the United Nations. See
United Nations Charter
Chaskalson, Arthur, 70–72, 249, 254
Chavez, Hugo, 15, 321
Chechens, rights of, 112
Chechnya: murders in, 1–2; and war,
156–57
Che Guevara, 261
chemical weapons, use of, 237

Cheney, Dick: and accountability, 272; and Afghanistan invasion, 133; on interrogation methods, 306; and Iran-Contra affair, 297–98, 304; "Meet the Press," interview with, 290; opponents of policies of, 236; and September 11, 2001, rights after, 294–96

Chernomyrdin, Victor, 277

Chiang Ching-Kuo, 181

Chiang Kai-shek, 181

Chile: arrests in, 209; civil rights violations in, 162–63; human rights abuses in, 178–80; military coup of, 3, 109, 162–63, 191; and Truth and Reconciliation Commission (TRC), 260, 262; and Vicaría de la Solidaridad, 167, 198. *See also* Pinochet, Augusto

China: Anti-Footbinding Society, 37; April 5th Incident in, 148; and Asia Watch, 215–16; challenges of, 328–30; children in, 85–86; and Communism, 147–50, 153–56, 329; crime in, 91; Cultural Revolution of, 29, 148; Democracy Wall movement in, 147–49; economic growth of, 88; economic power of, 231; economic progress, benefits of, 81; famine in (1958 to 1961), 29, 85; and "The Fifth Modernization," 148–50; and "Four "Modernizations, 148; "Great Leap Forward" policies of, 29, 85, 147; and HIV/AIDS, 91, 155, 229; human right movement in, 23; and information sources, 12; and National People's Congress, 154; and political prisoners, 241; power of government in, 90; and Qincheng prison, 149; and Sudan (Darfur), 310; trade relations with, 166; universality of rights in, 91–92

chivalry, age of, 118

CHRI. *See* Commonwealth Human Rights Initiative (CHRI)

Christian Church, 335n6; and war, 118

Christian Science Monitor, 267

Christie, Julie, 188

The Chronicle of Current Events, 142

Chun Doo Hwan, 180–81

CICC. *See* Coalition for the International Criminal Court (CICC)

Cicero, 30

citizen movements, 28–29

Citizens' Committee, 40

Citizens' Rights Association. *See* National Citizens' Rights Association

Civil Liberties Bureau, 46

civil rights violations, 161–62. *See also specific country*

Civil War (United States): abolitionist movement and, 37; coverage of, 120

Clarke, Richard, 288

Clarkson, Thomas, 33–34

Classified Information Procedures Act, 304

Clinton, Bill: China, trade relations with, 166; Kosovo intervention, 313; and Rwanda, 267

Clinton, Hillary, 228

Coalition for the International Criminal Court (CICC), 256–57

Cold War, 161–85; and competition between East and West, 13; ending of, 16–17, 334; hardening of lines during, 101; and 1970s events, 4, 10; threats of, 21, 289. *See also* Communism

Columbia Journalism Review, 239

Colville, Lord, 111

Commentaries (Blackstone), 33

Commission on Human Rights, 97

Committee of Cooperation for Peace, 163–64

Committee to Protect Journalists (CPJ), 8, 237, 239

Commonwealth Human Rights Initiative (CHRI), 249

Communism, 138–60. *See also* Cold War; *specific country*

Conference on Security and Cooperation in Europe (CSCE), 14

Congo. *See* Democratic Republic of the Congo

Congo Free State, 43

Congress of People's Deputies (Russia), 156

Constitution. *See* U.S. Constitution

Convention Against Torture and Other
Cruel, Inhuman or Degrading Treat-
ment or Punishment (CAT), 108, 109,
111, 299
conventional law. *See* Treaty law
Convention on the Elimination of All
Forms of Discrimination Against
Women (CEDAW), 108
Convention on the Elimination of All
Forms of Racial Discrimination
(CERD), 108
Convention on the Prevention and Pun-
ishment of the Crime of Genocide:
adoption of, 99–101, 218
Convention on the Rights of the Child
(CRC), 108
Cook, Robin, 268, 313
Coolidge, Calvin, 307
Costa Rica: marketable resources of, 89
Council of Europe, 158, 243
*Country Reports on Human Rights
Practices:* and Abrams, Elliott, 172,
230; critiques of, 236; first volume of,
168–70; September 11, rights after,
288, 304
*Courting Social Justice: Judicial Enforce-
ment of Social and Economic Rights in
the Developing World*, 74
Court of Cassation, 292
Court of Chivalry (England), 118
Cousins, Norman, 54
Cowper, William, *The Task*, 34
CPJ. *See* Committee to Protect Journal-
ists (CPJ)
craft unions, 336n6
CRC. *See* Convention on the Rights of
the Child (CRC)
Crimean Tatars, 140
Crimean War of 1854–56, 119–20
Croatia, war with Serbia, 283
Cronkite, Walter, 239
CSCE. *See* Conference on Security and
Cooperation in Europe (CSCE)
Cuba: and Americas Watch, 215; and
Catholic Church, 345n8; and Com-
munism, 151–53
customary law, 93

Czechoslovakia: intellectuals in, 13, 146–
47; and "Prague Spring," 141, 145
Czech Republic: Slovakia, separation
from, 65

Dallaire, Romeo, 313
Daniel, Yuli, 139–41
Darfur. *See* Sudan (Darfur)
Darrow, Clarence, 50
Davis, David Brion, 34, 36
Dayton, Ohio, peace negotiations in,
267–68
Declaration of Independence (1776):
concept of rights in, 58; language of,
96; opening sentences of, 27
"Declaration of Sentiments," 37
de Klerk, F. W., 16, 184
Defense Department, 305
DeGaulle, Charles, 248
Democracy Wall movement (China),
147–49
Democratic Republic of the Congo: and
accountability, 271, 273–74, 277, 284;
conflicts in, 17; different militias of,
356n36; and International Criminal
Court (ICC), 270–71; street children
of, 229
Deng, Francis, 112
Deng Xiaoping, 148–49, 154, 166
deniability, 261
Department of Bantu Education, 169
Department of Justice, 288–89, 305,
342n17
Derian, Patricia: aides, 345n9; appoint-
ment of, 170–71; successor to, 207;
and systematic human rights abuses,
limitations, 178
Dershkowitz, Alan, 220–22
detainees ("war on terror"): interrogation
of, 133; torture of, 135–36. *See also*
Abu Ghraib Prison
Detainee Treatment Act (DTA), 300
détente, 143–44
Dewey, John, 44, 98
disappearances, 208, 238, 253, 259–60
Disraeli, Benjamin, 42, 312
Doctors without Borders, 130, 311

Douglass, Frederick, 35, 37
DRC. *See* Democratic Republic of the Congo
Dred Scott case, 41
Dreyfus, Alfred, 47–48, 54, 247
Dreyfus case, aftermath of, 8, 9
D'Souza, Frances, 244
DTA. *See* Detainee Treatment Act (DTA)
DuBois, W. E. B., 44
Dulles, John Foster, 101, 112–13
Dunant, Henry, 119
Duvalier, Jean Claude ("Baby Doc"), 16, 172, 177
Dworkin, Ronald, 67, 78; *Taking Rights Seriously*, 70

East Asia, human rights abuses in, 180
Eastman, Crystal, 46
economic, social and cultural rights violations, 79–80
Economic and Social Council, 97–98
economic rights, 62–63
Egyptian Initiative for Personal Rights, 257, 319
Eisenhower, Dwight D., 101
Eldridge, Joseph, 239–40
El Salvador: abuses reported in, 209–11; human rights in, 173–75; and Lawyers Committee for International Human Rights, 236; murders in, 183–84; truth commission of, 260
Emancipation Proclamation, 35
eminent jurists panel, 322–23
England: antislavery movement (eighteenth century in, 7–10, 33–35, 42; and Declaration of Rights, 31–32. *See also* Britain
English Revolution, 31–32
Enzensberger, Hans Magnus, 193
Eritrea, independence of, 65
ERRC. *See* European Roma Rights Center (ERRC)
ESC violations. *See* Economic, social and cultural rights violations
Esenin-Volpin, Alexander, 141
Estemirova, Natalya: enlistment of, 9; murder of, 1–2, 5–6, 251; works of, 3

Ethiopia, Eritrean independence of, 65
ethnic cleansing: in Nazi Germany, 264–65; in Russia, 224
European Convention for the Protection of Human Rights and Fundamental Freedoms, 108
European Convention on Human Rights, 112, 158
European Court of Human Rights: and Council of Europe, 243; establishment of, 47; governments belonging to, 158–59; jurisdiction of, 115; and recognition as leader, 104
European Court of Justice, 104, 113, 243
European Roma Rights Center (ERRC), 249–50
European Union, influence of, 21
Evans, Gareth, 247
Exploration, 149
Extractive Industries Transparency Initiative, 246

Fang Lizhi, 154
Federalist Papers, 83, 295, 298
Fédération International des Droites de l'Homme (FIDH): described, 247–48; establishment of, 9; and international human rights, 102; outgrowth of, 54; and ties, 256; World War II, impact of FIDH on, 52
feminist movement (United States), 7
Ferguson, Plessy v., 44, 45
FIDH. *See* Fédération International des Droites de l'Homme (FIDH)
Fifteenth Amendment, 37–38
"Fifth Modernization, The" (China), 148–50
Figueres, José, 55
"Final Document on the Struggle Against Subversion and Terrorism" (Argentina), 226
First Amendment, 68, 104, 307–8
FISA. *See* Foreign Intelligence Surveillance Act (FISA)
FMLN, 173
Ford Foundation, 205, 228–29, 350n30

Ford, Gerald: and CSCE, 14; and détente, 143–44; on Pinochet's abuses, 165; and Section 502B of the Foreign Assistance Act, 168; Supreme Court nominees of, 347n1
Foreign Assistance Act, 165; adoption of, 94; Section 502B, 168–69
Foreign Intelligence Surveillance Act (FISA), 298–99
Foreign Relations Committee, 207
Forges, Alison des, 217
Forster, E. M., 52
Forum Asia, 249
"Four Modernizations" (China), 148
Fourteenth Amendment, 37, 41
Foxman, Abraham, 220
France: antislavery movement in, 34–35; and Court of Cassation, 292; and Declaration of the Rights of Man and of the Citizen, 31–32
France, Anatole, 47
Franco, Francisco, 126
Franco-Prussian War, 122
Frankfurter, Felix, 50, 338n37
Fraser, Donald, 164, 167
Freedom Defence Committee, 52
Freedom House, 234, 240–41
"Freedom John." See Lilburne, John ("Freedom John")
Freedom of Information Act, 291, 306
Free Speech League, 41
Frei, Eduardo, 55
French Declaration of the Rights of Man and of the Citizen of 1789: and "imprescriptible" rights, 86; language of, 96; opening sentences of, 58; on property rights, 105; rights set forth in, 60; and "second generation" rights, 63
French Revolution, and slavery, 34
Frost, David, 296
Fujimori, Alberto, 180, 280
Fund for Free Expression, 205
Fund for Humanitarian Law in Serbia, 250, 252–53

gachacha courts (Rwanda), 280
Gandhi, Indira, 51

Gandhi, Mohandas, 48–49
García, Romeo Lucas, 171, 180
Garrison, William Lloyd, 35–36, 336–37n16
gas warfare, 124–25
Gates, Robert, 14, 305
Gavras, Costa, 163
Gaza, 223; "Operation Cast Lead," 222, 325
Gbagbo, Laurent, 356n36
Geneva Convention (First), 119–20
Geneva Conventions (1949), 104; and accountability, 265; Additional Protocols (1977) of, 128–29, 265; and civil rights violations, 162; labeling of as "quaint," 132–33, 136; and September 11, rights after, 290–91, 294, 300–301; war, laws of, 128
genocide: Guatemala, 263; and Human Rights Watch, 221; and Sudan (Darfur), 275, 309–10; use of term, 309
Genocide Convention. See Convention on the Prevention and Punishment of the Crime of Genocide
Georgia: movement into South Ossetia, 224–26; Russia, war against, 17
Geremek, Bronislaw, 145–46
Germany: poison gas, use of, 124–25; war crimes of, 126, 128. See also Holocaust; Nuremberg headings
Ghana, repression in, 89
Gierek, Edward, 145
Ginsberg, Allen, 193
Gjelten, Tom, 221
Gladstone, William, "Bulgarian Horrors and the Question of the East," 42
Glendon, Mary Ann, 59
Global Fund to Fight AIDS, 247
Global Rights, 8
Global Witness, 245–46
Goering, Hermann, 127
Goldman, Emma, 50–51, 338n41
Goldman, Robert, 357n2
Goldstone, Richard, 266
Gonne, Maud, 188
Gonzales, Alberto: labeling of Geneva Conventions as "quaint" by, 132, 137; and September 11, rights after, 290, 298, 305

Gorbachev, Mikhail, 141–42
Gordimer, Nadine, 193
Grant, Frances, 55
Great Depression: Roosevelt, Franklin
    D., election of, 75; World War II, early
    days of, 127
"Great Leap Forward" policies, China, 29,
    85, 147
Grigorenko, Pyotr, 144, 194
Grootboom, 71–72, 74
Grotius, Hugo, 30, 118
Guantanamo, 290; closing of, 302–3,
    306; and constitutional law, 294–95;
    lawsuits related to, 300; and unitary
    executive theory, 298
Guatemala: accountability, 263–64;
    genocide, 263; human rights abuses,
    180
Gulf War (1991), 217, 219, 237
Gutman, Roy, 265–67

habeas corpus, power to suspend, 341n6
Hague, The, International Criminal
    Court (ICC) (see International
    Criminal Court [ICC]); and Sudan
    (Darfur), 19
Hague conferences of 1899 and 1907, 42
Hague Conventions: and Czar's initiative,
    122–23; and production of weapons,
    123–25
Haig, Alexander, 15, 206
Haiti, during Cold War, 177–78
Hajek, Jiri, 146, 147
Hamas, 219; Operation Cast Lead against,
    325
Hamdan, Salim Ahmed, 300–302
Hamdi v. Rumsfeld, 300–301
Hamilton, Alexander, Federalist Papers
    writings, 83, 295
Hammarberg, Thomas, 197–99, 347n14
Handicap International, 214
Hariri, Rafik, 279
Harkin, Tom, 164, 167
Harlan, John Marshall, 41
Harold of Hastings, 118
Harrington, Michael, 164
Harris, Arthur "Bomber," 127
Harun, Ahmed, 275, 276

Harvard Business School, 201
"hate speech," 327
Havel, Vaclav, 13, 146, 150
Hayner, Priscilla, 263
Haynes, Stephen, 136
Haynes, William III, 295, 298
Haynsworth, Clement, 347n1
Hays, Arthur Garfield, 54
"heckler's veto," 357n6
Helsinki Accords, 143–45, 147, 251, 256;
    signing of, 206
Helsinki Committees, 213
Helsinki Group, 3, 141, 145, 250–52
Helsinki meeting, 14
Helsinki Watch, 212; and Afghanistan,
    213; establishment of, 205–6; focus
    of, 214; leaders of, 206–7; monitoring
    abuses of, 350n29; and Turkey, 214–
    15. See also Human Rights Watch
Henkin, Louis, 235
Herodotus, 117
Hezbollah, war against, 17, 219–22,
    353n20
Hill, Christopher, 27–28
Hiroshima, 127–28, 142
Hitler, Adolph: and British Union of
    Fascists, 52; and Ossietzky, Karl von,
    247–48
Hitler-Stalin Pact, 51
HIV/AIDS, 333; in Burma, 314; in
    China, 91, 155, 229; and Global Fund
    to Fight AIDS, 247; and Nevirapine,
    72, 255; in Russia, 229; in South
    Africa, 72–75; and Treatment Action
    Campaign, 255
Hobbes, Thomas, 30
Hochschild, Adam, 43–44
Holbrooke, Richard, 178
Holder, Eric, 136, 342n17
Holder v. Humanitarian Law Project,
    307–9
Holmes, John Haynes, 44, 46
Holocaust: and Genocide convention, 99;
    ICRC, silence on war crimes of 130–
    31; and laws of war, 125–26
Hong Kong, civil liberties in, 90
Hopgood, Stephen, 200
"Hudood Ordinance," 255

humanitarian intervention concept, 312–13
Humanitarian Law Project, Holder v., 307–9
Human Rights Commission of Pakistan, 250, 255
Human Rights Committee (Moscow), 141
Human Rights Day, 99
Human Rights First, 8, 235, 303
Human Rights Watch, 204–32; in Africa, 216; and Amnesty International, 205; and armed conflict, 202–3; and Asia Watch, 215; attack on, 221–22; claims against, 12; and Communism, 138; creation of, 204; critiques of, 236; director of, 79–80; in El Salvador, 174; emergence of, 195; and genocide, 221; and genocide, use of term, 309; and Georgia, movement into South Ossetia, 224–26; and Helsinki Watch (*see* Helsinki Watch); and HIV/AIDS, 229; in India, 216; and international war crimes tribunal, call for, 265–66; and Israel, 219–24; and Israel Defense Forces, 219–21; and Kurds, 218, 237; and Middle East, 217; monitoring of abuses by, 350n29; origins of, 8; and post-September 11 detainees, 293; prisons, focus on, 228; report by, 87; in Rwanda, 217; shaping of, 209; shift in, 230; size of, 11; in Sudan (Darfur), 18–19; and Women's Rights Project, 228–29. *See also* Americas Watch
Humphrey, John, 97
Hungarian Revolution (1956), 13
Hunt, Lynn, 26–27, 60
Hussein, Saddam: al-Qaeda, link between, 133; and chemical weapons, use of, 237; execution of, 18, 280, 316; Kurds, slaughter of, 221; and Kuwait, invasion of, 217–18; victory over, 17
Hu Yaobang, 154
hydrogen bomb, 141

IAADF. *See* Inter-American Association for Democracy and Freedom (IAADF)

ICC. *See* International Criminal Court (ICC)
ICCPR. *See* International Covenant on Civil and Political Rights (ICCPR)
ICESCR. *See* International Covenant on Economic, Social and Cultural Rights (ICECSR)
ICG. *See* International Crisis Group (ICG)
ICJ. *See* International Commission of Jurists (ICJ)
ICRC. *See* International Committee of the Red Cross (ICRC)
ICTJ. *See* International Center for Transitional Justice (ICTJ)
ICTR. *See* International Criminal Tribunal for Rwanda (ICTR)
Idea of Justice, The (Sen), 75–76
Ifill, Gwen, 239
IHF. *See* International Helsinki Federation for Human Rights (IHF)
ILHR. *See* International League for Human Rights (ILHR)
"imprescriptible" rights, 86
independence and self-determination, 66–67
independent journalism, 335n3
Index on Censorship, 244
India, 49–51; and Commonwealth Human Rights Initiative (CHRI), 249; and Human Rights Watch, 216; and No Peace Without Justice (NPWJ), 269–70; Pakistan, separation from, 65
Indian Civil Liberties Union, 51
Indian Constitution of 1950, 69–70
Indian National Congress, 49
Indonesia, Reagan's visit to, 348n4
Initiative Group for the Defense of Human Rights, 141
Inter-American Association for Democracy and Freedom (IAADF), 54–55, 113
Inter-American Commission on Human Rights, 198
Inter-American Court of Human Rights, 47, 113, 115, 243

Inter-American Institute for Human Rights in Costa Rica, 164
Internal Security Act (Malaysia), 293
International Center for Transitional Justice (ICTJ), 242, 264
International Centre for the Protection of Human Rights, 242
International Commission of Jurists (ICJ), 102; described, 248–49; eminent jurists panel of, 322–23; funds of, 346n6; launching of, 102
International Commission on Intervention and State Sovereignty, 313
International Committee for Political Prisoners, 50
International Committee of the Red Cross (ICRC), 119, 130–31, 342n13
International Covenant on Civil and Political Rights (ICCPR): articles of, 63; generally, 109, 146; overview, 102–8
International Covenant on Economic, Social and Cultural Rights (ICESCR): Articles of, 106–7, 146; rights under, 62–63
International Criminal Court (ICC): and accountability, 269–81; adoption of, 123; Assembly of State Parties to, 349n16; establishment of, 8, 258–59, 285; and Georgia, movement into South Ossetia, 225–26; permanence, 227; punishments by, 314; in Sudan (Darfur), 19, 309–10
International Criminal Tribunal for Rwanda (ICTR), 77, 267
International Criminal Tribunal for the Former Yugoslavia (ICTY): accountability of, 266–69, 282; cases referred to, 280; creation of, 131–32; establishment of, 331; and fears of conflict, 278; functioning of, 110–12; and Human Rights Watch, 227; judge, serving as, 123, 356–57n2; Physicians for Human Rights (PHR), evidence of, 238
International Crisis Group (ICG), 246–47
International Foundation for Electoral Systems, 176

International Helsinki Federation for Human Rights (IHF), 212, 213, 348n5
international humanitarian law, 117–37
international human rights law, overview, 93–116; customary law, 93; treaty law, 93–94
International Human Rights Law Group, 239
International League for Human Rights (ILHR), 8, 54, 101–2, 235
International League for the Rights of Man, 240, 247
International Network of Civil Liberties Organizations, 256
International Republican Institute, 176
International Rights Law Group. See Global Rights
interrogations, 133, 306
Iran-Contra affair, 295–98
Iraq, medical care during war, 349n26
Iraq-Iran War of 1980s, 129–30
Iron Curtain. See Cold War; Communism
Israel: denunciation of, 111–12; Gaza conflict in, 223; Hezbollah, war against, 17, 221, 222; and Human Rights Watch, 219–24; Lebanon, engagement in, 219–20, 232; Palestinians, beatings by soldiers of, 237
Israel Defense Forces, 219–21
Izvestia, 157

"J'Accuse," 47
Jackson, Henry, 166
Jackson-Vanik Act. See Trade Act
Jahangir, Asma, 255
Jamaica: Americas Watch, 227
James II (king of England), 31–32
Japan: civil liberties, 53–55; standard of living, 88
Japanese-Americans: World War II, 307
Japanese Civil Liberties Union, 54
Jaruzelski, Wojciech, 212
Jefferson, Thomas, 58, 86
Jennings, Peter, 239
Jeppesen, Mohamed v., 308–9
Jerusalem Post, 220

Jewish "refuseniks," 144
Jiang Qing, 148
Jilani, Hina, 255, 356n2
"Jim Crow," 39–40
John, Augustus, 52
John (king of England), 26
Johnson, Lyndon B., 5
Josipovic, Ivo, 353n26
J. Roderick MacArthur Foundation, 244
Judiciary Committee of the House of
    Representatives, 296

Kagame, President Paul, 217
Kagan, Elena, 308
Kambanda, Jean, 18, 269, 279
Kampfner, John, 244
Kandic, Natasa, 252–53
Kant, Immanuel, 32–33
Karadzic, Radovan, 267–68, 277, 279
Kausikan, Bilahari, 86–88
Keepers of the Flame (Hopgood), 200
Kennedy, Anthony, 301, 309
Kennedy, Edward, 164–65, 167–68
Kennedy, John F., 186
Kenya, accountability, 277–78
KGB, 139
Khan, Irene, 200–201
Khieu Samphan, 18, 279
Khodorkovsky, Mikhail, 24
Khomeini, Ayatollah, 244, 297
Kibaki, President Mwai, 273
Kimberley Process Certification Scheme,
    246
King Leopold's Ghost (Hochschild),
    43–44
King Leopold's Soliloquy (Twain), 43
Kirkpatrick, Jeane: appointment of, 171–
    73; Carter administration, criticisms
    of, 182; and Castillo, Jaime, 344n4;
    and Helsinki Watch, 206; and human
    rights policy, 15; and Human Rights
    Watch, 230
Kissinger, Henry: and Chilean armed
    forces, 3, 163; and Country Reports,
    168; and détente, 144; and Watergate,
    165
Klein, Jacques, 268

Knightley, Phillip, 335n3
Kolakowski, Leszek, 13
KOR, 145–46
Korean War, 129, 180–81
Kosovo: independence of, 66; interven-
    tion in, 313; and lawyers, 252–53;
    NATO entry into war, 131; NATO
    intervention in, 17; and war, 277
Kouchner, Bernard, 311
Kovalev, Sergei, 141–44; commitment of,
    156–57; and Soviet abuses of rights,
    165
Kramer, David, 241
Krulak, Charles, 236
Krupp case, 124
Krushchev, Nikita, 139, 186
Ku Klux Klan, 39
Kurdish Human Rights Project, 243–44
Kurdistan Workers Party, 308
Kurds, Human Rights Watch, 218, 221,
    237
Kurland, Philip, 357n6
Kuron, Jacek, 145
Kushayb, Ali, 275, 276
Kuwait: invasion of, 217–18
Kyoto Treaty, 306

Latin America: Catholic Church, influ-
    ence of, 109; and "truth commissions,"
    260–61
Lauren, Paul Gordon, 27, 52–53
laws, overview, 93–116
Lawyers Committee for International
    Human Rights, 235–36, 317
Laxalt, Paul, 178
League of Women Voters, 39
Lebanon: and accountability, 277–78;
    Israel, engagement in 219–21, 232;
    justice, peace and, 353n20
Lefever, Ernest, 207–9
Legal Defense Fund of the NAACP, 47
Legal Resources Center in South Africa,
    250, 254–55
LeMay, Curtis, 127
Lemkin, Raphael, 99–100
Leopold II (king of Belgium), 43–44, 56
Lester, Anthony, 242–43

Letters from Russian Prisons (Baldwin), 51
Levellers, 28
Liberator, The, 35
Libya, and ICC, 276
Lieber Code, 120–22
Lieber, Francis, 120–22
Lilburne, John ("Freedom John"), 28, 32–33
Lincoln, Abraham: and Emancipation Proclamation, 35; habeas corpus, suspension of, 121; and Lieber Code, 120; town of, 44
Litvinov, Pavel, 141
Liu Xiaobo, 155–56, 159, 330
Locke, John: on French Declaration of the Rights of Man and of the Citizen of 1789, similarity of works, 58; *Second Treatise on Civil Government,* 30–32
Lundy, Benjamin, 35–36
lynching, 44
Lysenko, T. D., 141

MacArthur, Douglas, 53, 127
MacArthur Foundation, 205
MacBride, Sean, 188, 191, 346n6
MacKenzie, Lewis, 221
Macmillan, Harold, 186
Madison, James, 59
Magna Carta, 26
Malaysia: and democracy, 90; and wealth, 88
Malik, Charles, 98
Mamdani, Mahmood, 274
Mandela, Nelson: and accountability, 262; endorsement of, 266; release from prison of, 16, 184
Mansfield, William, 33–34, 47, 301
Mao Zedong, 128; death of, 29, 88, 148; "Great Leap Forward" policies of, 29, 85, 147
Marchenko, Anatoly, 144
Marcos, Ferdinand, 16, 178, 180, 236
Martens, Fyodor Fyodorovich, 123
"Martens clause," 122–24
Martinet, Louis, 40, 43
Marx, Karl, 60
Mary Stuart (queen of Scots), 31–32

Massimino, Elisa, 236–37
Massing, Michael, 239
Matteotti, Giacomo, 52
Mazowiecki, Tadeusz, 110, 146
Mbeki, President Thabo, 75
MCA. *See* Military Commissions Act of 2006 (MCA)
McCarthy, Joseph, 161
McGovern, George, 164
Media Legal Defence Initiative (MLDI), 245
Medico, 214
Meese, Edwin III, 296
Memorial (organization), 1–3, 156, 251
Memory of Solferino (Dunant), 119
Mendez, Juan, 112
Meném, Carlos Saúl, 260, 279
Mental Disability Advocacy Center, 250
Mental Disability Rights International, 240, 250
Menuhin, Yehudi, 188
Meron, Theodor, 123, 137
Methodist Church, 239–40, 242
Michnik, Adam, 13, 145, 150
Middle East: and Arab revolutions of 2011, 24; and Human Rights Watch, 217
Mignone, Emilio, 253–54
Military Commissions Act of 2006 (MCA), 301–2
Mill, John Stuart, *The Subjection of Women,* 38
Miller, George, 164
Milosevic, Slobodan: accession to power of, 66; and accountability, 279; death of, 17–18; indictment of, 277; and war, 268
Milosz, Czeslaw, 13
Milton, John, *Areopagitica,* 28
Mitford, Diana, 52
Mitterand, François, 221
Mladic, Ratko, 267–69, 277
MLDI. *See* Media Legal Defence Initiative (MLDI)
Mobutu Sese Seko, 172
Moffett, Toby, 164
Mohamed, Binyan, 308

Mohamed v. Jeppesen, 308–9
Moi, President Daniel Arap, 172
monitoring, 114–15
Montealegre, Hernán, 164
Monteneros, 261
Montgomery bus boycott, 161
Montt, Efrain Rios, 180
Moore, Henry, 188
Morel, Edmund, *West African Mail*, 43
Moreno Ocampo, Luis, 271–74
Morgenthau, Henry J., Sr., 49
Morrison, Toni, 205
Moscow: and Human Rights Committee, 141; and Olympics, 181; Pushkin Square in, 139–41; Red Square in, 141
Moscow Helsinki Group, 3, 141, 145, 250–52
Mosley, Oswald, 52
Mott, Lucretia, 37
Moyn, Samuel, 4, 338–39n48
Mubarak, Hosni, 103, 319
Mugabe, Robert, 314
Mukasey, Michael, 136
Munro, Robin, 216
Muslims: in Bosnia, 221, 352n11; detention of, in U.S., 103; as minorities, 326–27; in Netherlands, 357n4

NAACP. *See* National Association for the Advancement of Colored People (NAACP)
Nagasaki, 127–28, 142
Nation, 44
National American Women Suffrage Association, 38
National Archives, 306
National Association for the Advancement of Colored People (NAACP): establishment of, 10; founders of, 45; longevity of, 250; and lynching, 1909, 44–45; membership recruitment of, 41
National Citizens' Rights Association, 40–41, 44
National Civil Liberties Bureau, 46
National Council for Civil Liberties (NCCL), 52, 250
National Democratic Institute, 176

National Endowment for Democracy (NED), 176, 179, 234, 350n4
National People's Congress (China), 154
National Public Ratio, 221
National Women Suffrage Association, 38
"native rights," 28
NATO: and Dayton agreement, 268; humanitarian intervention, 312–13; Kosovo, entry into war, 17, 131; Serbia, defeat of, 281
natural law principles, 26–56
natural rights, 336n10
Nazi Germany: concentration camps, 96; and ethnic cleansing, 264–65; war crimes, prosecution, 42. *See also* Nuremberg Charter; Nuremberg trials; Nuremberg Tribunal
Nazi war criminals, prosecution, 42
NCCL. *See* National Council for Civil Liberties (NCCL)
NED. *See* National Endowment for Democracy (NED)
Nehru, Jawaharlal, 51
Netherlands, Muslims in, 357n4
Nevirapine, 72, 255
New Orleans, segregation, 40
New Republic, 220
Newsday, 265
New York Sun, 220
New York Times, 5, 223
New Zealand, suffragist movement, 38
NGOs: in India, 70; lobbying, 269; as targets, 24
Nicholas II of Russia, 122
Nigeria, Biafran war, 130
Nightingale, Florence, 120
9/11. *See* September 11, 2001
Nineteenth Amendment, 37, 56
Nixon administration, and Chilean coup, 169. *See also* Nixon, Richard M.
Nixon, Richard M.: and Chilean armed forces, 3, 163–64; and civil liberties, violations of, 161–62; forced resignation of, 165; and "Pentagon Papers," 5; staff, 296; and Supreme Court candidates, 347n1; and Watergate, 295. *See also* Nixon administration

Nizhny Novgorod, 213
Nobel Peace Prize: Amnesty International, 4, 8, 198–99; Cassin, René, 248; establishment of, 11; Liu Xiaobo, 155, 330; Obama, Barack, 332; Ossietzky, Karl von, 247–48; Sakharov, Andrei, 143; Sen, Amartya, 75
No Peace Without Justice (NPWJ), 269–70
norms, rights, 57–92
North Korea, and information sources, 12
Novy Mir (Tardovsky), 139
NPWJ. *See* No Peace Without Justice (NPWJ)
Nuremberg, as accountability model, 264–65
Nuremberg Charter, creation of, 100
Nuremberg trials, 42, 123, 127
Nuremberg Tribunal, 100; *Krupp* case, 124
Nyerere, Julius, 312

Obama administration: and Arab revolutions of 2011, reaction to, 320; and human rights, 323–24; and Human Rights Watch, 231; and International Criminal Court (ICC), 311; and September 11, rights after, 304–5
Obama, Barack: appointments by, 136, 276; on Guantanamo, 290, 302, 306; and human rights movement, 21; and Human Rights Watch, 230; military commissions, use of, 355n22; and Nobel Peace Prize, 332; Secretary of Defense post, appointment of, 14; and unitary executive, theory of, 298. *See also* Obama administration
Observer, 244
Observer Weekend Review, 187
O'Connor, Sandra Day, 300
Olympics: Moscow, 181
Omaar, Rakiya, 217
One Day in the Life of Ivan Denisovich (Solzhenitsyn), 139
Open Russia Foundation, 24
Open Society Foundations, 350n1
"Operation Cast Lead," 222, 325

Organization of African Unity, 64–65
Organization of American States, 198, 254
Organization of the Islamic Conference, 275
Orlov, Yury, 141, 144–45
Orwell, George, 13, 52
Ossietzky, Carl von, 52, 247–48
Ottoman Turks, 49–50
Ouattara, Alassane, 356n36
outcomes, predicting, 318–34
overview of the movement, 1–25

Pakistan: and Human Rights Commission, 255; human rights groups in, 250; India, separation from, 65
Palestinians, investigations of beatings, 237
Palestinian suicide bombers, 219
Palmer, A. Mitchell, 46
"Palmer Raids," 46, 50
Parliament of Paris-medieval, 118
Parocka, Jan, 146
Pasternak, Boris, 140
Pell, Claiborne, 209, 344n6
Penal Reform International, 245
Pentagon, attacks on. *See* September 11, 2001
"Pentagon Papers," 5
Percy, Charles, 208
Peru: and accountability, 263; human rights groups in, 250
Philbin, Patrick, 295
"Philhellenism," 312
PHR. *See* Physicians for Human Rights (PHR)
Physicians for Human Rights (PHR), 8, 214, 237–39, 350n4
Pillay, Navenethem, 112
Pinochet, Augusto: and Barnes, Harry, 15; and coup, 3, 109, 162–63; defeat of, 179–80; end of dictatorship, 262; end of rule, 198; generally, 171; human rights abuses by, 178–79; in London, 1998, 272; persecutions by, 150; successors of, 260; torture by forces, 164–65

Pisan, Christine de, 26
Plavsic, Biljana, 279
Plessy, Homer Adolph, 40–41
Plessy v. Ferguson, 44, 45
poison gas, use of, 124–25
Poland: Charter 77, 146–47; KOR, 145–46, 155
Polish Helsinki Committee, 212
Popper, Karl, 13
Powell, Colin, 309
Prague, entry of Soviet tanks, 13
"Prague Spring," 141, 145
Pravda, 144
Presidential Human Rights Commission (Russia), 156
prevention, 322–23
prisons, Human Rights Watch focus on, 228
Prohibition, 39
property rights, 105
Proust, Marcel, 47
provocation, 327–28
Proxmire, William, 344n6
"Publish What You Pay" campaign, 246
punishment, generally, 314, 322
Pushkin Square, 139–41
Putin, Vladimir, 157–58, 224, 251
Pygmies, 245

Qaddafi, Muammar, 258–59, 279, 311, 320, 331
Qincheng prison, 149
Queen's Counsel, 243

Rasul v. Bush, 299–300
Rather, Dan, 239
Read, Herbert, 52
Reagan administration: and Americas Watch, 211–12, 219; and Argentina, 171; criticisms of, 241; democracy, promotion of, 176–77; human rights policies, adoption of, 253; and human rights regimes, 172–75; and Human Rights Watch, 230; and Hussein, Saddam, 237. *See also* Reagan, Ronald W.
Reagan, Ronald W.: and apartheid, 184; and Castillo, Jaime, 344n4; democracy,

promotion of, 182–83; and distortions in reporting, 236; Germany, visit to, 100; and Helsinki Watch, 206–8; on human rights abuses, 111; and human rights policy, 15; Indonesia, visit to, 348n4; and Iran-Contra affair, 295–98; and South Africa rights movement, 16; and "war on drugs," 349n28; Westminster address, 175. *See also* Reagan administration
Red Crescent Society, 302–3
Red Cross. *See* American National Red Cross; International Committee of the Red Cross (ICRC)
redistribution, 82–83
Rejali, Darius, 191
"responsibility to protect," 311
Rice, Condoleezza, 288, 299
Rice, Susan, 276
Rieff, David, 222
rights, overview, 57–92
rights movements, 29
riots and demonstrations, Soweto, 169. *See also* Tiananmen Square
Rivera y Damas, Archbishop, 174
Rizzo, John, 305
Roberts, Adam, 125
Roberts, Justice John, 309
Rockefeller Foundation, 213–14
Roginsky, Arseny, 156
Rohde, David, 267
Roma: communities, attacks on, 325; deportations, 326; minorities, 327
Rome conference (1998), 272
Romero, Oscar Arnulfo, 173–74
Rome Treaty, 225; Coalition for an International Criminal Court, 270; International Criminal Court, establishment of, 8
Romulo, Carlos, 98
Roosevelt, Eleanor: Commission on Human Rights, establishment of, 97; and Freedom House, 241; protections of civil rights, 162; U.N., Human Rights Commission meeting (1952), 66; and Universal Declaration of Human Rights, 60–61, 99, 101

Roosevelt, Franklin D.: election of, 75; and Universal Declaration of Human Rights, 60–61

Roth, Kenneth, 79–81, 220, 229

Roth, Philip, 244

Rousseau, Jean Jacques, *The Social Contract*, 118–19

Rowlatt Act. *See* Anarchical and Revolutionary Crimes Act

R2P (responsibility to protect), 314–15

Rubenstein, Joshua, 193–94

Rumsfeld, Boumediene v., 301–3

Rumsfeld, Donald: opponents of policies of, 236; and September 11, rights after, 292, 305; vulnerability of to prosecution, 272

Rumsfeld, Hamdi v., 300–301

Rushdie, Salman, 244

Russell, Bertrand, 338n45

Russell, William Howard, 119–20

Russert, Tim, 290

Russia: Chechens, rights of, 112; and Congress of People's Deputies, 156; ethnic cleansing in, 224; Georgia, movement into South Ossetia, 224–26; and Georgia's war against, 17; and HIV/AIDS, 229; and Memorial (organization), 1–3, 156, 251; and Open Russia Foundation, 24; political repression in, 51; and Presidential Human Rights Commission, 156. *See also* Soviet Union

Russian Revolution (1917), 39, 307

Rwanda: *gachacha* courts, 280; Human Rights Watch, 217; mass murder, 76–77

Rwandan Patriotic Front, 281–82, 341n3

Saab, Georges Abi, 356n2

Saakashvili, Mikhail, 224, 226

Sakharov, Andrei: exile of, 213; influence of, 13; and Nobel Peace Prize, 143; and Soviet abuses of rights, 165; Wei's sentence, protesting, 150; works of, 141–43

Sanchez, Ricardo, 292

Sané, Pierre, 200

Sanger, Margaret, 39

Santa Cruz, Hernán, 98

Sarkozy, Nicolas, 250, 325

Satanic Verses, The (Rushdie), 244

Saudi Arabia, provision of religious freedom, 62

Scalia, Antonin, 296, 300–302, 309

Scammell, Michael, 244

Scanlon, Thomas, 78

Schell, Orville, Jr., 205

Schoultz, Lars, 198–99

Scotland, Articles and Ordinance of War, 123

"second generation" rights, 62–63

Second Treatise on Civil Government (Locke), 30–32

Section 502B of the Foreign Assistance Act, 168–69

segregation, early nineteenth century, 44–48; 1880s, 39–41

self-determination, 66–67

Sen, Amartya, 75–78, 88; *The Idea of Justice*, 75–76

Senate Foreign Relations Committee, 208–9

Sendero Luminoso, 180

Seneca Falls, New York convention, 37–38, 337n18

September 11, 2001: and Bush administration, 288–90, 294; and civil rights violations, 162; complexity of case, 134–35; and criminal convictions, 288, 305; period following, 20–21, 103, 202, 231, 323–25; rights after, 285–317; victims of attacks, 287; and war, laws of, departures from, 121; World War II, compared, 288–89. *See also* "war on terror"

Serbia, and accountability, 281–83; human rights groups in, 250, 252–53; NATO defeat of, 281

Sharp, Granville, 33

Shaw, George Bernard, 338n45

Shcharansky, Anatoly, 144

Shea, Nina, 241

Shotwell, James T., 53

Shultz, George, 177

Sierra Leone, Special Court, 277
Sihanouk (king of Cambodia), 214
Silva, Raúl Henriquez, 162–63, 167, 321
Singapore, wealth, 87–88
Sinyavsky, Andrei, 139–41
Sitwell, Osbert, 52
Slavery Abolition Act (England), 34
slaves and slavery, and voting rights, 38.
    See also abolition movement (United
    States); antislavery movement
Slovakia, separation from Czech Repub-
    lic, 65
Snow, Clyde, 238
SOAT. See Sudan Organization Against
    Torture (SOAT)
Social Contract, The (Rousseau), 118–19
social rights, 62–63
Socorro Juridico, 173
Solferino, battle of, 119
Solzhenitsyn, Alexander, 13, 140
Somerset, James, 33–34
Somerset case, 301
Somoza, Anastasio, 171, 174
Sontag, Susan, 193
Soobramoney, 71–74, 84
South Africa, 111–12; and accountability,
    261–63; apartheid in, 3–4, 13–14,
    184, 262–63, 351n7; equality, provi-
    sion of, 62; and HIV/AIDS, 72–75;
    human rights abuses in, 261–63; and
    ICC, 276; judicial system of, 48–49;
    and Legal Resources Center, 254–55;
    rights, overview, 70–75; rights move-
    ment, 16 of; and Treatment Action
    Campaign (TAC), 72–74, 80, 83; and
    Truth and Reconciliation Commis-
    sion (TRC), 198, 242, 262–63
South African Constitutional Court, 70–
    74, 82–85, 249, 322–23
South Korea: human rights abuses in,
    180–81; standard of living of, 88
South Ossetia, Georgia movement into,
    224–26
Soviet Union: Afghanistan, invasion of,
    213–14; Constitution Day in, 139;
    and détente, 143–44; disintegration
    of, 65; and Helsinki meeting, 14;

human rights after regime change,
    156–58; and human rights organiza-
    tions, 141–43; and hydrogen bomb,
    141; intellectuals in, 13, 140, 144–45;
    and Jewish "refuseniks," 144; Jews
    in, 166; and KGB, 139; and KOR,
    145–46; post World War II, 97;
    Prague, entry of tanks into, 13; Rea-
    gan denouncement of, 212; scientists
    and mathematicians in, 141–43; and
    Universal Declaration of Human
    Rights, 61–62. See also Cold War;
    Communism; Russia
Soweto, protests, 169
Spanish Civil War, 126
Sparta, 117
Special Court for Sierra Leone, 277
Special Rapporteur on Internally Dis-
    placed Persons, 112
Special Rapporteur on the Protection of
    Human Rights Defenders, 255
Special Rapporteur on Torture, 112
Spender, Stephen, 244
Spingarn, Arthur, 44
Sri Lanka, armed forces, 17
Stalin, Joseph, 53, 141
Stanton, Elizabeth Cady: and National
    Women Suffrage Association, 38; and
    Seneca Falls, New York convention, 37
Steffens, Lincoln, 41
Stevens, John Paul, 300
Stone, Harlan Fiske, 307
Stone, Lucy, 38
Stoppard, Tom, 244
Stover, Eric, 237–38
street children, 229
Streit, Clarence, 53
Stroessner, Alfredo, 103
Student Nonviolent Coordinating Com-
    mittee, 37
Subjection of Women, The (Mill), 38
Sudan (Darfur): and accountability, 317;
    conflicts in, 17–19, 335n6; crimes in,
    275–77; genocide in, 275, 309–10;
    prosecutions in, 273; R2P, 314–15
Sudan Organization Against Torture
    (SOAT), 276

suffrage movement (United States), 37–39
Sunstein, Cass R., 78–79
Sun Tzu, 117–18
Syria, news blackout, 234

TAC. *See* Treatment Action Campaign (TAC)
Tadic, Boris, 353n26
Tadic, Dusko, 266–67
Taiwan: political reform in, 181–82; wealth in, 87
Taking Rights Seriously (Dworkin), 70–71
Taliban, 135; and captured fighters, 133; strategy of, 17
Tamil Tigers, 17
Tanzania, intervention in Uganda, 312
Tarkunde, Justice, 51
Task, The (Cowper), 34
Taylor, Charles: and accountability, 279; indictment of, 277; trial of, 18
Terrorism Act of 2000 (United Kingdom), 293
terrorist attacks, 2001. *See* September 11, 2001
Thailand, detentions in, 293
Thatcher, Margaret, 16, 111
Thirteenth Amendment, 37
Thomas, Clarence, 296, 309
Thomas, Norman, 50
Tiananmen Square: aftermath of, 166; developments leading to, 153–54; and Human Rights Watch, 216; last to leave, 348n6; reasons for demonstration, 148; stakes at time of demonstration, 330
Tibet, Asia Watch, 215–16
Timerman, Jacobo, 208–9
Times of London, 119–20
Timor-Leste, 264
Tokyo, trials, 127
Tolbert, David, 242
torture: and Americas Watch, 209; Amnesty International's *Report on Torture*, 191–92; and Argentina, 259–60; and boycotts, 181; and Bush administration policies, 291–92, 306; and Chile,

164–65; and detainees ("war on terror"), 135–36; prohibitions against, 67. *See also* Convention Against Torture and Other Cruel, Inhuman or Degrading Treatment or Punishment (CAT); Special Rapporteur on Torture; Sudan Organization Against Torture (SOAT); United Nations Convention Against Torture
Tourgée, Albion Winegar, 40, 43, 44
Trade Act, 166
TRC. *See* Truth and Reconciliation Commission (TRC)
Treatment Action Campaign (TAC), 72–74, 80, 83, 255
treaty law, 93–94
Treaty of Versailles, 125
Treaty to Ban Landmines (1997), 8
Trujillo, Rafael, 55
Truman, Harry, 101
Truth and Reconciliation Commission (TRC): and Chile, 260, 262; leaders of, 198; and South Africa, 262–63; success of, 242
"truth commissions," 258, 260–61
Tunisian League for Human Rights, 319
Tupamaros, 261
Turkey, and Helsinki Watch, 214–15
Tvardovsky, Alexander, 139
Twain, Mark, *King Leopold's Soliloquy*, 43

Uganda, intervention by Tanzania, 312
Ukraine, European Court, 113
unalienable rights, 86
Unamuno, Miguel de, 52
U.N. Commission on Human Rights, 110
U.N. Council on Human Rights, 112
UNESCO, 191–92
unitary executive theory, 298–99
United Arab Emirates, 229
United Kingdom, Terrorism Act of 2000, 293
United Nations: Economic and Social Council, 97–98; High Commissioner for Human Rights, 114; Special Rapporteur on Internally Displaced Persons, 112; Special Rapporteur

United Nations *(cont)*
on the Protection of Human Rights
Defenders, 255; Special Rapporteur
on Torture, 112; 2005 world summit,
313–14; Universal Declaration of
Human Rights, adoption of, 59
United Nations Charter, 144; adoption
of, 95; Articles, 95–98; generally, 2;
war, laws of, 126
United Nations Convention Against
Torture, 295
United Nations General Assembly: meet-
ings with Krushchev, 186; Sihanouk
(king of Cambodia), speech by, 214;
Universal Declaration of Human
Rights, 63–64, 98–99
United Nations High Commissioner for
Human Rights, 111, 247, 352n14
United Nations Human Rights Commis-
sion, 208
United Nations Human Rights Council,
110, 231
United Nations Mine Action Center, 222
United Nations Security Council: and
International Criminal Court (ICC),
276; International Criminal Tribunal
for Rwanda (ICTR), creation of, 267;
International Criminal Tribunal for
the Former Yugoslavia, creation of, 131,
266; War Crimes Commission, 266
United States: abolition *(see* abolition
movement [United States]); abolitionist movement (nineteenth century),
10; feminist movement (nineteenth
century), 7; feminist movement
(twentieth century), 7
United States Marine Corps, 236
Universal Declaration of Human Rights:
adoption of, 54, 59, 62, 98–99, 143;
and Article 19, 244; articles of, 103–7;
fundamental rights recognized in, 21;
generally, 2; "human rights," evolution
of, 86–87; and ICCPR provisions,
102; overview, 60–64
USAID, 158
U.S. Army Field Manual, 306

U.S. Constitution: and abolitionists, 36;
enforcement of, 78–79. *See also specific
amendments*

Valdez, Julio de Pena, 189–90
Vanik, Charles, 166
Vaso Miskin Street, 221
Velikanova, Tatyana, 141–42
Versailles Peace Treaty, 64
Vicaría de la Solidaridad, 167, 198
Victores, Oscar Mejía, 180
Videla, Jorge, 18, 209, 279
Vietnam: Communism, 151; journalists
in, 5; repression in, 89
Vietnam Veterans Foundation, 214
Vietnam War: criticisms, 129; protests, 163
Villard, Oswald Garrison, 44
Vindication of the Rights of Women, A
(Wollstonecraft), 38
Vonnegut, Kurt, 205
voting: African Americans, exclusion of,
45; and slaves, 38; women's rights(*see*
suffrage movement [United States])

Walesa, Lech, 146
Walker, William, 183
Walling, William English, 44
"wall slamming," 135
Wall Street Journal, 219
Wanding, Ren, 153–54
war, laws of, 117–37; and atomic bombs,
127–28; and boundaries, 117; and
Holocaust, 125–26; and Lieber Code,
120–22; and "Martens clause," 122–
24; military necessity of, 121; poison
gas, use of, 124–25; sick and wounded,
treatment of, 125–28; weapons, production of, 123–25
war crimes, prosecution. *See* Nuremberg
Charter; Nuremberg trials; Nuremberg Tribunal
War Crimes Commission, 266
Warley, Buchanan v., 45
"war on drugs," 349n28
"war on terror": beginnings of, 236;
humanitarian law, application of,

133–34; and human rights, 231; launching of, 202–3; as metaphor, 295, 354n11; violations of civil liberties in name of, 20

Washington Office on Latin America (WOLA), 239–40

Washington Post, 5, 200–201

waterboarding, 135

Watergate, 5, 165, 295

WCTU. *See* Women's Christian Temperance Union (WCTU)

weapons, production of, 123–25

Weekly Standard, 220

Wei Jingsheng, 148–50, 153–54, 159

Wellington, Duke of, 35

Wells, H. G., 53

West African Mail (Morel), 43

Wilberforce, William, 33–34

Wilhelm II, 49

William of Orange (Netherlands), 31–32

Williams, Brian, 239

William the Conqueror, 118

Windsor, Jennifer, 241

Wise, Stephen, 44

Witt, John Fabian, 42–43

WOLA. *See* Washington Office on Latin America (WOLA)

Wollstonecraft, Mary, *A Vindication of the Rights of Women*, 38

Women's Christian Temperance Union (WCTU), 39

women's rights: and abolition movement (United States), 36–37; and suffrage movement, 37–39

Women's Rights Project, 228–29

Workers Defense Committee, 145

World Anti-Slavery Convention (London), 37

World Conference Against Racism in Durban, South Africa, 111–12

World Council of Churches, 102

World Jewish Congress, 102

World Trade Center: attacks on (2001) (*see* September 11, 2001); bombing (1993), 134

World War I: poison gas, use of, 124–25; United Nations Charter, adoption of, 95; United States entry into, protests, 45–46

World War II: atomic bombs, use of, 127–28, 142; Japanese-Americans during, 307; September 11, comparison, 288–89; sick and wounded, treatment of, 125–28; war crimes of, 100, 126, 128. *See also* Holocaust; Nuremberg trials; Nuremberg Tribunal

worldwide movement, 233–57. *See also specific organization*

Wu, Harry, 241

Xerxes, 117

Yeltsin, Boris, 156–57

Yew, Lee Kuan, 88

Yoo, John, 295, 298, 305

Yugoslavia: accountability, 264–65; International Criminal Tribunal, 18

Zalaquett, José (Pepe), 164, 198–99

Zhou Enlai, 146, 154

Zia-ul-Haq, 255

Zimbabwe: R2P, 314–15

Zola, Émile, 47

HUMAN RIGHTS AND CRIMES AGAINST HUMANITY

Eric D. Weitz, *Series Editor*

Echoes of Violence: Letters from a War Reporter
BY CAROLIN EMCKE

Cannibal Island: Death in a Siberian Gulag
BY NICOLAS WERTH. *Translated by Steven Rendall with a foreword by Jan T. Gross*

Torture and the Twilight of Empire from Algiers to Baghdad
BY MARNIA LAZREG

Terror in Chechnya: Russia and the Tragedy of Civilians in War
BY EMMA GILLIGAN

"If You Leave Us Here, We Will Die":
How Genocide Was Stopped in East Timor
BY GEOFFREY ROBINSON

Stalin's Genocides
BY NORMAN NAIMARK

Against Massacre: Humanitarian Intervention
in the Ottoman Empire, 1815–1914
BY DAVIDE RODOGNO

All the Missing Souls:
A Personal History of the War Crimes Tribunals
BY DAVID SCHEFFER

The Young Turks' Crime against Humanity
BY TANER AKÇAM

The International Human Rights Movement: A History
BY ARYEH NEIER